fifth edition

Early Childhood Language Arts

Mary Renck Jalongo

Indiana University of Pennsylvania

Boston   Columbus   Indianapolis   New York   San Francisco   Upper Saddle River
Amsterdam   Cape Town   Dubai   London   Madrid   Milan   Munich   Paris   Montreal   Toronto
Delhi   Mexico City   Sao Paulo   Sydney   Hong Kong   Seoul   Singapore   Taipei   Tokyo

Editor-in-Chief: Aurora Martínez Ramos
Associate Sponsoring Editor: Barbara Strickland
Editorial Assistant: Amy Foley
Vice President, Director of Marketing: Quinn Perkson
Executive Marketing Manager: Krista Clark
Production Editor: Annette Joseph
Editorial Production Service: Omegatype Typography, Inc.
Manufacturing Buyer: Megan Cochran
Electronic Composition: Omegatype Typography, Inc.
Interior Design: Omegatype Typography, Inc.

Credits and acknowledgments borrowed from other sources and reproduced, with permission, in this textbook appear on the appropriate page within the text.

Library of Congress Cataloging-in-Publication Data
Jalongo, Mary Renck.
   Early childhood language arts / Mary Renck Jalongo.—5th ed.
      p.   cm.
   Includes bibliographical references and index.
   ISBN-13: 978-0-13-704874-8 (pbk.)
   ISBN-10: 0-13-704874-2 (pbk.)
  1. Language arts (Preschool)   2. Language arts (Early childhood)   I. Title.
   LB1140.5.L3J35   2010
   372.6—dc22

                                                                      2010006186

Printed in the United States of America

10 9 8 7 6 5 4 3 2 1   RRD-VA   14 13 12 11 10

www.pearsonhighered.com   ISBN 10: 0-13-704874-2
                              ISBN 13: 978-0-13-704874-8

To the early childhood educators who function as advocates for every young child in their centers and classrooms, support all children's efforts to become literate, and sustain a commitment to developmentally effective practices and educational equity throughout their professional careers.

M. R. J.

Mary Renck Jalongo is a teacher, writer, and editor. As a classroom teacher she taught preschool, first grade, and second grade; worked with children and families of migrant farm workers; and taught in the laboratory preschool at the University of Toledo. Currently she is a professor at Indiana University of Pennsylvania, where she earned the university-wide outstanding professor award and coordinates the Doctoral Program in Curriculum and Instruction.

Dr. Jalongo has co-authored and edited more than 25 books, many of them textbooks in the field of early childhood education, such as *Creative Thinking and Arts-Based Learning* (5th ed., Merrill/Prentice Hall), *Exploring Your Role: An Introduction to Early Childhood Education* (3rd ed., Merrill/Prentice Hall), and *Major Trends and Issues in Early Childhood Education* (2nd ed., Teachers College Press). Recent publications for practitioners include two National Association for the Education of Young Children (NAEYC) books, *Learning to Listen, Listening to Learn* and *Young Children and Picture Books;* an edited book for the Association for Childhood Education International (ACEI), *The World's Children and Their Companion Animals: Developmental and Educational Significance of the Child/Pet Bond;* and *Planning for Learning: Collaborative Approaches to Lesson Design and Review.* She is also the author of two award-winning Position Papers for ACEI.

Since 1995 Dr. Jalongo has served as editor-in-chief of the Springer international publication, *Early Childhood Education Journal.* She also co-edits Springer's new book series, *Educating the Young Child: Advances in Theory and Research, Implications for Practice,* and has made presentations on various aspects of early childhood education throughout the world.

Contents

PART TWO   Oral Language

chapter four   Helping Young Children Become Better Listeners   73

chapter five — Supporting the Speaking Abilities of the Very Young   95

chapter six — Using Narrative and Expository Texts to Foster Growth in Literacy   124

PART THREE   Literacy with Print

chapter seven   Fostering Growth in
Emergent Literacy   147

chapter eight	Supporting Early and Independent Reading 174

PART FOUR   Written Language and Symbol Systems

PART FIVE   The Teacher of Language Arts

Preface

The word *literacy* has become increasingly difficult to define in an information society dominated by the powerful visual images found in the mass media.

> Here we stand between traditional forms of literacy and new forms that are continually appearing. What it means to be literate has become a moving target, one we can never completely define because information and communication technologies continually change. As the meaning of literacy changes, our role as literacy educators is also being fundamentally altered. (Leu, 1997, p. 62)

Contemporary early childhood classrooms demand the preparation of a new kind of early childhood educator. Today's teacher of very young children (from birth through age 8) is expected to be a much more knowledgeable and sophisticated professional than in years past. She or he is expected to possess the skills of professional collaboration, to teach in ways supported by scientific evidence, to integrate the perspectives of special education with those of early childhood education, and to supply evidence of children's growth as learners. Therefore, any textbook that hopes to serve as a resource for teacher preparation in the field of emergent and early literacy must reflect these understandings, trends, and goals. In response to rising expectations for early childhood educators' effectiveness and student achievement, six significant changes have been made to the fifth edition of *Early Childhood Language Arts*.

New to the Fifth Edition

Early Childhood Language Arts has been thoroughly revised; at least 30 percent of the material is new to the book.

- **References and Internet Resources.** The references have been completely updated, with the great majority of them published in 2001 or later. A wide array of online materials from authoritative sources have also been incorporated into the text.
- **MyEducationKit.** MyEducationKit is integrated right into the text. Look for the MyEducationKit logo in the margins, and follow the simple instructions to access the chapter objectives, study plan, assignments and activities, and web links on the MyEducationKit for this book (www.myeducationkit.com).
- **Links with Literature.** This new feature leads students to classic and contemporary high-quality children's literature across various genres. Rather than being given lengthy lists of books, students are directed to online sources from leading professional organizations that are continually updated as well as provided with

"Names to Know." For example, Chapter 1 Links with Literature focuses on multicultural, multiethnic, and international children's books and also provides links to multicultural and international resources.

- **English Language Learners.** This new feature provides the very latest research-based recommendations for working with students who are acquiring English.
- **How Do I . . . ?** This feature offers a step-by-step explanation of how to teach a particular skill, such as introducing new vocabulary words or planning a standards-based lesson.
- **Margin Notes.** These have been completely revised to address four different aspects of language arts instruction. **Standards in Education** provide standards of leading professional associations that govern instruction in the language arts. **Brain and Language** notes inform students of the implications of neuroscience research for early childhood educators. **Infants and Toddlers** provide a research perspective on the language development of the youngest learners. **Research and Report** notes suggest individual investigation outside the classroom that culminates in a small group, in-class activity focused on a timely topic related to each chapter's content.

Focus of the Book

In preparing this fifth edition of *Early Childhood Language Arts*, my experiences with newcomers to the field continued to serve as a touchstone. Throughout the revision process, I kept asking myself, "What do early childhood educators really need to know, do, and understand in order to work effectively and compassionately with the very young?"

Michelle, a former student, immediately came to mind. During her early childhood teaching career thus far, Michelle has had memorable experiences with diverse groups of young language learners that have contributed to her professional development. As a student teacher in a rural public school kindergarten, she found out firsthand how a pervasive developmental disorder such as autism affects a child's development in general and language development in particular. Five-year-old Kevin, a boy in her class, talked but rarely used language to communicate to or with anyone. Michelle would often notice Kevin mouthing letters or talking to himself about things that captured his interest. He was particularly fascinated by letters, numbers, maps, and globes, and Michelle was surprised to discover that his reading skills were very advanced.

During Michelle's first full year of teaching as a long-term substitute in first grade, her class included Krystall, a child who used a motorized wheelchair and a communication board with a voice synthesizer to communicate. One of Michelle's most treasured teaching moments was observing Krystall and her friend Madeline, a child who was hearing impaired, play together. Krystall would point to the icon on her electronic communication panel, Madeline would demonstrate the corresponding word using American Sign Language, Krystall would push the button so that the voice synthesizer would say the word, and both girls would giggle.

In her second year of full-time teaching, Michelle married and moved to California, where she took a job in a private preschool in an urban area. After she met her class for the first time, Michelle called me to say, "I have 15 children in my class, and there are 12 different languages represented! I'm going to learn so much this year!"

I share these stories about Michelle because they illustrate how important it is for teachers to be well informed about young children's language and the strategies used to support language growth. Consider how, in just 3 years' time, Michelle's knowledge of children's communication disorders and language development was enriched and enlarged. Consider also how she made the commitment to keep on learning and developing as a professional. I believe that Michelle was and will continue to be successful as an early childhood practitioner because she fully accepts her responsibility for fostering all young children's language growth and because she continually seeks professional development. As her former college professor, I would also like to think that the quality of her teacher preparation program made a significant contribution to her excellence as a teacher.

What was apparent from the start was that Michelle did not approach the diverse language learners in her class or center as an inconvenience or a burden. Rather, these new situations sent her in search of support from authoritative sources to learn more—from the child's family, the library, the Internet, experienced teachers, specialists from other professions, professional organizations, and community services. Michelle did not merely talk about being a facilitator of children's language; she put her philosophy into action and truly helped every child reach his or her potential as a communicator. With this, the fifth edition of *Early Childhood Language Arts*, I too sought to capture essential elements of what enables a novice teacher to mature into a master teacher.

Underlying Assumptions

I think that it is helpful for textbook authors to make their beliefs explicit to those people who are considering using the book. *Early Childhood Language Arts* is distinctive from many other early literacy books in that it includes oral language rather than only emphasizing literacy with print. Beginning with the first edition and continuing now with the fifth, my approach has always been to integrate not only the language arts (listening, speaking, reading, and writing) but also the other subject areas, including the fine arts. The language arts are incomplete without these important connections. We know that learners of language come to us with wide variations in background experiences and abilities; therefore, it only makes sense that we respond in kind with a repertoire of teaching strategies, rather than advocate one best method for all.

More specifically, some of the underlying assumptions that I make about young children as language learners include the following:

- The early years are "prime time" for language development; therefore, it is particularly important for young children's teachers to be knowledgeable about ways of fostering language growth.
- The communication environment has changed dramatically in recent years. In this complex environment, children need to know how to use multiple symbol systems.
- Language is, first and foremost, a tool for social interaction; children need to use language to achieve important purposes.
- Learning to read and write is challenging and requires motivation; high-quality literature is a major means of motivating children to become literate.
- Literacy during early childhood typically begins with oral language; therefore, it is important to give equal time to listening and speaking, rather than to focus exclusively on reading and writing.
- Literacy is more than mouthing words; children need dynamic role models to emulate so that they are "apprenticed" into literate behavior.
- High levels of literacy are expected in contemporary society; children and families need to be invited into literacy activities that will expand the range of options available to them in work and life.
- Becoming a competent teacher of young children requires knowing how to adapt to multiple demands; therefore, early childhood educators need to reflect deeply on their actions and the consequences of those actions for young learners.
- Early childhood educators cannot meet the needs of diverse groups of language learners alone; they need to collaborate with families and professionals in order to provide high-quality educational experiences.
- Literacy affects the ability of individuals to participate in society; therefore, a major purpose of literacy learning should be to enhance the power of individuals to influence institutions for the better.

Audience for the Book

Early Childhood Language Arts is intended for teachers of young children (birth through age 8). The text is most appropriate for a 4- or 5-year teacher preparation program that leads to certification or licensure. It is also appropriate for a graduate-level course for practicing teachers who are developing specialized expertise in the early childhood field.

Structure of the Chapters

This book has been designed with two audiences in mind. One audience is the instructor who is seeking to provide a high-quality, interactive course that moves beyond the traditional lecture format. The other audience is the college or university student who seeks to develop a more thorough understanding of language and literacy development during the early years. The following features were designed with both of these audiences in mind.

Fact File

Each chapter begins with a Fact File that serves as a support for the instructor by simultaneously synthesizing current research as well as addressing common misconceptions of students.

What Is . . . ?

Next, each chapter defines the key topic to be addressed, such as the home literacy environment (Chapter 2) or narrative and expository text (Chapter 6). After learning the terminology central to the chapter, students are invited to delve into the topic further via case material.

Collaboration with Families and Professionals

This section of each chapter contains real-world case material that enables students to see how teachers are expected to work with professionals in other fields, with families, and with children. These cases are designed to provide readers with experience in collaboration, promote reflective thinking, and generate class discussion.

Overview of . . .

Provides a developmental perspective on the chapter content.

Teacher Concerns and Basic Strategies

Every chapter contains sections that identify common concerns of teachers, basic strategies for effective language arts programs for the very young, and specific teaching activities that are developmentally appropriate.

Classroom Activities to Support . . .

An array of sound pedagogical practices that teach the content of each chapter is supplied.

Research-Based Literacy Strategies

Three instructional strategies that are supported by empirical research conclude every chapter. Each is described briefly and supported by empirical evidence.

Supplements for Instructors and Students

The following supplements comprise an outstanding array of resources that facilitate learning about early childhood language arts. For more information, ask your local Allyn & Bacon Merrill Education representative or contact the Allyn & Bacon Merrill Faculty Field Support Department at 1-800-526-0485. For technology support, please contact technical support directly at 1-800-677-6337 or http://247.pearsoned.com. Many of the supplements can be downloaded from the Instructor Resource Center at www.pearsonhighered.com/irc.

Help your students get better grades and become better teachers.

MyEducationKit: Dynamic Resources Meeting Your Needs

MyEducationKit is a dynamic website that connects the concepts addressed in the text with effective teaching practice. It is also easy to use and to integrate into assignments and courses. Wherever the MyEducationKit logo appears in the text, follow the simple instructions to access a variety of multimedia resources geared to meet the diverse teaching and learning needs of instructors and students. Here are just a few of the features that are available:

- Online study plans, including self-assessment quizzes and resource material
- Gradetracker, an online grade book
- A wealth of multimedia resources, including classroom video, expert video commentary, student and teacher artifacts, case studies, strategies, and lesson plans
- Web links to important national organizations and sites in your field

Study Plan   A MyEducationKit Study Plan is a multiple choice assessment with feedback tied to chapter objectives. A well-designed Study Plan offers multiple opportunities to fully master required course content as identified by the objectives in each chapter:

- **Chapter objectives** identify the learning outcomes for the chapter and give students targets to shoot for as they read and study.
- **Assessments** evaluate students' mastery of the content. These multiple choice and essay assessments are mapped to chapter objectives. Students can take these quizzes as many times as they want. Not only do these quizzes provide overall scores for each objective, but they also explain why responses to particular items are correct or incorrect.

Assignments and Activities   Designed to save instructors preparation time and to enhance student understanding, these exercises show concepts in action through videos, cases, and student and teacher artifacts. These help students synthesize and apply concepts and strategies they read about in the book.

Multimedia Resources The rich media resources you will encounter throughout MyEducationKit include:

- *Videos.* The authentic classroom videos in MyEducationKit show how real teachers handle actual classroom situations. Discussing and analyzing these videos not only deepens understanding of concepts presented in the text, but also builds skills in observing children and classrooms.
- *Student and Teacher Artifacts.* Real K–12 student and teacher classroom artifacts are tied to the chapter topics in your text and offer practice in working with the different materials teachers encounter daily in their classrooms.
- *Case Studies.* A diverse set of robust cases illustrates the realities of teaching and offers valuable perspectives on common issues and challenges in education.
- *Web Links.* On MyEducationKit you don't need to search for the sites that connect to the topics covered in your chapter. Here you can explore websites that are important in the field and that give you perspective on the concepts covered in your text.

General Resources on MyEducationKit The resources section on MyEducationKit is designed to help students pass their licensure exams; put together effective portfolios and lesson plans; prepare for and navigate the first year of their teaching careers; and understand key educational standards, policies, and laws. This section includes:

- *Licensure Exams.* Contains guidelines for passing the Praxis exam. The Practice Test Exam includes practice multiple choice questions, case study questions, and video case studies with sample questions.
- *Lesson Plan Builder.* Helps students create and share lesson plans.
- *Licensure and Standards.* Provides links to state licensure standards and national standards.
- *Beginning Your Career.* Offers tips, advice, and valuable information on:

  - Resume Writing and Interviewing: Expert advice on how to write impressive resumes and prepare for job interviews.
  - Your First Year of Teaching: Practical tips on setting up a classroom, managing student behavior, and planning for instruction and assessment.
  - Law and Public Policies: Includes specific directives and requirements educators need to understand under the No Child Left Behind Act and the Individuals with Disabilities Education Improvement Act of 2004.

Visit www.myeducationkit.com for a demonstration of this exciting, new online teaching resource.

Instructor's Manual and Test Bank

For each chapter, the instructor's manual features the chapter focus, chapter objectives, key terms, student learning experiences, and teaching and learning resources, along with a sample syllabus and a sample project. The Test Bank includes true/false, multiple choice, matching, and discussion/essay questions. Page references to the main text and suggested answers have been added to most questions to help instructors create and evaluate student tests. (Available for download from the Instructor Resource Center at www.pearsonhighered.com/irc.)

PowerPoint™ Presentation

Designed for teachers using the text, the PowerPoint™ Presentation consists of a series of slides that can be shown as is or used to make overhead transparencies. The presentation highlights key concepts and major topics for each chapter. (Available for download from the Instructor Resource Center at www.pearsonhighered.com/irc.)

Speak with your Allyn & Bacon Merrill sales representative about obtaining these supplements for your class!

Acknowledgments

As any author can attest, no book is entirely the product of one writer's efforts. I am indebted to the writings of other authors whom I admire and have cited here and to my college students, who have taught me how to be a better professor over the past 31 years.

I want to thank my editor, Aurora Martínez Ramos, for her keen insights into the changing marketplace and continuous support of this fifth edition. My sincere appreciation also goes to the following reviewers, who thoughtfully evaluated the revision plan and the earlier drafts of the fifth edition: Dr. Kathleen Bernhard, Hudson Valley Community College, and Annmarie Malchenson, HACC, Central Pennsylvania's Community College.

Also deserving of recognition are my editors for previous editions at Allyn & Bacon, including Virginia Lanigan, Sean Wakely, and Nancy Forsyth. Michelle Amodei, doctoral candidate at Indiana University of Pennsylvania, revised the Instructor's Manual and Test Bank for the fifth edition based on the work that Natalie Barnyak, faculty member at University of Pittsburgh, Johnstown, had done previously. Michelle Amodei also updated the PowerPoint™ Presentation and prepared the MyEducationKit.

Finally, I would like to thank my husband for his thoughtful commentaries on drafts of these chapters and for his forbearance as I pursued my passion for writing.

chapter one

Appreciating Diversity and Educating the Young English Language Learner

Lindfors Photography

FACT FILE on Diverse Language Learners

• There are nearly 21 million children under the age of 5 in the United States (Children's Defense Fund, 2008). California, Texas, and New York have the largest number of children; North Dakota, Vermont, Wyoming, and the District of Columbia have the fewest.

• Since 1990, the enrollment of English language learners (ELLs) in U.S. public schools has grown by 105 percent while growth in the general school population has been only 12 percent (Kindler, 2002).

• Over 4 million school-aged children are English language learners; they now consti-tute nearly 10 percent of the U.S. school-age population and are an increasingly diverse

1

group (Gollnick & Chinn, 2008; Ovando, Collier, & Combs, 2005; Zelasko & Antunez, 2000). In California the primary language of 60 to 70 percent of the children is not English (Roseberry-McKibbin & Brice, 2000).

• Over 400 different languages are spoken by young ELLs (Kindler, 2002). However, nearly 80 percent of the ELLs in the United States are children living in poverty whose first language is Spanish. The next most populous groups of ELLs in the United States are Vietnamese, Hmong, Cantonese, and Korean (Kindler, 2002).

• More than 1 in 6—13.3 million—children in the United States are from low-income backgrounds. There is great variation among the states, ranging from a low of 1 in 12 in New Hampshire to a high of almost 3 in 10 in Mississippi (Children's Defense Fund, 2008).

• As the student population has grown more diverse, the teaching force has become more homogeneous (Johnson, 2006). In 2003, nearly 40 percent of United States public school children were members of minority groups while less than 10 percent of their teachers were members of minority groups (Snyder & Hoffman, 2003).

• Although some languages are spoken by hundreds of millions of people (English is the native tongue of 400 million) and others by only a few thousand, one language is not judged superior to another simply because it is spoken by a greater number of people (Fox, 1997; Office for Standards in Education, 2008).

Did any of this information surprise you? If so, what? Why? How will you use this knowledge to educate and care for the very young?

What Is the Cultural Context and Home Literacy Environment?

Every group and every individual has beliefs about language and its use, values and ideas about language and its speakers, and expectations for language teaching and learning (Park & King, 2003). One highly influential type of cultural context that young children bring with them to school is the effect of the home literacy environment (HLE) (Burgess, Hecht, & Lonigan, 2002; Weigel, Martin, & Bennett, 2006). The home literacy environment is conceptualized in many different ways; however, the main idea is the amount of support that children get at home in their efforts to acquire literacy with print (Hood, Conlon, & Andrews, 2008; Nutbrown, Hannon, & Morgan, 2005, Phillips & Lonigan, 2009). To illustrate differences in the HLE, hearing parents of children who are deaf (Stobbart & Alant, 2008) or parents and families of children with severe visual impairments (Murphy, Hatton, & Erickson, 2008) may have very different concepts of their roles in supporting literacy. The home literacy environment has both immediate and long-term consequences for learning (Melhuish et al., 2008).

PEARSON
myeducationkit

Go to the Assignments and Activities section of Chapter 1 in MyEducationKit and complete the activity entitled "Knowing Families."

Although it may be customary to think of reading aloud and visiting the library, families engage in all types of activities that involve literacy tasks, such as making a shopping list, communicating with family members via e-mail, planning a community garden (Starbuck & Olthof, 2008), or consulting an information board at the local store about upcoming events (McTavish, 2007). Naturally, there is great diversity in the family members present in each home (Mui & Anderson, 2008), the type and amount of media in children's homes, the time devoted to reading versus television, and the kinds of practice with oral and written language that each child acquires prior to beginning school (Bracken & Fischel, 2008; Linebarger, Kosanic, Greenwood, & Doku, 2004; Sonnenschein & Munsterman, 2002).

> **Standards in Education**
> Two leading professional organizations have issued standards for diversity. Check out the Association for Childhood Education International Diversity Committee's (2008) standards at www.acei.org/diversityed_84_3_158f.htm and the National Association for the Education of Young Children's (2005) position statement on diversity at www.naeyc.org/about/positions/pdf/diversity.pdf.

Some of the home activities associated with better academic performance in school include engaging young children in conversation, reading and discussing books, providing writing materials, supporting play that incorporates literacy activities, demonstrating the purposes of literacy, and maintaining a joyful atmosphere around literacy activities (Denton, Parker, & Jasbrouck, 2003). If the home literacy environment and that of the school are dramatically different, it often makes literacy learning more difficult for the child. Rather than expect the child to switch to the middle-class values and attitudes that predominate in the school, the school needs to become more culturally responsive (Gay, 2000; Olsen & Fuller, 2007) and capitalize on each family's strengths (Carter, Chard, & Pool, 2009; González, Moll, & Amanti, 2005).

As a teacher of young children, you need to consider how each person's identity and community serves as a reference point, as a way of looking at the world. Consider, for example, how one educator described symbolically his experience of arriving at school with Spanish as his first and only language (quoted in Gutierrez & Larson, 1994):

> I came to kindergarten so excited and ready to learn. I came with my *maleta* (suitcase) full of so many wonderful things, my Spanish language, my beautiful culture, and many other treasures. When I got there, though, not only did they not let me use anything from my maleta, they did not even let me bring it into the classroom. (p. 33)

Situations such as this one help to illustrate why it is particularly important for teachers to look beyond their own family experiences and customary ways of thinking (Bornstein, 2009; Christian, 2006; Gonzalez-Mena, 2008a, 2009a; Jones & Nimmo, 1999). It is surprisingly easy to fall into the habit of thinking the group to which we belong sets the standard by which others should be judged. For example, preconceptions may cloud a teacher's views of a child with foster parents (Swick, 2007), a parent in prison (Clopton & East, 2008a, b), lesbian or gay parents (Patterson, 2006), grandparents responsible for his or her care (Kenner, Ruby, Jessel, Gregory, & Arju, 2007), or with parents who are recent immigrants and speak very little English (Moore & Ritter, 2008). A teacher's belief system might lead to favored treatment of or, conversely, unease with children from families for whom faith is of paramount importance to their family interactions and traditions or with children who may be participating in regular religious instruction (Peyton & Jalongo, 2008).

Children in today's classrooms are more culturally, socially, academically, and physically diverse than ever before because, the farther you go back in history, the more you would find children with special needs separated from their peers (McCormick, Loeb, & Schiefelbusch, 2002). In the 1930s and 1940s in the United States, most children with special needs were kept at home and did not attend school at all. During the 1950s and 1960s, they were completely isolated from peers in special classes. More often than not, these classrooms were located in the least well-equipped and most remote areas of the building. During the 1970s and early 1980s, children with special needs were brought from their special education classroom into the regular classroom periodically to work alongside peers, a practice called *mainstreaming*. In the 1990s and continuing into the new millennium, children with special needs are included, often full time, in the classroom with typically developing peers. This practice is referred to as *inclusion* (Hooper & Umansky, 2009; Mallory & Rous, 2009; Mogharreban & Bruns, 2009; Schwartz, 2005).

In the diverse early childhood settings you are going to encounter, some young children will have highly developed language and others will face serious language difficulties. Teachers cannot afford to "aim down the middle" with their teaching in the hope that they will successfully reach the average student, that the children who are struggling will somehow catch up, and that the students who are advanced will take care of themselves. Diverse settings require *child advocates*, teachers who are committed to championing the cause of every child. Overall, the research shows that inclusive early childhood programs work best when there is a clear philosophy, teacher support, a focus on the child, a continuum of services, and interprofessional collaboration (Sandall, Hemmeter, Smith, & McLean, 2005). A community of language learners emphasizes cooperation, collaboration, and mutual respect between and among children, parents, families, and professionals. High-quality early childhood language arts programs focus on the whole child. This means that there is attention to the child's physical, emotional, social, intellectual, and aesthetic growth (Foundation for Child Development, 2008). Figure 1.1 summarizes what a literacy community looks like in action. The National Council for Accreditation of Teacher Education (2007) asserts that high quality education is a fundamental right of all children and requires educators to demonstrate the knowledge, skills, and professional dispositions to work successfully with children of all races, ethnicities, disabilities/exceptionalities, and socioeconomic groups to assure high-quality education for all children. Figure 1.2 provides suggestions on working with English language learners that reflect this perspective.

When you find out that you will be responsible for a child with severe disabilities, it is natural to feel a bit anxious about your ability to help her or him or to react in a cautious manner at first. Such concerns often stem from the worry that you do not or will not have the support that you need. This is to be expected because meeting the needs of diverse language learners is not a goal that can be accomplished alone. It takes a team of professionals, all of whom are dedicated to the care, education, and support of the child and family (Division for Early Childhood, 2007). *Interprofessional collaboration* refers to "the communication, cooperation, and coordination that occurs

FIGURE 1.1 Literacy Communities in Action: What to Look For

Evidence of Collaboration with Parents, Families, Professionals, and the Larger Community

Teachers who seek to communicate with parents and families in a variety of ways, who strive to make them feel welcome, who use different times and occasions as opportunities to confer about the child's progress, and who use community resources to enhance learning opportunities for children.

What to Look For

Information boards, flyers, newsletters, displays of children's work, notices about special events, support services information, notes in backpacks, thank-you letters, invitations to participate, classroom volunteer schedule, videos/audio recordings/books created by the class that can be checked out, and parenting resource books.

Evidence of Support for Emergent Literacy and Reading

Teachers who are avid readers themselves, both of professional materials and children's books, and teachers who immerse children in print and high-quality literature to support emergent literacy and reading.

What to Look For

Independent reading, paired reading, reading aloud, choral reading, chants, raps, rhymes, reading "big books," song charts, dictated stories, poems, child-constructed books, Readers' Theater, Thought for the Day, classroom helper board, visual aids for instruction.

Evidence of Support for Drawing, Writing, and Spelling

Teachers provide support when they call children's attention to print; model the writing process for children; demonstrate enthusiasm for multiple symbol systems that children use to communicate; offer support and encouragement to children engaged in drawing, writing, and spelling; and use technology to support children's pictorial and graphic communication.

What to Look For

Children's handwriting, mailboxes with drawings and letters, stories accompanied by drawings, multimedia projects, scripts of plays, original picture books, class e-mail and web pages, message boards, word-processing software and computer printouts, signs and posters, peer editing, journal writing, class newsletter.

Evidence of Support for Oral Language

Teachers who talk and listen respectfully to children and families, who encourage conversations between and among children throughout the schoolday, and who provide time and materials for play and spontaneous language to support oral language.

What to Look For

Opportunities for peer interaction, extended conversations between adults and children, recorded books and equipment for listening to them, music center, literacy materials to use during play, props for dramatization, puppets, flannelboard cutouts, high-quality DVDs to view and discuss, computer software.

Note: See Wohlwend (2008) for additional resources.

FIGURE 1.2   Guidelines for Working with English Language Learners

Respect Families

Accept that children are members of diverse family and community systems and that they bring multiple gifts of language, culture, and wisdom. Recognize that families know their children in ways that can enrich and enlarge your understandings. Strive to build lines of communication among linguistically diverse families so that they can support one another.

Analyze Beliefs and Attitudes

Set aside negative myths and common misconceptions. Assure the child and family that their native language and culture are valued. Be aware that not all families are eager to have their children cared for outside the home and may not be entirely convinced of the value of early childhood education.

Acquire Specialized Skills

Seek out on-the-job training concerning issues such as the politics of race, language, and culture; strategies for furthering cross-cultural communication (e.g., effective use of translators); and assessment strategies suited to English language learners.

Reach Out to Families

Become better informed about each child's and family's language history. Make personal contact in the family's native language, if at all possible. Hold meetings at convenient times and in locations that families do not find intimidating, and give them support and incentives for participation (e.g., child care, transportation, snacks).

Offer Comprehensive Services

Take a family literacy approach and provide classes in English for parents/families so that they can participate more directly in literacy learning and see its positive effects.

Create a Sense of Community

Warmly welcome every member of the classroom community. Reflect diversity and give children authentic, integrated opportunities to participate in a vital learning community.

Become a Keen Observer

Collect evidence of the child's language use both in the native language and in English. Report these findings in ways that can be shared with families during conferences. Accept children's errors as a normal part of language development.

Be an Advocate

Endorse policies that address the needs of young, diverse language learners by working with organizations and leaders capable of addressing these needs.

Sources: Bouchard, 2001; Eihorn, 2001; Garcia, 2008; Harvey, 2001; Obiakor & Algozzine, 2001; Schwartz, 1996.

between members of two or more professions when they are dealing with client concerns that extend beyond the usual area of expertise of any one profession" (Gardner et al., 1998). The ability of a variety of professionals to share and collaborate effectively is crucial to program success.

Suppose, for example, that one of your students has had surgery for a cleft palate and needs support to learn to speak clearly. In order to respond, you would need to meet at various times with the child's parents or family and other educators. Additionally, you might work with other professionals, such as a pediatrician or a speech/language pathologist. Without the benefit of these blended perspectives, it would be exceedingly difficult to address the needs of the child.

A clear philosophy, commitment to every child, appropriate teacher support, and collaboration with families and professionals all make essential contributions to establishing a community of language learners. In the next section, you will meet Cheryl, my former student. Now a teacher, Cheryl illustrates how all of these principles can be put into practice.

Collaboration with Families and Professionals

PEARSON
myeducationkit™

Go to the Assignments and Activities section of Chapter 1 in MyEducationKit and complete the activity entitled "Culture and the Classroom Community."

Cheryl is a public school teacher in urban California. This year, her class includes Victoria, a child from Venezuela who speaks and writes Spanish but almost no English; Caitlin, a child with a severe vision impairment called *macular degeneration* that will eventually lead to blindness; and Mei, a bilingual Hmong child, the son of two Vietnamese graduate students at the university. Cheryl uses a wide variety of strategies to facilitate the language growth of these children and give them a sense of belonging.

In Victoria's case, Cheryl reads about ways to support dual language learners. By getting to know Victoria's extended family, she finds out that the first-grader has an aunt in high school who has been in the United States for several years. The schoolday for secondary students ends early, so Victoria's aunt volunteers each afternoon from 2:30 to 3:30, a plan that also benefits her because she is enrolled in the child-care training program at the vocational school.

For Caitlin, the child with the vision impairment, Cheryl builds her understanding of vision problems and consults with special education teachers in her school district to plan appropriate activities. Additionally, she works with the local Association for the Blind to get Caitlin's family in contact with a program that trains leader dogs for the blind so that Caitlin can get on the waiting list early.

In the case of Mei, who is fluent in two languages, Cheryl involves him almost like a teacher's aide to help other Hmong children in the school who are newly immigrated to the United States and are just beginning to learn English. This arrangement has provided Mei with many challenging activities, such as translating some easy readers and recording the accompanying audio. The book/audio combinations created by

Mei have been made available to be checked out of the library. Cheryl has also helped Mei locate a bilingual pen pal on the Internet.

As a result of Cheryl's efforts, all three of these children are progressing well in school and have a respected place among their peers.

Contributions and Consequences

- *Contributions of the teacher:* How did the teacher play an active role in the lives of these children?
- *Contributions of the family:* How did each family support their child and get involved?
- *Contributions of other professionals:* How did professionals in other fields contribute to addressing the needs of these children and families?
- *Consequences of collaboration:* If the adults had refused to work together, what might have been the effect on the children's literacy learning?

Clearly, Cheryl is making every effort to address these standards in her daily classroom practices. The remainder of this chapter provides detailed information about how you too can become a successful teacher in diverse early childhood settings. To begin, look at Figure 1.3 to get a preview of the general recommendations for working with diverse learners in the language arts classroom.

Meeting the Needs of Children with Language Differences

Without question, the United States is a diverse society, yet our nation's track record in working with language differences in the classroom is not a source of pride. When my mother, Felicia, attended public school in the city of New York in the 1930s, it was customary to punish children (e.g., force them to write "I will speak English at school" 1,000 times) for speaking their native languages. One day, Felicia was caught speaking Italian to a little boy who had just moved to the United States from Italy and asked her for help. While she stood frozen with fear, awaiting her punishment, her teacher said, "Oh, Felicia. You speak Italian. I think it would be wonderful to learn another language, especially one as beautiful as Italian!" When little Felicia shared this incident with her mother, the teacher was invited to the most sumptuous six-course lunch that my Italian grandmother could prepare, complete with her hand-crocheted table linens and real china and crystal!

Even though there were some enlightened teachers like this one, who went against standard practices, the prevailing attitude toward any language other than English prior to the 1960s was to get rid of it as rapidly as possible. As support for this point of view, educators pointed to the bilingual child's tendency to mix the two languages as if they were one, combining words from each (e.g., a Spanish-speaking child who says "I like el gato" for "I like the cat"). This *code switching*, as it is

Brain and Language

In a study of the young child's ability to perform short-term memory tasks, the researchers found that most preschoolers were capable of explaining the strategies they used to recall information (Visu-Petra, Cheie, & Benga, 2008). The children described, for example, practicing in their minds and using words to remember the pictures. How could a teacher coach children to do this? Visit the Dana Foundation (www.dana.org) website for the latest findings on neuroscience.

Attitude

Maintain a positive attitude and focus on children's strengths rather than their limitations, saying, for example, "Ask Jon. He can answer you on his Vox," rather than "Jon can't talk." Be patient and encourage children to do likewise.

Fairness

Realize that being fair is much more than "treating everyone the same." Actually, you will need to treat children differently while being fair and just. It isn't fair, for example, to criticize a child with Tourette's syndrome (a physiological disorder that causes people to have unpredictable verbal outbursts) for talking when you have asked children to listen quietly to the story.

Rules

Make expectations clear and establish a very small number of rules with the children. For instance, have rules about health and safety, such as "No hurting other people," to include hitting, biting, kicking, shoving, and so on.

Directions

Give directions in clear, concise, and sequential fashion and support the directions with demonstration. For example, *show* children how to use the listening center and walk them through the procedures, one step at a time, instead of merely telling them about it.

Manner of Presentation

Use concrete examples and demonstrate how to proceed whenever possible, such as showing children how to form the letters of the alphabet by writing with a finger dipped in paint, in sand, with a marker on chartpaper, on the chalkboard, with a laser pointer, on an overhead transparency, and so forth. Use multisensory approaches.

Time

Break up instructional time—for example, a 10-minute large-group discussion in the morning and 10 minutes at the end of the day, rather than 20 minutes at one time. Give children more time to complete a task if they need it.

Adaptations

Individualize activities; for example, a child who has great difficulty writing might be asked to write just the first letter of his or her name. Others in the class might be expected to write their entire names. Give every child a chance to be successful.

Narration

Interpret the behavior of special-needs children for the other students so that they begin to understand them better. For instance, you might say, "Shannon is coming over to play house with you. Look, she's starting up her wheelchair. Now she's ready to be the mother. Give her a baby doll to put on her tray."

Encouragement

Instead of using stock phrases (e.g., "very good," "good job"), give specific feedback that urges the child to move to the next level, such as "Tony, I noticed that you know so many things about trucks when we talked about our story today. I'm going to loan you this book to take home and show to your mom and grandma. Tomorrow, there will be a story about airplanes that I think you will like."

Small Spaces

Many children prefer small, comfortable spaces where they can read, work without distraction, or simply "get away from it all." Designate a quiet area. It could be a corner with pillows and a book center with low shelves, for instance.

Parents and Families

Dispel fears that the child will be excluded or caused to feel incompetent. Share successes often, so that parents and families can really see how their children are benefiting from the program.

Professionals

Know who to turn to for particular types of support and when it is appropriate to do so. Do not consider it a personal failure if you cannot "make it all better" for a child who has profound problems.

Celebrations

Celebrate successes, large and small. For a child with autism, it might be a note that reads "Gabriel talked today! He knew the answer to a subtraction problem."

PEARSON
myeducationkit™

Go to the Assignments and Activities section of Chapter 1 in MyEducationKit and complete the activity entitled "Meeting the Needs of Children with Language Differences."

called, used to be cited as evidence that a child's first language interfered with learning English, but studies now document that skill in one language supports and complements learning another language (Conteh, 2007; Jalongo & Li, 2010).

Historically, the dominant social group has made a deliberate effort to make children conform and abandon their first language. When young children are immersed in a culture where one language is associated with high prestige and social success, their first language may be sacrificed (Fillmore, 1991; National Association for the Education of Young Children, 1996a). There are many personal accounts of children from different cultures who have felt pressured to abandon their first language. Yet if they do this before they have mastered English, they often become fluent in neither language. Moreover, when children abandon their native tongue, it is in some ways a rejection of the culture represented by their first language (Fillmore, 1991; Ogbu, 1988). Nevertheless, many places throughout the world continue to violate children's linguistic rights and fail to respect their first language (Cummins, 2003; Reyes & Azuara, 2008).

As teachers, we must be aware of our language biases. Why is it that the same adult who cringes to hear an Appalachian child say "I didn't do nothing" or a Hispanic child pronounce *chocolate* as "shoclate" is thoroughly charmed to hear a British child pronounce *schedule* as "shedule" or finds the New England pronunciation of *idea* as "idear" appealing? Evidently, some language differences win social approval because they tend to be associated with individuals who have higher social status.

Infants and Toddlers

According to the Children's Defense Fund (2008), one in five children under age 3 in the United States is poor. Look into a program called Women, Infants and Children (WIC) at www.wicworks.ca.gov. What are the program's goals, and why is it important to offer supplemental nutrition to the very young?

If you doubt that you have such biases, consider what occurs when a college teacher is not a native speaker of English. College students will sometimes complain about or even ridicule instructors who do not speak English as their first language and protest that they do not understand them. It is more often the case that some college students are not willing to make the extra effort to communicate, have a certain arrogance about being fluent speakers of English, and/or feel superior because their families "were here first." Everyone possesses some language biases; the challenge for teachers is to be aware of these prejudices and make a genuine effort to change.

Early childhood educators are required to respect the child's home language, even if no one in the community speaks that language (Nemeth, 2009a, b). Some excellent resources on second language learning are in the ELLs feature of this chapter on pages 20–22.

Overview of Children's Language Differences

Six major categories of linguistically different children can be identified.

Autism Spectrum Disorders

Autism spectrum disorders are developmental disabilities that have a pervasive effect on verbal and nonverbal communication as well as social interaction (Branson, Vigil, & Bingham, 2008; Hyman & Tobin, 2007). Autism is generally evident before age 3 and is believed to be the result of a neurological disorder that occurs in nearly 1 in 100 births (Centers for Disease Control and Prevention, 2010). Autism ranges in severity from total absence of speech to language that is adequate in form but disordered from the perspective of social appropriateness and meaning (Hall, 2009; Zager, 2004); for this reason, it often is referred to as a spectrum. About half of children on the autism spectrum do not speak at all, while others have some speech but may avoid social interaction and eye contact. Children with autism spectrum disorders may have difficulty being understood by others because they do not make the connections between old and new information explicit. Some behaviors displayed by children with autism may include repetitive movements (e.g., rocking, waving fingers in front of the face), meaningless repetition of language (called *echolalia*), a resistance to environmental change or change in routines, unusual responses to sensory experiences, and an inability to interpret and respond appropriately to social cues. Some children on the autism spectrum are gifted in one or more of the curricular areas.

PEARSON

myeducationkit™

Go to the Assignments and Activities section of Chapter 1 in MyEducationKit and complete the activity entitled "Understanding the Dimensions of Multiculturalism."

English Language Learners

The designation *English language learner* is commonly used to refer to children who do not have English as a first language and are working to acquire proficiency in English. The most common example is the newly immigrated child who is enrolled in a school where English is the dominant language of instruction.

Children with Gifts and Talents in Language

Children with high verbal/linguistic intelligence may evidence exceptional strengths and abilities that set them apart from peers. These children use language in ways that are more advanced and more creative than most peers; therefore the language activities in which the child is engaged need to offer intellectual challenges. Characteristics of these children may include mastering the letter symbols and sounds early, exhibiting intense curiosity, displaying extraordinary memory, showing great persistence at language tasks, learning multiple languages, or attaining highly advanced conversational abilities. It is also possible to have both a "gift" and a disability (Feeney, Moravcik, Nolte, & Christensen, 2009).

Language Delay

My first experience with a child's language delay involved twin sisters who had created their own unique language that others could not understand, a phenomenon called *idioglossia*. As a result, the twins' ability to communicate was lagging far behind that of their preschool peers. A child with a language delay is acquiring and using spoken language at a much slower rate (usually a year or more behind) than that of agemates. For example, most young children speak their first recognizable words around 12 months of age. If a 2-year-old child who appears to be developing normally in other ways has not yet begun to use expressive language, it is generally considered cause for concern. Often these delays are attributed to undetected middle ear infections that interfere with the ability to hear and process language.

Language Disabilities

This category includes a wide variety of influences that affect a child's ability to use language. It may be a learning disability that makes it difficult for the child to write. It could be a physiological problem, such as deafness, that impedes the child's ability to use speech. It could also be a language processing problem caused by difficulties in sustaining attention (Biederman, 2005). Serious language problems can be caused by stress as well, as in the case of children who are neglected and deprived of normal opportunities to develop language or who are terribly abused and shut themselves off from the world by remaining silent.

Dialectical Differences

Dialectical differences refer to variations in the way the same basic language is spoken, such as an African American child who speaks African American English (AAE). Some characteristics of this dialect may include substituting an "f" sound for a "th" in the middle or at the end of a word ("toof" for "tooth"; "aufor" for "author"), dropping the verb ending (e.g., "He see it" for "He sees it"), differences in the verb forms of *are* (e.g., "She be bringing it" rather than "She is bringing it"), and different pronunciations for particular words (e.g., "liberry" for "library" or "exspecially" for "especially"). Languages also have regional dialects; for example, people from the southern United States speak English differently from those in England, Australia, or even other parts of the United States.

 ## Teacher Concerns and Basic Strategies

Three teachers made the following comments about the children in their classes with language differences:

> This year, for the first time, I worked with a 3-year-old foster child who was exposed to "crack" cocaine during his prenatal development. At first, he was wild. I have to admit that when I saw him come into the front door of my family day care, I wanted to run right out the back. But as he learned to use language to express himself, his behavior started to get under control. It's funny, because at first, I had many sleepless nights thinking that it would be impossible to work with him. But now he fits in so well.

> When I heard that Jesus, a 4-year-old boy with spina bifida who could not speak and was not toilet trained, would be in my prekindergarten class, I was worried that the children would make fun of him. But his mother would bring him just for the afternoon

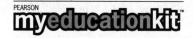

Go to the Assignments and Activities section of Chapter 1 in MyEducationKit and complete the activity entitled "Teaching to Promote Self-Esteem."

session, fresh from his bath and smelling of baby powder. The special education teacher worked with me to build my confidence and skill. Jesus would respond to us by smiling and cooing. He won all of our hearts.

This year, I volunteered to teach in the school district's summer program. There were two boys from Mexico who did not speak English assigned to my class. The first day, I overheard one of the boys say to the other, "La rubia dice que" ("The blonde says that"). I realized that they were referring to me! I hadn't even introduced myself. That night, I took out my old Spanish books from college and tried to refresh my memory. Then I borrowed a Spanish course on CD-ROM from the library. I am using more visual aids than ever before and watch these boys to see if they are getting the gist of the activities. They are certainly quicker at learning English than I have been at learning Spanish, even though I studied it previously.

The following basic strategies will guide you in creating a sense of community in your early childhood language arts program.

1. *Examine personal attitudes and beliefs about children and families that are linguistically and culturally different.* This is an essential starting point in establishing a culturally responsive curriculum that values human diversity. Do not assume that children who speak other languages live only in large urban areas. Just think about some of the situations that may bring dramatic language differences into your classroom or center. It might be children who are adopted from other countries, whose parents are on student visas and enrolled in college studies, who are indigenous peoples (e.g., Native American tribes), who live in regions of the country (e.g., the Southwest) where another language is spoken, who have lived abroad and become fluent in another language, or who have studied a language as part of their religious training (e.g., Hebrew). These are just a few of the possibilities, and the teacher's role is to support them all (Dixon, 2008).

Teachers must accept linguistically diverse learners and believe that learning content takes precedence over studying English as a subject (Suarez, 2003). In order for all students to have equal opportunities for education success, teachers must be aware not only of what children need to learn but also of the knowledge and skills that they bring from their own linguistic and cultural backgrounds (Fillmore & Snow, 2002; Park & King, 2003).

2. *Confront your language biases.* It is not possible to work effectively with English language learners without first genuinely welcoming them into classroom communities, treating them with respect and kindness, and advocating for their needs (Houck, 2005; Parker & Pardini, 2006). As teachers, we must be aware of our language biases. The daily routines, traditions, and expectations for school of children and families from the nonmajority culture often can be a source of surprise to white, middle-class teachers (Baghban, 2007a). Rather than imposing the dominant culture's "agenda" on others, teachers need to be open-minded and willing to learn from others.

3. *Strive to learn about and understand language differences.* There is a difference between behaviors that occur naturally during second-language acquisition and those that are indicative of learning problems. Without knowledge of such differences, teachers can misdiagnose young children as having learning disabilities. Approach language differences positively, rather than viewing them as problems (Volk & Long, 2008).

4. *Embrace different methods of communication.* One important responsibility of teachers is to accept children's efforts to communicate; every child's language has to be valued and respected.

Kindergarten children, for instance, are delighted to discover that they can use gestures to communicate a simple message: "I (point to self), want (extend arms forward, palms up, and bring hands up toward chest in a grasping gesture), cookies (do the motion of cutting out a cookie with a cookie cutter, using the left hand to represent the dough)." Teaching children some American Sign Language, allowing them to try out communicating with a picture board, or typing messages are all ways to help children respect alternative forms of communication.

5. *Allocate time for peer interaction.* Children's language when engaged in play with peers tends to be varied, complex, and sophisticated. Therefore, it is important to give children a chance to engage in spontaneous and natural conversations.

6. *Create a language-rich environment that gives students a chance to engage in meaningful activities.* Evaluate the classroom environment to make certain that books, supplies, postings, newsletters, and equipment convey positive messages about language diversity and disabilities. Provide models of good English language use as well as of the languages spoken at home by children and their families.

Cummins (2003) offers the following general principles about English language learners:

- Children's native language is fragile and easily lost in the early years of school. In the absence of strong support for their first language, children can lose their ability to communicate in it within 2 to 3 years of starting school (Soto, Smrekar, & Nekovei, 2001).
- Bilingualism has positive effects on children's linguistic and educational development.
  - A child's level of development in his or her first language (L1) is a strong predictor of development in a second language (L2).
  - A well-implemented bilingual program can promote literacy and subject matter knowledge in a minority language without having any negative effects on a child's development in the majority language.
  - To reject a child's language in the school is to reject the child.

For the latest on bilingual education, visit James Crawford's Language Policy Website (http://ourworld.compuserve.com/homepages/JWCRAWFORD).

7. *Develop a family-centered friendly program.* Establish a schoolwide support group of teachers, staff, families, and community members that meets regularly and frequently

Research and Report
Visit a school's website and search for information about the students' performance on tests of reading. Then use your college library or search engine to consult the publication *Education Week's Quality Counts* annual report (or access it via the free website at www.edweek.org/ew/qc/2008/18src.h27.html). This group "grades" every state on various quality indicators and its report is called the Nation's Report Card. How does your home state compare with others?

to promote the goal of effective programs for students with different languages and language abilities. The teacher has a responsibility for fostering language and needs to maintain high expectations for all students.

8. *Use a multifaceted approach to assessment.* Combine different types of assessments—particularly observations of the child during play and in informal conversation with peers—to get a well-rounded picture of each child's language capabilities.

Classroom Activities to Support Diverse Language Learners

I Can . . .   Highlight children's achievements beyond English on a bulletin board. For example, abilities such as: "I can count to 10 in English and Spanish," "I can say please and thank you in Farsi, Chinese, and Hmong," "I can write your name in Arabic," or "I can teach you some sign language" all encourage children to seek out the skills of their classmates so that they can contribute to the display. Many different types of texts produced by children can be a way to communicate with families as well (Lee, 2006). For example, a kindergarten class was studying pairs of opposites so children drew and labeled one half of the page while their families drew and labeled the other. One grandfather sent back a humorous self-portrait labeled with "my nose is long" in response to his grandson's drawing of "my hair is short."

PEARSON

Go to the Assignments and Activities section of Chapter 1 in MyEducationKit and complete the activity entitled "Classroom Activities."

Let Children See Themselves in Books   Picture books by Ann Morris (*Loving; Shoes, Shoes, Shoes; Hats, Hats, Hats*) celebrate the universal as well as the particular. Likewise, books about food by Norah Dooley (*Everybody Cooks Rice, Everybody Brings Noodles,* and *Everybody Serves Soup*) show the many variations of these items. Activities that are familiar, yet somewhat different, help children to be more accepting of the differences they encounter. Book series such as those by Mary Lankford (*Hopscotch around the World, Dominoes around the World, Birthdays around the World, Mazes around the World, Jacks around the World*), Beatrice Hollyer (*Wake Up, World! A Day in the Life of Children around the World* and *Let's Eat: What Children Eat around the World*), or Edith Baer (*This Is the Way We Go to School* and *This Is the Way We Eat Our Lunch*) are sure to start discussions.

Our Names For   There are a surprising number of names for family members; for example, grandparents might be called abuela, papa, mawmaw, grandpa, dadima, grand-pap, pap, poppi, papap, and so forth. Talk with children about the different names for mothers, fathers, siblings, and other family members. Emphasize that those differing from their own are not strange; rather, they are a reflection of that family's traditions.

Text Translation   Check out a free website called Babelfish (babelfish.yahoo.com). Type the text of a favorite children's book into the box, page by page, and number the pages accordingly. After the book has been translated, ask a volunteer with proficiency in the child's first language to proof it for errors. Make a copy of the book, paste the translated text below the English, and give it to the child to facilitate following with the story as the book is read. An online source of international children's stories can be found at http://en.childrenslibrary.org.

Job Descriptions   Have children think about the classroom duties that need to be performed and the skill set best matched to each role; for example, what abilities are important in tending to classroom pets? How about plants? What about line leader? Story editor? Meet with small groups of children to develop job descriptions for each responsibility.

Seek Out Multicultural Concept Books   Alphabet books such as the African *Ashanti to Zulu* (Musgrove, 1992), the British *The Queen's Progress: An Elizabethan Alphabet* (Mannis, 2005), the African American *K Is for Kwanzaa* (Ford, 2003), the Native American *Many Nations: An Alphabet of Native America* (Bruchac, 2004), and two in both Spanish and English, *Gathering the Sun/Cosecha de Sol: An Alphabet in Spanish and English* (Ada, 2001) or *F Is for Fiesta* (Elya, 2006) encourage children to think beyond their own experiences. Likewise, counting books that expand children's experiences beyond their immediate environment such as *We All Went on Safari: A Counting Journey through Tanzania* (Krebs, 2004) introduce children to cultures beyond their own. *Mung, Mung: A Fold Out Book of Animal Sounds* (Park, 2004) introduces children to the different ways that animal sounds are interpreted by various cultures.

Proverbs That Teach   Older students or children who have high verbal/linguistic intelligence will find this to be a challenging task. Ask them to interview older family members and collect proverbs, adages, sayings, or (as in Spanish) *dichos*. For example, "Don't cry over spilled milk," Don't put all your eggs in one basket," or "The early bird gets the worm." After they have discussed and understood the meanings of the expressions with their family members, have them illustrate each saying and make them into a big book or e-book to share with families at conference time. For websites devoted to proverbs throughout the world, see Proverbs by Country of Origin (www.famous-quotations.com/asp/origins.asp), Proverbs from 300 Countries and Cultures (http://creativeproverbs.com), or CogWeb's Proverb Resources (http://cogweb.ucla.edu/Discourse/Proverbs/index.html).

Which Traditions?   As Balaban (2007) points out, teachers cannot assume that families who immigrate to the United States observe all of the traditions of their culture. So a family from Mexico may be familiar with but not necessarily participate in the festivities that are depicted in *Clatter Bash! A Day of the Dead Celebration* (Keep, 2008). On the other hand, a family may elect to make some of the mainstream culture's traditions a new part of their family's traditions, such as having a birthday cake or celebrating the 4th of July with a picnic. Instead of assuming that you know, ask the child if and how traditions are observed. Put yourself in the role of learner.

Conclusion

As you consider your role in working with diverse language learners, keep in mind what Boyer (1996) referred to as the "centrality of language":

> We have this wonderful capacity to communicate with one another, using the most intricate systems of symbols. One of the most critical responsibilities of the elementary school is to help children lay the best possible foundation for a deeper understanding of the symbols of words and numbers and the arts that together make up language. (p. 6)

PEARSON myeducationkit To check your comprehension on the content covered in this chapter, go to the MyEducationKit for your book and complete the Study Plan for Chapter 1. Here you will be able to take a chapter quiz and receive feedback on your answers.

Research-Based Literacy Strategies

Story Retelling Using Technology

After children are familiar with a story, they can retell it in their own words. Research suggests that story retelling is particularly effective with children who come from cultures with rich oral traditions (Au, 1993; Mason & Au, 1998). Inviting children to retell is an open-ended activity that allows for differentiation; children's versions of the story can range from simple to complex and therefore adjust to their developmental levels (Riley & Burrell, 2007; Sadik, 2008). Retelling is a good test of a child's memory, story comprehension, and attention to plot. Stories on CD-ROMs (see Shamir & Korat, 2006, for selection guidelines) are an avenue for retelling (Pearman, 2008); so are teacher-made electronic books (Rhodes & Milby, 2007). An online source for award-winning international books in various languages is found at http://en.childrenslibrary .org. Word-processing programs can also be used to generate computer images that stimulate children's imaginations and invite them to retell stories as well as build on the stories produced by peers. A worksheet to accompany retellings is posted at www.really goodstuff.com/pdfs/136442.pdf and a scoring rubric to use with older students is at www.louisianavoices .org/unit5/edu_unit5w_story_retelling.html.

Books for Children with Low Book Interest

Parents and families sometimes report that their young children are disinterested in picture books.

One way of bridging the gap between playing with toys and reading books is to choose picture books that invite participation, such as print copies of books with flaps to lift, parts that move, cutouts to peer through, and textures to touch, such as those by David Carter, Eric Hill, Dorothy Kundhardt, Steve Jenkins, Chuck Murphy, Jan Pienkowski, and Robert Sabuda. Some suitable for toddlers and preschoolers are *Dear Zoo* (Campbell, 2007), *Open the Barn Door* (Santoro, 1993), *Pat the Bunny* (Kundhardt, 1994), *Ten Bright Eyes* (Hindley, 1998), *How Many Bugs in a Box?* (Carter, 2006), and *Peek-a Who?* (Laden, 2000). For kindergarten/primary children, try *ABC 3-D* (Bataille, 2008) and *Gallop* (Seeder, 2007). Kaderavek and Justice (2005) found that such books generated longer sentences and more questions from children during in-home readings of storybooks.

The opportunity to manipulate books offers English language learners a chance to label not only pictures but also their actions while operating the book. In addition, interactive books often are predictable—with repeated phrases, rhymes, verses, or questions—and this supports children with language difficulties. Books based on familiar folktales or songs provide another source of support for children with language delays or disorders. Teachers will find the free Instant Multilanguage Translator at www.freetranslation.com to be a great resource for converting the texts of these books produced by children into the first language of other children.

Dolch Sight Word List

Approximately 50–75 percent of the words used in everyday reading are called "sight words" because readers are expected to quickly identify the word and its meaning (Smith, 2006). The Dolch sight word list consists of 250 sight words that often are used on spelling lists, flashcards, and various tests of knowledge of the English language (Liebert, 1991). It takes many, many repetitions of these words in order for them to become part of a sight word vocabulary, particularly for children with attention deficits and language disorders/ delays. Working with the Dolch list over time can support English language learners as they build a larger sight word vocabulary in their visual memory. Children who are advanced in language can master the Dolch sight word list at a rapid pace as a way to increase their reading fluency. Activities to practice the words are posted at http://reading .indiana.edu/ieo/bibs/dolchwordlist.html. Visit www .mrsperkins.com/dolch.htm to download Dolch lists suitable for different grade levels, in different formats (e.g., Word, pdf, worksheets, computer software).

Links with Literature
Books That Celebrate Diversity

What Is a Picture Book That Celebrates Diversity?

Part of the appeal of children's literature is identification with the traditional story elements of characters, settings, plot, and theme. Where nonfiction is concerned, books about other cultures, ethnic groups, and geographic regions build interest and inform the reader beyond his or her immediate experience. For these reasons, children's books that portray diversity are an essential part of any early childhood program (Braus & Geidel, 2000). Some guidelines for choosing and reasons for using *multicultural, multiethnic, and international literature* include the following:

Accuracy
- Does the information in both text and illustrations accurately depict the culture?
- Is the information in stories with contemporary settings up-to-date?

Portrayal of Characters
- Are the characters portrayed as unique individuals, rather than stereotyped representatives of a culture?
- Is the language spoken by the characters accurate and appropriate to their backgrounds and the social situation in which the action takes place?

- Do the characters have names that are authentic within their cultures?
- Are the characters' lives enriched and guided by their cultural backgrounds?
- Do characters demonstrate the ability to be leaders, to solve problems, to take the initiative?

Language
- Is the text free of words and images that are demeaning and offensive?

Perspective
- Is cultural diversity viewed as an asset?
- Does the book make it clear that it is not necessary to give up nonmainstream culture in order to be successful?
- Are characters from diverse cultures viewed as part of American society, rather than as outsiders?

Illustrations
- Are the images culturally accurate? Do they avoid stereotypes and caricatures?
- Do the illustrations show a variety of physical features among members of a group?
- Do the illustrations present specific rather than generic aspects of the culture?

Overall Effect
- Does the book contribute to the self-esteem of members of the culture portrayed?

- Does the book inform and enlighten members of other cultural groups who read the book? Can they relate to the characters in the book?
- Does the story invite multiple interpretations and avoid preaching a message?
- Is the book worthy of repeated rereading and extended conversations about it?

Sources: Glazer & Giorgis, 2008; McName & Mercurio, 2007; Norton, 2008.

How to Use Children's Books about Diversity

- Culturally diverse literature needs to be presented throughout the schoolyear, not governed by the calendar.
- Rather than singling out books about diversity, try grouping them with other related books.
- Strive to pronounce words in other languages accurately. Ask a native speaker of the language to assist you in pronouncing words and phrases.
- When reading books that are written in dialect, practice the dialect until you know it or do not attempt to read it that way.
- Be specific when referring to stories, authors, and illustrators.
- Invite children to participate in elaborating and contributing to the group's understanding of the elements within the book.
- Maintain good records of what you have read so that you can achieve a balance of topics.

Print Resources for Multicultural Books

Akrofi, A., Swafford, J., Janisch, C., Liu, X., & Durrington, V. (2008). Supporting immigrant students' understanding of U.S. culture through children's literature. *Childhood Education, 84,* 209–229.

Baghban, N. (2007). Immigration in childhood: Using picture books to cope. *Social Studies, 98,* 71–77.

Barr, C., & Gillespie, J. T. (2007). *Best books for children, supplement to the eighth edition: Preschool through grade 6.* Englewood, CO: Libraries Unlimited.

Blaska, J. (2003). *Using children's literature to learn about disabilities and illness.* Moorhead, MN: Practical Press.

Dyches, T. T., & Prater, M. A. (2008). *Teaching about disabilities through children's literature* (2nd ed.). Englewood, CO: Libraries Unlimited.

Freeman, J. (2006). *Books kids will sit still for 3: A read-aloud guide.* Englewood, CO: Libraries Unlimited.

Glasgow, J. N., & Rice, L. J. (Eds.). (2007). *Exploring African life and literature.* Newark, DE: International Reading Association.

Hadaway, N. L., & McKenna, M. J. (2007). *Breaking boundaries with global literature.* Newark, DE: International Reading Association.

Harris, V. J. (2008). Selecting books that children will want to read. *The Reading Teacher, 61*(5), 426–430.

Levin, F. (2007). Encouraging ethical respect through multicultural literature. *The Reading Teacher, 61*(1), 101–104.

Lima, C. W., & Lima, J. A. (2008). *A to Zoo: Subject access to picture books* (8th ed.). Englewood, CO: Libraries Unlimited.

McClellan, S., & Fields, M. E. (2004). Using African American children's literature to support literacy development. *Young Children, 59*(3), 50–54.

McClure, A. A., & Kristo, J. V. (2002). *Adventuring with books: A booklist for Pre-K–Grade 6.* Urbana, IL: National Council of Teachers of English.

Morrow, L. M., & Gambrell, L. B. (2004). *Using children's literature in preschool.* Newark, DE: International Reading Association.

National Association for the Education of Young Children. (2001). *Books to grow on: African American literature for young* children [Brochure #568]. Washington, DC: Author.

Norton, D. E. (2008). *Multicultural children's literature: Through the eyes of many children.* (3rd ed.). Upper Saddle River, NJ: Prentice Hall.

Odean, K. (2002). *Great books for girls: More than 600 books to inspire today's girls and tomorrow's women.* New York: Ballantine.

Quintero, E. P. (2004). Will I lose a tooth? Will I learn to read? Problem posing with multicultural children's literature. *Young Children, 59*(3), 56–62.

Rand, D., & Parker, T. T. (2001). *Black books galore! Guide to more great African American children's books.* New York: John Wiley.

Schon, I. (2002) *Books to grow on: Latino literature for young children* [Brochure #581; Available in Spanish #581S]. Washington, DC: NAEYC.

Silvey, A. (2005). *Best books for children: A parent's guide to making the right choices for your young reader, toddler to preteen.* Boston: Mariner/Houghton Mifflin.

Steiner, S. F. (2001). *Promoting a global community through multicultural children's literature* (2nd ed.). Englewood, CO: Libraries Unlimited.

Yokota, J. (Ed.). (2001). *Kaleidoscope: A multicultural booklist for grades K–8* (3rd ed.). Urbana, IL: National Council of Teachers of English.

Zambo, D., & Brozo, W. (2008). *Bright beginnings for boys: Engaging young boys in active literacy.* Newark, DE: International Reading Association.

Zbaracki, M. D. (2008). *Best books for boys: A resource for educators.* Englewood, CO: Libraries Unlimited.

Internet Sources

Celebrating Cultural Diversity through Children's Literature
www.multiculturalchildrenslit.com

Children's Books Online: The Rosetta Project Library
www.childrensbooksonline.org/library.htm

Children's Literature Reviews
www.childrenslit.com/childrenslit/home.html

International Books Online
http://en.childrenslibrary.org

International Children's Digital Library
www.icdlbooks.org

ELLs

Who Is the Young English Language Learner?

Teachers need to learn about language backgrounds of students, including: What languages are spoken in the community? In the home? For worship? For school activities? In which language is a given child's receptive language strongest? Expressive language? Is the child's first language firmly in place? (Tabors, 2008). Although it is customary to assume that young English language learners are from families that have left desperate circumstances to pursue a better quality of life or that they reside only in urban areas, this describes only some of our immigrant population. Thus, the 10 million children in the United States who speak a language other than English at home can be surprisingly diverse, not only in terms of their national origins and the amount of exposure to and practice with the English language they've amassed but also with respect to their socioeconomic circumstances and the educational levels of other family members (Federal Interagency Forum on Child and Family Statistics, 2006). To illustrate just a few frequently overlooked categories of young English learners, they may be: children of international adoption who have varying levels of familiarity with their native language (Meacham, 2007); children whose first language (L1) actually consists of two languages (e.g., a tribal language and a national language); economically privileged children whose parents are employed in international trade, politics, science, or medicine; or young children who use one language for worship and a second for conversation.

ELLs with Strong Academic Preparation

- Are at or above equivalent grade levels in the school curricula and are literate in their native language
- Need English language development so that they can keep up with academic content demands
- Can transfer their educational knowledge to their new experiences, but young ELLs may not have much experience with distinct subject areas (e.g., social studies, science)

Implications for Instruction

These children will be able to use their mastery of the L1 as a "scaffold" on which to build their knowledge of English; therefore, learning English becomes an additive process and ELLs' L1 is considered a valuable asset (Cárdenas-Hagan, Carlson, & Pollard-Durodola, 2007). Strategies for developing vocabulary in English are essential (August, Carlo, Dressler, & Snow, 2005). Effective instruction draws on the sum of ELLs' experiences in listening, speaking, reading, and writing as a whole for their literacy growth (Vandergrift, 2006). The support of teachers, volunteers, and peers with proficiency in both languages helps children in making connections between languages and mastering content across the curriculum (Parker & Pardini, 2006).

ELLs with Limited Formal Schooling

- May not have attended school due to war, poverty, or geographic isolation and may need additional time to become accustomed to school routines and expectations

- Are not literate in their native language; therefore, it has limited value as a scaffold for learning English
- May have significant gaps in their educational backgrounds across the subject areas
- Need literacy skills, English language development, and content area knowledge

Implications for Instruction

In order for English to be understandable, instruction for ELLs with limited school experience begins with the enactive and iconic modes (Bruner, 2004). The enactive mode engages them in actually doing something in order to connect it with language (e.g., using a spoon to eat soup in combination with the words *spoon, eat,* and *soup*). The iconic mode uses concrete objects (e.g., fruit or plastic replicas of fruit) or pictorial representations of objects (e.g., photographs, clip art) to support vocabulary growth and make the language that is heard more understandable. Gradually, children can begin to connect the symbolic mode (e.g., letters, words, numbers, and other abstract symbols) with the enactive and iconic.

ELLs Raised in the United States Who Speak a Language Other Than English at Home

- May not be literate in L1 or L2 or may be literate in their home language but need to expand their knowledge of English at school
- May rely extensively on child care and school settings as the opportunity to learn and practice English
- May be members of "linguistically isolated households" defined by the U.S. Bureau of the Census (2003) as homes in which no one has proficiency in English
- May be called on by parents to serve as spokespersons or interpreters in English or even in L1

Implications for Instruction

Family literacy programs that address the language skills of parents as well as children are valuable (Saracho, 2008). Inviting volunteers into the classroom

who can speak the child's L1 can be an important form of support for young ELLs. Offering special classes or workshops to raise parents' awareness of the importance of supporting children's learning at home, or offering family literacy programs can increase the opportunities for families to learn together.

Adapted from *Literacy Development for Language Minority Children*, Presented at the First Annual OELA (Office of English Language Acquisition, U.S. Department of Education) Summit, Washington, DC.

Online Resources for Teaching English Language Learners

Asher, J. J. (2000). *Year 2000 update for the Total Physical Response, known world-wide as TPR.* Los Gatos, CA: Sky Oaks Productions.

www.tpr-world.com/tpr-y2k.html

Ballantyne, K. G., Sanderman, A. R., & McLaughlin, N. (2008). *Dual language learners in the early years: Getting ready to succeed in school.* Washington, DC: National Clearinghouse for English Language Acquisition.

www.ncela.gwu.edu/resabout/ecell/earlyyears.pdf

English Language Instructional Support for English Language Learners (ODE)

www.ode.state.or.us/cifs/english/ellstandards.pdf

English Second Language (AskERIC)

http://ericir.syr.edu/cgibin/print.cgi/Resources/Subjects/Foreign_Language/English_Second_Language.html

ESL Department (NWREL)

www.nwrel.org/sky/department.asp?ID=3D0&d=3D15

ESL resources (from Blue Web'n)

www.kn.pacbell.com

Espinosa, L. (2008). *Challenging common myths about young English language learners.* Policy Brief no. 8. January. New York: Foundation for Child Development.

www.fcd-us.org/resources/resources_show.htm?doc_id=660789

EverythingESL.net

http://everythingesl.net

Michael Krauss

www.lclark.edu/~krauss

National Clearinghouse for English Language Acquisition in the Classroom

www.ncela.gwu.edu

Online Directory of ESL Resources

www.cal.org/ericcll/ncbe/esldirectory

World Class Instructional Design and Assessment (WIDA): A Resource Guide

www.wida.us/standards/Resource_Guide_web.pdf

World Class Instructional Design and Assessment (WIDA): CAN DO Descriptors

www.wida.us/standards/CAN_DOs/index.aspx

Print Resources for Teaching English Language Learners

Akhavan, N. L. (2006). *Help! My kids don't all speak English: How to set up a language workshop in your linguistically diverse classroom.* Portsmouth, NH: Heinemann.

Cary, S. (2004). *Going graphic: Comics at work in the multilingual classroom.* Portsmouth, NH: Heinemann.

Crawford, J. (2007). *Educating English learners: Language diversity in the classroom* (6th ed.). Los Angeles, CA: Bilingual Educational Services.

Freeman, Y., & Freeman, D. (2006). *Teaching reading and writing in Spanish and English in bilingual and dual language classrooms* (2nd ed.). Portsmouth, NH: Heinemann.

Menyuk, P., & Brisk, M. E. (2005). *Language development and education: Children with varying language experience.* Hampshire, UK: Palgrave Macmillan.

Nemeth, K. N. (2009). *Many languages, one classroom: Tips and techniques for teaching English language learners in preschool.* Beltsville, MD: Gryphon House.

Samway, K. D. (2006). *When English language learners write.* Portsmouth, NH: Heinemann.

Uribe, M., & Nathenson-Mejia, S. (2008). *Literacy essentials for English language learners: Successful transitions.* New York: Teachers College Press.

Van Sluys, K. (2005). *What if and why? Literacy invitations in multilingual classrooms.* Portsmouth, NH: Heinemann.

How Do I ...

Find High-Quality Picture Books Using the Internet?

High-quality picture books are a tremendous resource for planning lessons and designing learning activities that are well suited to children's developmental levels (Dwyer & Neuman, 2008). As a first step, review the "10 Quick Ways to Analyze Children's Books for Racism and Sexism" from the Council for Interracial Books for Children posted at www.birchlane.davis.ca.us/library/10quick.htm.

Consider the following questions when selecting books for children:

- Does the book compare favorably with other picture books of its type?
- Has the picture book received the endorsements of professionals?
- Are the literary elements of plot, theme, character, style, and setting used effectively?
- Do the pictures complement the story?
- Is the story free from ethnic, racial, or sex-role stereotypes?

- Is the picture book developmentally appropriate for the child?
- Do preschoolers respond enthusiastically to the book?
- Is the topic (and the book's treatment of it) suitable for the young child?
- Does the picture book appeal to the parent or teacher?

Additional evaluation questions consider the illustrations:

- Are the illustrations and text synchronized?
- Does the mood expressed by the artwork (humorous or serious, rollicking or quiet) complement that of the story?
- Are the illustrative details consistent with the text?
- Could a child get a sense of the basic concepts or story sequence by looking just at the pictures?
- Are the illustrations or photographs aesthetically pleasing?

- Is the printing (clarity, form, line, color) of good quality?
- Can children view and re-view the illustrations, each time getting more from them?
- Are the illustrative style and complexity suited to the age level of the intended audience? (Huck, Kiefer, Hepler, & Hickman, 2003)

Online Lists of Best Books

American Library Association Notable Books for Children
www.ala.org/booklist/index.html

Award-Winning Links
www.magickeys.com

Award-Winning Picture Books and Recommended Authors/Illustrators
http://childrensbooks.about.com/od/ages610 learningtoread/u/new_readers.htm#s3

Bank Street College of Education
www.bnkst.edu/bookcom

Best Children's Books by Age
www.parents.com/family-life/entertainment/ childrens-books

Children's Literature Sites
www.col.k12.me.us/teachers/sites.html

Children's Literature Web Guide
www.acs.ucalgary.ca/~dkbrown

Classic Picture Books
www.kidsreads.com/lists/pic-classic.asp
http://childrenspicturebooks.info/picture_book_link.htm

International Reading Association "Children's Choices" and "Teacher's Choices"
www.reading.org/Resources/Booklists/ ChildrensChoices.aspx
www.reading.org/Resources/Booklists/ TeachersChoices.aspx

Kirkus Reviews
www.kirkusreviews.com/kirkusreviews/images/pdf/ BestChildrens.pdf

National Association for the Education of Young Children
www.naeyc.org/families/childrensbooks.asp

National Education Association (NEA)
www.teachersfirst.com/100books.htm

New York Public Library
http://kids.nypl.org/reading/recommended.cfm

New York Times
www.nytimes.com/slideshow/2008/11/06/books/ 20081109ILLUSTRATEDBOOKS_index.html

Notable Books for a Global Society (International Reading Association)
www.csulb.edu/org/childrens-lit/proj/nbgs/intro-nbgs .html

Publishers Weekly Children's Bestseller List
www.bookwire.com/AboutB/inside.html

Reading Rainbow
www.pbs.org/readingrainbow/index.html

PEARSON myeducationkit™ Now go to Chapter 1 in the MyEducationKit (**www.MyEducationKit .com**) for your book, where you can:

- Find Chapter Objectives.
- Complete Assignments and Activities that can help you more deeply understand the chapter content.
- Extend knowledge with content-specific Web Links.
- Check your comprehension on the content covered in the chapter by going to the Study Plan. Here you will be able to take a chapter quiz, receive feedback on your answers, and then access resources that will enhance your understanding of chapter content.

chapter two

Optimizing Every Child's Language Growth through Family Literacy

Annie Pickert/Pearson Education

on Families

- The federal poverty line for a family of four in 2008 was $21,200. Almost 1 in 13 children in the United States—5.8 million—lives in extreme poverty, defined as a household income below $10,600 for a family of four (Children's Defense Fund, 2008).
- The percentage of children under age 18 living with two married parents fell from 77 percent in 1980 to 68 percent in 2007. In 2007, 23 percent of children lived with only their mothers, 3 percent lived with only their fathers, 3 percent lived with two unmarried parents, and 4 percent lived with neither of their parents (Federal Interagency Forum on Child and Family Statistics, 2008).

- While the population age 5 and over grew by 25 percent from 1980 to 2000, the number who spoke a language other than English at home more than doubled (U.S. Bureau of the Census, 2003, p. 2).

- The most common languages spoken at home in the United States are, in descending order, English, Spanish, Chinese, French, and German. In recent years, Mandarin Chinese has jumped from the fifth to the second most widely spoken non-English language in the United States (U.S. Bureau of the Census, 2003, p. 3).

- Preschool children from homes where literacy is supported have an estimated 1,000 to 1,700 hours of informal reading and writing encounters before coming to school, while children without such family support have only 25 hours of such experiences during the preschool years (Adams, 1990). National survey data suggest that children from literacy-rich homes are able to recognize letters and perform better in reading (Denton, West, & Walston, 2003).

- Literacy development is greatly influenced by family life. Studies have shown that children's literacy skills are enhanced when their family members read to them at home, model reading to children, make reading and writing materials available at home, and stimulate children to raise and respond to questions (Gillanders & Jiménez, 2004; Hood, Conlon, & Andrews, 2008; Swick, 2009).

- More that one-third of children in the United States enter school with significant deficiencies in language, early literacy skills, and motivation to learn that place them at risk for developing long-term reading difficulties (Carter, Chard, & Pool, 2009; Hart & Risley, 1995; Neuman, 2006).

- The percentage of prekindergarten children ages 3 to 5 read to frequently by a family member increased from 78 percent in 1993 to 86 percent in 2005. The percentage of children whose family members frequently told them a story increased from 43 to 54 percent. Family members who taught their children letters, words, or numbers rose from 58 to 77 percent (National Center for Education Statistics, 2006).

- The percentage of school-age children (ages 5–17) whose parents had completed a bachelor's degree or higher increased from 19 percent in 1979 to 35 percent in 2006 (National Center for Education Statistics, 2008).

- Families influence literacy development through interpersonal interactions related to literacy, the physical environment and literacy materials in the home, and attitudes toward literacy, which affect emotions and the motivation to become literate (Braunger & Lewis, 2005; Lane & Wright, 2007; Neumann, Hood, & Neumann, 2009; Swick, 2009).

Did any of this information surprise you? If so, what? Why? How will you use this information to become an effective teacher of young children?

What Characterizes Family and Community Engagement in Schools?

Traditionally, educators have assumed that it is the parents' responsibility to attend school functions, such as meetings and performances by children, as well as to volunteer time to perform simple tasks, such as planning games for a party or chaperoning a field trip. Many of these expectations are problematic.

First of all, they tend to exclude nontraditional families and fathers or other male family members (McBride & Rane, 1997; Pattnaik, in press; Saracho, 2008). When a child-care center hosts a mother/daughter breakfast, for example, where does that leave the foster child or the child being raised by a single father? Another problem involves holidays. If the only times schools invite volunteers are connected with religious holidays (e.g., a Christmas pageant), where does that leave parents and families who are members of other religious groups? Evidently, some of the traditional activities that continue to be a part of many early childhood programs do more to communicate white, female, middle-class, Christian perspectives than to promote a sense of family participation in schools. It is important for early childhood educators to work to build a sense of community, not only in the classroom but also beyond (Knopf & Swick, 2008; Rule & Kyle, 2009; Scully & Howell, 2008).

Without a doubt, parents/families play a significant role in children's education (McCarthey, 2000; Pena, 2000). Today, members of the extended family—grandparents, siblings, aunts, uncles, cousins, foster families, and others who accept responsibility for the child—are invited to support children's growth in literacy. The common denominator of such efforts is that everyone who contributes comes away with this clear, consistent message (Cavaretta, 1998): "My work counts. My voice is heard. I've made a difference in the lives of these children."

Where acquiring literacy with English is concerned, parents and families who do not have a strong command of English and who have no one in their household or community who can help them on a regular basis often find it difficult to communicate with school personnel (Batalova, 2006). According to the U.S. Bureau of the Census (2003), a linguistically isolated household is one in which no person age 14 or over speaks English at least "very well" and, using that criterion, 4.4 million households, encompassing 11.9 million people, are linguistically isolated. As you read about the teachers in the next section, think about what you can do as a teacher to support literacy learning for young children.

Collaboration with Families and Professionals

Linda, a Head Start teacher who works with 4-year-olds, conducts home visits with families. No matter what time she arrives at some homes, the television set is blaring, even if no one is watching. Even if families have an opportunity to eat a meal at the same time, they do so in silence. Often, the children are shushed to be quiet or even pulled away because they block the screen while adults are watching a talk show, the news, a soap opera,

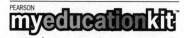

music videos, or some favorite program. She knows that some of her students are missing opportunities to develop language.

Linda decides to address the issue at the first large-group meeting held with parents in the fall. She wants to make parents aware of high-quality children's programs and recordings, to encourage them to limit the amount of TV, and to show them how to use the closed-captioned option so that, where available, families can see the words in English while they are listening in their first language. Next, she enlists the support of a newspaper, a bookstore, the public library, and community college students enrolled in a commercial art course. Linda serves as the content expert, based on her review of the research on the adverse effects of too much television (Erwin & Morton, 2008). Her collaborators provide the financial backing and design the materials that she needs.

With the support of this group, Linda is able to produce a professional-looking packet of materials that includes an attractive informational brochure; a list of books dealing with the topic of "taming the television monster" that includes *Fix-It* (McPhail, 1984), *Mouse TV* (Novak, 1994), *The Bionic Bunny Show* (Brown & Brown, 1984), and *The Berenstain Bears and Too Much TV* (Berenstain & Berenstain, 1984); and recommended TV programs to support literacy (see Moses, 2009). As a culminating activity, she puts all of the parents' and families' suggestions on alternatives to television watching into a booklet called *100 Things That Are Better for Your Child Than Watching Television.* Parents and families have included suggestions such as read a book, take a walk, visit a friend, cook together, play Go Fish, and so forth. Finally, Linda adds some materials written for families about early literacy that emphasize the importance of literacy activities at home.

Contributions and Consequences

- *Contributions of the teacher:* What role did the teacher play in taking positive action?
- *Contributions of the family:* How did families support the project and get involved in it?
- *Contributions of other professionals:* How did professionals in other fields contribute to addressing the needs of the child and family?
- *Consequences of collaboration:* How might this story have ended differently if the adults had never reached consensus?

Overview of Parents' and Families' Contributions to Early Literacy

Parents and families affect the child not only through heredity but also through the type of language environment they provide in the home. Their attitudes toward education

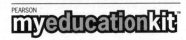

Go to the Assignments and Activities section of Chapter 2 in MyEducationKit and complete the activity entitled "Family Literacy Programs."

and aspirations for their children, the language models and literacy materials they supply, and the activities they encourage all make a substantial contribution to children's language development (Burningham & Dever, 2005; Schaller, Rocha, & Barshinger, 2007; Souto-Manning, 2007). As Comer (1998) observes:

> Some families are closed out of the economic mainstream, and they cannot give their children the language experience, the social experience, the confidence that grows out of being able to operate in the society. Their children go to school unable to present themselves in a way that enables people to see their ability or potential. Teachers have lower expectations as a result. And so children lose their skills, their aspirations, and the potentials that were there, and they achieve at a lower level. A child's intelligence level is not fixed at birth. Young children are "underdeveloped" or "differently developed." (p. 12)

Brain and Language

Hearing two languages from birth may shape babies' brains in ways that provide advantages in early learning. In a study of families in the Trieste area of Italy, infants who were immersed in Italian and Slovenian from birth had more advanced language than peers from single-language households (Mehler & Kovacs, 2009).

Four fundamental roles support and promote children's language development. These roles are initiated in the home and later reinforced in the educational setting (DeBruin-Parecki, 2009). Those parents and families who are able to give their children the best chance at becoming literate have learned to observe children thoughtfully, arrange the environment to support language development, interact with children in ways that advance language growth, and motivate or encourage the child's efforts to master language (Goodman & Goodman, 1979).

Figure 2.1 provides an overview of roles that parents, families, and community members can fulfill to support children's literacy growth.

Engaging Families as Observers of Children

When parents and families function as observers, they monitor their children's progress, build on their strengths, and help them to meet new challenges in language. For example, in the following transcript of a tape recording of parents interacting with their 29-month-old child, notice how her parents observe what Georgie (short for Georgianna) does and then respond to her needs:

Georgie: I baby. (Singing.) Mary had a little lamb.

Father: Go ahead.

Georgie: How you talk about on it? Huh?

Father: Say what you want to say. (Adults tell her to move closer to microphone.)

Georgie: No. I don't want to. Hold it this way? Two hands. How Mummy talk? (Pause.) Hi Mama. Hi Mommy. What's my friends' names, huh?

Mother: Debbie, Dana, Kristy, Marty, Michelle, Tammy.

Father (asking Georgie):   Who else?

Audience Members for Literacy Events. In this role, parents, families, and community members are appreciative audiences for children's demonstrations of their emerging literacy abilities. An example would be parents attending a puppet play children have created or family members attending the graduation of parents who have successfully completed their high school diploma equivalency test (General Education Diploma [GED]).

Classroom Volunteers and Translators. Parents with fluency in a child's first language can assist by providing explanations in L1 or supporting the child's efforts to translate the words they want to write or read. For example, one official language of the Philippines is Tagalog. An adult fluent in English and Tagalog could offer invaluable support to a child with Tagalog as L1.

Volunteers for Literacy Events and Programs. In this role, parents, families, and communities give of their time to assist children in becoming literate individuals. For example, adults might volunteer to help children "publish" their stories by typing each child's dictated story or by helping children to assemble their paper or digital books.

Literacy Teachers at Home. In this role, parents, families, and community members contribute to a child's education at home. An example would be establishing a bedtime story routine or participating in a program at the library.

Paraprofessionals in Support of Language Learning. In this role, parents, families, and community members undergo specialized training so that they can take on responsibilities for teaching. For example, they might agree to go through a training program that will enable them to serve as adult literacy tutors to help children's parents and families acquire workplace literacy.

Decision Makers on Literacy Issues. In this role, parents, families, and community members serve on committees or serve in an advisory capacity. For example, they might be representatives to a committee that deals with censorship issues and responds to complaints about educational materials or serve on a committee to evaluate the reading program.

Literacy Learners. In this role, parents, families, and community members advance their own literacy learning as a way to support children's literacy learning. They might return to take a class for English second-language learners, take a Saturday workshop on "How to Read to Your Child," or join a book discussion group.

Contributors of Literacy Resources. In this role, parents, families, and community members donate resources to the program. It might consist of something simple, such as donating books that their children have outgrown or reading and recording a story read-aloud. It could also be more involved, such as getting financial support from a local business or writing a proposal to obtain funds from the federal government or a private agency.

> **Georgie:** And Glen.
>
> **Father:** And?
>
> **Georgie:** Who?
>
> **Father:** How about who lives over here? (Gestures next door.)
>
> **Georgie:** I don't know—Heidi.
>
> **Mother:** What about her baby brother? What's his name?
>
> **Georgie:** Baby brother.

When families learn to take notice of what children can do, children get the support they need to build confidence and skills as learners of language.

Engaging Families as Environment Arrangers

Parents also contribute to children's growth in literacy by creating a print-rich environment (Schickendanz, 2008). This richness need not come from costly materials; it can include books borrowed from the library, recycled paper, and simple writing implements.

The Morrell family is a good example. They recently returned from a family reunion/camping trip a few hours' drive from their urban home. Four-year-old Carl has been using the snapshots that were taken to identify family members and the activities they shared together. His mother suggests that they make a book about their vacation, and with a little glue and some pieces of cardboard salvaged from her hosiery packages, they assemble a durable booklet, complete with captions dictated by Carl. Before long, Carl has learned to read the entire book aloud. Carl's parents have provided an environment for literacy.

Engaging Families as Interactors

When parents carry on extended conversations and really listen to what their children have to say, they are functioning as interactors. The following conversation occurred between David (nicknamed Boomer), who is 3 years 8 months old, and his mother as she was cooking dinner. Although this rural Appalachian family's income falls far below the poverty line, it is clear that Boomer has rich opportunities to develop his oral language skills.

> **Boomer:** I'm gonna be like Daddy when I grow up.
>
> **Mother:** How will you be like Daddy?
>
> **Boomer:** Simple, change fur (meaning that he will have body hair) and my hair will be black. My legs will be big, and even my foots will be big.
>
> **Mother:** What are you going to do when you're a daddy?
>
> **Boomer:** Fix things and play with you when I'm a dad.
>
> **Mother:** What else?
>
> **Boomer:** An' maybe take a glue gun an' fix stuff.

Mother: Are you going to have kids?

Boomer: Yeah.

Mother: Boys or girls?

Boomer: Oh, simply I'll play with Steve when I grow up.

Mother: You're going to play with Steve when you grow up like Dad?

Boomer: I hate Steve and I like Steve. (Steve is a neighbor who is 2 years older and has been calling Boomer a "pipsqueak.")

Mother: You hate Steve and you like Steve. Yeah, that's probably the way it is with a lot of friends, huh. What else are you going to do when you're a daddy?

Boomer: Oh, when I grow up, you're going to hang on my arm.

As this dialogue illustrates, young children need others who function as interactors.

Engaging Families as Motivators and Encouragers

In their role as motivators and encouragers, parents and teachers recognize children's functional language needs, stimulate children's interests, and encourage and respond to their efforts to communicate. Marjorie, age 3, is visiting her aunt and an elderly neighbor. The preschooler looks at the neighbor curiously and then hands her red Mickey Mouse sunglasses to her aunt and says, "Here, hold these." After the aunt obliges by folding the glasses and placing them on her lap, a conversation follows.

Marjorie: No, not fold, hold.

Aunt: But I am holding them.

Marjorie: No, I wanna hold them like Peg's.

Aunt: Oh, you mean you want them to hang around your neck, like Peg's?

Peg: Honey, they're on a chain. See? (She lifts the collar of her dress while Marjorie inspects.)

Marjorie: I want one of those so I can hold my sunglasses.

Later, when they leave to go to a discount store, Peg takes Marjorie's aunt aside, gives her some money, and says, "Buy Marjorie the gaudiest chain you can find at the dollar store, and tell her it's a present from me."

 Teacher Concerns and Basic Strategies

Nancy, a first-grade teacher, had this to say about early literacy:

> Because I teach in a wealthy suburban school, people sometimes assume that my job must be easy. But just because children have all the material things, that doesn't mean they don't have problems. Working with the children of financially successful parents, many of whom are lawyers, creates a different set of challenges. My major concern is

PEARSON
myeducationkit™

Go to the Assignments and Activities section of Chapter 2 in MyEducationKit and complete the activity entitled "One Teacher's Experience."

the pressure that I see on the very young. They are overscheduled, with some sort of lesson or structured activity almost every night. They sometimes arrive at school exhausted, and it seems to me that they don't have much time just to be kids.

Adults usually pressure children because they are fearful of the highly competitive future children face, are anxious to have their children help with responsibilities, or want to live through their children and fulfill their own needs for achievement in particular areas (Hills, 1987). Language learning can put pressure on children in these ways:

- By emphasizing being the best and competing fiercely with others, such as when a parent says, "You're in the top reading group and you'd better stay there."
  - By comparing one child with another, such as when a parent says, "He should be reading at third-grade level. His brother could read almost anything at his age."
  - By criticizing and punishing, such as when a parent says, "You should know how to read that word. I want you to sit right there until you remember it."
  - By exposing children to developmentally inappropriate practices at home, such as when a parent says to a kindergartner, "Look, I bought you a second-grade reading workbook at the store. If you do a couple of pages every night, you'll be ahead of everyone next year."

Infants and Toddlers
The very young child may be more reliant on gestures. Rowe and Goldin-Meadow (2009) found that 14-month-olds produced 25 meanings through gesture within a 90-minute session. Their conclusion is that adults need to attend to gestures just as much as vocalizations when interacting with toddlers.

High-pressure tactics inhibit children and frequently impede them in becoming more fully literate. If children are afraid to take risks, their progress in literacy will surely be thwarted, because language learners need to "experiment freely and try things unashamedly" (Shuy, 1981, p. 107).

Sean, who works with children in the Title I reading support program, expresses another common teacher concern:

> Our turnout for parent meetings is usually disappointing. Sometimes, after we have worked hard to offer a program that the parents said they wanted, only two or three people show up. I can't figure out what to do.

When developing programs, take into consideration the particular characteristics and circumstances of the families being served by the program. Treat parents and other members of children's families as real people with multiple roles to fulfill, rather than defining them only in terms of their relationship with the child in your class (e.g., Chad's mother, Chelsea's grandfather).

Create a simple survey so that families can respond anonymously. What are their informational needs? What are their concerns? What services and supports do they need? Might they contribute their time to an activity that would support the program? Which activities do they prefer? Important questions to ask parents and families at the beginning of the year during a home visit are: What are your hopes for your child this year? and How can we help? You might find that they would love to have a hotline to call with their questions about events and services. You might find that they would appreciate a calendar of summer learning activities, lists of recommended picture books, or a workshop on family stories.

It may not make sense to parents who have little time to spend with their children to leave them with a babysitter and go to school for a meeting. It might make more sense to plan some activities that parents and children can enjoy together. Furthermore, a parent's or family's definition of an "expert" on early childhood may differ considerably from your own. Parents may feel that someone who has successfully raised a large number of children is more credible than a person with an advanced degree, for example. So you might get a better response with a panel discussion of parents whose children are successful. Generally speaking, if parents and other family members can see how what they are asked to do will provide direct benefit to the child, they will be more likely to participate enthusiastically.

Educators and families also need to work together to arrive at a consensus about what constitutes a quality education for young children.

Classroom Activities to Support Family Literacy

PEARSON
myeducationkit™

Go to the Assignments and Activities section of Chapter 2 in MyEducationKit and complete the activity entitled " 'My Tooth.' "

Research and Report
Interview several parents who have something in common (e.g., parents of infants/toddlers, newly immigrated children, children beginning kindergarten). Also invite them to ask your class questions about young children's language and literacy growth. Then use your text and other resources to formulate answers and present them via a newsletter, brochure, or bulletin board.

Library Cards   Some families may not use the resources of the public library. If families lack prior experience with the concept of a lending library then they may not understand that materials are loaned free of charge, that libraries offer nonprint media, that materials in languages other than English are sometimes available, or that free programs (e.g., storytime) are offered there. Even when families have knowledge about library services, the fear that they will not be able to afford the fines if a child destroys or misplaces an item borrowed from the library or worries about revealing immigration status to apply for a library card may be a deterrent (Margolis, 2001). Work with your parents and families to address these concerns and get them library cards so that children have access to these services and resources.

Everyday Conversations   When parents and families want to help their children, they sometimes overlook naturally occurring opportunities for children to listen, watch, and participate in language (Beals, 2001). Provide parents/families with suggestions on how to make mealtimes the basis for talk about a variety of topics, including such things as favorite meals and reasons for liking particular food items; vocabulary for utensils, foods, and colors; and how foods were selected, purchased, and prepared.

Birthday Packets   Ms. Spewock (1991), a reading specialist, creates birthday packets that she sends to the parents of every child in the district. The first packet is sent to the hospital shortly after the mother gives birth, and the packets continue each year right through the primary grades. Parents of adopted children and children who are new to the district receive them, too. Each packet contains child development information, suggested learning activities, recommended books available at the local library, and, beginning when the child turns 3, a birthday card.

Original Story Tapes   Ms. Freeman, a first-grade teacher, initiated a project to make children's homes more print rich with wordless picture books. First, she shared several wordless books with her students, and they invented group stories to go along with the pictures. Then the children selected their own favorite wordless books and wrote their own texts to accompany the illustrations. Each child edited and wrote the final copy on self-adhesive notes, which could be placed inside the book without damaging it. Finally, the children made audiotapes of themselves reading their books. Ms. Freeman sent the books and the tapes home, along with a letter explaining the project and asking the parents to invite their children to share what they had done and provide a brief comment.

Visiting Class Mascot   Ms. Malcolm's private nursery school had a panda as its mascot, so she sent home with different students at different times a stuffed toy panda and a diary. The child and his or her parents kept a journal of the panda's adventures while it spent a week in their home. It was understood that these adventures could be real or imaginary and that the child was expected to participate in creating the journal entries. When the panda diary was returned to the classroom at the end of each week, it gave the teacher some insight about the various families with whom she was working. This activity also encouraged parents and children to engage in literacy events throughout the week. (For more ideas on family journals, see Edwards & McMillon, 2008 and Harding, 1996.)

Information Board   Mr. Thornton, a teacher in an infant/toddler center, created an information board for parents. The bulletin board included brochures from physicians, nutritionists, counselors, psychologists, and various community service organizations that he had gathered during a health fair at the local shopping mall. A calendar of upcoming events in the classroom, school, and community was maintained, as well as a daily "good news" item. Parents were asked to suggest other items that would be helpful, and soon there was a "swap" section for toys, clothes, and baby furniture as well as a lost and found section.

Adopt-a-School   Work with local businesses to support school efforts by, for example, providing tips on how adults can promote literacy (perhaps inserted in pay envelopes), donating funds or materials to the school, or volunteering time at literacy events.

Bookworm Program   Seniors, high-schoolers, family members, and community members can collect donated books, read aloud, share a talent related to a book theme, help assemble and keep track of bookpacks, staff a toy/book lending library, or talk with children about the books they have read.

Creating with Catalogs   Mail-order catalogs provide a free, colorful, and plentiful supply of pictures that can be used for various purposes that support language. Newman (1996–1997) suggests such activities as creating a picture dictionary, selecting an outfit of clothes suitable for the weather, making a picture shopping list, using catalog pictures to illustrate a story, playing classification games (e.g., sorting pictures by colors, shapes, sizes, uses), collecting pictures from different seasons or climates, making a collage of pictures of hobbies and activities in other parts of the world, and filling out an order form.

Conclusion

Too often, there is an implicit assumption that the schools have all the knowledge about how to further children's learning. Actually, educators can learn much from families about a more natural style of learning. There are at least five reasons that homes can be excellent learning environments (Tizard & Hughes, 1984):

1. There is an extensive range of activities within the home, as well as various types of excursions from the home.
2. The parent and child share a common life that links past with present and present with future.
3. The interaction is usually one to one.
4. The daily experiences in the home have great personal significance for the child.
5. There is an intense loving, caring, sharing, trusting relationship between the adult and child.

In these activities and in any others you might initiate, remember that the real challenge for parents/families and teachers is building mutual trust and respect. Parents/families need to appreciate the teacher's ability to see the child in comparison to other students at the same grade level. The teacher needs to value the child's family members' ability to round out his or her view of the child by contributing a perspective on home and family. By blending these two very different viewpoints, we can gain a clear picture of the child and make well-informed decisions that further a child's development.

PEARSON **myeducationkit** To check your comprehension on the content covered in this chapter, go to the MyEducationKit for your book and complete the Study Plan for Chapter 2. Here you will be able to take a chapter quiz and receive feedback on your answers.

 ## Research-Based Literacy Strategies

Providing Access to Books through Pediatricians

Several studies have concluded that children who struggle with reading often have limited access to interesting materials (Krashen, 1997, 2001). One strategy that has been surprisingly effective is enlisting the support of pediatricians who advise parents/

families to share picture books with their young children and distribute age-appropriate books, free of charge.

One of the best known programs is Reach Out and Read (ROR), in which well-child visits to the clinic are used as an opportunity to encourage reading to young children, to distribute developmentally and culturally appropriate books to the families when the child is between 6 months and 5 years of age, and to have volunteers model reading aloud to children in clinic waiting rooms. For this program and others like it, the impact has been remarkable and significant (Weitzman, Roy, Walls, & Tomlin, 2004).

For some English language learners, picture books distributed in this way may be among the only English language materials in their homes or the only materials written at their level of understanding. Access to books that the children own, rather than borrow, can promote book sharing and prepare them for literacy experiences at school. To illustrate the impact of programs that involve pediatricians, after low-income Hispanic American families were provided by their pediatricians with appropriate children's books, easy-to-read suggestions for sharing books with toddlers, and encouragement for reading aloud at home during a well-baby checkup, the families were 10 times more likely to read with children at least 3 days a week in comparison with parents in a control group (High, LaGasse, Becker, Ahlgren, & Gardner, 2000).

The practice of sharing books at home and at school is a major mechanism for supporting linguistically diverse learners.

Training Parents and Families as Reading Partners

Teachers should not assume that parents and families already know how to share books effectively with children (Strickland, 2004). Programs that coach families in effective ways of reading aloud to children have shown positive and significant outcomes (Annett, 2004; Roberts, 2008; Sylva, Scott, Totsika, Ereky-Stevens, & Crook, 2008). Families involved children in more literacy activities after they were taught how to: read aloud expressively; ask open-ended, friendly questions; and invite the child to participate (e.g., taking turns reading portions of the text, echo reading). Some of the materials and activities that were most appreciated by parents were erasable writing boards, parent handbooks, a presentation by a professional storyteller, modeling of read-alouds, literacy games that could be played by the whole family, a zoo visit that led to a language experience story, and group trips to the library (Cook-Cottone, 2004).

By providing training and using materials such as those by Seedling Publications (www.seedlingpub .com), parents/families can see their children enjoying books and will be more inclined to make the time to do more reading (Yaden & Paratore, 2002). If parents and families have computer access at home or at the public library, they can find a wealth of resources, e-mail discussion listservs (such as Parenting-L), submit questions to be answered, or read an interactive electronic magazine focused on family literacy at the National Parents' Information Network (NPIN). NPIN also provides strategies called Keeping Kids Reading and SMART PARENTING On-Line. Other online sources include the Electronic Schoolhouse, Family Village, Parents as Teachers National Center, Parents' Place, and Family World.

Building Vocabulary by Reading Aloud

Although it has been argued that children under the age of 6 months are not ready to attend to a story being read to them (Murkoff, Eisenberg, & Hathaway, 2003), research indicates that when infants are read to by parents and caregivers important literacy skills such as book awareness, print awareness, vocabulary development, fluency, and comprehension are developing (Armbruster, Lehr, & Osborn, 2003; Manning, 2005). In a study involving several hundred parents who documented their 2-year-olds' vocabularies, the range was enormous. Parents reported that their toddlers knew between 50 and 550 words (Fenson et al., 1994).

One way of building vocabulary in a meaningful context is reading aloud. Justice, Meier, and Walpole (2005) found that kindergartners who had been identified as at risk of academic difficulty were able to learn vocabulary effectively while sharing books. Moreover, the most effective way of accelerating vocabulary was for the adult to elaborate on the words in the story. In fact, the children with the lowest vocabulary made the greatest gains when the adult talked about the new words the children encountered in the book. For more on the connection between reading aloud and vocabulary development, visit www.uth.tmc.edu/circle/read_aloud .htm. For a discussion of the effects on reading aloud for second-language acquisition, see www.indiana .edu/~reading/ieo/bibs/vocabrng.html.

Links with Literature
Multicultural Bookpacks

What Is a Bookpack?

A bookpack is an assortment of children's books suitable for reading aloud and a selection of accompanying materials in some sort of easily transportable container (e.g., a totebag, a backpack, a large plastic bag, or small suitcases). It is circulated to children, parents, and families as a sort of miniature lending library (Cohen, 1997; Creamer & Baker, 2000; Reeves, 1995; Richardson, Miller, Richardson, & Sacks, 2008). The purpose of the bookpacks is to support literacy activities at home and give families access to high-quality picture books. Bookpacks are designed by teachers to suit the developmental characteristics of children. Topics and activities are matched to particular needs. Bookpacks also give children and families an opportunity to respond to the materials provided by evaluating their home literacy experiences with the bookpacks on various topics or themes.

What Is Included in a Bookpack?

A bookpack should contain the following six items:

1. *A note to the parents and children introducing the bookpack.* This note should (1) state the purpose of the theme; (2) list ways that this particular theme/bookpack will support children's growth in literacy; (3) be clear, concise, and free of errors; and (4) encourage families to participate in the bookpack project.
2. *Books specifically chosen for your students.* Include books that represent a range of reading abilities; for example, you might include a wordless book so that the nonreader can use the illustrations to tell a story and an easy reader with controlled vocabulary to support the emergent reader. It is also important to include dual-language books (Sneddon, 2008a, b) to support book sharing by families that do not have English as their first language.
3. *An inventory card listing the bookpack's contents.* This card will be used to keep track of what each pack contains and revised as the bookpack's contents are further developed.
4. *A story prop that children can play with and retell the story.* Select toys or invent games that complement the theme and the books you have selected. Ideally, these materials should encourage the child to engage in story play and retell the stories.
5. *A collection of children's books and other materials related to the theme.* Carefully select additional books that go along with the theme. You may want to collaborate with the school and public libraries to produce these lists. For additional information see Zeece and Wallace (2009b).

Names to Know

Vera Aardema, Karen Ackerman, David A. Adler, George Ancona, Jan Brett, Marcia Brown, Ashley Bryan, Eve Bunting, Ann Cameron, Eric Carle, Lorinda Bryan Cauley, D. Chocolate, S. Choi, Shirley Climo, Donald Crews, Demi, Baba Wagué Diakité, Leo and Diane Dillon, Nora Dooley, Arthur Dorros, Lois Ehlert, Tom Feelings, Candice Fleming, Valerie Flournoy, Mem Fox, Nikki Giovanni, Eloise Greenfield, Ann Grifalconi, Ann Herbert, Mary Hoffman, Beatrice Hollyer, Rachel Isadora, D. B. Johnson, Barbara Joosse, Ezra Jack Keats, Eric Kimmel, Rikki Levinson, Patricia MacLachlan, Patricia McKissack, Pat Mora, Ann Morris, Walter Dean Myers, Linda Sue Park, Brian Pinkney, Patricia Polacco, Faith Ringgold, Cynthia Rylant, Robert D. San Souci, Allen Say, Gary Soto, John Steptoe,

Simms Taback, Pamela S. Turner, Karen Williams, Vera Williams, Jane Yolen, and Ed Young.

Recommended Books about Families

A Chair for My Mother (Anniversary Edition) (Williams, 1984) or the Hmong version, *Ib Lub Rooj Rua Kuv Nam* (Williams, 2001); *Families* (Morris, 2000); *In Daddy's Arms I Am Tall* (Steptoe, 2001); *My Dadima Wears a Sari* (Sheth, 2007); *The Family Book* (Parr, 2003); *What a Family* (Isadora, 2006); *And*

Tango Makes Three (Parnell, 2005); *Jin Woo* (Bunting, 2001); *I Love You Like Crazy Cakes* (Lewis, 2000); *Rabbit's New Baby* (Horse, 2008); *Flying!* (Luthardt, 2009); *Hey Daddy! Animal Fathers and Their Babies* (Batten, 2002); *Fathers, Mothers, Sisters, Brothers: A Collection of Family Poems* (Hoberman, 2001); *My Family* (Kincade & Global Fund for Children, 2006); *Your Own Big Bed* (Bergstein, 2008); *Welcome Baby! Baby Rhymes for Baby Times* (Calmenson, 2002); *I Can't Talk Yet, But When I Do* (Markes, 2003).

ELLs
Internet Resources for Promoting Print Awareness at Home

Parents who continuously interact with and read to their children enhance their children's overall language development (Barton, 2004). Using the questions below as a starting point, interview several parents who have something in common (e.g., parents of infants/toddlers, bilingual children, children beginning kindergarten).

Questions for Parents and Families

1. How do you usually prefer to be contacted by the school (written messages, telephone calls, or face-to-face conferences)?
2. Have you participated in any of the parent involvement activities at your school (such as conferences, PTA meetings, programs presented by the children, fund-raising activities)? What influenced your decision about whether or not to participate?
3. What support services does your school offer? Are you aware of any programs that are specifically designed to promote early literacy?
4. Is there any item, contact, event, or program that you found particularly helpful or useful? Why did you find it particularly useful or helpful?
5. What suggestions do you have for improving home–school communication and cooperation?
6. What questions do you have about children's early language development?

Now interview your peers in the class with the following questions:

1. What questions did families have about children's early language development and literacy growth?
2. What efforts are you making to prepare yourself to work with parents, families, and communities? Have you been involved in any volunteer or service activities where you interacted with parents and families?
3. What goals and expectations do you have for your program in terms of working with families? What supports would you hope to see in place?
4. How are you going about understanding the various ethnic groups, cultural backgrounds, languages, customs, values, ceremonies, and symbols of the children and families in the community?
5. Have you done anything thus far in your studies or work that supports parents/families? What was a source of pride to you as an early childhood educator?

Teachers will also find materials designed specifically for parents and families that offer information on early language development and advice on improving young children's listening skills to be a valuable resource (Lu, 2000; Smith, 2008). National organizations, such as the American Speech-Hearing-Language Association (www.asha.org), the

International Reading Association (www.ira.org), and the National Association for the Education of Young Children (www.naeyc.org) offer free or inexpensive developmental charts, brochures about early literacy topics, and a variety of other resources, some of which have been translated into Spanish. Creating an attractive display of these materials or sending them home so that parents and families with limited resources can access them easily helps to explain and reinforce the work that teachers are doing at school to promote English language learning.

Websites for Parents and Families

ERIC Clearinghouse on Elementary and Early Childhood Education
www.ericeece.org

ERIC Clearinghouse on Reading, English, and Communication
www.indiana.edu/~eric_rec

Even Start Family Literacy Program
www.ed.gov/offices/OESE/CEP

Family Education Network
http://familyeducation.com

Family Strengthening Resources
www.cisnet.or/pubs/facts/webres.html

I Am Your Child
www.iamyourchild.org

National Institute for Literacy (NIFL)
www.nifl.gov

National Parent Information Network (NPIN)
www.npin.org

No Child Left Behind for Parents
www.nochildleftbehind.gov/parents/index.html

Parenting Site
www.parentsoup.com

Partnership for Family Involvement in Education
www.pfie.ed.gov

The Partnership for Reading
www.nifl.gov/partnershipforreading

How Do I ...
Conduct Meetings with Families?

Suggestions for a Start-to-School or Back-to-School Night

The purpose of this meeting is for parents/families to (1) see the classrooms where their children will be assigned, (2) get to meet the school staff, (3) learn about the school and the instructional program, and (4) set a positive tone for the remainder of the year. For very young children, you may want to try a "simulated day," in which parents/families/children arrive together and children take them on a walking tour of what they do at school (Laverick, 2008).

Create a Friendly Environment

• Invite parents in person, in writing, and on the telephone so that knowing about the meeting does not depend on their proficiency in reading English.

• Provide name tags and wear one yourself.
• Give family members an opportunity to tour the classroom. Display samples of children's work, label centers, and create a photo essay of what children have done (or will do) during the year.
• Consider using technology, such as a video of classroom projects or a multimedia/computer presentation.
• Provide a web or map or month-by-month calendar of the curriculum, and make copies of the daily and weekly schedule.

For a Group Meeting

• Open with a sincere welcome for the family members. Mention that you understand how busy they all are and appreciate their willingness to give of their time.

- Present an overview of the daily routine and year-long plans. Consider including some short film clips that capture the essence of what children will be learning in your class.
- Explain general policies and procedures (e.g., child guidance strategies, attendance, assessment practices, and so forth).
- Prepare a handout, handbook, or brochure on other important information (e.g., contacting parents/families when a child is ill, permission for walking field trips, and so forth). Make certain that the tone of these materials is positive and supportive and arrange to have them translated if some parents/families would benefit.
- Encourage parents to contact you with any questions or concerns, emphasizing that it is better to contact you early, before a small issue becomes a big one.
- Thank them for attending and end on a positive, caring note that stresses the importance of open communication and working as a team.

General Speaking Tips

- Present a professional image in terms of your attire, posture, and manners. Be warm and gracious but do not speak with parents/families in an overly casual and familiar way.
- Have everything set up and arranged (e.g., PowerPoint presentation, handout packets, student work portfolios) well in advance of the event. Practice your presentation several times. Do not read from a script.
- Walk around and meet and greet people before the large-group presentation begins. This will relax you and help your audience feel more connected with you. Try to speak with everyone instead of engaging in an extended conversation with a few familiar faces.
- As you are presenting, draw on all of your best teaching behaviors (e.g., avoid distracting habits, use gestures, project confidence and enthusiasm, make a few comments that let them know you as a person committed to support all children's learning, get in close physical proximity to the audience, speak to people by name, avoid speak-

ing in a monotone). If something unforeseen happens (e.g., the power goes out), just smile and go on.

Holding Parent/Family Conferences

The purpose for parent/family conferences is to give family members a chance to talk specifically about their child's academic progress, behavior, and social relationships with early childhood staff. Follow these guidelines:

- Devote time to learning more about the cultural backgrounds of your students. Learn what is considered to be a sign of respect and make it part of your interaction with families.
- Get children involved in preparing for the conferences by selecting samples of their best work, making displays of their projects, preparing signs, planning the refreshments, and participating directly in the conferences. Explain the reason that parents/families and teachers meet to talk about a child's progress, and give children an opportunity to ask questions or air concerns about upcoming conferences.
- Prepare parents and families for the conferences by asking them to make lists of anything they want to discuss.
- Prepare your early childhood setting for the event by making it look, sound, and smell inviting. Be certain that every child's work is displayed prominently. Try to make centers and materials self-explanatory with posters, signs, directions, and explanations.
- When you meet, provide adult-size chairs for the parents/families. Do not position yourself at your desk and put them in a child-sized chair; this can be demeaning.
- Gather data such as your observational notes, individualized educational programs (IEPs), student portfolios, attendance records, progress reports, and so forth.
- Become thoroughly familiar with the policies and procedures of the school or center, outline your main points, and prepare your responses to the most typical question. (How is my child doing in comparison to others?)

- Develop a schedule that meets the needs of busy working parents and families and provides different time options. Collect parents'/families' first, second, and third time slot preferences so that a master schedule can be produced. Allow approximately 20 to 30 minutes, on average, for each conference. If you see that a conference is going to take much longer than anticipated, plan a follow-up meeting rather than having a long line of parents and families waiting. Save a difficult conference for a time right before a break or at the end of the day so that you can take additional time if necessary. To minimize interruptions, make and post a sign that reads "Please do not disturb. Conference in progress."

- Greet family members at the door and introduce yourself. Do not make assumptions that can backfire, such as assuming that a child has the same last name as parents, assuming that a man with gray hair is the child's grandfather, or assuming that a teenager is a sister.

- Begin by reviewing the agenda so that the parents/families know what to expect. Remember that everyone is there for the same reason—to support the child. Use the "criticism sandwich": If you have some difficult information to share, sandwich it in between positive or neutral information so that the conference begins and ends on a positive note. Reassure the families that their children are in good hands.

- Try to be specific in your comments, and avoid educational jargon. Listen closely and accept feelings and attitudes, ask for families' opinions, and encourage collaboration. Give families ways to help that emphasize "everyday literacy," or using literacy to get relevant, real-world tasks accomplished.

- Use positive body language (e.g., leaning forward slightly, smiling, nodding). If the parent/family member becomes angry, refrain from defending yourself. Hear the family out and avoid being judgmental. When the conference closes, recap. Above all, don't "tell tales out of school" and complain to others about parents and family members. Recognize that information about a child's progress is confidential and should not be shared with anyone other than the parent or person legally responsible for the child.

Extensions of Meetings and Conferences

- Plan for follow-up. Send an email, written note, or call family members to thank them for participating. Try to keep the lines of communication open and stay in touch. Keep copies of all correspondence and records of contacts with families. Use both scheduled and opportune times (e.g., when parents pick up a child after school) to continue to build a working relationship. Plan workshops that give families ways to support literacy that are easily integrated into family life, such as cooking together and making a rebus recipe or working on letter identification with magnetic letters on the refrigerator door.

- Orient the families to the next transition. Prepare families for important events in their child's life, such as starting kindergarten or first grade. You might create a simulated schoolday for families or work with colleagues to create a tour of the next grade level and record it so that children and families can see it even if they cannot attend the meeting.

- Look into family literacy initiatives. These programs offer literacy instruction to families, broadly defined to include parents, caregivers, siblings, and young children. Family literacy programs are founded on the belief that one family member's growth in literacy affects everyone else in the family.

Resources: Brown & Jalongo, 1986; Ediger, 2008; Edwards, 2009; Neuman, Caperelli, & Kee, 1998; New Jersey Education Association, 1997; Swick, 2009.

PEARSON myeducationkit™ Now go to Chapter 2 in the MyEducationKit (**www.MyEducationKit** .com) for your book, where you can:

■ Find Chapter Objectives.

■ Complete Assignments and Activities that can help you more deeply understand the chapter content.

■ Extend knowledge with content-specific Web Links.

■ Check your comprehension on the content covered in the chapter by going to the Study Plan. Here you will be able to take a chapter quiz, receive feedback on your answers, and then access resources that will enhance your understanding of chapter content.

chapter three

Understanding Language Development in Early Childhood

Frank Siteman

FACT FILE on Language Development

- According to the National Institute on Deafness and Other Communication Disorders (2009), the first 6 months are the most crucial to a child's development of language skills.

- Babies' early speech sounds during the first 6 months of life typically include many sounds that are not used in their native language. During the second half of the first year, their babbling begins to sound more like the language or languages spoken in their homes (Trawick-Smith, 2009).

- Infants who are taught American Sign Language go through a babbling stage of experimenting with language, using hand signs rather than oral language (Pettito & Marentette, 1991).

43

- Expressive and receptive language performance at 10 months and at 2 years are predictive of cognitive and language skills in later childhood (Hohm, Jennen-Steinmetz, Schmidt, & Laucht, 2007; Marchman & Fernald, 2008).

- By age 2, children produced an average of 338 comprehensible utterances per hour, but the range was enormous: from 42 to 672. The 2-year-olds used approximately 134 different words per hour, with a range of 18 to 286 (Hart & Risley, 1995, 2003).

- Knowledge of any language can serve as a jumping-off point for subsequent language learning, because most children apply what they know about their first language (L1) to their second language (L2) (Parke & Drury, 2001). If two languages are spoken in the home, it is common for a toddler 18 months or older to use both languages and to know which family member uses which language. At times, words from both languages (e.g., "please" in English, "bitte" in German) are combined and used simultaneously (e.g., "bitteplease") (Trawick-Smith, 2009).

- By the age of 2 years 6 months, children have a vocabulary consisting of approximately 600 words. At age 3, children begin linking words to connect new words to objects or events known to them. This process is known as "fast-mapping" (Boyd & Bee, 2010).

- Beginning at about age 3, young children learn an estimated 6 to 10 new words per day (Spodek & Saracho, 1993).

- When many families in the community speak a particular language, schools are more apt to provide instruction in that language (e.g., Spanish). However, literally hundreds of other languages and dialects are spoken in American homes, and, as a result, approximately two-thirds of second-language children get little support for language learning (La Fontaine, 1987).

- A few thousand words account for 90 percent of the spoken vocabulary anyone uses or hears on a regular basis (Hayes & Ahrens, 1988). A highly educated adult has a listening/speaking vocabulary of about 10,000 words but likely knows nearly 10 times as many words in reading and writing, or about 100,000 words (Byrnes & Wasik, 2009).

- Because the production of speech involves control of the tongue, lips, and breathing, the development of fine motor skills and of speech are connected (Singh & Singh, 2008).

- Language affects not only cognitive growth but also social competence (McCabe & Meller, 2004). Children who learn to speak and interact successfully with others tend to develop more effective learning strategies and literacy skills. Children who have problems communicating and becoming literate are at risk for social isolation and other academic difficulties in school (Kostelnik, Whiren, Soderman, & Gregory, 2008).

Did any of this information surprise you? If so, what? Why? How will you use this knowledge to become an effective teacher of young children?

What Is Language?

Of all the characteristics that human beings possess, language is the one that most defines us and differentiates us from other forms of life. The National Council of Teachers of English and the International Reading Association (1996) define *language* broadly, meaning not only mastery of the systems and structures of language but also how to apply knowledge of various language forms and functions, depending on the task at hand. However, the definition of language developed by these two major professional organizations goes even beyond the forms and functions of oral and written language to include visual communication as well.

If you think about a contemporary child's life, it makes sense to include visual literacy. Young children are "awash in a cosmic soup of language, numbers, images, music, and drama. Television, radio, movies, billboards, print media, electronic media, packaging, grocery stores, malls, and restaurants" all require them to become consumers and users of symbol systems, or what researchers call *signs* (Berghoff, 1997, p. 316). The child of today, more than ever before, is expected to become an expert user of multiple symbol systems, moving between and among signs when representing ideas, feelings, and events (Leland & Harste, 1994).

Children's lives are deeply affected by their literacy learning, as Genishi (1988) explains: "As we use language with others, it shapes our identities and social lives. The way our own language sounds to listeners leads them to make judgments about where we are from, what our occupation is, how friendly or clever we are" (p. 78).

Thus, learning language is much more than an academic achievement. Human language is, first and foremost, a social instrument. Indeed, learning language is perhaps the most social of all types of learning (Fillmore, 1997). We know this because in horrible examples of deprivation, isolation, and abuse, young children do not learn to talk. One of the most extreme and publicized cases was that of Genie, a child who was kept isolated and confined to a room without any human interaction (Fromkin, Rodman, & Hyams, 2006). Even though she was obviously intelligent and received extensive language instruction, Genie never really mastered language at a level that would enable her to function independently in the world after her rescue. Unlike the character in the movie *Nell*, this real child who was deprived of language early faced major linguistic and social hurdles throughout life and was ultimately institutionalized.

Learning language is a challenge because not only are children expected to learn *about* language, but they are also expected to learn *through* language (Egan-Robertson & Bloome, 1998). Early childhood is the most rapid period of language development. If the young child fails to get support as a language learner an irreplaceable opportunity may be lost. Young children's confidence and skill as language learners and users can be damaged by carelessness or the absence of educational opportunities. Language difficulties often reverberate throughout the child's experience beyond the realm of academic achievement. The child who cannot use words to disagree may resort to aggressive behaviors; the child who cannot be understood may withdraw into silence; and the child who struggles with reading may give up on pursuing an education. For all of these reasons, an early childhood practitioner bears an awesome responsibility for facilitating every child's language to the maximum extent possible.

All existing forms of human language have several features in common:

PEARSON
myeducationkit™

Go to the Assignments and Activities section of Chapter 3 in MyEducationKit and complete the activity entitled "Benefits of Peers to Language Development."

- *Language is communicative.* It enables us to both transmit and receive messages. These messages include thoughts, emotions, ideas, and values expressed in words that can be recombined in nearly limitless ways.
- *Language is abstract.* It uses sounds, words, gestures, and graphic symbols that stand for something else, whether it is American Sign Language, Farsi, or braille. Because it is abstract it can be used to refer not only to objects, events, and situations in the present but also to the past or future.
- *Language is rule governed.* Every language has a system of rules that determine word order, meaning, and the formations of different words.
- *Language is social.* Even before infants can speak words, they can use gestures, noises, and crying to communicate. The main purpose of language is to facilitate interaction with other people.
- *Language is versatile.* It can be arranged and recombined in limitless ways. It is even possible to use language to communicate about things that do not yet exist, such as a science fiction author who creates a completely imaginary world.

Keep these features of language in mind as you read about Jacob, a preschooler with special needs for language support.

Collaboration with Families and Professionals

This year, Mr. Conway's preschool class will include Jacob, a 4-year-old who has a birth defect that has resulted in an inability to speak. Mr. Conway works with Jacob's family and three professionals as part of a transdisciplinary team to give Jacob the services that he needs. These specialists include a speech/language pathologist, the school social worker, and a special educator.

After conducting a home visit, interviewing the family, and observing Jacob in his home environment, Mr. Conway and the other professionals have determined that Jacob could benefit immensely from assistive technology (Judge, 2006; Mistrett, Lane, & Ruffino, 2005). The federal government defines assistive technology as "any item, piece of equipment or product system, whether acquired commercially or off the shelf, modified, or customized, that is used to increase, maintain, or improve functional capabilities of individuals with disabilities" (IDEIA, 2004). Assistive devices enable children to perform tasks that would not be possible without the devices (Parette, Peterson-Karlan, Wojcik, & Bardi, 2007). Available technology ranges from low-tech (e.g., a pencil grip) to high-tech (e.g., an electric wheelchair) (Parette, Blum, & Boeckmann, 2009). Mr. Conway's team investigates the assistive technology guidelines at Able Net

Standards in Education
Review the National Association for the Education of Young Children (NAEYC) Code of Ethical Conduct at www.naeyc.org/about/positions/PSeth05.asp. How will your work be a reflection of these important standards?

(www.ablenetinc.com) with an emphasis on support for young children's language (Center for Technology in Education Technology and Media Division, 2005; Watts, O'Brian, & Wojcik, 2004).

Jacob needs the high-tech assistive technology of an augmentative and alternative communication (AAC) system, which is a specially configured computer. When each key/icon on the keyboard is pressed, a voice synthesizer pronounces the word, and these individual words can be combined into messages.

There are many different types of systems. The team needs to decide which one should be used. The speech/language pathologist investigates several different systems and arranges a demonstration. After the family decides on a system, there is the issue of cost. The school social worker contacts the university researcher who invented the new equipment and works with the local Jaycees to raise the money. After the equipment arrives, Jacob works individually with a special educator to learn how to use the assistive technology.

According to Jacob's individualized educational program (IEP) and the agreement made with his family in an individualized family service plan (IFSP), the major goal this year is for Jacob to be able to communicate with others using his AAC device. This goal is further broken down into stages, beginning with single-word icons, then two-icon combinations, and finally sentence-like sequences.

About this experience, Mr. Conway says, "I never realized what a world of difference AAC could make in the lives of children. It provides not only academic support but also a mechanism for social and emotional growth. It has helped me too. I have learned from working with everyone. Now I really make an effort to keep up on new inventions to help children with special needs."

Contributions and Consequences

- *Contributions of the teacher:* How did the teacher play an active role in this situation?
- *Contributions of the family:* How did the family support the child and get involved in furthering the child's literacy growth?
- *Contributions of other professionals:* How did professionals in other fields contribute to addressing the needs of the child and family?
- *Consequences of collaboration:* How might this story have ended differently if the adults had not worked together?

How Do Children Learn to Communicate?

Linguistics refers to verbal (oral and written) language and its study. Basically, two means of communication are available to the young child: paralinguistics (nonverbal) and linguistics (verbal). *Paralinguistics* are those nonverbal means of communication that are related to language, such as facial expressions, gestures, body postures, and voice intonation (Menyuk, 1988). These nonverbal forms of communication play a

Brain and Language

The PBS documentary *The Brain* reported that, only four weeks into gestation, the first brain cells (neurons) are forming at the rate of 250,000 every minute. For more facts linking neuroscience and education, visit the Research Network on Early Experience and Brain Development (www.macbrain.org)— the group funded by the MacArthur and McDonnell foundations.

significant role in language comprehension, particularly when verbal expression is just developing. In fact, it is possible to get the essence of a message without any words at all. A toddler who has been taught not to touch the CD player, for instance, might play a mischievous game, whereby she pretends to touch it and then looks expectantly at her mother, who responds by shaking her head and looking solemn. Even though no words are spoken by the child or adult, communication occurs.

Let's look at how Katie, a 2-year-old, uses both nonverbal and verbal means of communication. She sees a battery-operated toy with three plastic penguins that climb up a staircase, zoom down a sliding board, and then repeat the whole process all over again, complete with chirping noises. She points to the toy and says "Birdies! Birdies!" while beckoning toward the toy with her fingers. "See it?" she asks in a hopeful voice. When the toy is placed within reach, Katie asks, "Touch it?" The toddler deftly picks up each penguin, inspects it closely, and then puts it back in place. She is delighted by this newfound ability to intervene in the penguins' rhythmic climbing and roller-coaster descent. Finally, she pats her chest with her hands and asks, "Have it?"

Katie's behavior illustrates the strides that are made in children's language development in just two years. When she was a newborn baby, her only means of communication was crying. How did she manage to travel this far in her ability to communicate? How will she progress to the conversational ease of a typical 5-year-old child or the complex sentences of a second-grader?

At some point during your school career, you no doubt studied and learned that the communication process includes a sender, a message, a medium for conveying that message, a receiver of the message, and a context in which that message is transmitted. How does this communication process apply to the language learning of the young child? Lauren, a 3-year-old who is meeting a couple of her parents' friends for the first time, provides a good example. Lauren hides behind the curtains and then behind a visitor's chair. "She's a little shy at first," Lauren's parents explain, "and sometimes difficult to understand." The preschooler comes out from behind the chair and looks admiringly at the woman visitor's necklace. Then Lauren says with perfect pronunciation and a tone of command in her voice, "I want to wear it."

Lauren's behavior illustrates the communicative process. It includes a sender (Lauren), a message ("I want to wear it"), a medium (spoken words), a receiver (the visitor), and a context, both physical (the living room) and social (verbal interaction with friends of the family who are unfamiliar to Lauren).

When two people are communicating with one another, the one who sends the message also expects some response on the part of the receiver. A baby who cries expects someone to appear in the doorway, ready to provide comfort. The child who is experimenting with a paper-cup-and-string "telephone" expects the person on the other end of the line to listen and talk back. The child who sends text messages to her or his grandparents awaits a reply. Thus, human communication is "a person sending a message to another individual with the conscious intent of evoking a response" (Johnson, 1972, p. 11).

Scientists have continued to debate the question of whether language is a uniquely human characteristic. No one doubts that animals can *communicate*, meaning that they can send messages through any of the sensory perception channels—visual (sight), auditory (sound), olfactory (smell), gustatory (taste), or tactile (touch). We know that animals communicate in many different ways, such as a mourning dove who calls to her mate or a newborn kitten who finds its mother through smell, taste, and touch.

It would be difficult to argue that animals—even those animals that have remarkable systems of communication, such as dolphins—are capable of something comparable to human language. Koko, a mountain gorilla who was taught American Sign Language and who has been the subject of several popular children's picture books, exemplifies some impressive language abilities. She was remarkably intelligent and communicated complex ideas to her trainer—such as her wish for a pet kitten—yet her repertoire and her skill with symbols was limited. Furthermore, if human reinforcement ceased, her sign language would fade. Despite extensive training, Koko's sign language ability still lagged far behind that of a typical 3-year-old human.

Components of Language

PEARSON
myeducationkit

Go to the Assignments and Activities section of Chapter 3 in MyEducationKit and complete the activity entitled "The 'Science' of Teaching Language."

There are four equally important dimensions of human language. Simultaneous attention to all four of these features is what makes the mastery of a language difficult. Figure 3.1 reviews these four components of language: (1) pragmatic (social context), (2) semantic (meaning), (3) syntactic (structural), and (4) graphophonic (the alphabetic, orthographic, sound/symbol aspects).

Pragmatics

Pragmatics has to do with the social context for language. It deals with who can speak, to whom they can speak, what they can say, how they should say it, when and where it is said, and the medium used to communicate (Hymes, 1971). Pragmatics includes such considerations as what is polite or rude, how turns are taken during a conversation, when silences become uncomfortable, and the efforts speakers make to repeat or adapt information to make it understandable to their listeners. In Spanish, for instance, addressing a person as *usted* (you) is more polite, while *tu* (you) is used with more familiar persons. Even nonverbal considerations are included, such as how far we stand apart (e.g., when are people invading our space?), the role of eye contact (e.g., looking down is a sign of respect in some cultures, but others think that making eye contact shows confidence and honesty), how we make gestures (e.g., is it impolite to point?), and whether touching is offensive (e.g., when is hugging okay?).

To illustrate how pragmatics affects language, think about how you would express disagreement with your supervisor, your parent, your classmate, or a preschooler.

FIGURE 3.1   Components of Human Language

Dimension/Definition	Behaviors of Child
Pragmatics	*Comprehension of social implications of utterances*
Mastery of the social interaction system of language	Example: Knowing that "Help! Help!" is a way to attract attention and get assistance in an emergency
Production of utterances appropriate to the social situation	Example: Learning to say "please" and "thank you"
Semantics	*Comprehension of meanings*
Mastery of meaning system	Example: Associating the words "bye-bye" with departures
Production of meaningful utterances	Example: Saying the word "truck" when a truck passes by
Syntax	*Recognition of structure in utterances* .
Mastery of grammatical system	Example: Realizing that plural nouns often end in s
Production of correctly structured utterances	Example: Learning noun/verb order to ask a question: "Why can't he play?" instead of "Why he can't play?"
Graphophonics	*Comprehension of sounds*
Mastery of sound system	Example: Hearing the words "You can bring your bear" and responding appropriately
Production of sounds	Example: Learning to say the word "no"

Source: Adapted from Levin, 1983.

One of the best ways to assess children's understanding of the social side of language is by observing them during play. The following play text illustrates pragmatics at work. Two preschool girls are playing with miniature toy people. One empty plastic coffee container is a "house" (with toy bedroom, bathroom, and kitchen fixtures inside) and another is a "school" (with toy desks and chairs). Maria plays the roles of teacher and mother, while Luan plays the parts of the three children.

> **Maria (Teacher—in an authoritative voice):**   "OK children." (She switches back to her normal voice and says to her playmate, "Pretend they are talking to each other.") "No chewing gum in school!"

Luan (playing all three children and using a silly voice): "Chomp, chomp, chomp!" "But that's fun!" (Picks up one figure.) "Teacher, I have to go home now. I don't feel good!" (Moves the figure to the home.) "Mom, Mom!" (Returns the figure to the school.) "OK, I'm back now!" "I just have a cold, achoo!" (Moves the figure back home again.) "Hi, Mom!"

Maria (switching roles to become Mother): "Take a bath!"

Luan (puts figure into tub): "I'm finished, Mom! Achoo, achoo, achoo! Now there's three absent from school."

Maria (still playing Mother): "Stay home and stay in your beds."

Luan: "But Mom! Oh Mother, oh Mother, oh Ma Ma Ma Moooother!!" (Clean-up time is announced by the teacher.)

Semantics

Semantics, the second component of language, refers to the meanings of words. Consider, for example, the word *potato*. Three-year-old Lee looks at her dinner plate and sees a small white mound. It tastes bland and has a smooth texture. "Do you like your potatoes?" her father asks. The next day, her family stops at a restaurant, and she eats some white circles covered with an orange, rubbery substance—potatoes au gratin. "You like potatoes, huh?" her mother comments. On Saturday, Lee goes to the grocery store and watches a woman who is handling brown, dirty objects in the produce section. She overhears the woman say, "I think I'll get a couple pounds of potatoes." Some weeks later, Lee visits relatives and sees her cousins playing a game they call Hot Potato with a pillow in the living room. Then her aunt says to a group of relatives who are watching television, "Time for lunch, you couch potatoes!" The variety of Lee's experiences with just one word during a few weeks illustrates why learning word meanings can be troublesome for beginning language learners.

Typically, children's difficulties with word meanings, or semantics, fall into one of three categories: (1) not knowing the correct word, (2) interpreting words or phrases literally, or (3) mistaking one word for another. The following vignette illustrates the importance of knowing the correct term. Anna is playing by her sandbox and calls to her teenage sister, "There's a worm, a big worm. Help me, sissy. I don't want it to get me." "Anna," her sister replies, "worms don't bite. Don't worry about it." "But it's a big black worm with a head," Anna continues. "I can see it looking at me." Anna's sister climbs down from the porch, sees a six-foot black snake, screams, and they both run inside. Based on this experience, Anna learns the difference between the words *snake* and *worm*.

Another common difficulty with language is the literal interpretation of words. *Idiomatic expressions* have figurative, rather than literal, meanings, such as "I'm all tied up" and "He let the cat out of the bag." When Nicole's father comments to his friend "I see you got a haircut," Nicole looks at the man curiously and whispers to her father, "I think you're wrong, Daddy. He got a whole bunch of hairs cut."

Children also mistake one word for another. Usually, this happens because they are trying to make sense out of whatever they hear. Sometimes these misunderstandings result in invented forms, or words that children make up based on their effort to make sense of what they have heard. Four-year-old Anita is at a family reunion picnic where cole slaw is being served. She likes it and wants more, except that she refers to it as "cold slop." In some ways, Anita's label for this food is more descriptive than its real name!

Syntax

Syntax refers to the set of rules or the grammar of a language. Mickey, a kindergartner, knows something about the rules of language. He explains how to form plurals to a classmate like this: "Because, Vickie, when you have lots of stuff, like more than one stuff, then you put an *s* at the end."

Word order is another syntactical aspect. In English, the noun usually precedes the verb (e.g., "The boy ran," rather than "Ran the boy"). The use of inflections, or word endings, is another syntactical rule. Children learn that the past tense of a regular verb usually is formed by adding *-ed*. If a child says, "We goed to Sea World," that child has learned the rule. It just happens that *go* is an irregular verb that has *went* as its past tense. The same is true for the formation of plurals that Mickey was explaining to a classmate. A child who says, "I need new slippers for my foots" has learned some of the rules about forming plurals.

Although these examples might be viewed by adults as mistakes, they are evidence of *overregularization*, in which children apply the rules without exception (e.g., "Look at the deers" or "She teached us about animals"). The English language is full of irregular forms like these. That is one reason that English is considered to be a difficult language to learn and another reason that children's mastery of language is such an impressive accomplishment.

Graphophonics

The *graphophonic* system refers to the letters and sounds that constitute a language. Most babies are actually more sensitive to slight differences in language sounds than adults. When babies are given a specially designed pacifier that records their responses, research shows that their sucking slows down to a steady rate as they hear the same sound repeatedly and that they begin to suck rapidly when a new sound is introduced. This response is a sign that they have detected the new sound and are interested again. This heightened speech perception evidently narrows over time (Trawick-Smith, 2009).

A child who learns another language during early childhood usually speaks it without an accent. An adult who acquires a second language, however, often has a heavy accent that reflects the characteristics of his or her native language. Japanese adults, for example, often have difficulty discriminating between the English sounds *l* and *r* (e.g., saying "rike" for "like"), whereas Japanese infants can detect this difference.

After children acquire language, they continue to explore the sounds of language. Here is a text of 5-year-old Mark's talk as he plays in the blocks corner:

> One, two, three. (He counts the blocks as he picks them up.) I wonder if this will fall if I put three more blocks on top? (He is stacking blocks on the roof of his garage. As he puts

the second block on the stack, he bumps it and it all falls down.) Oooohh! What'd ya fall for? (He begins to build it again but doesn't stack so many on this time.) That's done. (He finishes it and grabs a toy car.) Are you gonna fit? Verrrroom! (He drives his cars around and makes car noises.) Hi, Sandy! Hi, Bill! Let's go to the ice cream place. OK. Vrrroooom, almost here, eerrrch! Let's get out. I want a biiggg ice cream cone! OK. Hey lady, gimme a five-scoop ice cream cone. Thanks. Here, Sandy. Now gimme a six-scoop ice cream cone. Thanks. Let's go. That was good! Veroom! (He drives to the garage and pretends to get gas; changing his voice to a lower pitch.) I have to get some gas, honey. (Switches to a higher pitch.) OK, Billy, buy me some gum while you're in there.

Mark uses words that imitate sounds, repeats phrases he has heard, and varies the pitch of his voice. When he says "oohh" and "veroom," for example, the resonance (amount of vibration in his vocal chords) changes, too. The emotional tone in his voice changes when he gives a command or asks himself a question. Mark's language emphasizes some words and includes slight breaks or pauses between words and sentences. When he says "OK, Billy, buy me some gum," he stresses *gum* and there are pauses after *OK* and *Billy*.

These features of the sound system of language are one reason that a computer voice usually sounds so flat and mechanical in comparison to a human voice. Most of us find a monotone difficult to listen to because our ear for language expects variation. As Mark matures, he will strive to match the sound units in his oral language, called *phonemes*, to the written units of language, called *graphemes*. Among the challenges in this process might be how to represent a sound like "veroom" in written language.

Teachers who consider all four components of language are able to make the most significant contributions to children's language growth.

Overview of Language Development

When does a child officially become a speaker of the native language? In the United States, we tend to confer the status of a beginning speaker on a child who can say "Mama" and "Dada." In U.S. society, most children begin to use recognizable words around the time that they begin to take their first steps, or around 12 months of age. Five young learners of language enrolled in a child-care center will help to illustrate the stages through which typically developing young children progress.

Prelinguistic speech refers to all of the nonword utterances that babies make. Angie is a 5-month-old who makes sounds that are similar to syllables. She babbles, making consonant/vowel sounds like "ma," "ta," "da," and she coos, making vowel sounds like "uuh." Kaoru, an 11-month-old in her class, is stringing these sounds together in wordlike ways. He uses the intonation and gestures of speech, but no actual words are discernible. Basically, Kaoru's vocalizations are English sounding, but no real words are spoken. This flow of gibberish with speechlike characteristics is referred to as *expressive jargon*.

Infants and Toddlers

Gestures play a vital role in early communication. In a study of 50 families with 14-month-olds, the toddlers produced 13 to 25 meanings through gestures in 90 minutes (Goldin-Meadow & Rowe, 2009). In a study of the gestures 3-year-olds made in response to music, children's gestures revealed their thinking (Nyland, Ferris, & Dunn, 2008). What are the implications for practice?

PEARSON
myeducationkit

Go to the Assignments and Activities section of Chapter 3 in MyEducationKit and complete the activity entitled "Children with Special Language Needs."

Figure 3.2 is a timeline of the general sequence for infant/toddler language development. Knowing this information will give you some sense of the way that language progresses. Such knowledge should not be used to label children as "above average," "average," or "below average," however. The teacher's role is always to support and facilitate language development in ways that further the child's competence, regardless of the age at which particular language behaviors appear.

Linguistic speech begins with first words and lasts until maturity. Even though 13-month-old Eileen uses expressive jargon, her language is interspersed with a few sounds that are identifiable as words, including "mama," "dada," "keekot" (kitty cat), and "buh-bah" (bottle). These one-word utterances are called *holophrases*. By 13 to 15 months, most infants have acquired about 10 words. Usually, their first words refer to things they can experience directly or act on in some way—family members, pets, favorite foods, or toys (Nelson, 2007). Sometimes they choose action words, such as "up" or "bye-bye," or engage in social games like Patty Cake. Occasionally, they use modifiers such as "bad" or "pretty," as well as words that enable them to obtain information (e.g., "whazdat?" for "what is that?"). Children sometimes pronounce words in surprising ways, which is responsible for many nicknames—like Christie, who was called "Crisit" by her baby sister.

As children progress through linguistic speech, they begin to link words together. If we listened in as 2- and 3-year-olds were playing together, we would hear many chil-

---

FIGURE 3.2   Timeline of Infant/Toddler Language Development

The first form of communication is crying. There are actually different types of cries. A painful cry is often signaled not only by the intensity but also by the number of pauses or how long babies hold their breath between cries.

As babies get older, they make sounds and gestures. At first, babies make the vowel sounds using their mouths (e.g., "ooooh," "aaaah"); by 4 or 5 months, they begin to use the back of their throat to make consonant sounds. At around 12 months, they connect vowels and consonants together, a type of utterance called *lallation* (e.g., "mamamama"). These consonant/vowel syllable sequences make up about half of babies' noncrying sounds from 6 to 12 months.

Babies' ability to understand language is much more developed than their ability to produce (expressive) language. Between 8 months and 1½ years, babies use expressive jargon, a flow of jibberish with languagelike intonation. At about the same time, babies begin to use single words (*holophrases*) that are understandable to others.

Toddlers and 3-year-olds tend to use telegraphic speech, words linked together without verb endings (e.g., *-ed, -ing*), articles (e.g., *the, and*), prepositions (e.g., *on, in*), and pronouns (e.g., *I, she, him*). Although children's language varies widely, the toddler's receptive (listening) vocabulary is often as much as four times his or her expressive (speaking) vocabulary. Two-year-olds are just learning how to converse and typically do not extend a conversation beyond two turns and do not sustain a topic for long.

Source: McCormick, Loeb, & Schiefelbusch, 2002.

dren combining words into the simplest of sentences, such as "Billy cry" to mean "Do something, Teacher. Billy is crying," "Look book" to mean "Please read this book to me now," "Portia sammich" to mean "I want to have my lunch now and eat my sandwich," and "Me go too" to mean "I want to go outside and play with the big kids." This type of language, reduced to its most essential elements, is referred to as *telegraphic speech* because it is comparable to the way we communicate when we are trying to save words, as in a telegram. Most of us would not write, for example, "I am desperately in need of cash. Please send money as soon as you possibly can," when economy of expression is the goal. If text messaging, we might write "HELP! SEND $!" The child's telegraphic speech does much the same thing: It distills the message into its essential elements, mostly nouns and verbs.

Notice that in all these cases, the children omit the auxiliary verbs and verb endings ("Billy cry" instead of "Billy is crying"), the prepositions and articles ("book" instead of "at the book"), and the pronouns ("Portia" instead of "me" or "I" or "my"). Gradually, even that telegraphic speech becomes more elaborate, as when a neighbor asks a 2-year-old if she wants to take a walk with her and her daughter. The toddler points to her mom and then points to herself and says, "My ask my mommy my 'llowed," meaning "I'll ask my mommy if I am allowed to go with you."

As children mature, of course, their speech begins to sound more and more like that of adults. They use increasingly complex sentences that eventually incorporate all of the features that were omitted in telegraphic speech. Still, language presents many challenges. Expressions for temporal relations (*yesterday, after, then*), causality (*if, because*), and quantity (*few, less, many*) are particularly troublesome because they require sophisticated thinking about sequences, causal relationships, and comparisons or relative amounts (McCormick, Loeb, & Schiefelbusch, 2002). So it would not be unusual for a child who can carry on a conversation reasonably well to confuse *yesterday* with *tomorrow*, saying, "Is there a party yesterday?"

Figure 3.3 is intended to give rough estimates of when various language milestones might be achieved in typically developing children, birth through age 8. It should not be regarded as a set of rigid standards to which every child is expected to adhere because a child's age does not tell us everything we need to know about her or his language development. Although language behavior informs us about what a child has learned, it does not explain why or how language learning occurs. That question has intrigued people for centuries. Some contemporary theorists have emphasized the importance of heredity, some have stressed the importance of environment, and still others have suggested it is the interaction of the two.

Theories of Language Acquisition

Whether you realize it or not, you already have some theoretical leanings. Complete the following sentence stem—"I think that children learn to talk primarily through . . ."—and then compare your answer with the statements that follow:

1. Children learn to talk primarily through imitation. They make certain sounds and are rewarded or reinforced for producing words.

FIGURE 3.3 Language Milestones

Stage 1: Prelinguistic—Speech-Type Sounds But No Words (approximately birth–11 months)

Birth	Crying is the major way of communicating needs.
2 weeks	Less crying, more random gestures and vocalizations.
6 weeks	Squeals, gurgles, and coos (makes vowel sounds such as "uhh").
2 months	Uses smile to communicate.
3 months to 6 months	Child *babbles* (makes consonant/vowel syllable sounds like "ma," "de," "da").
6 months to 9 months	Accidentally imitates sounds, more repetition of syllables (such as "ah-ba-ba"); utterances express emotions.
9 months to 11 months	Deliberately imitates sounds; shows definite signs of understanding some words and simple commands; uses *expressive jargon*, a flow of gibberish that has the intonation of real speech.

Stages 2 to 4: Linguistic Speech—Uses Language in Increasingly Complex Ways (approximately 1 year and up)

Stage 2: One-Word Utterances (approximately 1–2 years)

At approximately 12 months	Child uses *holophrases* (one-word utterances); complex meanings can underlie one word; vocabulary of three to six words.
12 months to 18 months	Intonation is complex and speechlike; extensive use of nouns. *Vocabulary:* 3 to 50 words. *Social:* Child does not attempt to convey additional information or show frustration when not understood.

Stage 3: Making Words into Phrases (approximately 2–3 years)

Around 2 years	Great strides in receptive language; child uses *telegraphic speech*, two- or three-word utterances. *Vocabulary:* 50 to 200 words. *Social:* Definite increase in communicative efforts; beginnings of conversation, although toddlers rarely extend conversations beyond two turns or sustain topics.
3 years	Often considered to be the most rapid period of language growth. *Vocabulary:* Many new words acquired daily; 200- to 300-word vocabulary. *Social:* Child strives to communicate and shows frustration if not understood; the ability of unfamiliar adults to understand the child increases.

FIGURE 3.3 Continued

Stage 4: Using Complete Sentences (approximately 4–6 years)

4 years	Pronunciation and grammar improve.
	Vocabulary: 1,400 to 1,600 words.
	Social: Child seeks ways to correct misunderstandings; begins to adjust speech to listener's information needs; disputes with peers can be resolved with words and invitations to play are more common.
5 to 6 years	Complex, grammatically correct sentences; uses pronouns; uses past, present, and future verb tenses; average sentence length per oral sentence increases to 6.8 words.
	Vocabulary: Uses approximately 2,500 words, understands about 6,000, responds to 25,000.
	Social: Child has good control of elements of conversation.

Stage 5: Using Language Symbolically (reading and writing) (approximately 6 years and up)

6 to 7 years	Uses more complex sentences more adjectives; uses "If . . . then" conditional clauses; average number of words per sentence is 7.6.
	Vocabulary: Speaking vocabulary of about 3,000 words.
7 to 8 years	Uses adjectival clauses with *which*, more gerunds, subordinate clauses.

Sources: Cruger, 2005; Dale, 1976; Loban, 1976; Maxim, 1989; McCormick, Loeb, & Schiefelbusch, 2002; Otto, 2008; Papalia, Olds, & Feldman, 2007; Tabors & Snow, 2001; Thal & Flores, 2001.

2. Children learn to talk because it is part of their normal progression of development, which is greatly influenced by heredity.
3. Children learn to talk because the human brain is "wired" for language. They seem to pick up language naturally.
4. Children learn to talk because of the interaction between their emerging abilities and their experiences. They are constantly striving to make sense out of their world.
5. Children learn to talk primarily because they need to communicate. Their emotional and social drives greatly affect the process of language development.
6. Children learn to talk because language is a part of the culture. Through language, children learn the social norms and expectations that enable them to participate in society.

PEARSON
myeducationkit™

Go to the Assignments and Activities section of Chapter 3 in MyEducationKit and complete the activity entitled "Expressive Language Disorders."

Which of these statements is most closely aligned with your own ideas? Perhaps it was difficult to decide. Some of them may sound familiar because they include theoretical orientations you have encountered previously. The first statement, as you may have guessed, is a behavioral theory. Item 2 reflects a maturational theory, 3 a preformationist theory, 4 a cognitive developmental theory, and 5 and 6 sociocultural learning theory.

Behaviorists, such as B. F. Skinner, emphasize the influence of the environment on language development. The stimulus/response dynamic is the essence of a behavioral theory of language acquisition. A 9-month-old pats the family dog while saying "duh-duh-duh." Her father gets excited and says, "Yes! That's right—it's a doggie. Say dog-gie." Then he calls to his wife in the next room: "Hey, honey! Come here. Alison just said doggie!" This situation offers one possible answer to the question of language acquisition. The child makes random sounds, certain sounds are reinforced, and after thousands of such experiences, the child begins to talk.

Maturationists emphasize individual biological readiness. Children's language, according to a maturational view, gradually unfolds in accordance with the child's "inner clock," just as a plant moves predictably from bulb to flower but does not necessarily bloom at the same moment as every other bulb. Individual children may vary considerably from that timetable without having any language problems. One child might talk exceptionally early at 8 months, and another child might not begin talking until 20 months. Despite these initial differences, it is often the case that both children are doing well in school 4 years later, and it might be difficult at that point to ascertain who was the first to talk. The conviction that children are on their own schedules, so to speak, is a maturational point of view.

Innatists or *preformationists* believe that the brain is "wired" for language acquisition. The basic sequence of language acquisition is the same regardless of the specific language being learned by the child. Whether a baby learns English, Japanese, or Balinese, the steps in language acquisition tend to move from babbling and cooing, to expressive jargon and holophrases, to telegraphic speech, to simple sentences, and finally to increasingly complex sentences. For the vast majority of children around the world, this task is accomplished during the preschool years, and if it is not accomplished during that time, language ability often suffers. Even though children do attain these language milestones at their own pace, the markers along the way remain relatively consistent (Chomsky, 1988).

Thus far, you have seen two theories that emphasize heredity (innatist and maturationist) and one that emphasizes environment (behaviorist). Next are two theories that emphasize the interaction between heredity and environment.

Cognitive developmental theory emphasizes this interaction in assuming that the organism (in this case, the child) both changes the environment and is changed by the environment. Also essential to the theory is the understanding that children go through a series of steps or stages in their language learning. The basic premise of cognitive developmental theory is *constructivism.* According to this theory, children do not simply soak up the language around them. Rather, they actively build or construct their understandings about the world.

The behavior of Marjorie, a 12-month-old, will help to illustrate the dual processes that are used to construct knowledge about language—assimilation and accommodation. Marjorie created the word "fuh-fuh," which she used to describe the faux fur collar on her mother's winter parka, a white dog puppet, and a faded yellow blanket. Evidently, this word described a category of objects that could be labeled as "white, furry things." In *assimilation*, existing mental structures keep expanding to include new concepts. If Marjorie indiscriminately referred to everything as a "fuh-fuh," she would be engaging in pure assimilation; her mind would operate like one giant file cabinet without any dividers or separate files. In *accommodation*, new mental structures are formed. If Marjorie created a new category every time she encountered something unfamiliar, she would be practicing pure accommodation; her mind would be like a file cabinet with separate dividers for each and every thing.

For children to form new mental structures that are useful and meaningful, assimilation and accommodation must work together. If Marjorie sees a toy horse with a mane and tail of white hair, where does she "file" it—as a "fuh-fuh" or a horse, or does it warrant a whole new category? She decides that the features of "horseness" in this particular item supersede its furriness and categorizes it as a horse. From a cognitive developmental perspective, children are, just like Marjorie, actively building their understandings about language. They use language as a tool to think with.

From a *sociocultural* perspective, language use and development is an inner thought process (psychological) and a means of interaction with others (social) that occurs in a variety of contexts (cultural). Opportunities for social interaction within a particular cultural context are the primary motivation for children to learn language.

For an illustration of this theoretical perspective, let's return to Marjorie. One morning, she toddles into the kitchen, points at her face, and says "Fuh-fuh, Mama." Her parents are completely mystified by this statement. What does the white and furry category have to do with her face? Marjorie is attempting to use language for social interaction, but no one can fathom her meaning. The question is answered after Marjorie develops an upper respiratory problem and the pediatrician discovers she has pushed a piece of frayed blanket fuzz into her nostril!

So even though the toddler has mastered only a handful of words, mostly nouns, these words are being used for social interaction, not merely as labels. Marjorie is striving to communicate, even if adults fail to understand her. Marjorie's behavior also reflects an understanding of the norms of her culture. She has learned that pointing at something is a way of focusing the attention of others on it, and she has tried to combine this gesture with her very limited vocabulary to get her message across.

Because sociocultural theory emphasizes the ways that humans learn and use language, it emphasizes pragmatics. As discussed earlier in this chapter, *pragmatics* refers to the different types of language that are socially appropriate with different people and different social contexts.

In recent years, theorists who regard language as a cultural phenomenon have gained greater recognition. Russian theorist Lev Vygotsky (1962) set forth a novel perspective on the role of language in thinking and learning. Whereas Jean Piaget (1963), a cognitive developmental theorist, argued that thought comes before language, Vygotsky argued that the child must first acquire language to have something to think with; language is a "tool for the mind" (Bodrova & Leong, 2007). An important aspect of Vygotsky's theory is the *zone of proximal development* (ZPD), or the distinction between what the child can do independently and what the child can do with social support. Usually, that social support comes from adults and from more competent peers. With support, children can function at a higher level in language. From a Vygotskian perspective, language development becomes more than an inner mental activity; it becomes a cultural phenomenon.

Even though theorists may disagree about the most important influence on the child's language development, most agree on the basic chronology of language learning and all agree that heredity and environment both play a role. Perhaps the best way of balancing these theoretical orientations is to use Genishi's (1988) explanation: "Language occurs through an interaction among genes (which hold innate tendencies to communicate and be sociable), environment, and the child's own thinking abilities" (p. 1).

Language is sometimes categorized as *receptive*, meaning language that is taken in (listening/reading), or *expressive*, meaning language that is produced (speaking/writing). Figure 3.4 (on pp. 62–65) provides an overview of receptive and expressive language activities for use with children in elementary school.

Teacher Concerns and Basic Strategies

Teachers who talked about children's speech development raised several issues. For instance, Lisa, a kindergarten teacher, said:

> Whenever I am working with young children, I find that they sometimes want to go on and on telling about something. I hate to cut them off, but sometimes their comments detract from a story or cause the other children to fidget. What should I do?

This teacher is right to think that it is not appropriate to disregard children's comments. With a younger child, you may want to suggest that she or he draw a picture to describe the event that was so exciting. With an older child, you might gracefully move on, saying something like "It sounds like you had a very interesting experience. It would be a good one to write about in your journal" or "Maybe you shouldn't tell us the end of your story yet. You could save it and write about it this afternoon."

Charles, who teaches third grade, raised another common concern.

> I feel so uncomfortable when the children all begin to talk to me at once. I don't want to hurt anyone's feelings. I'm never sure how to handle this. When I am teaching, I ask the children to raise their hands. But when the kids are waiting for the bus, on the playground, or in the cafeteria, I sometimes don't know who I should respond to first.

Less formal talk situations do sometimes create multiple demands on the teacher's attention. You may want to set aside some special reserved times to talk with individual children. Post a child's name on a helper's board to be your assistant and have your undivided attention when you are on bus, cafeteria, or playground duty. Another solution is to use a first-come, first-served approach and gently remind children to take turns.

Knowing how to approach shy students is also of concern to many teachers. Ming, a preschool teacher, commented:

I suppose that I have a special bond with children who are shy because I was so shy myself as a young child. I wonder how to help these children express themselves.

One thing to remember when drawing out shy young children is to avoid focusing too much attention on them. If you know that the child is reticent, consider meeting with the child and parent or family member together. Talk with the parent or family member, instead of talking directly to the child. Talk about things that you know would interest the child. Usually, if shy children feel secure and have something to say, they will join in the conversation. It may be a comment whispered to the caregiver, but it is participation nevertheless. When working with shy children, avoid situations that put children on the spot (e.g., "What color is this?" "Show me how you can spell") or that ask them to offer opinions that seem risky (e.g., "Are you ready to start school in the fall?" "How do you like your new baby brother?"). Stay calm and quiet long enough to get them to enter the conversation.

Classroom Activities to Support Language Development

Long before babies can talk, adults need to interact with them and talk to them:

Research and Report
Visit the National Association for the Education of Young Children website at www.naeyc.org. Choose information for teachers or families, then select a topic from the menu. Print out the brochure or position statement and bring it to class; share the highlights with the group.

Talking to Babies and Toddlers   When you speak with very young children, remember to simplify sentences, limit vocabulary, use here-and-now language, and repeat words and phrases. Talking to a baby during daily routines such as feeding, changing diapers, and bathing is an excellent way to build vocabulary and stimulate language growth. Studies show that caregivers who communicate well with infants and toddlers raise the pitch of their voices, exaggerate their facial expressions and speech, are very animated, and engage the child in interaction.

PEARSON
myeducationkit™

Go to the Assignments and Activities section of Chapter 3 in MyEducationKit and complete the activity entitled "Teaching Phonics."

Combine Sensory Stimulation with Talk   Babies are at Piaget's sensorimotor stage, a time when they are particularly sensitive to sensory input. Try experiences such as listening to music while you hold and gently dance with the child, stroking the baby's fingers and toes with different textured fabrics. Games such as Peek-a-Boo or action rhymes such as "This Little Piggy" also provide sensory stimulation.

Ping-Pong   When the infant or toddler makes a sound or says a word, imitate the child's vocalizations, and respond when the child vocalizes back to you.

FIGURE 3.4 Receptive and Expressive Language Strategies

Child's Desired Behaviors	Teacher's Verbal Prompts	Classroom Activities
Receptive Language Strategies		
Speaks in complex sentences	"I'm not sure what you mean. Tell me more." "Start with _____ and tell me again." (Give child appropriate word or phrase with which to start a complex sentence.) "Do you mean _____? Can you tell me _____?" (Give child appropriate sentence for repetition.)	• Read aloud literature that contains descriptive language and complex sentence forms. • Perform choral reading/speaking activities so children can hear and use expressive language. Young children can use poems with repetitive phrases. Older children can enjoy Paul Fleischman's *Joyful Noise: Poems for Two Voices.* • Memorize chants and rhymes. Tap out rhythms to improve fluency.
Uses specific vocabulary such as names, pronouns, possessive markers	"I asked _____ [where/when/who/how many/ etc.]. Tell me a _____ [place/time/name/ number/etc.]." "You said she. What person do you mean? Tell me her name." "Who does that belong to? Is it Susan's or is it Tom's?"	• Role-play situations in which children ask questions of others. • Have children generate questions and then interview peers or adults. Record interviews for later review. • Use cooperative groups to solve mysteries by connecting clues to answers: who, what, when, where, and so on. Children can create questions for other groups. • Encourage dialogue through class meeting, cooperative group work, and literature discussion. • Use a Who-What-When-Where analysis chart for literature. Young children can chart these with the teacher. • Play 20 Questions: Teacher or child thinks of a secret topic. Children can ask up to 20 yes/no questions to solve the mystery topic.

Skill	Example phrases	Strategies
Joins in conversations with peers and adults	"Please tell ___ to ___." (Give the child practice approaching and speaking to others.) "You're going to be a team leader. Who would you like in your group?" (Choose an activity in which the child succeeds easily; ask the child privately to name classmates with whom she/he feels comfortable.) "Ms. ___ wants someone to teach her children to ___. I know you are good at that. Let's pretend you are teaching this puppet to ___. How would you teach this puppet to ___?"	• Teach bridging phrases such as "I agree with Julie because . . ." or "In addition to what you said, I . . ." to facilitate discussion. • Have the children respond to each other's stories during Author's Chair time. • Teach cooperative group skills. Assign each group member a role and task (e.g., leader, recorder, encourager, presenter) and have children complete a group project. • Use math manipulatives to develop strategies for problem solving. Have children share their reasoning with each other.
Provides more information when asked	"I don't understand. Can you tell me with different words?" "Do you mean ___?" (Requires only yes/no response.) "Do you mean ___ or ___?" (Requires child to rephrase original statement.)	• Have children ask and answer questions during Author's Chair time, sharing time, or book discussions. • Have children respond to questions from teacher/peers in dialogue journals (written or recorded) or during editing activities. Have children explain their strategies and/or reasoning when giving an answer or comment. • Encourage questions and answers after oral presentations or during sharing time.
Participates appropriately in conversations (takes turns, stays on topic, does not interrupt others)	"We are talking about ___ [e.g., going to the grocery store]. What can you tell us about that?" "It's your turn now. Can you tell us ___?" (Gain child's attention and repeat question to prompt memory.)	• Class meetings: Use a "turn stick" that children pass to the person whose turn it is to talk. • At the beginning of a discussion, give each child three tokens. A child spends one token per turn. Turns are over when all of the tokens have been spent. • Cooperative group work: Assign roles of leader, recorder, questioner, and so on, to ensure that each child has a participatory role. • Use round-robin techniques for brainstorming. Drawing names from a holder ensures each child has an opportunity to speak.

(continued)

FIGURE 3.4 Continued

Child's Desired Behaviors	Teacher's Verbal Prompts	Classroom Activities
Expressive Language Strategies		
Signals when information is not understood	"Show me with your hands: Do you want a lot of help, a little help, or no help?" "Show me with your hands: Did you understand all of that, a little of that, or none of that?" "Tell me as much as you can. I'll help if it gets confusing."	• Seat a child in front row or close to teacher; establish a signal for the child to indicate a need for help (e.g., tap on teacher's shoe, tug on right ear). • Have children paraphrase and repeat directions. • Give incomplete directions: "What else do you need to know?" Children ask for information. • Give incomplete information for an activity: Children work in cooperative groups to determine what additional information is needed.
Gives appropriate responses when asked questions	"That tells me _____. Right now I want to know _____. Can you tell me _____?" (Credit child with answering a question but clarify desired information; then repeat/reword original questions.) "I can tell you're trying, but I want to know _____. Could you tell me _____?" (Credit child's effort, clarify, and repeat/reword original question.) "That's interesting. Sounds like you were reminded of _____. But right now, we're discussing _____. Tell me _____." (Credit effort and association with general topic but clarify specific topic and repeat/rephrase question.)	• Practice peer interviews for a Meet Your Classmate book. • Have children keep dialogue journals in which the teacher responds to children's reflections. In addition, have both teachers and children write at least one question per entry for the reader to answer. • Read and discuss *Martha Speaks* by Susan Meddaugh, in which Martha the dog gains the ability to speak by eating alphabet soup.

64

Follows multistep instructions without visual cues or repetition of directions	"Tell me what you have to do." "Tell me what you will do first." Have child signal teacher as soon as step is completed. Gradually expand the number of steps child completes before signaling teacher. "Great!" You have already followed the first direction. Now you have to _____. Tell me what you must do now." (Credit partial success, repeat next step(s). Immediately check for understanding.)	• Have children retell stories in proper sequence. Have children give explanatory "how-to" speeches for completing tasks like tying shoes and folding origami cranes. • Tell/write narratives of the steps followed to get ready for school, make Jell-o, etc. • Play Simon Says using more than one command (e.g., "Simon says to touch your toes and wave your hand").
Recognizes and adapts to subtle changes in classroom activities	"What did I do differently today? What do you think that means?" "I changed something this morning. Point to what I changed." "We have a visitor coming today. How should we change our schedule?"	• Use nonverbal cues such as a bell, music, or clapping to signal transition times in the classroom. • Develop a signal that children can use to help manage the classroom (e.g., a voice-level chart, traffic signal, or bell to signal when classroom is too noisy). • Use signs or other visual cues.

Source: Howard, S., Shaughnessy, A., Sanger, D., & Hux, K. (1998). Let's talk! Facilitating language in early elementary classrooms. *Young Children, 53*(3), 37–38. Reprinted with permission from the National Association for the Education of Young Children.

Thank You Games   Practice social routines, such as requesting an item ("Can I hold the baby doll?") and then giving it back to the child quickly while saying "Thank you."

Name and Narrate   Provide the child with labels as you do things together—for instance, while dressing the child to go outdoors. "First we'll put on your boots. Now your coat. Here's your hat. Now one mitten. Now the other mitten."

Embedded Teaching   Experts recommend using familiar contexts as a support for making language more understandable (McMullen, 1998). For instance, it is more understandable to the child to learn words associated with foods and meals if they are discussed during snack or lunchtime.

Fill-Ins   Instead of completing a sentence for the child, leave part of it blank so that the child can fill in the rest of the information. A simple example is "This is a . . ." To offer a greater challenge, you could say something more like a riddle. For instance, while at the grocery store, you might say "I need something for breakfast. It's something you eat with maple syrup."

Conclusion

Contrary to popular opinion, adults do not "teach children to talk." That phrase implies that the child is a passive repository for adult language or that language is somehow bequeathed to the child. We now know that children are far from being passive recipients of adult language. Children are the primary agents in the process of acquiring language. Adults may invite, encourage, or support, but the child is the learner who is striving to communicate.

myeducationkit   To check your comprehension on the content covered in this chapter, go to the MyEducationKit for your book and complete the Study Plan for Chapter 3. Here you will be able to take a chapter quiz and receive feedback on your answers.

Research-Based Literacy Strategies

Phonological Awareness and Learning to Recognize Rhymes

Phonological awareness is the ability to recognize, manipulate, and produce the sounds in spoken words. For the very young child, the emphasis is on playing with the sounds of language, rather than working with print. Activities such as listening to and chiming in on nursery rhymes are both ways of building phonological awareness (Byrne, Freebody, & Gates, 1992; Neuman, 2004). Children's phonological sensitivity and recognition of rhyme affects later literacy development. Based on longitudinal data gathered from young children, sensitivity to rhyme is a good predictor of which children will acquire phonological skills with print later on (Anthony & Lonigan, 2004). In a longitudinal study, 227 preschoolers were given an IQ test and a test of phonological awareness (PA). By the end of year two, only one child in the good PA group had become a poor reader (Heath & Hogben, 2004).

Clusters of words can be used to assess children's ability to detect rhyming words. A teacher might begin by asking children to find the words that "match" and saying "Tree, bee. Do they sound alike?" "Tree, sock. Do they sound alike?" "Tree, duck. Do they sound alike?" Following some practice with items such as these, clip art can be used to make matches that can be illustrated (e.g., *box/fox, star/car, moon/spoon, bat/cat, sock/clock, run/sun, pig/wig*).

Another way of fostering phonological awareness is to get children involved in acting out nursery rhymes. This helps to build phonological awareness, teach children the traditional rhymes, support speaking and listening skills, and encourage creative expression (Roush, 2005). Teachers should include the nursery rhymes of other cultures as well. These need to be shared in the original language because it preserves alliteration, rhythm, rhyme, and repetition. Therefore, when listening to nursery rhymes from other cultures, it is best to hear them as they are spoken in the intended language. Volunteers and tutors who speak the child's first language can share nursery rhymes in this authentic way and point out the words that rhyme. For a discussion of the research on phonemic awareness, visit www.reading a-z.com/research/phonological.html.

Using Environmental Print

Environmental print refers to the language and images that are everywhere in the child's environment—traffic signs, logos, food wrappers, and so forth. Children often recognize certain items, such as the appearance of a particular fast-food restaurant chain's billboard, long before they are independent readers. Environmental print activities capitalize on these "words that surround us" (Fingon, 2005) and encourage children to perform a variety of activities with them (Aldridge, Kirkland, & Kuby, 2002). Studies show that providing environmental print is an effective way of supporting emergent literacy (see National Council of Teachers of English, 2005). Collages, bulletin boards, and teacher- or child-made books are just a few ways to take in-

ventory of the environmental print that each child knows.

For English language learners, environmental print examples can be gathered in the child's first language as well as in English. In addition to merely collecting examples of environmental print, these materials can be made more challenging by turning them into guessing games or alphabetizing them (Rule, 2001). Because environmental print activities adapt readily to different levels of ability, teachers may want to structure one of their learning centers with an environmental print focus. For more on using environmental print with young children, see Xu and Rutledge (2003).

Using Children's Names to Foster Language Development

Throughout the world, the naming of children has special significance. In fact, many cultures have particular rituals associated with names, such as a ceremony during which the child's name is selected (www.ericdigests.org/2001–3/development.htm). Therefore, it is particularly important for teachers to learn each child's name and to check with the parents/family to be certain about the correct pronunciation.

Even before children know how to read or write other words, they often recognize and try to write (or have learned to write) their names. Research suggests that children's efforts to write their names are useful indicators of their literacy acquisition (Green, 1998). Toddlers and preschoolers often delight at hearing their names in stories or songs as well. By building on this familiarity, children can begin to understand the functions of print, increase their awareness of sound/symbol correspondence in words, and identify letters (Kirk & Clark, 2005).

Children are motivated to recognize one another's names in school. Flashcards that feature all the children's names can be used to take attendance and create a natural, meaningful context for practicing literacy skills. The teacher can hold up a card and ask, "Whose name is this? Is this student here today?" With practice, children will soon begin to recognize their classmates' names, often relying on the first letter or the general word outline shape (called *configuration*) as a cue for guessing. With daily practice, children will learn to recognize more and more names of those in the class. Children's books about the importance of names, such as *My Name is Yoon* (Recorvitz, 2003), are another resource in learning about names.

When children can recognize their names on sight, Denton, Parker, and Jasbrouck (2003) suggest reading simple sentences into which children's names are inserted, using the following procedure:

1. *Introduction.* Tell the children that they will read sentences made up of words that they know or can sound out; include students' names in the sentences.
2. *Teach the sight words.* Teach the words *a, and, the, he, she, we, it, was,* and *is.* If the children don't recognize the word, say the word (in a pleasant voice) and have them say it with you. Practice until they can identify the words quickly and accurately; point out their classmates' names in the sentence.
3. *Read the sentences.* Have the children practice reading the sentence several times until they can read it smoothly; create additional sentences with other students' names included.
4. *Evaluate individual progress.* Time each student in reading sentences for one minute, subtract any errors made, and record the number of words the child knows (adapted from Denton et al., 2003).

Another advantage to learning classmates' names is that children can use them to send drawings and writings to other students in their individual mailboxes or by computer. For more on using children's names as a teaching strategy, see Haney (2002) and McNair (2007). A variety of across-the-curriculum teaching activities are posted at www.kinderkorner.com/names.html.

Links with Literature

Books for Infants and Toddlers

What Is a Book for a Baby?

Suitable books for infants and toddlers are

- *Simple.* Books for babies often depict familiar objects (teddy bear, ball, kitten) or routines (bathtime, mealtime). Simple, uncluttered illustrations are also characteristic of the books babies like.
- *High contrast.* Books suited to babies attract their attention by using clear shapes that stand out from the background. Some ways of providing high contrast are to use black and white, primary colors, simple geometric shapes, or brightly colored photographs with uncluttered backgrounds.
- *Durable.* Books for babies and toddlers are designed to withstand hard use. Often, they are constructed of cardboard, fabric, or heavy plastic. These materials also make it easier for babies to turn the pages by themselves.

- *Appealing.* Picture books for the youngest child are matched to the interests of the very young. Topics such as enjoyable activities (e.g., going to the grocery store, playing with toys), relationships with caregivers, and all types of mothers and babies (including those in the animal world) are typical.
- *Suitable for sharing.* Some books are designed for parents to use with infants and toddlers, rather than for babies to manipulate themselves.

Why Read to Infants and Toddlers?

Senses. Books build babies' sensory awareness as they look (focus, track, and recognize objects), listen (enjoy the sounds of language), and touch (point to objects, feel the textures).

Imagination. Books extend babies' experiences beyond the already familiar and stimulate creative thinking.

Vocabulary. Books reinforce basic concepts and introduce new vocabulary.

Motivation to read. Book sharing lets children see an enthusiastic reader and causes them to associate warmth and closeness with reading.

Preparation for reading. Lap reading teaches children the following reading skills:

- Book handling behaviors (how to turn the pages, left to right, front to back)
- Book terminology (*pages, cover, author, pictures, print*)
- The similarities and differences between spoken and written language
- The understanding that marks on paper have meaning
- Basic story elements (setting, characters, plot)
- How to ask and answer questions (Butler, 1998; Kupetz & Green, 1997)

What Types of Stories Are Suitable for Infants and Toddlers?

In her classic case study of a child with multiple handicaps, *Cushla and Her Books,* Dorothy Butler (1975) discusses four basic qualities of books for the very young (infancy to 3 years old):

1. Appropriateness of theme and subject matter
2. Use of words that have precision and yet explore the resources of language, deftly and eloquently setting the scene and moving action along
3. Plots that proceed in a straight line (with no tangents)
4. Stories that build to a satisfying conclusion

Names to Know

Jess Alborough, Ted Arnold, Keith Baker, Byron Barton, Suzanne Bloom, Sandra Boynton, Margaret Wise Brown, John Burningham, Eric Carle, David A. Carter, Eileen Christelow, Lucy Cousins, Andrea Davis-Pinkney, Bruce Degan, DK Publishing, P. D. Eastman, Lois Ehlert, Mem Fox, Paul Galdone, Global Fund for Children, Eric Hill, Tana Hoban, Shirley Hughes, Pat Hutchins, Karen Katz, Annie Kubler, Dorothy Kundhardt, Nina Laden, Christine Loomis, Bill Martin, Jr., Jeanne Marzollo, Sam McBratney, Margaret Miller, Helen Oxenbury, Leslie Patricelli, Al Perkins, Roger Priddy, Dr. Seuss, Helen Siefert, Nancy Tafuri, Martin Wadell, Rosemary Wells, Audrey Wood, and Charlotte Zolotow.

A Sampler of Books

To see illustrated lists of The All-Time Best Books for Babies and The All-Time Best Books for Toddlers, visit the *Parents' Magazine* website (www.parents.com).

In addition to these classics, additional books for babies and toddlers include *Global Babies* (Global Fund for Children, 2007); *Head, Shoulders, Knees and Toes and Other Action Rhymes* (Newcome, 2000); *Diez Dededitos: Ten Little Fingers and Other Play Rhymes and Action Songs from Latin America* (Orozco, 1997); *Piggies* [board book] (Wood & Wood, 2005); *Whoever You Are* (Fox, 2007); *Ten Little Fingers and Ten Little Toes* (Fox, 2008); *Snuggle Me Snuggly!* (Baicker, 2004); *Daddy Kisses* (Gutman, 2001); *Hushabye* (Burningham, 2001); *Yummy Yucky* (Patricelli, 2003); *What Do You Hear Dear?* (Kleinberg, 2008); *Who Said Moo?* (Ziefert, 2002); *Hug* (Alborough, 2004); *Bright Baby Colors* (Priddy, 2004); *If You're Happy and You Know It* (Cabrera, 2005); *Ha Ha Maisy!* (Cousins, 2005); *My First Body Board Book* (DK Publishing, 2004); *This Little Piggy and Other Rhymes to Sing and Play* (Yolen, 2006); *Silly Sally* [board book] (Woods, 2007); *I Love You Like Crazy Cakes* (Lewis, 2003); *Max Cleans Up* (Wells, 2000); *Wake-ity Wake* (Baicker, 2004); *There's a Cow in the Cabbage Patch* (Beaton, 2002); *My Big Animal Book* (Priddy, 2002).

Online Resources for Families:

Reading to Infants and Toddlers
 www.highreach.com/pdfs/ITTM579005-Reading.pdf

Tips for Reading to Infants and Toddlers
 www.nea.org/readacross/resources/
 infantsandtoddlers.html

ELLs

The Affective Filter

Emotions play a role in second-language learning. Early childhood educators cannot hope to improve the situation for young English language learners without first genuinely welcoming them to classroom communities; treating them with respect and kindness; advocating for their needs; and valuing the funds of knowledge represented by their families, cultures, and communities (Houck, 2005; Parker & Pardini, 2006; Saracho & Spodek, 2007; Tabors, 2008). The feeling tone associated with second-language learning—the "affective filter"—exerts a powerful influence on its success (Coltrane, 2003; David, Onchonga, Drew, Grass, Stuchuk, & Burns, 2006; Krashen, 2003; Linquanti, 1999; Nieto, 2002). If, for example, children are corrected by teachers and ridiculed by peers, these negative associations can lead to a debilitating fear of making mistakes and slow the process of L2 acquisition (see Krashen, 2003, and Northwest Regional Educational Laboratory, 2003, for an overview).

The source of bias against young Spanish-speaking children in the United States often has more to do with the socioeconomic status of their families than proficiency in English. Language learning and fear get connected in a young English Language Learner's mind in the same way that classical conditioning operates. An initially neutral stimulus (e.g., speaking in English) is repeatedly paired with a noxious unconditioned stimulus (e.g., teacher judgment, peer ridicule) and, as a result of this pairing, an association between the stimulus and negative emotions is formed.

To illustrate, suppose that a child who is learning English is called on to read a short passage of text out loud. The task activates the amygdale, the part of the brain which elicits an immediate sense of dread and fear. The pressure to perform in language also activates the brain's cortex, which is slower to respond. As the feelings of worry and alarm mount and images of worst-case scenarios escalate, appraisal emotions kick in. This is the brain's assessment that the situation is indeed threatening.

After this occurs, the child's ability to concentrate is seriously compromised, and both short-term and long-term memory suffer. This happens because reasoning processes take place in an area called the visual work form area (VWFA)—the "mental workspace" of the brain. When that space is consumed with the task of exercising control over powerful emotions, it leaves little space available for other types of reasoning.

Young ELLs need the support of teachers, volunteers, and peers with proficiency in both languages if they are expected to make connections between languages and master content across the curriculum (Parker & Pardini, 2006). Support in the child's native language should be provided at some level (Thomas & Collier, 2002); even when the language is not spoken by any school personnel, teachers need to reach out to identify community volunteers who can assist. However, this is not always possible. The reality is pure supply and demand; schools with large groups of students who speak the same L1 tend to provide services. Speakers of languages shared by few or no other volunteers or peers find less accommodation for their needs. Young ELLs under these circumstances are expected to figure it out for themselves; if their teachers seek assistance, the responses invariably include a short list of modifications that will not cost the district any money, such as "use collaborative learning." Producing positive outcomes from pairing ELLs with monolingual peers, however, depends on such variables as the ELLs' language proficiency (both in L1 and L2), the nature of the task, and the skills and attitudes of the non-ELLs (Genesee et al., 2005). If these peers treat the ELL as immature, odd, or incompetent, this will raise the young ELL's affective filter, lower self-esteem, and may engender negative attitudes toward learning English. As Lightbown (2000) notes, there is no acceptable substitute for programs that consider the particular needs of individual ELLs:

No matter how sound the research on which new ideas, materials and techniques are based, pedagogical innovations must be implemented and adapted according to local conditions, the strengths of individual teachers and students, the available resources, the age of the learner, and the time available for teaching. (p. 454)

How Do I ...
Teach Phonological and Phonemic Awareness?

Phonological awareness is sensitivity to the sounds of language (Yopp & Yopp, 2009). Phonological awareness does not involve written letters. Even a 4-week-old baby can detect the difference between the letter sounds of *g* and *k*, for example (Richgels, 2001). Most 2-year-olds can detect the subtle differences between the words *hot*, *not*, and *lot* or *cat*, *cut*, and *cot* (Goswami, 2001). The following generalizations can be made about the phonological awareness of very young children.

Newborns
- Startle to loud, sudden sounds.
- Relax to comforting sounds (e.g., a lullaby, a heartbeat).
- Become interested again when a sound played repeatedly is changed.

Infants and Toddlers
- Experiment with sounds.
- Respond to familiar rhymes.
- Participate in action rhymes.
- Show interest in books that include pictures of familiar objects.
- Attempt to name objects or make the sounds of animals that are pictured.

As children gain experience, they begin to notice the sounds of particular words. A child's understanding of the sounds of language tends to progress from whole words to analysis of individual letter sounds. For example, a 3- or 4-year-old might be able to answer a question such as, "Which is bigger, an ant or hippopotamus? Now, which word *sounds* longer, ant or hippopotamus?" Or, while listening to a story read aloud, a young child might remark that the words *hop* and *top* sound "alike," meaning that the words rhyme. Children can do this without looking at the words,

even without knowing the alphabet. Gradually children become aware of syllables, the "breaks" that we hear in a word such as *mon/key*, for instance. Kindergartners often can detect these breaks and clap to them in their names and those of their peers.

Early Preschoolers
- Enjoy songs, stories, rhymes, and fingerplays.
- Recognize their names.
- Recognize rhymes (sound-alikes).

Kindergartners/First-Graders
- Are aware of sound/symbol relations (e.g., "*Macaroni* begins with *m*, like my name").
- Blend phonemes and split syllables (e.g., splitting the beginning sound of *d* from the word *duck*).

Phonemic awareness is more difficult because the child needs to recognize phonemes, the smallest units of sound in language (e.g., cat has three phonemes: c/a/t). Generally speaking, the progression is that children recognize beginning sounds, then ending sounds, and finally, sounds in the middle. Consonants are heard before vowels; for example, a child attempting to spell the word *picture* might write it first as *pr*; later as *pktr*; later still as *picter*; and finally, write it as *picture*. Knowing this general progression enables you to plan activities suited to the children's skills in detecting the sounds of language.

First-Graders to Third-Graders
- Segment phonemes in spoken words and manipulate phonemes to form different words (e.g., *man, fan, pan*).
- Learn to apply rules such as "When two vowels go walking, the first one does the talking and the second one is silent" (e.g., *neat, please*) and that an *e* at the end of a word often signals a long vowel sound (*bake, pine, use*).

Phonics instruction is an instructional approach that teaches children how to match the sounds of language to the letters that visually represent those sounds.

Now that you understand the basics, you may want to learn more about

- The development of phonological and phonemic awareness (Anthony, Williams, McDonald, & Francis, 2007; Cassady, Smith, & Putnam, 2008; Easterbrooks, Lederberg, Miller, Bergeron, & Connor, 2008; Mann & Foy, 2007)
- Teaching strategies (Cunningham, 2008; Enz, 2006; Manyak, 2008; McGee & Ukrainetz, 2009)

- Sample lesson plans: Read/Write/Think (www.readwritethink.org/lessons/lesson_view .asp?id=120). If you click on the category called "Picture Match," you'll find a wide range of lessons and resource materials. Try working in small groups with these resources to develop a lesson on phonological or phonemic awareness.
- Tasks that assess children's phonemic awareness (www.chapman.edu/soe/faculty/piper/resource/ informal.htm)

PEARSON myeducationkit Now go to Chapter 3 in the MyEducationKit (**www.MyEducationKit .com**) for your book, where you can:

- Find Chapter Objectives.
- Complete Assignments and Activities that can help you more deeply understand the chapter content.
- Extend knowledge with content-specific Web Links.
- Check your comprehension on the content covered in the chapter by going to the Study Plan. Here you will be able to take a chapter quiz, receive feedback on your answers, and then access resources that will enhance your understanding of chapter content.

chapter four

Helping Young Children Become Better Listeners

Lindfors Photography

FACT FILE on Listening

• Although listening is the language art that hearing children and adults use the most, it is the one taught least—an inverse relationship between the real world and the classroom (Smith, 2003a, b). As a result, listening has been known as the neglected or forgotten language art for more than 50 years (Tompkins, 2008).

• In a British policy paper on language instruction for young children, an independent research team concluded that far more attention needs to be given to listening skills so that children build their vocabularies and learn to listen attentively (Rose, 2006).

- From the earliest days of life, infants startle to loud sounds and are sensitive to pitch (Saffran & Griepentrog, 2001). The critical period for the development of auditory–neural connections in the brain is during the first 3 years of life; however, auditory abilities continue to develop until about 15 years of age (Robinshaw, 2007).

- In toddlers with and without hearing loss, there was a positive relationship between word production and opportunities for pretend play (Brown, Rickards, & Bortoli, 2001).

- It is estimated that the young child's receptive vocabulary often is four times that of his or her expressive vocabulary so listening is the basis for literacy. There is a correlation between children's ability to hear and decode sounds and the spelling skills they acquire later on (Lewis, Freebairn, & Taylor, 2002).

- Across historical eras, observational studies estimate that between 50 and 75 percent of students' classroom time is spent listening to the teacher, other students, or audio media (International Listening Association, 2008; Smith, 2008; Strother, 1987; Wolvin & Coakley, 1988, 2000). Even in more developmentally appropriate classrooms, the percentage of children's time spent listening to teachers and peers is about 25 percent. Outside school, approximately 45 percent of children's time is spent listening (Hunsaker, 1990).

- The most common cause of early reading difficulty is weakness in children's ability to apprehend, manipulate, and use the sound structure of spoken language (Stojanovik & Riddell, 2008). When children experience difficulty in cracking the alphabetic code that links the smallest units of sound (phonemes) with the corresponding smallest units of writing (graphemes), struggles with learning to read often result (Lonigan, 2005).

- Researchers found that 56 percent of students with learning disabilities and 28 percent of students who had not been identified as having learning disabilities had problems completing homework assignments. For students with learning disabilities, homework problems are often attributed to poor receptive language and memory deficits, both of which interfere with understanding or remembering what has been assigned (Bryan & Burstein, 2004).

- The ability to listen also affects social development. There is a relationship between preschool children's receptive language skills and acts of aggressive behaviors (Estrem, 2005). In particular, boys who demonstrated higher rates of physical aggression tended to have less developed receptive language skills.

- Preschoolers and children in the primary grades appear to be capable of identifying the behaviors associated with effective listening in their conversational partners. Interestingly, they identify grandparents as the best models of effective listening (Imhof, 2002).

- In children without significant hearing loss, common causes of listening difficulties include recurrent ear infections, lack of appropriate models for listening and learning, learning disabilities, attention deficits, behavior disorders, specific language impairments in the area of comprehension, and difficulty in adapting to the classroom's academic language (Jalongo, 2008b).

- Several variables that exert a negative effect on children's listening comprehension at school include the rapid rate of speech of some teachers; background noise, distractions, and interruptions in the classroom; and language or dialect differences between the child and teacher or peers.

- An intervention in which parents of children with communication difficulties were supplied with home activity packets to promote shared listening reported positive effects on parental attitudes and children's listening skills (Stevens, Watson, & Dodd, 2001).

Did any of this information surprise you? If so, what? Why? How will you use this knowledge to educate and care for the very young?

What Is Effective Listening?

PEARSON

Go to the Assignments and Activities section of Chapter 4 in MyEducationKit and complete the activity entitled "Listening to Learn Language."

A fussy newborn baby calms at the sound of her caregiver's voice singing a lullaby. A preschooler smiles and claps his hands at the lilting rhyme of his favorite fingerplay. A third-grader strains to hear every word from a book about baseball that a high school student is reading to the class. In all of these situations, children are trying to transform the sounds that they hear into meaning in their minds. A workable definition of *listening* includes three elements:

1. *Hearing,* a physiological response that includes auditory acuity (the ability to hear) and auditory perception (the ability to discriminate among sounds, to blend sounds together, and to hold sequences of sound in memory)
2. *Listening,* an act of perception that includes focusing, becoming aware, and selecting cues from the environment
3. *Comprehending,* an act of cognitive processing that includes getting meaning from what is heard; associating sounds with words already known; and organizing, imagining, and appreciating what is heard (Jalongo, 2008b)

When children were asked to describe "good listening" at school, a first-grader said that being a good listener/student means that you "don't talk," and a third-grader said that "a bad listener is someone who is confused and has to ask for help" (McDevitt, 1990). In fact, effective listeners focus attention, filter out distractions, process information, make pertinent comments, and ask relevant questions (Brent & Anderson, 1993).

Listening well plays an essential role in learning, but expecting children to listen *more* is not the solution. Instead, teaching them how to listen *better* is what's needed (DeHaven, 1988). Naturally, medical conditions and environmental circumstances that interfere with hearing have consequences for listening, as the following scenario about Gerardo illustrates.

Collaboration with Families and Professionals

PEARSON

myeducationkit

Go to the Assignments and Activities section of Chapter 4 in MyEducationKit and complete the activity entitled "Documenting Work Habits."

Standards in Education
Locate a particular state's language arts standards by searching on the Internet. Just type in the state name and the words "department of education" to search for language arts standards. What is it that young children are expected to accomplish in listening by the time they reach fourth grade?

Two-year-old Gerardo was adopted from an orphanage in Guatemala. Unlike most children his age, Gerardo has not started to talk. His adoptive parents are concerned, but they have faith that providing a loving and language-rich environment at home and in group child care will enable Gerardo to overcome his language delay. They interact with their child, even before he tries to speak, and they make time for visits to the library and to read a bedtime story every night. Yet when Gerardo begins to talk, he is unintelligible and grows increasingly frustrated when others do not understand him.

Based on her observations, Gerardo's teacher, Ms. Kelly, wonders if there might be a physiological problem and asks the parents to meet with her and the speech/language pathologist to discuss the situation. Ms. Kelly shares her detailed written observations of behaviors by Gerardo that prompted the referral, such as speaking loudly, moving up close during stories, and difficulty repeating words during songs or rhymes. After the parents give permission for a hearing test (audiometric assessment), it is discovered that Gerardo has a previously undetected hearing impairment caused by a buildup of fluid in his middle ear. After further consultation with the pediatrician, a referral is made to an otologist (eye, ear, nose, and throat doctor), who recommends surgery to put drainage tubes into the child's ears.

The surgery is a success. Gerardo hears better, his receptive language improves, and gradually his expressive language follows. One of his first words is *carseat*, a word that he associates with family outings. When Gerardo asks for his favorite drink of apple juice, he pronounces it "appleshoosh," but he says it clearly enough that just about everyone recognizes it. Gerardo's favorite book has bright pages of farm animals, and he usually reads it from back to front so that he can make the pig noise first.

By the time Gerardo is 3, he is making simple sentences such as "Swing low, swing high" in response to being pushed on a swing in the park. At age 4, when they pass a Mexican restaurant, Gerardo asks his Dad, "Did you get paid?" because going to the restaurant together is something the family does on Fridays. Clearly, this child has made impressive progress in his language learning.

Contributions and Consequences

- *Contributions of the teacher:* How did the teacher take an active role in this situation?
- *Contributions of the family:* How did the family support the child and get involved in the process?

- *Contributions of other professionals:* How did professionals in other fields contribute to addressing the needs of the child and family?
- *Consequences of collaboration:* How might this story have ended differently if the adults had failed to communicate effectively?

Why Is Listening Important?

Brain and Language

Some young children with significant hearing impairment can benefit from a cochlear implant if the surgical procedure is done early (Eisenberg, Fink, & Niparko, 2006). Although neuroimaging shows that children with cochlear implants process speech differently, within one year of getting a cochlear implant, toddlers' ability to understand simple sentences increased by 50 percent, and their ability to remember and follow through on sequence of instructions increased by 30 percent (Lee, Huh, Jeung, & Lee, 2004).

Of all the language skills that human beings acquire, listening is the one they will use the earliest and the most often throughout life. The sense of hearing functions even before birth, and the hearing child amasses extensive experience with listening long before speaking, reading, or writing. As soon as the hearing organs of the fetus are fully formed and functional, the child is able to listen. We also know that newborns respond differently to different types of sounds. As anyone who works in a hospital nursery or infant care can attest, infants are usually calmed by sounds that are similar to those heard inside the womb and distressed by the sound of other infants crying. Even infants on respirators breathe more rhythmically when music with a strong beat, rather than lullabies, is played softly in the background (Bayless & Ramsey, 1990).

Listening is the foundation for speaking, reading, and writing in children without hearing impairments (Jalongo, 2008b). When children are silent but attentive, it is common to speak of them as "taking it all in." Linguists put it somewhat differently, saying that young children need "meaningful aural input" in order to master language. A child may remain silent during a song or story or fingerplay, for example, and then suddenly begin to participate with great enthusiasm. Thus, receptive language experiences are a resource for expressive language.

As popular wisdom would have it, we "listen and learn." How much learning is based on these language skills? Children with receptive language difficulties will likely also have expressive language difficulties, as shown by Gerardo's story. They will struggle in school because they cannot easily learn in typical classroom conditions. These children cannot always keep up with the pace of verbal instruction, because they may not consistently understand the content of ideas being discussed and do not have strong skills for communicating what they do or do not know. When children do not hear or understand what is being discussed, they can become withdrawn in school or appear inattentive because they lose their focus (Cruger, 2005).

Infants and Toddlers

Most babies are born with the ability to perceive phonemes. Aaron Hannon's research found that at 6 months, babies responded to all rhythms; however, by 12 months, they responded differentially to familiar ones from their culture. View a video about this research at the Proceedings of the National Academy of Science site (www.livescience.com/common/media/video/player.php?videoRef=nas1040_Baby MusicM).

Even though listening is a frequent activity, it is seldom taught or poorly taught (Smith, 2003a). Students develop listening skills by example, particularly by having someone listen to them. Listening is actually something students have to be taught to do well, yet it has been virtually ignored in the preschool/primary curriculum. Why? Perhaps it is because teachers' preparation for teaching listening skills to children is inadequate. So even though teachers may recognize the value of listening, they may not know how to develop children's listening abilities.

Listening is a way of communicating respect. When children listen to one another, when teachers listen to children, and when children listen to teachers, a firm sense of community is built. A teacher discovered this when children who were deaf enrolled in her kindergarten class. When both of the children were out of the room to meet with the speech/language pathologist, the teacher took the opportunity to let the other children ask their questions.

"When did they get deaf?"

"How do you know what Timmy and Chris are saying?"

"When will they learn to talk?"

"Do they live in the same house?"

By listening to her 5-year-old students, the teacher was able to do a much better job of helping them to understand that both of the boys had been deaf since birth, that there are many ways of communicating, that their deafness was irreversible, and that the boys were not related.

Overview of Children's Listening Development

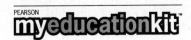

Go to the Assignments and Activities section of Chapter 4 in MyEducationKit and complete the activity entitled "Toddlers at Play."

Katya and Shirelle are two nursery school students who are playing with clay. Note how their conversation reveals not only hearing and listening but also comprehending.

Shirelle: I'm making pot pies.

Katya: Need some more? (She offers Shirelle a chunk of modeling clay.)

Shirelle: Okay, this is hard. (Each girl reaches inside the clay bucket, takes out a mound of clay, and then drops it onto her own pile.) Mine, plop, plop. (Both girls giggle loudly.)

Katya: I'm making a pie instead.

Shirelle: Me too. I'll ripple wopple it off (she says this while trimming off the excess with a plastic knife) and put it in the bowl. Now I'm gonna make pies.

Katya: Anyway, how do you make pies?

Shirelle: First you take it, and you roll it out. This is how you make it, and you roll it out. Then you cut, cut, cut, and cut. Then you go rut, rut, rut, rut, and there's some pot pie!

Shirelle's sensitivity to the rhythm and sounds of language is called *phonological aware-ness*. She is not yet reading and knows about 10 letters of the alphabet; however, she can detect patterns of sound that are more pleasing to the ear than ordinary talk.

Many factors influence listening behavior. First and foremost is capacity. *Capacity* includes physiological influences such as *auditory acuity* (i.e., the ability to hear)

PEARSON
myeducationkit

Go to the Assignments and Activities section of Chapter 4 in MyEducationKit and complete the activity entitled "Screenings for Young Children."

and *auditory perception* (i.e., the ability to discriminate among sounds, blend sounds together, and hold sequences of sound in memory). Children with severe hearing impairments, for example, often have a sensorineural hearing loss caused by damage or disease to the inner ear, auditory nerve, or neural pathways. Sounds may not reach the brain at all or may arrive in a highly distorted form. Neither amplification nor medical and surgical procedures can correct the problem (McCormick, Loeb, & Scheifelbusch, 2002). Other influences on capacity include such conditions as attention disorders, emotional disturbances, prenatal drug exposure, and language proficiency.

There is little in this category of preexisting influences that teachers can control or change. There is much that they can do, however, about three other influences on children's listening behavior: motivation, habits, and contextual variables.

Motivation has to do with the relevance of the listening and the child's willingness to focus on the task at hand. Is there a real reason to listen? Children will strive to listen in the classroom if they can recognize an immediate, tangible benefit. For example, if a child listens to instructions during a cooking experience, the product will be edible. If a child listens to peers respond to his or her story while sitting in the Author's Chair, the story can be appreciated and improved. When children know that they will be held accountable for listening by being expected to perform specific, interesting tasks, they will be more motivated to listen.

Habits affect listening. Children who have acquired ineffective listening skills can be coached. Productive listening habits include making predictions, watching the speaker, striving to understand, formulating questions, identifying and summarizing main ideas, and responding to what is heard. Teachers thus need to incorporate all of these habits when teaching.

The listening *context* is another aspect that teachers can control. Children's re-actions to confusion are affected by the setting as well as social relationships with speakers that cause them to think it is not their place to ask for clarification. Figure 4.1 provides an overview of developmental milestones in children's listening.

By the time young children enter kindergarten, they have already acquired sig-nificant listening skills, such as learning to use and respond to the signals speakers give to listeners, connecting what they hear with what they see, and relating what they hear to their own experience. Additionally, they have learned ways of getting others to listen to them and initiate a conversation ("Guess what . . ."). They have learned to ask questions when what they hear is difficult to understand ("Mom, what's a ghost whisperer?" "Is a hospital a sad or a happy place?"). They have also learned to use *prestarts*, words or phrases that have little substance but that indicate to listeners that the speaker is about to take conversational turn (Siefert & Hoffnung, 1999). Prestarts

FIGURE 4.1 · Developmental Milestones and "Red Flags" in Children's Listening

Infancy to 1 Year

- Startles to loud or strange noises.
- Orients head in direction of sound.
- Responds differentially to different types of music (e.g., lullaby vs. lively tune).
- Vocalizes in response to music and other sounds.
- Looks at speaker.
- Begins to understand words accompanied by appropriate gestures (e.g., *up, hi, more*).

Developmental "Red Flags" for Infants

- The infant does not react to sounds by blinking, widening the eyes, startling, or crying.
- At 4 months, the baby does not orient toward a sound outside her or his view.
- At 7 months, the baby does not immediately turn toward the sound of a voice across the room.
- At 9 months, the baby does not babble or stops babbling.

1 to 2 Years

- Recognizes own name.
- Associates words with actions.
- Understands simple instructions that include familiar key words (e.g., "Bring me your book" or "You can ride in the [grocery] cart").
- Learns simple games like Peek-a-Boo and Pat-a-Cake.
- Understands *no, bye-bye*.
- Points to body parts (e.g., eyes, nose, mouth).
- Listens to and attempts to join in nursery rhymes and songs.
- Listens to books for babies that label common objects (e.g., *Pat the Bunny*).
- Responds correctly to basic questions (e.g., "Where is your blanket?").
- Attempts to imitate words even when not fully understanding them, often dropping or confusing syllables or letters (e.g., "kepical" for "skeptical").
- Distinguishes pronouns (e.g., *her, him, we*).
- Understands there is a category of things called *colors* and may know an example or two, but does not necessarily match colors with words accurately (e.g., uses the word *red* in every situation where a color is called for).

Developmental "Red Flags" for Toddlers

- At 12 months, the baby does not respond to simple words like *no* and *bye-bye*.
- At 18 months, the child's speech does not have a natural quality to it. It may be particularly loud, soft, nasal, high pitched, or monotone. It may lack the prosody (musical quality) of speech.
- The toddler's speech does not include a variety of vowels and consonants. People outside the immediate family find the child's language incomprehensible.
- The child is not yet using telegraphic speech, putting together two words (e.g., "Mommy work," "more cheese").
- The child has difficulty with simple directions. Children with moderate hearing losses often mistake one word for another (e.g., returns with book after an adult says, "Go and get your ball").
- At 2, the child often turns up the sound on the TV or radio.

FIGURE 4.1   Continued

3 to 4 Years

- Memorizes simple fingerplays that have been repeated often (e.g., "Eeency Weency Spider").
- Understands simple concepts *(big/little, today, bedtime)*.
- Enjoys hearing the same story repeated again and again.
- Incorporates words and phrases from earlier discussions of books into later discussions of the same book.
- Points to different animals when named.
- Understands two-part directions (e.g., "First, put on your coat; then put on your hat").
- Matches distinctive musical sounds for the instruments that produced them (e.g., guitar, drums, piano).
- Responds appropriately to questions during conversation.
- Holds up correct number of fingers in response to a question ("How old are you?").
- Understands and defines objects by their use (e.g., "What do you need to eat your cereal?" or "A hole is to dig in").
- Understands simple comparisons (e.g., *big, bigger, biggest*).
- Understands conditional statements (e.g., *if/then, because*).
- Understands "just pretending" versus real.
- Is learning words that relate to past (e.g., *yesterday*), present (e.g., *today*), and future (e.g., *tomorrow*).
- Can talk briefly about what he or she is doing.
- Emulates significant adults' style of speech.

5 to 6 Years

- Identifies basic colors and shapes.
- Can demonstrate understanding of spatial relations *(on, under, near, behind)*.
- Perceives differences in pitch *(high/low)* and can conceptualize them as "stairsteps."
- Can follow more involved instructions (e.g., operate piece of computer software).
- Listens to longer stories and identifies with story characters.
- Understands and uses all types of sentences and clauses (e.g., "Yes, you can go outside but first you need to put on your boots").
- Retains information in the correct sequence (e.g., can retell a familiar story in considerable detail).

Developmental "Red Flags" for Preschool/Early Primary

- The child seems to get more confused when in a noisy environment or seated at a distance from the speaker.
- The child does not respond to statements or questions that would normally excite children in the group (e.g., "Who wants to help feed the rabbit?").
- The child says "What?" or "Huh?" frequently.
- The child has more difficulty following instructions when not watching the speaker's face.

Source: Adapted from Lerner, Lowenthal, & Egan, 2003.

can help a speaker signal to listeners that he or she wants to continue talking ("and, uh," "I mean"), acknowledge or affirm ("Yeah," "Um-hmm," "Me too"), or move the conversation forward by commenting on a previous statement ("Yes, but . . ." "You say . . ." "Well, I think . . .").

Another listening ability of children is connecting *aural input* (what they hear) to *visual input* (what they see). Listening activities can be related to real objects, to pictures, and to words. The cue cards for "The Opposite Song," by Mitzie Collins, for example, depict pairs of antonyms that rhyme (see Figure 4.2).

Another basic type of listening skill is the children's ability to connect what they hear with personal experience. This skill is learned primarily through listening to stories and discussing them with adults. Nelson (1989) gives the example of telling a story called "The Tailor" (Schimmel, 1978). When she shared the story with children, she used a puppet that changed its clothes to go along with the plot. In this tale, a tailor who has been

FIGURE 4.2   The Opposite Song

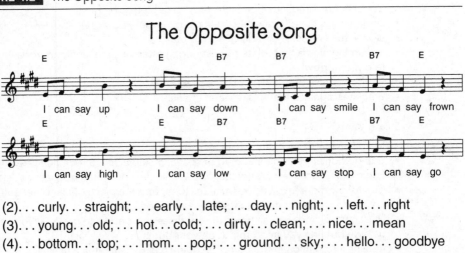

(2) . . . curly . . . straight; . . . early . . . late; . . . day . . . night; . . . left . . . right
(3) . . . young . . . old; . . . hot . . . cold; . . . dirty . . . clean; . . . nice . . . mean
(4) . . . bottom . . . top; . . . mom . . . pop; . . . ground . . . sky; . . . hello . . . goodbye

FIGURE 4.2 Continued

curly   straight   early   late

day   night   left   right

young   old   hot   cold

dirty   clean   nice   mean

bottom   top   mom   pop

ground   sky   hello   goodbye

Source: Adapted by Mitzie Collins, 1982, for the recording and companion book *Sounds Like Fun.* Sampler Records, Ltd. www.samplerfolkmusic.com. Used with permission.

too busy to make himself a fine coat finally decides to make one. He then wears the coat proudly all over town. When the coat becomes worn, he makes it into a jacket. When the jacket's sleeves become frayed, he makes it into a vest. Time passes and the vest gets old and worn. But the tailor cannot bear to part with the fabric (which reminds him of his coat, jacket, and vest), so he creates a hat. Eventually, the hat gets old and worn, too. At the conclusion of the story, the resourceful tailor goes back to his shop and emerges holding a fabric-covered button. Whenever he holds that button, he is reminded of that lovely fabric and the coat, jacket, vest, and hat he made for himself long ago.

After listening to the story, the teacher shared Sharon, Lois, and Bram's (1995) song and video for "I Had an Old Coat," which has a similar message. After children listened to the story of "The Tailor" and learned the lyrics to the song using a song chart, they listened to a picture book version of the tale, *Joseph Had a Little Overcoat* (Taback, 1999). They also heard *Wilfrid Gordon McDonald Partridge* (Fox, 1989) and discussed treasured objects and personal mementos.

Teacher Concerns and Basic Strategies

Alice, an experienced teacher, related her problem with keeping children's attention at certain times:

> My biggest problem has to do with discussion and sharing times in kindergarten. Usually, the children listen while I am teaching or reading a story. But whenever I expect them to listen to one another, I spend most of my time trying to keep their attention and reminding them to listen. This really bothers me, and I haven't found a solution.

PEARSON
myeducationkit™

Go to the Assignments and Activities section of Chapter 4 in MyEducationKit and complete the activity entitled "Listening for Understanding."

Remember that adults teach children to listen, first and foremost, by being good listeners themselves (Malaguzzi, 1994). In a study that supplied young English language learners who had recently emigrated to the United States with disposable cameras to document their lives outside of school, Keat, Strickland, and Marinak (2009) found that children tried to communicate with their teachers during individual conferences when teachers sat close to the child, looked at the child with a caring facial expression, and showed genuine interest in the child's efforts to communicate; conversely, if the teachers overwhelmed the child with "a tsunami of words" and persistent questions, the children usually fell silent. As an experienced teacher explained, "Listening to our students is an essential skill for teachers to have, because when we listen, the kids feel valued. As the expression goes, 'Kids don't care how much we know until they know how much we care.'"

This issue has as much to do with developmentally appropriate practice as it does with listening. Young children are active and relatively inexperienced as group members, so they seldom function well in large groups that leave them waiting to participate. They will have a better chance to succeed as listeners if the teacher keeps the group small (8 to 10 children) and makes sure that they stay involved. Too often, teachers use the old Show-and-Tell format for discussions, in which one child talks and the other children are expected to sit still and stay quiet. A better way to promote active listening is Show-and-Ask, in which a child shares a simple, inexpensive object and invites questions from the group about it. Of course, the teacher will need to model the behavior of an interested listener and teach the difference between a question and a comment (i.e., a question has an answer, the questioner does not already know the answer, and the response to the question comes from the speaker).

Another teacher, David, shared this experience:

I have been teaching second grade for 4 years, and I had a very challenging group this year. There were often times when I found myself talking over children's voices, and by the end of the day, I was tired and hoarse from struggling to quiet them down. The problem was particularly evident at the start of school and after recess, lunch, and gym class.

This issue has as much to do with managing classroom transitions as it does with listening. There are many ways to get children refocused and ready to listen following a boisterous activity. The teacher needs to establish some inviting, comfortable routines that get students focused:

- A sign-in sheet posted outside the door each morning and an interest table from which children can choose an activity
- A pleasant sound/signal (wind chimes, lights dimmed, battery-operated candle lit) for an after-lunch read-aloud
- A shy puppet/mascot who will not venture out until the children are quiet
- A "menu" of events throughout the day in bright colors

You can also begin with a real object, a brainteaser, a song, choral speaking, or creative dramatics. Whatever routine you choose, select something that attracts the children's attention and requires their attentive listening in order to participate.

Another concern with listening was brought up by Tracy, who teaches second grade:

After hearing myself repeat directions three, four, and maybe more times, I decided that I needed help. I hope there is a magic wand, so that with one wave, my students will listen and comply.

The most important step in getting children to listen to directions is to make the directions very clear in the first place. If you give complicated, confusing instructions that need to be sorted out to be understood, children will tune out and wait for a better explanation. Think through instructions carefully, trying to troubleshoot any aspects of the process that might be difficult or confusing for students. Tell children that you will be giving the instructions one time only, and use a simple visual aid to highlight each step in the procedure. Alert children to the organizational structure of your message, and tell them what to listen for—for example, "Today you will be working in groups on the class newspaper. There are four things that every group is

Research and Report

Visit the American Speech-Hearing-Language Association website (www.asha.org/topicindex.htm) and select a topic from the A to Z list that is designated as "Information for the Public" or as a Tip Sheet for teachers. How might you use some of these resources with families?

expected to accomplish during the next hour." Call on children to rephrase ("Now, who can explain the first step?"), question ("I have just explained the second requirement. Is there anything that you do not understand?"), recap ("Could someone summarize the four requirements—without looking at the board?"), and take responsibility ("If you need help as you work in your groups, do three things in this order: (1) Reread the list I've posted on the board. (2) Discuss it with your group. (3) See me. I'll be circulating around the room."). If teachers communicate more clearly and check for understanding periodically, children's apparent inability to follow instructions will diminish.

Classroom Activities to Support Listening

Building children's listening skills is something that teachers need to do throughout the schoolday, rather than at one designated time. Some recommended activities follow:

Play a Variety of Musical Selections   Listening to music can develop literacy skills, including focusing attention, listening without interrupting, associating words with actions, predicting outcomes, grasping central ideas, remembering details, interpreting what is heard, and enjoying listening selections (Russell, Ousky, & Haynes, 1967). Ms. Martin's brother plays the flute in the high school band, and she invited him to perform for the children. First, he played a square dance tune, "Turkey in the Straw." It sounded, in one child's words, "pretty, but different" from the fiddle version the children had heard on a recording. Then the flutist played Kenny G's "Songbird." Once again, the children generated lists of descriptive words. Finally, they selected their favorite and wrote a paragraph explaining why they enjoyed it the most.

Make Picture Book and Music Connections   Mrs. Yeagley has planned a unit around several distinctive examples of classical music and their picture book counterparts, including *Peter and the Wolf* (Voight, 1980), *Swan Lake* (Fonteyn, 1989), and *The Nutcracker* (Hoffman, 1984). A traditional story and music combination is the picture book *Inch by Inch: The Garden Song* (Mallett, 1997) and the recording by Maria Muldair. As they listen, children are directed to think about how music is used to create a mood and enhance the story.

Explain How Something Functions   During cooking experiences, a teacher noticed that her students were absolutely fascinated by some common kitchen gadgets, such as a hard-boiled egg slicer, a garlic press, a melon baller, an eggbeater, a wire whisk, an egg separator, a cheese slicer, and an orange juicer, to name a few. The teacher told the students, "Find out everything you can about this object. Think about how it works. I will explain how it works, and you will listen. Then you will explain how it works to someone else."

Reenactment of Imaginary Scenes and Everyday Events   During a teacher-initiated enactment, the children are invited to respond to various events they have observed or imagined. After the children have mastered some simple pantomime-type activities (e.g., pretending to be a cat, pretending to open a present), they are ready to move on to somewhat more involved imagination stretchers. One teacher used the following creative drama activity as part of a unit on pets:

> Let's pretend. Let's pretend about puppies. Close your eyes and think about a basket full of cute and cuddly puppies. There's one that is very playful and one that is sleepy. Open your eyes. Let's see how you would pet the puppies. Remember, they're very small. Okay, let's look at the playful one. Show how you would pick her up. Be careful! She's really squirming around! Now she's trying to lick your face. Put her on your lap, and let's look at the sleepy one. He's a little bit bigger and isn't quite awake yet. Let's pick him up. Oh, he looks like he wants to go back to sleep. Let's see how you will hold him. Which puppy will you choose? Why?

Conversation Station This is a learning center for no more than two or three children and one adult that uses vocabulary picture cards at a tabletop pocket chart to encourage thoughtful listening. No more than two to three children and one adult. A sign is posted: "Let's talk about . . ." Other materials are theme props, the Story Time book, and writing materials (Bond & Wasik, 2009).

Tell a Story After children have heard a story many times, they can demonstrate their listening skills by retelling the story in their own words. In Mrs. Ramirez's first grade, the children wore a special storyteller's cape adorned with miniature toys that represented various folktales. There was a tiny stuffed bear for "The Three Bears," a pom-pom chick to represent "Chicken Little," and a plastic pig for "The Three Little Pigs." When a child donned the hat and cape, he or she would go into a "recording booth" (a large cardboard box set up with a chair and a cassette recorder) and make an audiotape of the story. As the year progressed, more stories and objects to represent them adorned the cape. The teacher listened to the children's stories every day on her drive home as a check on their listening comprehension. Then the tapes became part of a listening library for children, as they enjoyed one another's stories.

Sound Effects Mr. Antonucci demonstrated several old-fashioned radio sound effects to his third-graders. He rustled a piece of cellophane to mimic a crackling fire and wiggled an old cookie sheet to imitate a roll of thunder in the distance. Then the children listened to Tom Paxton's (1984) song "The Marvelous Toy" and recorded their own version, complete with appropriate sound effects. For preschool children, creating the realistic animal noises of "Down on Grandpa's Farm" (Raffi & Whiteley, 1985) is a good listening activity.

Play the Police Officer Game This game requires two toy telephones, a tricycle, and a police officer's cap. It begins with the police officer circling the group while riding the tricycle and then going where he or she cannot see the other children. Next, two children are selected—one to play the parent's role and one to be the child. The parent describes the person selected to be the child over the phone. The police officer listens to the description and tries to locate the "lost" child. Then the lost child hops on the back of the tricycle for a happy reunion with the parent.

I Tell, You Do In this listening activity, children work with partners. One person has clay, and the other person tells her what to do to the clay to create an item he has in mind. A second way to use this partnering system is to have one child listen to a description of something very familiar given by another child, such as his or her house, pet, or teddy bear and attempt to draw the item to the speaker's specifications. Afterward, the picture can be revised based on additional information.

Story Line   Children can practice their listening comprehension of a story by arranging copies of the pages and key events from the book in the correct sequence on a clothesline. A good choice for this activity is *Bye, Bye Baby: A Sad Story with a Happy Ending* (Ahlberg & Ahlberg, 1990), in which a baby who is all alone goes on a quest to assemble an entire family.

Translate Sounds   Have children convert what they hear into written, graphic, musical, or dramatic form. Ms. Crawford, a first-grade teacher, and Ms. Cribbs, a sixth-grade teacher, collaborated on a cross-age tutoring project. Their goal was to make favorite books come alive by creating a "story land," complete with a guided tour. Each station highlighted a particular book and presented it in a different way: puppet show, storytelling apron, flannelboard, and so on. The "story land" was cooperatively designed and presented by the children, and the entire school went on the guided listening tour.

Compare/Contrast   Children can listen to a recording of the song "The Wheels on the Bus" (Sharon, Lois, & Bram, 1980) and then listen to a picture version of the same song in a book with movable parts (Zelinsky, 1990). They then compare/contrast the two in terms of the words, number of verses, and visual imagery.

Summarize Information   Information books, or books that tell all about something real in a factual way, are good resources for summarizing information. *Ant Cities* (Dorros, 1987), for instance, gives instructions on how to create an ant farm. After listening to the story, children can make a chronological list of the steps.

Story Map   After listening to a story, have the children make a large chart or map on the floor that shows the story character's travels. Planning the map begins with a question about the setting, then questions about the main character that focus on his or her goals, and finally the steps the character takes to achieve those goals. A good book title for this activity is *Hazel's Amazing Mother* (Wells, 1995).

Participatory Listening   Mr. Callahan told students the familiar folktale "Sody Salyratus" with guitar accompaniment. In the story, a series of characters go in search of some sody salyratus (baking powder) to make biscuits. Each character is devoured by a bear, until a little squirrel outwits him. Mr. Callahan also taught the children a little song to sing on cue throughout the story: "So-dy, So-dy, So-dy Salyratus."

Cause/Effect   Stories that present the consequences of a character's actions, such as *Feathers for Lunch* (Ehlert, 1990a), can be used to help children recognize causes and effects. A structure such as "Somebody wanted . . . and so . . . and then . . ." can be used to highlight causes and effects and check students' comprehension.

Audio Recipe   Listening to an audio of a simple, no-bake recipe is a highly motivating listening activity. Children can also create their own rebus recipe after listening to recorded instructions.

Directed Listening/Thinking Activity   The directed listening/thinking activity (DLTA) is a listening-based literacy strategy (Barclay, 2009; Strickland & Morrow, 1989). The DLTA has three basic parts:

1. Prepare for listening with questions and discussion.
2. Read the story.
3. Discuss the story after reading.

Figure 4.3 is an example of a DLTA using a humorous book suitable for the primary grades, *Two Bad Ants*, by Chris Van Allsburg (1988). In this story, two ants leave the group and go through some terrifying "ant's-eye-view" adventures during someone's breakfast.

FIGURE 4.3   Directed Listening/Thinking Activity with *Two Bad Ants*

1. Prepare for listening with questions and discussion.

   • Introduce the story with background information: "Today I'm going to read a story called *Two Bad Ants* (Van Allsburg, 1988). I wonder what ants could do that would be 'bad.' Any ideas?" "This book has puzzles in it because it shows how ants would see and talk about things, instead of the way that people would see or talk about things. Let's look at the pictures and try to predict what this story is about." Encourage children to respond as you turn the pages.
   • Focus the children on the objective for the reading with a statement such as "This story's about two ants who leave the group and go exploring on their own. While I'm reading it, see if you can tell whether the ants will want to go on another adventure soon."

2. Read the story.

   • Practice reading the book ahead of time for ease and expression. Show illustrations from the story as you read and ask children how a person would describe what the ants are describing. Pause at natural breaks for children's reactions, comments, or questions.
   • Tie your questions in with your objective: "Do you think that the ants are enjoying their adventure? How will they decide whether they want to do this again?" Ask children to look at the pictures and predict what will happen next.

3. Discuss after reading.

   • Guide discussion by the objective for your reading—in this example, inference and judgment: "Why do you think that this story was called *Two Bad Ants*? What decision did the ants make? What would you have decided if you were one of the ants?"

Conclusion

Based on listening research, we know that good listening does not occur automatically, that listening skills can be taught, that there is a direct relationship between listening and learning, and that listening needs to be part of the total curriculum. Young children do not need to put on their "listening ears." Rather, they need to participate in challenging, meaningful listening activities to develop their listening abilities. Listening is a true curricular basic. By examining our own effectiveness as listeners, appreciating the connection between active listening and learning, understanding the child as a listener, and integrating listening activities throughout the day and across the curriculum, we can do a better job of teaching children to listen effectively. As educators, we need to think of listening as the foundation for language development; otherwise, it will continue to be the neglected language art.

PEARSON myeducationkit To check your comprehension on the content covered in this chapter, go to the MyEducationKit for your book and complete the Study Plan for Chapter 4. Here you will be able to take a chapter quiz and receive feedback on your answers.

 # Research-Based Literacy Strategies

Audiobooks

Audiobooks, sometimes known as "books on tape," are professionally recorded, unabridged versions of fiction and nonfiction books. They may be available as tapes (either regular audiocassettes or four-track cassettes that require a special player) or as CDs. They are also available as downloads for mp3 players or iPods. According to the American Association of Publishers, audiobook sales totaled 331 million in 2008 (http://booksahead.com).

Audiobooks are a resource for teachers because they support listening comprehension and promote an interest in reading. Audiobooks give children independent access to literature and enable them to practice reading as many times as they wish with a book (Grover & Hannegan, 2005). For all students, audiobooks offer excellent examples of expert male and female narrators who convey appreciation for literature and model expressive reading. Older students often are inspired to create their own recorded versions of favorite books, complete with appropriate background music and other embellishments.

Audiobooks enable students with visual or physical disabilities to experience literature by listening (Holum & Gahala, 2001). For emergent or beginning readers, audiobooks enable children to work with texts that are above their actual reading levels. In addition, ELLs can listen and follow along in the printed text, thereby building fluency and expanding vocabulary. To maximize the effectiveness of audiobooks as a teaching tool, it is important for students to be able to control the rate of narration (Bergman, 2005). For children with attention deficits, recorded books typically include other audible "extras" that promote active listening, such as an audible signal to turn the page, music and sound effects, and interviews with authors (Mediatore, 2003).

The print sources that review audiobooks are *Audio Books on the Go, Words on Cassette, Audio File, BookList, Library Journal, Publishers Weekly,* and *BookPage.* Some resources for children's audiobooks include the Audio Publishers Association (www.audiopub.org), *AudioFile Magazine* (www.audiofilemagazine.com), Books On Tape (www.bookson tape.com), and Recorded Books (www.recorded books.com). Some Internet sites that offer free audiobooks include Aesop's Fables, Online Collection, All Free Online Children's Books, and Kids' Corner at Wired for Books.

For more on audiobooks, see Varley (2002) and Johnson (2003) and www.audiobookshelf.com/teachwith.html.

Technology to Support Listening

Auditory processing disorder is a condition in which an individual cannot process words or sounds (or both) in the traditional way (Phelps Deily, 2009, p. 10). Technology to support listening can be low-tech (e.g., a paper megaphone used to amplify spoken language for the listener), medium-tech (e.g., using the PowerPoint-based Ready-to-Go program to produce custom-made phonics worksheets), or high-tech (e.g., a cochlear implant that enables a child with a hearing impairment or deafness to hear). The resources of the American Speech/Hearing/Language Association (www.asha.org) report the latest research findings on applications of technology for individuals with hearing impairments or deafness. Use these resources in your work with families.

Directed Listening/Thinking Activity (DLTA) and Discussion Web

Teaching children to actively visualize information during listening and reading is a common strategy to develop and improve comprehension and memory (Harvey & Goudvis, 2007). As Headley and Dunston (2000) point out, the directed listening/thinking activity (DLTA) is a way to promote children's listening comprehension and ability to make inferences (Stauffer, 1975). By combining the DLTA with a discussion web (Alvermann, 1991) that is completed by small groups of children, students learn to form, state, support, discuss, and adjust personal opinions. The procedure is as follows:

1. Prior to reading a book aloud to the children, the teacher identifies the gist or underlying message of the story and writes a single question to focus the children's listening comprehension. In addition, the teacher identifies three to six stopping points, where students will reflect on the story and make predictions.
2. Students respond to the discussion web statement by working with their partners for approximately 5 minutes. They argue both sides of the issue and provide reasons for their thinking.
3. When time is up, students form groups of four by having one pair join another, and then they present each member's opinion and justification. For approximately 10 minutes, group members discuss all views presented.
4. A spokesperson from each group presents the group's views. For yes/no questions, responses can be tallied to determine the general opinion of all groups in the class. Students are encouraged to justify their thinking and question the thinking of classmates.
5. After discussion, students respond to additional questions.
6. On completion, comparisons are drawn between the ending of the story and the students' predictions (adapted from Headley & Dunston, 2000).

Links with Literature
Song Picture Books

What Is a Song Picture Book?

Music throughout the schoolday supports literacy development (Moravcik, 2000; Wiggins, 2007). A song picture book consists of song lyrics that have been illustrated and published as a book. Song picture books are particularly useful for learning language because there are clear connections between language development and musical development in young children (Paquette & Rieg, 2008).

How Are Emergent Literacy and Musical Development Connected?

Consider the following ways in which literacy with print and musical abilities are interrelated:

reading:	pretending to read favorite books based on familiar text
music:	attempting to sing along, pretending to play an instrument
reading:	connecting drawing and writing
music:	connecting music with movement
reading:	learning to track print (left to right and top to bottom)
music:	beginning to watch musical notation, perceiving patterns (e.g., "stairstep" of the scale)
reading:	knowing critical jargon related to reading
music:	learning the basics of musical terminology: tempo (fast/slow), pitch (high/low), dynamics (loud/soft)
reading:	recognizing familiar words
music:	identifying familiar melodies
reading:	identifying words that sound alike, rhyme, or begin with a common initial sound
music:	identifying pitches that match, connecting instruments to the sounds they make (*Sources:* Allington & Walmsley, 2007; Jalongo & Stamp, 1997)

Why Use Song Picture Books?

Song picture books support emergent literacy by

- Building on familiarity and enjoyment
- Providing repetition and predictability
- Expanding vocabulary and knowledge of story structures
- Promoting critical thinking and problem solving
- Fostering creative expression and language play

Source: Jalongo, 2004b; Jalongo & Ribblett, 1997.

Names to Know

Aliki, Ted Arnold, Jim Aylesworth, Karen Beaumont, Ashley Bryan, Eve Bunting, Carol Jayne Church, Susan Jeffers, Ezra Jack Keats, Stephen Kellogg, Mary Ann Kovalski, John Langstaff, Kadir Nelson, José-Luis Orozco, Tom Paxton, Merle Peek, Bryan Pinkney, Robert Quackenbush, Raffi, Glen Rounds, Pete Seeger, Kenneth J. Spengler, Peter Spier, Nadine Bernard Wescott, Jeanette Winter, and Paul O. Zelinsky.

A Sampler of Song Picture Books

Little White Duck (Zaritsky, 2005); *Sunshine on My Shoulders* (Denver, 2003); *Puff the Magic Dragon* (Yarrow & Lipton, 2007); *Grandma's Feather Bed* (Denver, 2007); *Baby Beluga* (Raffi, 1992); *All the Pretty Horses* (Sapport, 1999); *Just the Two of Us* (Smith, 2001); *Elvis Presley's Love Me Tender* (Presley, 2003); *Over the Rainbow* (Harburg & Arlen, 2002); *Summertime* (Heyward & Gershwin, 2002); *This Land Is Your Land* (Guthrie, 2002); *Don't Worry, Be Happy* (McFerrin, 2001); *America the Beautiful* (Sabuda, 2004); *Island in the Sun* (Belafonte, 2001); *Turn, Turn, Turn* (Seeger, 2003); *Coat of Many Colors* (Parton, 1996); *Cumbayah* (public domain); *Hush Little Baby* (Long, 1997); *The Train They Call the City of New Orleans* (Goodman & McCurdy, 2003); *Head, Shoulders, Knees and Toes* (Kubler, 2002); *I Know an Old Teacher* (Bowen, 2008).

ELLs
The Listening Environment

In terms of auditory development, young children are less adept than adults at "filling in the blanks" when messages are incomplete, garbled, or ambiguous (Stelmachowicz, Hoover, Lewis, Kortekaas, & Pittman, 2000). When attempting to evaluate listening environments, there are three key variables:

1) the listener's auditory development, 2) the quality and intensity of the acoustic signal relative to the presence of competing sounds, and 3) the listener's experience with the linguistic components contained in the signal (Nelson, Kohnert, Sabur, & Shaw, 2005). On all three counts, young ELLs are at high risk of failing to understand the messages that they hear. Most developmental charts of second-language acquisition begin with a stage called "silent" as ELLs often remain quiet for a period of time before attempting to produce utterances in L2 (Ellis, 2007). The demands placed on listening skills are magnified in second-language contexts, where the receiver has incomplete control of the language (National Capital Language Resource Center, 2008). Due to the role that listening plays in children's early literacy development and academic success, effective listening skills and strategies merit far more attention in work with young ELLs (Jalongo & Li, 2010).

With respect to environmental variables that interfere with hearing a message, even an empty classroom is apt to be a poor listening environment due to noise from HVAC systems, the reverberation of sounds off hard surfaces, and noises from out-

doors (Knecht, Nelson, Whitelaw, & Feth, 2002). Once the early childhood classroom is populated by groups of active young children and their teachers, the signal-to-noise ratios make listening difficult, even for children with normal hearing and English as their first language (Rogers, Lister, Febo, Besing, & Abrams, 2006). For young children listening to an unfamiliar L2, the listening demands are even greater, leaving them at "a distinct disadvantage in classrooms with typical noise and reverberation" (Nelson et al., 2005, p. 219).

To create a positive listening environment for ELLs, teachers should

- Make an effort to speak distinctly, slow their rate of speech, and use more visual aids.
- Make instructions clear, concise, and sequential.
- Strive to minimize background noise and disruptions.
- Reinforce messages with pantomime, demonstration, and print material.
- Rephrase (rather than just repeat) when children ask a question or appear to be confused.
- Enlist the support of peers to provide explanations.

How Do I ...

Teach Onsets and Rimes (Word Families)?

One way that children can get the most from studying phonics and improve their spelling is through understanding onsets and rimes, sometimes referred to as "word families." An *onset* is the letter or letters at the beginning of the word; for example, a teacher might ask what letter would need to be added to *e* to make the word *me* and then guide the children in forming other words by changing the onset, such as *he*, *we*, or *she*. This sort of natural clustering helps children to get several instances of basic concepts in phonics. A *rime* is the pattern at the end of the word—for example, *-in*, *-et*, *-op*, *-un*, *-oat*, *-ight*, *-all*, *-ope*, *-eal*, *-eed*, *-oice*, *-ide*, *-ike*, *-uck*, *-oil*, *-ook*, *-oon*, *-ink*, *-ish*, and so forth. The idea is that if phonics elements are taught directly, children will recog-

nize them when they hear and see them (Moseley & Poole, 2001).

Gunning (1995, p. 486) explains how to teach onsets and rimes in a five-step process. For example, to teach the *-at* pattern, a teacher would use the following strategy:

1. *Build words by adding the onset.* Write *at* on the board, and have several students read it. Ask what letter should be added to *at* to form the word *sat*, and then show how to form *hat* by adding *h* to *at*. Form the words *mat*, *fat*, *rat*, *cat*, and *that* in the same way. Have students read all the *-at* words and tell what is the same about all of them. Have students note that all the words end in the letters *a-t*, which make the

sounds heard in *at*. Then have them tell which letter makes the /a/ sound and which letter makes the /t/ or ending sound in *at*.

2. *Build words by adding the rime.* Write *s* on the board, and have students tell what sound it stands for. (Saying consonant sounds in isolation distorts them, but it helps students, especially those who are having difficulty detecting individual sounds in words.) Ask students to tell you what you would add to /s/ to make the word *sat*. After adding *at* to *s*, say the word in parts (/s/ /at/) and then as a whole. Pointing to *s*, say /s/; pointing to *a* and *t*, say /at/. Running your hand under the whole word, say "sat."

3. *Select another model word.*

4. *Provide guided practice.*

5. *Apply the onset/rime strategy to a book that features a word family.*

Additional practice might use the "make and break technique," in which children construct, break apart, and reconstruct words. The teacher chooses a word (*and*, for instance) and spells it with magnetic letters; then the teacher says the word and

has the child say it. The teacher then jumbles the letters and has the child reassemble the word and say it. This is repeated until the child constructs and reads the word with ease. The teacher then puts an *s* in front of *and*, explaining that the word now spells *sand*. The teacher removes the *s* and explains that the word now says *and*. This process is repeated with *band* and *hand* (Gunning, 1995, p. 486). In addition, children can play sorting games with these word clusters after gaining familiarity with them. Evidently, children often figure out new words by relating them to words they already know, and teaching rimes such as *-ake*, *-ile*, and *-ate* is an efficient way to support this.

To view a podcast of this process, download "Phonics through Shared Reading" from www.reading.org/resources/podcasts/index.html (Gill, 2006). For numerous examples of onset and rime activities, visit www.breakthroughtoliteracy.com. For a free download of songs that teach onsets and rimes, visit www.songsforteaching.com/phonemicawareness.htm. For sample lessons on word sounds see Starfall at www.starfall.com and www.readwritethink.org/lessons.

PEARSON myeducationkit™ Now go to Chapter 4 in the MyEducationKit (www.MyEducationKit.com) for your book, where you can:

- Find Chapter Objectives.
- Complete Assignments and Activities that can help you more deeply understand the chapter content.
- Extend knowledge with content-specific Web Links.
- Check your comprehension on the content covered in the chapter by going to the Study Plan. Here you will be able to take a chapter quiz, receive feedback on your answers, and then access resources that will enhance your understanding of chapter content.

chapter five

Supporting the Speaking Abilities of the Very Young

Annie Pickert/Pearson Education

FACT FILE on Speaking

- Oral language refers to the corpus of words in a child's vocabulary as well as his or her ability to use those words to understand and convey meaning (i.e., syntactic and narrative skills) (Lonigan, 2005, p. 11).

- There are about 6,900 languages spoken worldwide, but only 153 have written forms (Gordon, 2005). In Africa alone, there are 1,000 different tribal languages (Gollnick & Chin, 2008).

- On any given day in the United States, about 80 different languages are spoken in the public schools (Wiles, 2004). Other than English, Spanish is spoken more than any other language in all regions of the United States. The number of Spanish speakers has grown by about 60 percent (U.S. Bureau of the Census, 2003, p. 4).

• The 10 most common languages of children in the United States who do not speak English are Spanish, Russian, Vietnamese, Arabic, Tagalog, Haitian Creole, Navajo, Hmong, Cantonese, and Korean (Sundem, Krieger, & Pikiewicz, 2009).

• The English language consists of approximately 40 phonemes (units of sound), categorized as vowels and consonants (McCormick, Loeb, & Schiefelbusch, 2002). English is largely a Germanic language in its grammar or structure and more of a Romance (Latin-influenced) language in its vocabulary.

• Researchers have identified at least four factors that influence how quickly young children master a second language: (1) motivation, (2) exposure, (3) age, and (4) personality (Tabors & Snow, 2001). Young children's language skills develop best in natural settings, such as in play-based experiences (Saracho & Spodek, 2007).

• Children's overall oral language proficiency, as well as their phonological skills, influence the course of their reading development. Children with average or above-average oral language and above-average phonological short-term memory are far more likely to become good readers (Mann & Foy, 2007; Nation & Snowling, 2004).

• Attention-deficit hyperactivity disorder (ADHD) is characterized by developmentally inappropriate levels of hyperactivity/impulsivity and/or inattention symptoms that are pervasive across time and settings and impair daily functioning. Children with ADHD tend to have difficulty with oral language tasks that require relatively higher degrees of vigilance, effort, and controlled processing (McInnes, Humphries, Hogg-Johnson, & Tannock, 2003).

• Oral language delays and disorders have been shown to have a negative impact on young children's development of prereading skills such as vocabulary knowledge and word identification skills (Wise, Sevcil, Morris, Lovett, & Wolf, 2007).

Did any of this information surprise you? If so, what? Why? How will you use this knowledge to educate and care for the very young?

What Is a Positive Talk Environment?

Go to the Assignments and Activities section of Chapter 5 in MyEducationKit and complete the activity entitled "Tasting Apples."

Throughout history, children's talk has not been fully appreciated by adults. Children's talk was disparagingly referred to as "prattle," and children were supposed to be "seen and not heard." Moreover, adults often disregarded children's words as inaccurate, fanciful, or inconsequential. Even today, some teachers and administrators insist on quiet and treat much of children's talk in classrooms or centers as an annoyance.

As a first step in this examination of children's talk, consider your characteristic ways of responding to young children's talk. Do you take delight in children's words? Do you enjoy the expressions of their imaginations through talk? How do you feel about children being permitted to talk while they work in groups? How will you manage the common situation of children all wanting to talk at once or for an extended period of time in a larger group?

These are just some of the issues that you will need to think about when you consider children's speech. What you decide will have far-reaching consequences for the type of early childhood classroom that you create (Kontos & Wilcox-Herzog, 1997; Wilcox-Herzog & Ward, 2009).

As a start, reflect on your talk experience as a child:

> What I needed as a child in school was a teacher who wanted to hear my voice, my ideas, the words that were always present but never spoken; a teacher who would have given me the support and safety and a space in which to project that voice, . . . a teacher who would have valued my voice just because it was mine, not because it provided the right answer. (Gallas, 1994, p. 14)

Establishing a positive talk environment requires early childhood educators to

- Express a sincere commitment to and compassion for all children.
- Send congruent verbal and nonverbal messages.
- Invite children into extended conversations and interactions with peers and adults.
- Listen attentively to what children have to say.
- Use children's interests as a basis for conversation.
- Speak respectfully to children.
- Plan or take advantage of spontaneous opportunities to talk with each child informally.
- Refrain from making judgmental comments about children, either to them or within their hearing (Kostelnik, Whiren, Soderman, & Gregory, 2008).

Notice how Ms. Jamie, a child-care provider, supports productive talk by using the open-ended questioning strategies in Figure 5.1 to discuss a field trip with her students:

Ms. Jamie: What is a *hospital?*

Missy: A place where you go when your head cracks open.

Adam: Like when you get sick and get an ear infection.

Jared: A place where they got to make sure your heart is beating.

Aaron: A place where you get stitches or a cast.

Ms. Jamie: What is a *cast?*

Missy: It is something that keeps you dry and safe so it can heal.

Matt: To keep your arm healthy.

Ms. Jamie: How would you get to the hospital?

FIGURE 5.1   On the Value of Open-Ended Questions

What Is an Open-Ended Question?

An open-ended question cannot be answered with a simple yes or no.

> Not Open-Ended: "Is Goldilocks afraid of the bears?"
>
> Open-Ended: "Goldilocks ran away. Why?"
>
> Not Open-Ended: "Is the Little Red Hen working hard?"
>
> Open-Ended: "Why did all the animals change to saying 'I will' instead of 'Not I'?"
>
> Not Open-Ended: "Do the pigs trust the wolf?"
>
> Open-Ended: "Why did the pigs decide to keep the wolf out?"

There are three basic types of open-ended questions, ranging from literal to abstract:

1. *Right-there questions* call on children to think literally and give short answers that could be found right in the story—for instance, "How many kittens lost their mittens?" or "Which little pig has the strongest house?"
2. *Inference questions* call on children to read between the lines and fill in information that is not directly stated—for instance, "Why did Little Jack Horner think he was a good boy?" or "What do you think will happen next?"
3. *Personal connection questions* invite children to connect books with their own lives and experiences, such as, "Do you know anybody else who is learning to swim like Froggy?" (*Froggy Learns to Swim*, London, 1995).

Benefits of Open-Ended Questions

- Let children know that they have your undivided attention.
- Allow children to participate more fully in conversations and talk more.
- Require more elaborate answers and longer sentences from children than a simple yes/no answer.

Opportunities to Ask Open-Ended Questions

- When the child shows an interest in a particular object or thing
- When sharing books together (e.g., turning the pages, pointing to pictures, noticing patterns in a story)
- During quiet, relaxed times such as families and children riding in the car together, when the first few children arrive at the school or center, when chatting informally out on the playground, and when you see children around town and stop to chat

---

Source: McNeill & Fowler, 1996. For more on questions, see Siemens, 1994.

Avanti: Drive in a Corvette or bicycle.

Kellen: You could drive there and get a Popsicle while you wait.

Ms. Jamie: Who would you see there?

Missy: Doctors, nurses, an X-ray person, babies, and parents.

Ms. Jamie: What would they do there?

Sammy: Give you X-rays and shots that really hurt.

Avanti: Take your blood pressure.

Matt: I have an idea. You could ride in a wheelchair.

Ms. Jamie: How would you feel before you went?

Kellen: Sad, mad, and happy.

Avanti: Nervous!

Matt: Terrible!

Ms. Jamie: How would you feel after you were there?

Avanti: Fine, happy, much more better.

Notice how the children were encouraged to talk about what made an impression on them, rather than guess what the teacher wanted them to say.

Collaboration with Families and Professionals

When Ms. Donovan thinks about the talk of the children that attend her preschool in a thriving suburb of northern Virginia, the most striking feature is the different languages, cultures, and ethnic groups they represent. There is Graziella, who recently immigrated to the United States from the Philippines; Mwongoli, a girl from Kenya who speaks English, Kiswahili, and her tribal language; and Li, who speaks a Cantonese dialect of Chinese and has very little prior experience with English.

PEARSON
myeducationkit™

Go to the Assignments and Activities section of Chapter 5 in MyEducationKit and complete the activity entitled "Managing Goodbyes."

There is little question that Li is struggling with all of the adaptations he has to make to his new country and language. Both of his parents are graduate students at a local university and know English, even though they do not speak it at home. Because Li had not yet begun to study English in his native country, coming to the United States meant instant and complete immersion in a foreign language as well as culture shock. As Ms. Donovan notes, "Li is extremely quiet and reserved at school. He stands on the sidelines and watches the other children intently. Some of the children have concluded that he 'can't talk,' and I was so upset to find out that Li has been teased and ridiculed by some older students while waiting for the school bus."

Ms. Donovan knows that Li needs special support in acquiring English, but none of the teachers at the school knows how to speak or write Chinese. When she meets with Li's family, it is clear that they, too, are very concerned and are already trying to help Li practice his English. They also have strong ties to the Chinese community. There is an undergraduate student from China who is studying early childhood education at the university. Ms. Donovan contacts his field experience supervisor and makes arrangements for the student to complete his case study of a child's literacy development in her class with Li. Now Li has a translator, an English tutor, and an adult male protector when he waits for the school bus!

Contributions and Consequences

- *Contributions of the teacher:* How did the teacher play an active role in this situation?
- *Contributions of the family:* How did the family support the child and get involved in the process?
- *Contributions of other professionals:* How did professionals in other fields contribute to addressing the needs of the child and family?
- *Consequences of collaboration:* How might this story have ended differently if the adults had not collaborated?

How Do Young Children Use Speech?

Speech is the *expressive* form of oral language; listening is the *receptive* form of oral language. Speech is a tool for conveying oral language (Lerner, Lowenthal, & Egan, 2003). This may all sound simple enough, but acquiring speech is actually a remarkable achievement (Fields, Groth, & Spangler, 2007). Because so many young children arrive at school ready, willing, and able to talk, there is a tendency to overlook the many different parts of the body involved in producing speech.

Brain and Language
A common misinterpretation about research on the brain is that there are "critical periods" after which development cannot occur. Actually, the brain has remarkable plasticity and, unless there is severe and extensive damage, other parts of the brain can work to make all sections of the mind work together (Thomas, 2003). What are the implications of this for educators?

Speech production depends on precise physiological and neuromuscular coordination of respiration, phonation, resonance, and articulation. Respiration is the act of breathing; phonation is the production of sound by the larynx and vocal fold; resonance is the vibratory response that controls the quality of the sound wave; and articulation is the use of the lips, tongue, teeth, and hard and soft palates to form speech sounds. Exhaled air from the lungs is modified by the vocal folds in the larynx and/or the structure of the mouth to produce speech sounds. Speech is willed, planned, and programmed by the central nervous system, the brain, the spinal cord, and the peripheral nervous system, which includes the cranial and spinal nerves. The different parts of the nervous system are bound together by neurons to form a complex information exchange network that transmits motor impulses to and from the muscles of the speech mechanism. (McCormick et al., 2002, p. 6)

Children's ability to talk is often taken for granted unless difficulties arise. Allan, a first-grader, was referred to the speech/language pathologist, who found him to be a very unusual case. He understood others, so his receptive language was good. His concept of conversation was, if anything, advanced. The only problem was in his unusual pronunciation and articulation of words, which was unlike the speech immaturities commonly observed in young children. When Allan's single-parent mother was called in, she indicated that Allan had begun to talk early, so there was no indication of a language delay. It was not until his two elderly grandparents, who were Allan's primary caregivers, came to school that the mystery was solved. Both of Allan's grandparents had severe dental problems and, as a result, moved their mouths as little as possible when speaking. Allan had learned to talk the same way. Because he lived in a remote rural area and had limited contact with others, he had few other models for language. Allan gradually changed his speech to make himself better understood by others. Of course, differences in the language used at home and at school are not always so dramatic as Allan's, but the influence is there nonetheless. Figure 5.2 summarizes the various influences on young children's language development.

Ms. Praisner teaches 3- and 4-year-olds. Here are some questions and comments from her students that she recorded in her journal:

Dusty (age 3): (Puts a top on the desk and gives it a spin; then twirls around himself.) I can move like a tornado. I saw 'em on TV. I like 'em. (Teacher: "But didn't it show on TV how tornadoes hurt people and wreck buildings?") Yes, but they don't know that people are in the houses when they knock 'em down, do they?

Rene (age 3): Why do they always put water under bridges?

Teddy (age 3): It rains, the sun comes out, and there is a rainbow.

Whitney (age 4): See this nail polish? My mom put it on because I have a 3 o'clock appointment.

Bradley (age 4): I saw a man who made horses today. When we got there, he was nailing on the feet.

At any given point in the typical patterns of language development, children's ability to imitate what they hear is greater than their ability to produce language independently, and their ability to produce language is ahead of their ability to comprehend it fully (Lovel, 1968). Understanding that discrepancies exist among imitation, production, and comprehension will be important to you as you interact with young children. You will need to ask questions to find out what children really mean because they may use words that they do not understand, overestimate the clarity of their communication, or assume that everyone shares their interpretations of language. The behaviors of three children will help to show how imitation and production precede comprehension:

When 3-year-old Lizbeth overhears her family talking about an ice hockey game at the Civic Arena, she hears the sounds and tries to imitate them, even though she cannot produce the words independently and does not comprehend their meaning. To Lizbeth, it is the "Civvie Carrena."

Four-year-old Darlene lives in Pennsylvania. Her aunt lives in California, and she knows it is far away. When her family decides to move from an apartment to a house about 15 miles away, a neighbor asks where they were going. Darlene says, "Oh, a long way. Clear to Calipania! You're not gonna see me anymore." Darlene is not just imitating sounds she has heard; rather, she is able to produce a word that sounds like the names for states she already knows.

FIGURE 5.2   Factors That Influence Speech Development

Neurological Factors

Cognitive development. In order for children to speak, they need sufficient intelligence and maturity. Even a child who is a genius does not begin to talk that much earlier than peers because he or she needs to acquire experiences in order to attach words to those experiences. Part of being able to speak is being able to preplan what we say.

Information processing strategies. In order to talk, children need to learn how to focus attention, to discriminate between and among sounds, and to hold sounds in memory so that they can be reproduced later.

Motor output capabilities. Speech requires carefully coordinated movements of the lips and tongue as well as the voice. For most of us, these movements have become so automatic that we barely notice them. Usually, we become aware of these demands only when speaking a different language that includes different pronunciations or when illness (e.g., laryngitis) or injury (after oral surgery) interferes with normal speech.

Socioemotional development and motivation. Because language is a social instrument, part of what builds speech is human interaction. From the earliest months of life, babies respond and try to elicit responses from their caregivers even when their only language is a cry.

Structural and Physiological Factors

Sensory acuity. Acuity in all of the senses, not only hearing, can affect speech. A child who cannot experience things directly through the sense of sight will necessarily build vocabulary differently than a sighted child. The same holds true for a child whose sense of taste, touch, or smell is affected. Without direct experience, it is difficult to put words to these ideas and feelings.

Oromuscular capabilities. Human speech involves using the muscles of the throat as well as control over the lips and tongue. Medical conditions that interfere with this control interfere with language.

Speech transmission mechanisms. Speech also relies on respiration, the ability to breathe. If, for example, paralysis has affected that portion of the body, then the ability to project the voice will be very limited.

Environmental Factors

Sociocultural variables. Research has shown that although talk is ordinarily a part of the home environment at all socioeconomic levels, the perceived purposes for that talk and the applicability of that prior experience to the classroom differ markedly.

Experiences. Children's speech is affected by caregivers' responsiveness and opportunities for nonverbal and verbal interaction. In order to master speech, children need comprehensible linguistic input.

Physical context. Having things to talk about is another influence on children's speech. Pets, toys, objects to manipulate, picture books to share, and other materials can stimulate conversation.

Source: McCormick, Loeb, & Schiefelbusch, 2002.

Five-year-old Stephan is going for a ride in his grandfather's "talking car." His grandfather demonstrates how the computerized voice announces that the lights are on, the keys were left in the ignition, and so on. When the car announces "Door ajar," Stephan looks disgusted and says, "Grandpa, this car is silly. A door is not a jar!" Stephan's comments show that he can imitate, produce, and comprehend words, even though he interprets the single word *ajar* as two words.

Overview of Children's Speech Development

Communicative and Noncommunicative Speech

Young children's speaking abilities may be clustered into two broad categories: communicative and noncommunicative. *Noncommunicative speech* is nonconversational; it is not directed toward or adapted to listeners. Three types of noncommunicative speech commonly observed in children under the age of 6 or 7 are (1) repetition, (2) monologue, and (3) dual or collective monologue (Piaget, 1959).

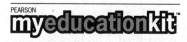

Go to the Assignments and Activities section of Chapter 5 in MyEducationKit and complete the activity entitled "Conversations."

Go to the Assignments and Activities section of Chapter 5 in MyEducationKit and complete the activity entitled "Communicating within a Group."

Repetition occurs when the child plays with the sounds for the sensual pleasure of talking. A 3-year-old girl rhythmically repeated these sounds as she rocked back and forth in a wooden, boat-shaped toy: "Row the boat, row, row, row the boat. Row, row, row. Rock the boat row. Rock, rock, rock the boat. Row, row, row."

Monologue occurs when the child talks as though thinking aloud yet makes no attempt to address anyone. This is also referred to as *private speech*. Private speech is talk that children address to themselves. The period between wakefulness and sleep is often a time for monologues, such as that produced by Anthony, an 18-month-old: "See the doggie. Dee the doggie. I see the doggie (said two times in a falsetto voice). Kitty likes doggie" (Gardner, 1980). Older children continue to use monologues. In a kindergarten class that had just returned from a hospital field trip, one boy talked to himself as he painted a picture, saying things like the following:

"There's the elevator we rode on."

"I need green for the old lady in the wheelchair."

"I liked those cookies they gave us. Mommy's aren't that big."

"I'm not going to be there, but it would be fun to play with all those toys."

Note that when children engage in private speech, the same words that adults once used to regulate children's behaviors are now used by children themselves for the purposes of self-regulation. Studies of private speech have found a direct link between children's use of private speech, self-regulatory speech, and self-control (Zaslow & Martinez-Beck, 2006).

A *dual* or *collective monologue* occurs when the child talks aloud in the presence of others and takes turns talking but without truly conversing. In a dual or collective monologue, children speak aloud about separate topics. In the following example, which takes place in the housekeeping corner, two different play themes are in progress. Melissa is playing the role of queen, while the other children are playing house. If you read Melissa's words separately, you can see that her speech is on a completely different topic from that of her peers:

Melissa: I'm the queen.

Leesha: Are you gonna eat? (Referring to Carolyn)

Carolyn: There's an egg stuck in here.

Leesha: Well, you're just gonna have to leave it there!

Carolyn: If anyone would like the salt and pepper, this is the salt and pepper. (She holds up the shakers.)

Melissa: Uh-oh. I better get this stapled again. (Referring to her crown)

Leesha: (Speaking to Carolyn) I think it's time to go to bed. This baby is sleepy. Will you put my baby to bed?

Carolyn: Do you have a blanket? Let's tuck her in.

Leesha: (Picks up a plastic carrot and offers it to the baby.) Do you need a carrot?

Carolyn: Babies drink milk. They don't eat carrots!

Melissa: This kingdom has lots of queens.

In this collective monologue, Melissa is using noncommunicative speech.

Communicative or *socialized speech* occurs after young children begin to acquire a sense of audience and grasp the social interaction aspect of conversation. Observing a child's spontaneous language use during play is generally the best indicator of her or his level of language functioning. There are six types of socialized speech:

1. *Play talk*, in which children express personalities other than their own during play
2. *Negotiation talk*, in which children attempt to join in activities, establish rules, and surmount challenges
3. *Excluding talk*, in which children deny another child entry into a game or activity
4. *Challenge talk*, in which children disagree with the definitions and rules of others
5. *Empathic talk*, in which children put themselves in a troubled child's position and offer solace and support
6. *Information and understanding talk*, in which children converse with others, raising questions about issues and topics of importance and meaning (Kliewer, 1995)

Each of these forms of socialized speech is evident in the following police-and-criminals play text recorded in a kindergarten classroom:

Heidi: Let's play police. I'll be the cop and you be the bad guy. (*Play talk—taking on roles*)

Michael: Can I be real bad? I know, I'll have a gun and kill people. (*Information and understanding talk, play talk, negotiation talk*)

Heidi: No, that's too mean. Just rob a bank or something. (*Excluding and negotiation talk*)

Michael: I want to be a killer. If I can't, I won't play cops with you. (*Challenge talk*)

Heidi: Well, OK, let's start now! I'll come to your hideout to get you. (*Play talk*)

Michael: Who is it?

Heidi: It's the cops.

Michael: What do you want?

Heidi: I'm here to 'rest you. Come out with your hands up. I'm going to throw you in jail. (*Play talk*)

Michael: Oh no you're not, I'll get away, 'cause you're a girl. (*Challenge talk*)

Heidi: Wait, you don't play fair. I'm the cops, you can't get away. (*Challenge talk*)

Michael: You don't play fair. I don't wanna play with you anymore. (*Exclusion talk*)

Heidi: Let's play house instead then. (*Empathic talk*)

Communicative language requires the speaker to coordinate a wide array of skills and abilities:

• *Mastery of nonverbal behavior.* Nonverbal forms of communication can replace the spoken word (e.g., thumbs up to mean "good" or "go ahead"), reinforce the spoken word (e.g., nodding while saying "Yes!"), or contradict the spoken word (e.g., looking serious while joking).

• *Familiarity with conversational rules.* A conversational partner needs to master the constraints and conditions of conversation, such as taking turns, adjusting to changes in the conversational topic, correcting misunderstandings, sticking to relevant topics, using questions appropriately, and mastering techniques for initiating or terminating a conversation.

• *Ability to sequence.* Conversation demands the ability to think back or reflect on experience and then link it with past, present, and future objects, situations, and events.

• *Capacity to interpret messages.* Before children can engage in conversation, they need to realize that a message is being delivered to them. Young children who are unaccustomed to being part of a group will sometimes fail to understand this. If the teacher announces, for example, "Let's all put our toys away now," the young child may not understand that this message is intended for him or her.

• *Ability to formulate and produce a response.* Children engaged in conversation need to generate an appropriate response.

In the play text that follows, five girls, ages 5 to 7, demonstrate all of these conversational skills. Because they routinely play together in Tangi's basement, where her mother's beauty shop is located, they have had ample opportunity to acquire a specialized vocabulary and observe the routines. Kelly and Heather are playing the roles of hairdressers, Tangi and Jennifer are the customers, and Justine is the cashier:

Kelly: Have a seat, ladies.

Heather: What will it be today? (Speaking to Tangi and Jennifer)

Tangi: Oh, our usual cut and perm.

Heather: Well, you ladies came at a good time. Today is our special on perms.

Kelly: What size curlers would you ladies like?

Heather: Do you want the full perm or the partial perm?

Tangi: I would like the pink curlers, and I want the full perm.

Jennifer: I would like the yellow curlers, and I want the partial perm. Just the top of my head is to be curly.

Kelly: Please cover your eyes with this towel while I put the solution on your hair.

Tangi: How much does a style cost?

Jennifer: Is it extra or part of the sale price?

Heather: It's not extra. The styling cost is included in the sale price of perms.

Kelly: It's time for you ladies to have your hair rinsed and curlers taken out.

Heather: How much do you want cut off?

Tangi: I want just the end tips cut off.

Jennifer: Leave enough for me to curl my hair with a curling iron. Cut off as much as you can.

Kelly: How would you like your hair styled?

Tangi: Style my hair the way you think best, so that it looks good with my face.

Kelly: How do you ladies like your hair? Is it to your satisfaction?

Tangi: I like mine.

Kelly: How about you, Jennifer?

Jennifer: I like mine, too.

Justine: Tangi, your perm comes to $49.95. Jennifer, your perm comes to $56.95. Here's your change, ladies. Have a nice day.

Tangi: Thank you. Jennifer, let's go out for lunch. What do you say?

Jennifer: Alright, Tangi, that sounds like fun—let's go!

As this play episode illustrates, children can be amazingly adept conversational partners. They are, of course, greatly affected by the cultural context in which they live.

Understanding Young Children's Language Challenges

How would you respond to these situations?

- A 3-year-old named Robbie pronounces his name as "Wobbie."
- Alaina tells you that she saw cows standing in a "grassture" during her trip to Kentucky.
- Carin, a kindergartner, says, "You teached us how to do that already."
- Stan, a first-grader, shares a joke with the elementary principal. When the principal laughs and teases him a bit, Stan says, "Shut up."

Would you refer Robbie to a speech therapist? Tell Alaina that there's no such thing as a "grassture"? Insist that Carin say "taught" instead of "teached?" Inform Stan that he has been very rude? Would you assume that any of these children had an inadequate language background?

Actually, all of the behaviors just described are common in young children. Each relates to one of the components of language discussed in Chapter 3: *graphophonics* (the sound and symbol system of language), *semantics* (the meaning system of language), *syntax* (the structure of language and its grammatical rules), and *pragmatics* (the social appropriateness of language).

Robbie's pronouncing an *r* as a *w* is not uncommon. Many young children display such speech immaturities (e.g., speech difficulties that gradually disappear without intervention). Figure 5.3 highlights some of the most common pronunciation problems in young children's speech.

FIGURE 5.3   Common Articulation Difficulties of Young Children

Articulation Difficulty	Example
th for *s* or *z*	Kerri (age 4) is offered candy and says, "No, thanth. I had thum candy yetherday."
d for *g*	Neesha (age 2) says, "Me doe now" for "Me go now."
w for *l*; *d* for *th*	Crystal (age 4), shopping for toys: "I could wike one of dem."
b for *v*	Maria (age 3) asks for "beaumbilla" (vanilla) ice cream.
w for *wh*; *d* for *th*	Paco (age 2) asks, "Was dat?" for "What's that?"
w for *r*	Jennifer (age 3) asks if they can go to the Italian restaurant: "I wanna go to the Woma Woom" (Roma Room). Then when referring to a book she says, "The wabbit wan awound the twee."
th for *ch*; *ch* for *sh*	Mei (age 3), commenting on his new puppy's misbehavior: "Doggie thoo my chew."
sh for *ch*	LaQuira (age 4), on Sunday morning: "Me going to shursh."

| **FIGURE 5.4** | Examples of Children's Invented Words |

long ago plus *once upon a time*	"onceago"
because plus *except*	"becept"
two of them	"toodum"
twins, Becky and Brenda	"Beckyenda"
nice and clean	"nickaneen"
upset plus *excited*	"upsited"
a couple of minutes	"comitz"
Pledge of Allegiance	"Plegiance"

Alaina has never heard of a *pasture*, but experience tells her that horses eat grass, so she makes the word fit her understanding about horses—*grassture*. Children often make creative errors like these, called *invented forms*. A child who says, for instance, "I'm barefoot all over" shows that she has grasped the concept of being naked. The child who says, "We're not big shots; we're little shots" knows something about opposites. Several interesting examples of children's invented forms are given in Figure 5.4.

Carin's comment, "You teached us," has to do with syntax, or the structure of language. It includes such things as inflections (word endings), word order, forming plurals and possessives, making comparisons, and conjugating verbs. Once again, children's knowledge of the rules is often evident. A child who says, "Mine is more better" or "This is the bestest present I ever got" knows that *-er* and *-est* are usually used to compare things. It just happens that *good-better-best* is an exception. Young children face a particularly difficult syntactical challenge when they try to form negatives. Figure 5.5 shows the developmental progression in learning to convert a sentence into its negative form.

Stan's mistake of telling the principal to "shut up" is an example of pragmatics, the social appropriateness or inappropriateness of language. A child who playfully tells family and friends to "shut up" may generalize that behavior to other social situations. This does not mean that he or she is deliberately being rude or defiant; it is just a use of language that is not acceptable in a more formal context.

Even though language immaturities such as these are commonly observed, there are times when young children do not grow out of their language problems. They may have a language delay, meaning that they achieve various milestones much later than peers. They may also have a language disability that interferes with their reception, processing, or production of language. As was described in Figure 5.1, the difficulty can be primarily physical, environmental, social, or any combination thereof. One of the most common sources of language problems in young children is an undetected

---

FIGURE 5.5 Developmental Sequence in Forming Negatives and Questions

At about 2 years, puts *no* or *not* at the front of the sentence.

- Not more.
- No can do it.

At approximately 24 to 28 months, uses a repertoire of negatives but only in present tense and with no contractions.

- Kitty no scratch.
- Mommy not go.

At approximately 26 to 32 months, relies mainly on rising intonation to denote a question; may begin using *what* or *where* to begin a question.

- He sad?
- What that?
- Where it go?

At approximately 3 years, uses *why, where,* and *what* at the beginning of the sentence. May have difficulty with selecting the correct pronoun. Often mistakes *what* questions for *why*.

- Where the ball now?
- What he crying?
- Why she can't sit down?

At approximately 4 or 5 years, asks yes/no questions by placing the verb first in the sentence (e.g., *Is grandma coming too?*). Often uses phrases such as *You know what . . . ?* Uses contractions. Uses past-tense negatives.

- Didn't she take a nap?
- You know what? Daddy isn't really sleeping.
- That park wasn't clean.

Source: Song & Fisher, 2005.

Infants and Toddlers

Research has found that when toddlers were intensely engaged with an activity and concentrating on the nonverbal aspects, they spoke less. When toddlers were more casually involved with an activity, they tended to produce more spontaneous speech (Wiener-Margulies & Rey-Barboza, 1996, p. 65). What are the practical implications of these findings?

hearing problem. If the child has chronic ear infections, a very common ailment, it interferes with comprehensible input. When the input is garbled, the child's speech can be difficult to understand. Sometimes the delay or disorder seems to be related to an understimulating environment, in which a child has few opportunities to talk or is encouraged to use "baby talk."

Another example of an expressive language disorder is stuttering. For some children, stuttering is a speech immaturity. In preschool children, it tends to occur when they are excited and their thoughts are moving faster than their language can express. Usually, a child who is supported rather than criticized and taught to slow down gains greater mastery over language and the stuttering disappears. For other children, stuttering is a more persistent and serious difficulty, one that requires professional help. Some new drug therapies also are available to treat stuttering. In every case, a thoughtful evaluation of the child's language in various contexts is warranted.

Teacher Concerns and Basic Strategies

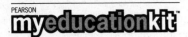

Go to the Assignments and Activities section of Chapter 5 in MyEducationKit and complete the activity entitled "Playing in a Restaurant."

Adults can use several basic principles to improve their communication skills with children (Faber & Mazlish, 1999):

Instead of denying feelings, put them into words. If a child says, "Teacher, I hate Ricardo!" we might be inclined to respond with "That's not a very nice thing to say." A better strategy is to accept the child's feelings and help him or her put them into words: "It sounds like you are angry because Ricardo knocked over your blocks."

Instead of scolding, give information. Think about your reaction to these two statements from teachers:

Scolding: "Lisette, how many times do I have to tell you to be gentle with the gerbil? If you don't learn how to be more careful, you won't get to hold him anymore."

Giving information: "Lisette, gerbils are very small animals, and they can be hurt if they are held too tightly. She is tame and will stay in your hand if you make it into a little cup shape, like this."

Clearly, the second strategy is more helpful and communicates more effectively.

Instead of demanding a confession, describe the problem. If the teacher uses an accusing or commanding tone ("All right! Who made this mess?"), the children will tend to deny their involvement in order to avoid punishment. If the teacher states the problem instead, it encourages the children to engage in problem solving. For instance, the teacher might say, "Oh, there is water all over the floor near the sink. It needs to be mopped up so that nobody slips and falls." Usually, one child will volunteer and several others will follow. If not, the teacher should begin mopping and say, "If somebody would help me mop, then we could have our snack." In this way, children see how their helping behavior can result in a positive outcome for everyone.

Instead of giving orders, offer choices. "After we read this book together, you may do one of three things: go to the listening center and hear the story again, go to the art center and make something that you thought about during the story, or go to the library and read a book with a partner." This third-grade teacher does not overwhelm children with alternatives ("Find something to do"), nor does she completely restrict their options ("Copy the new vocabulary words from the chalkboard, and write a sentence for each word").

Instead of lecturing, say it briefly. Keep it simple and place the responsibility with the child. Compare the following:

> "Melanie, come and get this puzzle and put it on the puzzle rack right this minute. You know that it belongs there when you are finished with it. Remember, children, you are all supposed to put the toys away after you play with them. I always have to remind some of you."

> "Melanie, the puzzle belongs on the shelf."

The second approach gets Melanie thinking. She has to reassemble the puzzle again and slide it into the puzzle rack. When appropriate, use just a word or two, such as saying "Your jacket" to a child who is going outside without his or her coat on.

Instead of emphasizing children's difficulties, describe their successes. Instead of saying "Greg can't spell his last name yet," try "Greg, I see that you printed your first name on your painting." This second statement encourages Greg to keep on writing, while the first one makes him feel inadequate. Also try to be descriptive of children's successes by saying, for instance, "Cherisse, you made your puppet's voice sound like a witch's voice, and your puppet looks wicked too!" rather than "That's a nice puppet."

Instead of talking, put it in writing. Kindergarten and primary-grade classrooms should have "mailboxes" so that teachers and children can communicate with one another. The mailboxes can be made out of recycled containers (such as milk cartons or soft drink bottles with the tops cut off and laid on their sides), snack food cans, or cardboard boxes with dividers inside. Children can communicate through drawing, writing, or any combination thereof with peers and with the teacher, and the teacher can send positive messages to the children.

Instead of being "judge and jury," solve the problem together. Listen to this class discussion about a toy that is the subject of frequent disputes. When the teacher begins the discussion by asking "What's good about the new tricycle?" the children comment: "It's red," "You can hook the wagon on to it and pull stuff around," "I don't have one at home," and "It's nicer than the old one." When the teacher asks what is bad about it, the children say, "Kids fight about it and try to push you off sometimes," "You want to play with it for a long time but you can't," and "Some people won't share unless you tell the teacher." Finally, when the teacher asks what can be done, the children suggest, "Get more tricycles," "Make everybody share," "Tell the teacher if somebody doesn't take turns," and "Use the egg timer like we did when we got the wagon." Using this strategy allows everyone to participate in the solution.

Research and Report
Reread the guidelines from Faber and Mazlish (1999) on pages 110–111 and locate additional expert advice on effective family/child communication. Prepare a brochure for families that would encourage them to communicate more effectively with their children. Use the templates on a word-processing program to produce a professional-looking brochure.

Classroom Activities to Develop Children's Speaking

Many different activities can support the development of children's speech.

Children's Narration of Drawings   Individual children can use dictation to create stories, as Camille did when she narrated the story to accompany her drawing in Figure 5.6.

FIGURE 5.6   Camille's Drawing

Camille, age 7, talks about her drawing:

This is my Grandma's farm I went to for my birthday. And this is the barn (pointing to various objects on the paper). The roof is all dirty and gonna fall apart. These are the cats that live in the barn, and this one doesn't have a tail and Grandpa calls it "Stubby." This is one of the cows in the barn and he SMELLS! These spots are his black spots; he has black spots all over his body. And these are the big black birds that fly around the barn, and this is the hay outside of the barn that Grandpa has.

PEARSON
myeducationkit™

Go to the Assignments and Activities section of Chapter 5 in MyEducationKit and complete the activity entitled "Use Your Words."

Group Discussions Many teachers find group discussions difficult to direct. Hendrick and Weissman (2009) provide these general guidelines for guiding group discussions:

- Convey enthusiasm and enjoy interacting with the children.
- Keep the group small and stable.
- Minimize tensions and distractions.
- Plan carefully yet be flexible.
- Begin promptly when children start to gather.
- Adjust the pace and include variety.
- Encourage discussion through supportive comments.
- Ask skillful, open-ended questions.
- Draw the group to a close before it falls apart.
- Focus on children's communication, rather than their material possessions.
- Model the kinds of behaviors you want to see in the children.
- Recognize that young children's contributions may be wish fulfillment, rather than factual reporting.
- Allow children to take the lead and say what they want to say, rather than quiz them.

In general, the younger the group, the more necessary it is to limit the size and duration of the group. For example, sharing centers may be more effective than whole class sharing time (Dailey, 2008).

Interviews With interviews, children have an opportunity to formulate and rehearse questions in advance. Try inviting school personnel—such as the secretary, bus driver, janitor, or a cafeteria worker—to the classroom so that children can find out about the jobs these people do. Ask parents and other community members to visit and be interviewed. When Ms. Thomas invited the principal to be interviewed by her kindergarten class, one of the children asked, "Are you the boss of the school?" and another asked, "Do you pack or buy your lunch?" When a child asked the principal, "What's your telephone number?" and the adults asked why the boy wanted to know this, he replied, "So I can call her if I get lost!"

Co-Playing Enter into the children's dramatic play when they seem to be losing interest or having difficulty getting started. You can stimulate children's speech by taking on a role ("Hello, I'm the postal carrier and I have a package to deliver to this house"), using an object symbolically ("We can use this cardboard tube for a firefighter's hose"), incorporating new vocabulary ("How do I make an appointment for my dog in this veterinarian's office?"), making suggestions ("If they're going to speed around on those bikes and you're the police officer, you might want to write some tickets or put up some traffic signs for them to obey"), and asking questions ("I'm a very hungry customer. What can you get to eat at this restaurant?"). Co-playing gives teachers a chance to assess children's speech in different contexts.

Mystery Boxes This strategy begins with an object that children cannot see because it is inside a closed box. The main purposes are for children to learn a strategy for raising questions, receive guidance from the teacher in making inferences, and build skills in oral expression. For example, if the children begin with broad categories ("Is it a toy?" "Is something to eat?") they will be more successful at guessing than if they are specific ("Is it a ball?" "Is it a toy truck?"). Children also learn to listen more carefully. Gradually, students begin to realize that if they ask, "Is it a teddy bear?" after the teacher has already answered no to "Is it a toy?" then they are wasting one of their questions. See Rule (2007) for detailed instructions on playing this very intellectually challenging game with young children.

Think-Alouds   A think-aloud is exactly what it sounds like—a person making her or his thought process accessible to others by giving a play-by-play account of the reasoning taking place. For example, if you were writing you might say, "Hmm. What's a good story that I'd like to share with others? I know, I'll write about my new kitten and use photos to illustrate the story. A good title for the story might be 'A First-Grade Teacher's First Kitten.' This kitten did not have a mom so I fed it with a bottle until it was big enough to eat food by itself. . . ." Think-alouds let others in on our internal mental states. For many examples of lessons and activities to help children use think-alouds, see Block and Israel (2004) and Oczkus (2009).

Guided Play and Role-Play   "Imagine that it's a freezing cold day," the teacher says, "and you are going to have a cup of hot chocolate. It's sitting on the table right in front of you. Watch out! It's very hot and the mug is very full, with marshmallows bobbing around on top. Let's see how you would taste it." In this example, children are presented with a problem. If you were observing the class, you would see many different responses: some pretending to use a spoon, some blowing on the cup, and some trying to sip it without picking up the mug. For more on guided play to support children's conversational competence, see Tsao (2008).

Play with Puppets   Puppets are recommended because they speak a universal language, encourage cooperation, improve communication skills, and integrate the curriculum. A group of preschool children are watching a puppet play of "Little Red Riding Hood" performed by the librarian. The wolf puppet turns to the audience and says slyly, "I think I'll take a shortcut over to Granny's and wait for that sweet little girl to arrive. Now don't tell her. Promise?" "Yes," the children dutifully reply. The moment that the wolf disappears from the stage and Little Red comes on stage, the children begin to shout, "Don't do it!" "Run!" and "The wolf's gonna get you!" These children identified with the story and used their expressive language to help, even though they are breaking their promise to the Big Bad Wolf. After children have experience with puppets, try using familiar stories and predictable books as the foundation and let children improvise a script. The puppets themselves need not be elaborate. Figure 5.7 illustrates several types of simple puppets. Also see Crepeau and Richards (2003), Hunt and Renfro (1982), Minkel (2000), and VanSchuvver (1993) for more about puppetry in the classroom.

FIGURE 5.7 Simple Puppets

RECYCLABLES

FOOD CONTAINERS

PAPER PLATES

OLD ARTICLES OF CLOTHING

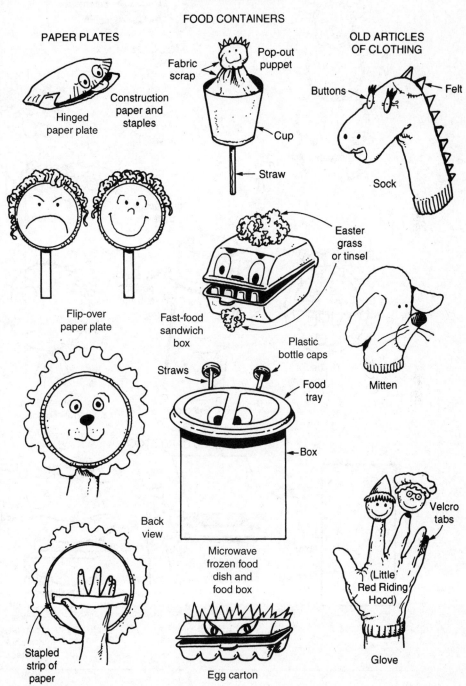

Hinged paper plate

Construction paper and staples

Fabric scrap

Pop-out puppet

Cup

Straw

Buttons

Felt

Sock

Flip-over paper plate

Easter grass or tinsel

Fast-food sandwich box

Mitten

Plastic bottle caps

Straws

Food tray

Box

Back view

Microwave frozen food dish and food box

Stapled strip of paper

Egg carton

Velcro tabs

(Little Red Riding Hood)

Glove

(continued)

FIGURE 5.7 Continued

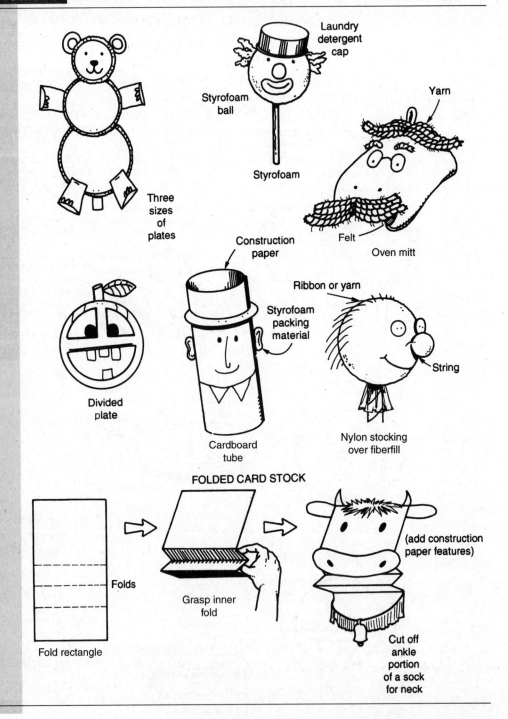

If you are working with a group, try this procedure:

- Select a simple, familiar, and predictable story with several characters that the children have heard many times.
- Make a list of the main characters and ask children to use puppets that were purchased (Folkmanus is a source for beautiful puppets) or have the children make a simple puppet for each character.
- To get started, put the children in a line that corresponds to the story sequence, read the story aloud, and have children step forward and move their puppets when the character's name is mentioned. Stories that are cumulative, such as *Move Over, Rover* (Beaumont, 2006) are a good choice. Stories with a definite plot sequence are suitable as well, such as *Too Much Noise* (McGovern, 1967) and *One Fine Day* (Hogrogian, 1971).
- Model for the children how the puppet invents dialogue, based on the story. Stories in question-and-answer format, such as *Where Are You Going? To See My Friend* (Carle & Iwamura, 2003), *What Do You Say, Dear?* (Joslin, 1958), *Where Does Joe Go?* (Pearson, 2002), and *The Grouchy Ladybug* (Carle, 1977), are good choices.
- As a next step, pose the questions from the story and give children turns to answer back in the character of their puppets. Consider using *Baby Bear, Baby Bear, What Do You See?* (Martin, 2007), *Have You Seen My Duckling?* (Tafuri, 1986), or *From Head to Toe* (Carle, 1999).
- Progress to dramatizing short scenes and eventually to enacting the entire story using their puppets and retelling skills. Some good choices are *The Empty Pot* (Demi, 1990) and *The Sign Maker's Assistant* (Arnold, 1992).

Narrated Theater   Narrated theater is often used with children who are not yet reading. In narrated theater, the teacher reads the story while the children enact it. As the children gain familiarity with the story, the teacher stops at various points and lets them improvise pieces of dialogue. When books have repetitive phrases, such as *Possum Come a-Knockin'* (Van Laan, 1990), the entire group of children can recite that portion in unison. The text of the story used in narrated theater may also be printed on a large sheet of chartpaper or be accompanied by a "big book" version. This enables children to become more familiar with the story and gradually take over the narrator's role. Some suggestions for narrated theater are *Caps for Sale* (Slobodkina, 1940), *The Cat Who Loved to Sing* (Hogrogian, 1988), *Rabbit Makes a Monkey of Lion* (Aardema, 1990), and *Anansi and the Moss-Covered Rock* (Kimmel, 1990).

Scripted Drama   Generally speaking, scripted drama is more appropriate for older children. The following questions can help guide you in using plays with young children:

- Is the script suited to the children's reading abilities?
- Is the idea of performing a play initiated by the child or children?
- Does the performance take place in a familiar, supportive environment (e.g., the classroom) rather than an unfamiliar, high-pressure situation (e.g., on stage in an auditorium)?
- Is the story one that the children have selected or invented?

Voice Amplification For children who are shy, speak softly, or need voice amplification due to some physical condition, consider using an inexpensive toy microphone and public address system, walkie-talkies, a karaoke machine, a cheerleader's megaphone, or a megaphone made out of a gallon plastic milk jug with the bottom cut off. Children can practice speaking or singing along using these aids and gradually build their confidence about speaking and projecting their voices.

Reciprocal Teaching Reciprocal teaching is a strategy that is well supported by the research. It involves having children listen to a story and then assigning them to one of four roles during the small-group discussion that follows—(1) reteller, (2) summarizer, (3) questioner, and (4) predictor. Myers (2005) adapted the strategy for kindergartners by using puppets to model each role: (1) The Princess Storyteller, (2) Clara Clarifier, (3) Quincy Questioner, and (4) the Wizard. This strategy is an excellent way to encourage students to participate in interactive read-alouds, to assess prior knowledge, and to evaluate students' comprehension of the book that was read aloud.

Say Something About . . . *Say Something*, a poetic book by Mary Stolz (1993), can be used to give children an opportunity to express themselves through beautiful words. Inspired by the book, a first-grader was asked to say something about space and stars. She said, "Space never ends," "Space is the hat for God," and "Stars are the pictures of space" (Quintero & Rummel, 1996).

Conclusion

When teachers build on all of the oral language learning that has already taken place at home, children will learn to speak more competently and confidently. By appreciating the rich diversity in the language of students and emphasizing functional language activities, teachers can make a significant contribution to children's expressive language abilities.

myeducationkit To check your comprehension on the content covered in this chapter, go to the MyEducationKit for your book and complete the Study Plan for Chapter 5. Here you will be able to take a chapter quiz and receive feedback on your answers.

Research-Based Literacy Strategies

K-W-L Plus

The K-W-L strategy gets children involved in completing a three-column chart with column heads titled "Know," "Want to Know," and "Learned." In K-W-L Plus, children get involved in organizing, integrating, and summarizing the information they have acquired from the text (Ogle, 1986). Using K-W-L Plus with informational texts in the early elementary grades may influence students' reading choices in the upper elementary grades (Headley & Dunston, 2000). Stages in K-W-L Plus are as follows:

1. The teacher previews a book, choosing a topic that has sparked children's interest. During

this reading of the book, the teacher identifies several stopping points where a particular concept requires elaboration or terminology needs clarification.

2. The teacher assesses children's prior knowledge on the book's topic before reading. In the K (What We *Know*) column of the chart, the teacher and students construct a list of what they think they know about the topic, even ideas that are incorrect (to be revised later, after reading). This step may be completed as a total group, with small groups, or by pairs of students. Teachers can take dictation for not-yet-writers, pair independent writers with partners who cannot write, or have pairs of child writers take turns writing.

3. Sort the material into meaningful categories. The teacher demonstrates how categories are formed by thinking aloud to organize the information. If reading about animals, for example, some categories might be physical appearance, habitat, food, and so forth.

4. The W (*Want* to Know) column of the chart is filled with questions generated by the students. It, too, is completed prior to reading as a way to set purposes for listening to the story or reading it independently. Seeing the questions appear in print as they are asked provides additional support for children who struggle with reading and for English language learners.

5. The teacher reads the book aloud as the students listen for words and phrases that answer their questions. These are recorded by the teacher or, if writing independently, by the students, in the L (What I *Learned*) column. Students are also free to add questions to the W column. The group summarizes the questions that were answered and those that were not.

6. The *Plus* part of the activity gets children involved in categorizing the information that they learned under the headings from the first (*Know*) column. Students may revise their categories at this point, as necessary.

7. With these categories in place, students generate a map or web of ideas with the topic of the book in the center of the chart. The main categories radiate out from the center, and the details are listed below. Lines are used to il-

lustrate the relationship of the main topic to the categories, and the teacher can use chart templates from computer software to integrate technology during this step.

8. Students number the categories in order of preference or importance, and these maps become the basis for children's oral or written summaries of the text (adapted from Headley & Dunston, 2000).

Speech-to-Text Software

The purpose of speech-to-text programs is to convert children's oral language into printed text almost as quickly as the words are spoken. Speech-to-text programs are a form of technology designed to take the place of a teacher or volunteer taking dictation for the child. For children who are struggling with reading, speech-to-text offers concrete, immediate feedback on the connections between spoken language and printed text. These "talking word processors" are a resource for teaching other languages to English speakers or for reinforcing the first language of English language learners and are available in Spanish, German, French, and Italian versions. Examples of speech-to-text programs include Kurzweil Voice and VoicePad, VoiceText, Dragon Dictate (for IBM) and PowerSecretary (for Macintosh), IBM VoiceType 3, Simply Speaking, and the Philips Dictation systems (including Speech Magic and Speech Note). Keystone is one of a very few programs that offers both speech-to-text and the reverse—written text converted to spoken words, or text-to-speech.

Electronic Talking Books

Electronic talking books for children typically offer a digitized reading of the text; click-accessible definitions, background information, and animation; questions for the children to answer; special features designed to support children's reading (e.g., pronunciations of new terms); and activities to extend the experience (e.g., suggesting actions to accompany the story or play activities to complete afterward). Electronic talking books are available on CD or DVD as well as on the Internet. While these books cannot replace reading aloud with parents/families, electronic talking books can provide enrichment

(Mol, Bus, & DeJong, 2009). Electronic books allow young children to hear a story read and correlate the spoken words with the printed words as many times as they wish. Many electronic books also highlight each word as it is pronounced so that the child can follow along in a word-by-word fashion. For English language learners, the opportunity to get immediate feedback on a word's pronunciation as they read the text on screen provides comprehensible input.

Some electronic books are equipped with a tracking system that can provide feedback to the teacher on the words that were problematic as the child attempted to read aloud, thus providing words for further study (Holum & Gahala, 2001). Some electronic books may offer searchable text that enables children to locate and revisit information with ease. For children with minor visual impairments, the text often can be displayed in a larger font.

Links with Literature
Poetry and Stories in Verse

If children are to hear, use, and appreciate the beauty of language they need opportunities to speak beautiful words. By using their speaking voices as instruments, children can recite poetry, stories, and chants in a number of different ways.

- *Chants and raps.* Some books are written as a chant. After children have learned the words to the book, these chants can be recited. Children can use the rhyming structure of rap songs to create their own raps.
- *Fingerplays.* In one of the first kinds of choral speaking used with young children, a fingerplay, children use their hands to make gestures that accompany the poem. For example, *Playtime Rhymes for Little People* (Finch, 2008) is a collection of fingerplays accompanied by a music CD.
- *Action rhymes.* Children recite while performing actions that usually involve the whole body in enacting or interpreting a short poem or chant.
- *Echo poems.* Another simple form of choral speaking, in which the children simply repeat after the leader.
- *Line-a-child.* Another strategy for choral speaking that works very well with cumulative poems. If the children design pictures or masks or costumes to accompany the poem, each child can step forward and speak his or her line.
- *Unison.* One or a few children begin reading, gradually adding more and more children's voices until the poem becomes louder and more forceful. Or, it can move from loud to soft.

- *Refrains.* A type of choral speaking that involves a leader who speaks most of the poem or chant, with the group responsible for the part that is repeated. This repetition may occur at the beginning, or the refrain can conclude each page.
- *Choral speaking and story songs.* After nearly all of the children can recite a poem, tell a story, or sing a song from memory, this can become the basis for drama. Children may enact the story themselves or they may use different types of visual aids such as simple puppets, a story scroll, a flannelboard, cue cards, or an illustrated chart. For more ideas about books that invite participation, see Grover and Hannegan (2005).

Names to Know (Poets, Poetry Compilers, and Authors of Stories Told in Rhyme)

Arnold Adoff, Dorothy Aldis, Claire Beaton, Marc Brown, Nancy Carlstrom, John Ciardi, Chris L. Demarest, Beatrice deRegniers, Ed Emberley, Tom Feelings, Aileen Fisher, Paul Fleischman, Douglas Florian, Mem Fox, Nikki Giovanni, Eloise Greenfield, Nikki Grimes, Mary Ann Hoberman, Lee Bennett Hopkins, Paul B. Janeczko, X. J. Kennedy, Ruth Krauss, Karla Kuskin, Nancy Larrick, Betsy Lewin, Reeve Lindberg, Myra Cohn Livingston, Anita Lobel, Bill Martin, David McCord, Eve Merriam, Walter Dean Myers, Iona Opie, Jack Prelutsky, Dr. Seuss, Diane Siebert, Rosemary Wells, Elizabeth Winthrop, Audrey Wood, and Jane Yolen.

Online Resources

To view many different resources on teaching the traditional nursery rhymes in Head Start—including dozens of free, nicely illustrated versions of nursery rhymes and seasonal alphabet books to send home with the children—visit a web site called Webbing into Literacy (http://curry.school.virginia.edu).

Go to the Public Broadcasting Service's poetry-theme website for teachers at www.pbs.org/ teachers/earlychildhood/theme/poetry.htm to view episodes of children's educational programs on poetry, play a game with the characters from Marc Brown's Arthur series that enables children to join Fern's Poetry Club, or create poems and pictures at the Between the Lions site.

ELLs

Respecting Cultural Differences in Conversation

The chart below summarizes some the cultural and ethnic differences in nonverbal and verbal communication (Scollon & Scollon, 2000). Take these into consideration as you interact with children, families, and other community members.

Nonverbal

Eye contact.   Is looking someone in the eye a sign of confidence and honesty or a sign of disrespect? For many Native Americans, Asians, and Africans, bowing the head is a sign of respect.

Proximity to the listener.   When do we feel that the physical distance between conversational partners is appropriate? When do we feel that a person is invading our personal space? Americans tend to like a space of at least 18 inches between them and the person they are talking to. People of other cultures often prefer to stand closer when talking.

Body posture.   Do we lean closer when discussing a confidential topic or stare off into space? For many Japanese, the latter would be more appropriate when discussing a sensitive subject.

Gestures.   How do we gesture to someone else to walk in front of us, for example? With a sweep of the arm? By stepping back several paces? By a thrust of the chin? Some of the gestures that are obscene in one culture have no such meaning in another—for instance, using the middle finger to point.

Touch.   Is a light touch on the arm interpreted as warm and caring or as overly familiar? In France, for example, it is common to greet someone with a kiss on both cheeks, something that makes many Americans uncomfortable.

Verbal

Amount of talk. Does silence make us uncomfortable? How much talk is too much? People from some cultural or ethnic backgrounds may talk much more than others.

Beliefs about the reasons for talking. Is the primary purpose of talking to get to know someone, or must you know someone before you feel comfortable talking? Many middle-class Americans feel that talk is a way to get acquainted, for instance.

Ways in which authority figures and others interact. Is it the person in authority's role to talk, or is it the other person's role to try and create a favorable impression on the person in authority? Some of the parents you will meet, for example, may expect men to be administrators and women to be teachers.

How speakers present themselves. Do you put your best foot forward or expect others to uncover your strengths? Some of the parents and families you will meet from other cultures may teach their child to do the latter.

Who controls the topic. Does the person who initiates contact have control over the topic? In the United States, the person who initiates a telephone call is expected the take the lead in the conversation.

Amount of explicitness. Do we paint a vivid, detailed picture, or do we expect listeners to fill in the blanks? Many middle-class Americans tend to be impatient with long, detailed explanations and feel that the speaker is telling them more than they want or need to know.

Concepts of politeness. Is it always impolite to interrupt? It is not unusual for Italians to interrupt and see it as the sign of a lively conversation.

Ways of expressing ideas. Should we reveal ourselves to the listener or try to keep our feelings confidential? In this age of "confessional" journalism and talk shows in the United States, we discuss things openly that people in many other cultures would consider to be very private.

Time lapses between speaking turns. Is there a critical point at which the listener feels that the conversation is moving too slowly? Some people tend to want the dialogue to move quickly and are impatient or uncomfortable with lapses in conversation.

Departure rituals. Are there ways of signaling that the conversation is over? If these ways are violated, is the listener offended? For instance, when talking on the telephone, are we insulted when a person simply hangs up without saying good-bye?

 HOW DO I ...

Encourage Extended Conversation with a Young Child?

The secret to conversing with a young child is to step back and listen (Stephenson, 2009). Conversing with a young child is an important skill that will require you to

- Identify with children's needs, interests, and perspectives.
- Follow the child's lead and make all of your statements related to what the child just said.
- Support children as they move back and forth between their inner thoughts and speaking about their thoughts.

This can be accomplished through four basic strategies (McNeill & Fowler, 1996).

Expansions, in which the adult elaborates on what the child has to say. For instance, if the child says, "Read my book," you might respond, "Oh, you want me to read your favorite book to you now."

Extensions, in which the adult adds new information. For example, if a child says, "We're getting fish at school," the adult might say, "Yes, I heard that you are going to have goldfish and that everyone is going to take turns taking care of them."

Clarifying questions, which show adults expressing genuine interest in what the child has to say.

Clarifying questions should relate to topics that children know something about—ideally, the child should know even more about the topic than the teacher does (Hendrick & Weissman, 2009). For example, after a child says, "And I can jump rope really good," the teacher might ask, "What rhymes do you say when you are jumping rope? . . . I'll have to listen and watch at recess today!"

Answers to questions, which can be simple answers to simple questions (e.g., "When is story time?"). However, when you answer children's questions, try to "listen between the lines" and figure out what the child really wants to know. The child who asks, "Why is your belly big? Are you pregnant?" is not trying to pry or insult the adult. Rather, the child is simply curious about why that person looks different. When you respond to children's questions, always strive to make the connection clear between what the child is asking and your response.

To test your skills in conversing with a child, do the following:

1. Arrange to conduct an extended conversation with a young child. You will probably want to choose a child who has sufficient speech to communicate (ages 3–8).

2. Your goal is to really converse with the child, so try to meet with a child who knows you and feels comfortable talking with you. Get the parents' permission to record the conversation in writing or on audio or video.

3. Collect some pictures that are likely to interest a child. You may want to bring some children's books along. Make certain that all of your materials and equipment are ready.

4. Begin by introducing yourself. Tell the child that you want to talk with him or her about favorite things. Allow the child to select whatever picture he or she likes and begin the conversation.

5. During the course of the conversation, relate every one of your comments and questions to whatever the child just said.

6. Use all four of the research-based strategies to enhance children's speech: expansions, extensions, clarifying questions, and answers to the child's questions.

7. List the strategies in item 6 above and transcribe excerpts from the recording that illustrate how you used each one.

8. Be prepared to share your example of each language strategy in class.

PEARSON myeducationkit™ Now go to Chapter 5 in the MyEducationKit (**www.MyEducationKit .com**) for your book, where you can:

- Find Chapter Objectives.
- Complete Assignments and Activities that can help you more deeply understand the chapter content.
- Extend knowledge with content-specific Web Links.
- Check your comprehension on the content covered in the chapter by going to the Study Plan. Here you will be able to take a chapter quiz, receive feedback on your answers, and then access resources that will enhance your understanding of chapter content.

Shutterstock

chapter six

Using Narrative and Expository Texts to Foster Growth in Literacy

FACT FILE on Narrative and Expository Texts

• Young children develop autobiographical memory through discussing personally significant events. When there is no one with whom to share family stories, autobiographical memory does not develop fully because children's recollections are not reinforced (Nelson, 1999, 2007).

• In the United States, various ethnic and cultural groups have strong oral storytelling traditions (Heath, 1983). Storytelling is an important way to preserve traditions and transmit the values of specific cultural groups such as aboriginal people (Gomez & Grant, 1990;

McKeough et al., 2008). Often, these stories are accompanied by ceremonies, art, dance, and important lessons (De Marrais, Nelson, & Baker, 1994).

• One way of demonstrating respect for other cultures is to include distinctive community storytelling styles in the curriculum (Lotherington, Holland, Sotoudeh, & Zentena, 2008; McKeough et al., 2008; Meesook, 2003; Park & King, 2003; Riojas-Cortez, Flores, Smith, & Clark, 2003).

• European Americans tend to tell stories with a single topic focus and a definite beginning, middle, and end. The stories of African American children tend to include more than one topic, flow freely from one event to the next, and emphasize personal meaning and engagement (Bloome, Champion, Katz, Morton, & Muldrow, 2001; Hale-Benson, 1986). Unfortunately, their narrative abilities may be judged as inferior by educators with different assumptions about what constitutes a good story.

• In 2002, the federal government enacted the No Child Left Behind Act into law (www .ed.gov/policy/elsec/leg/esea02/index.html). Every state was required to develop academic standards, and as these standards were implemented, a greater emphasis was placed on children's ability to understand and produce the language of information, or *expository texts* (Snow, Griffin, & Burns, 2005).

• The use of nonfiction literature in primary classrooms offers a variety of instructional opportunities such as teacher-directed instruction, scaffolded student investigations, or independent student investigations (McInnes, Humphries, Hogg-Johnson, & Tannock, 2003; Palmer & Stewart, 2005).

• It is important for teachers to present informational texts interactively, particularly for English language learners, so that children are engaged in the material (McGee & Morrow, 2005; Ranker, 2009). Working with factual material supports young children in building vocabulary and comprehension skills (Read, Reutzel, & Fawson, 2008; Yopp & Yopp, 2004).

• The use of expository texts in the early childhood years may help children to better transition into the increased use of informational textbooks as they enter third and fourth grades (Best, Floyd, & McNamara, 2008).

Did any of this information surprise you? If so, what? Why? How will you use this knowledge to educate and care for the very young?

What Are Narrative and Expository Texts?

The term *narrative* refers to event-structured material—in other words, *stories* (Engle, 1995). Stories may be real, such as biographies, or imaginary, such as fairy tales. Narratives include sharing accounts of relatively recent personal experiences, retellings of traditional or familiar stories, or original stories that are products of the imagination.

PEARSON
myeducationkit™

Go to the Assignments and Activities
section of Chapter 6 in MyEducationKit
and complete the activity entitled
"Studying Birds."

Expository texts are very different. They are not plot driven, like stories; rather, they are designed to explain, describe, or present a logical argument. If you visited your local bookstore and went to the sections on cooking, self-help, home repairs, sports, and politics, you would be looking at expository texts.

To further explain the difference between narrative and expository texts, consider two books about dogs. A child could listen to the true tale of *A Lucky Dog: Owney, U.S. Rail Mascot* (Wales, 2003) or hear an imaginary account of a family's decision to visit a shelter and adopt two dogs, *"Let's Get a Pup!" Said Kate* (Graham, 2003). Both of these books are narratives because they are structured by the events in the story. On the other hand, if a child were to read a story about how to choose or train a puppy, that would be an expository text. Figure 6.1 (on pp. 128–129) compares and contrasts narrative and expository picture books with multicultural themes.

As children gain more experience with the language of explanation, they learn to interact more productively with expository-type text (Duke & Kays, 1998). Educators are therefore being urged to read not only story books but also information books aloud to children, to discuss these books with children, and to guide children in understanding the different features and expectations for readers that are associated with expository texts (McGee & Morrow, 2005; Richgels, 2003).

Even though the primary purpose of an expository text is to present new information, one of the trends in children's literature is to combine both narrative and expository texts in the same book. The Magic Schoolbus series, which presents science facts through stories about Miss Frizzle's class field trips, is a good example of this blend of story and information. The How Do I? section in this chapter on pages 145–146 provides guidance on selecting and using information books.

Stories are equally important in the lives of children. All around the world, in hundreds of different languages, children speak these same words: "Tell me a story." Why are children so enthralled by stories?

> Stories think for themselves, once we know them. They not only attract and light up everything relevant in our own experience, they are also little factories of understanding. New revelations of meaning open out of their images and patterns continually, stirred into reach by our own growth and changing circumstances. (Hughes, 1988, pp. 34–35)

We use stories to reflect on, organize, and communicate what it means to be human (Jensen, 2006; Nelson, 2007). Stories make important contributions to children's lives and literacy growth. Why do children beg adults to tell and read stories? One author imagined that if young children could put into words what they gain from stories, they might say things like the following:

> Read me a story so that I can travel beyond my world. Read me a story so that I can imagine pictures of unseen things. Read me a story so that I can hear words—words to ponder, words to reside inside my head, words that I safely tuck away until I create my own story someday. (Terry, 1989, p. 49)

Let me read stories so that I can discover how real writers write. Let me discuss stories so that I can learn the secrets of story making. Let me write stories so that I can grow and develop as a writer. Let me share my stories so that I may enjoy the pleasure of authorship. (adapted from Terry, 1989, p. 56)

After children have heard many different stories, they learn how to formulate and share their own stories. Although we may use the word *story* in everyday conversation to refer to event-structured material, when the word is used to talk about children's literature, the meaning is more specific. Where children's literature is concerned, two elements are introduced: nonliterality and change. *Nonliterality* means that the story is more than a factual report of a real-life event. The second element, *change*, is equally important. If no changes take place as a character pursues the goal, then it is not a story. A "story is something happening to someone you have been led to care about. . . . Whatever its subject matter, every story is about change" (Shulevitz, 1985, pp. 7, 47). Narrative and expository texts have a common goal, for whether the child is reading a fairy tale or a "how-to" book about gardening, the ultimate goal is for him or her not only to comprehend various types of texts but also to produce them (Duke, 2003).

Collaboration with Families and Professionals

Craig works in a before-and-after-school child-care program for children in the primary grades. As a project for his children's literature course at the community college, he has decided to focus on the two major types of texts: narrative and expository.

Standards in Education
Each year, the National Council for Social Studies publishes a list of notable children's books that can be downloaded free at www.socialstudies.org/notable. Each book is reviewed using quality standards, annotated (briefly described), and keyed to the social studies standards. The most appropriate grade levels are indicated as P = Primary (pre-K–2) and I = Intermediate (3–5).

PEARSON myeducationkit
Go to the Assignments and Activities section of Chapter 6 in MyEducationKit and complete the activity entitled "Understanding Disabilities."

As an introduction to narrative text, Craig works with the children to develop a web or map of ideas and clusters their understandings about stories into three categories: (1) different kinds of stories (stories in books, family stories, fairy tales), (2) why people like stories (funny, surprising, interesting characters, exciting), and (3) ways to tell stories (storytellers, books, puppets, films, plays). Craig decides to mobilize all of the resources in his community to make the storytelling theme come alive. Among the people he contacts are the children's services librarian, a troupe of storytellers from the college who use sign language to tell stories, a college professor of early childhood education who is a storyteller, family members (particularly grandparents) who can be interviewed about family stories, and a master's degree student who did her thesis on multicultural stories. Additionally, Craig refers to several print and Internet sources, including a unit on storytellers in *Teaching Young Children Using Themes* (Kostelnik, 1991), *Stories in the Classroom: Storytelling, Reading Aloud, and Role Playing with Children* (Barton & Booth, 1990), and the Handbook for Storytellers website (http://42explore.com/story.htm).

FIGURE 6.1 Comparison of Narrative and Expository Texts

Narrative Texts	Expository Texts
Texts that are event structured and in story form, both oral and written	Texts that offer factual information and explanation, both oral and written
Features	**Features**
Has characters with whom children can identify	Offers general statements about characteristics of and relations among events and objects
Illustrations are often fanciful	Illustrations are realistic (e.g., diagrams, figures, visual models)
Frequently uses a chronological order	Uses various text patterns—question/answer, cause/effect, compare/contrast, problem/solution
General Examples	**General Examples**
Biographies, autobiographies, folk and fairy tales	"All-about," "How-to," and "How-it-works" books

Multicultural Children's Literature Examples

Race

Black Is Brown Is Tan (Adoff, 1997, 2002). A poem about the different skin colors in a loving interracial family.

All The Colors We Are: The Story of How We Get Our Skin Color (Kissinger, 1997). A simple explanation of how melanin determines skin color; illustrated with photographs of children.

Art

Marianthe's Story: Painted Words and Spoken Memories (Aliki, 1998). A new English language learner struggles to communicate with her new classmates until she discovers the language of art.

The Art Book for Children (Ruggi, 2005). A child's introduction to art, illustrated with reproductions of paintings by famous artists across the ages.

Weaving

Abuela's Weave (Castaneda, 1995). A Guatemalan child learns about love, family, and the craft of weaving from her grandmother.

One Little Lamb (Greenstein, 2004). A simple, step-by-step account of how wool turns into clothing.

The Chief's Blanket (Chanin, 1998). A story set in the 1800s about a young girl who learns the craft of weaving from her grandmother.

Songs from the Loom: A Navajo Girl Learns to Weave (Roessel, 1995). A photo essay of contemporary Navajo blanket weavers from the We Are Still Here: Native Americans Today series.

FIGURE 6.1 Continued

Piñatas

A Piñata in a Pine Tree: A Latino Twelve Days of Christmas (Mora, 2009). A twist on the traditional counting rhyme that incorporates vocabulary in Spanish.

Piñata! (Emberley, 2004). Following a brief factual explanation, this book tells the story of piñatas.

The Piñata Maker (El piñatero) (Ancona, 1994). This bilingual photo essay explains how piñatas are constructed.

Cut Paper Art

The Origami Master (Lachenmeyer, 2008). A Japanese artist uses his creations to keep him company and finds a new friend in this tale illustrated with cut paper art.

Magic Windows (Ventanas Mágicas). (Garza, 1999). Instructions on making eight different folded and cut tissue paper designs.

Dolls throughout the World

The Magic Nesting Doll (Ogburn, 2005). A matryoshka (Russian nesting doll) has the power to grant three wishes in this fairy tale.

Cornhusk, Silk, and Wish-Bones: A Book of Dolls from Around the World (Markell, 2000). A photo tour of 26 different dolls from five continents that shows the array of materials dolls are made of and where each type of doll is made on a world map.

The Wheat Doll (Randall, 2008). In nineteenth-century Utah, a young girl loses her beloved doll during a storm but finds it once again.

Babushka's Doll (Polacco, 1995). A Russian doll comes to life in this fanciful story.

Navajo Dance

Jingle Dancer (Smith, 2000). A young girl learns how to make her regalia and participate in the traditional dance of her people.

The Navajo (Santella, 2002). A factual account of the tribe from the True Books: American Indians series.

Clay

Gugu's House (Stock, 2001). A child from Zimbabwe lives in a thatched-roof house that is covered with abstract patterns and clay sculptures. The rain washes the colors away.

Big Messy Art Book (Kohl, 2000). Instructions on art projects that include painting and working with clay.

As an introduction to expository text, Craig invites the children to generate a list of things they want to be able to do or know more about. Their list includes playing baseball, baking a cake, growing vegetables, riding a dirt bike, and so forth. For each topic, Craig invites speakers and works with the librarian to collect an assortment of books. In addition, family members bring in treasured objects and tell or write the stories of those objects. These items are put in a lighted display case in the hallway, and parent volunteers work to translate and type cards that briefly tell why each item has significance for the family.

About this project, Craig says, "By focusing on narrative and expository forms of writing, we were able to celebrate differences as well as sense our common bonds. Because children helped to plan the theme, they were very excited about both types of reading and writing."

Contributions and Consequences

- *Contributions of the teacher:* What role did the teacher play in this project?
- *Contributions of the family:* How did the families get involved?
- *Contributions of other professionals:* How did professionals in other fields contribute to the project?
- *Consequences of collaboration:* How might this story have ended differently if the various adults had not shared and supported the project?

Overview of Children's Narrative and Expository Styles

PEARSON
myeducationkit™

Go to the Assignments and Activities section of Chapter 6 in MyEducationKit and complete the activity entitled "Storytime with Miss Joan."

PEARSON
myeducationkit™

Go to the Assignments and Activities section of Chapter 6 in MyEducationKit and complete the activity entitled "Becoming a Surgeon."

Narrative Text

By the time children reach the age of 3 to 4 years, most begin to tell stories. Children's stories give adults a glimpse into their higher-level cognitive processes, their representations of themselves, their understandings of tasks, and their inferences about their listeners (Engle, 1995; Nelson, 2007; Nelson, Aksu-Koc, & Johnson, 2001). Children's own stories tend to begin at home and gradually move farther away (Applebee, 1978). Very young children's narratives are usually about home and family. Here is 3-year-old Nicholas telling his cat's story:

> I have a Cat name Sammy Cat 'cause I like it. My dad wanted me to name Sammy Cat "Top Cat," but I want Sammy name better. Mummy likes mine name better for Sammy too.

Here is Sarah, age 4, telling about her puppy:

> I got a new puppy, Mommy-Daddy got me a new puppy. We all got to name him and, uhm, his name is Rusty. Mommy gets all mad when he pees on the new carpet. But, but I play with him and I throw him his ball and he chews on my shoes.

With ample opportunities to enjoy stories, a child's use of literary style may emerge quite early. By the age of 5, most children with experience listening to stories use these elements of literary style:

- They give titles to their stories.
- They begin using a formal opening ("Long ago and far away") and closing ("The End").
- They use the past tenses of verbs to describe story events.
- They use their voices expressively when telling their stories so that listeners will pay closer attention.
- They begin to use elements of surprise and suspense.

Brain and Language

There are correlations among brain development, language acquisition, and cognition (Wasserman, 2007). Brain research suggests that children raised in nonacademically oriented environments tend to communicate more about the immediate context and rely on concrete visual images, physical activities, and symbolic representations (Rushton & Larkin, 2001). How might narrative texts and the dramatic arts—puppetry, storytelling, and creative drama—be used to build on the strengths of children with few prior school-like experiences?

The characters in children's stories generally reflect the following progression (Nicolopoulou & Richner, 2007). At first, characters are like action figures—they are all about the physical actions that they perform and sometimes seem to be involved in a never-ending series of adventures (Gardner, 1980).

Next, the characters in children's stories become "agents" with hints of the characters' mental states. Often it is not until age 5 or 6 that the characters in children's stories express thoughts, intentions, and feelings. Here is 6-year-old Courtney's story about a duck character:

Once upon a time there was a little boy, and the little boy had a little duck. The duck's name was Quacker, and the boy's name was Tommy. Every morning and night, Tommy fed his little duck. And one morning the duck has three babies, two boys and one girl. The boy's name was Mike, and one of the girl's names was Cindy. The other girl's name was Bethany. The end.

Kindergarten and early primary-grade narratives often have a unifying theme that connects events and attempts to explain when and why (Stadler & Ward, 2005). The settings tend to venture beyond home (school, the zoo, the museum) or indefinite places (such as the forest, outer space, or the jungle). Here is 6-year-old Justin's account of his heart surgery:

I had a pink robe and a bed with three yanks [an adjustable bed]. I was hooked up to an IV. One day a nurse came in and said, "Justin, we're going to take your picture." It got put in the newspaper. Mommy bought me a new tractor. I was real sick and nauseated. I had the flu with a bad fever. I ate lots of Popsicles. I wasn't scared—just sick! There were 25 doctors. I was there 3 days. I saw a guy with a broken leg in a wheelchair. They took my blood. They had a big needle and stuck it in my arm [he demonstrates]. My dad was there and it didn't hurt a bit.

The picture Justin drew about his hospital stay is shown in Figure 6.2.

Children's stories may simply stop without any feeling of conclusion or "wrapping up," as in the following story by Mitchell, age 6:

Chester and the Leprechaun

One day after a big rain in Connecticut, Chester was hopping along. Then, all of a sudden, he saw a rainbow. He figured he would hop over and see if anybody was there. All he found was a big, black pot. On the pot he saw a little man dressed in green, with a

FIGURE 6.2   Justin's Account of His Hospital Stay

hat that had a three-leaf clover on it. He remembered what Tucker had told him about a leprechaun before he had left.

By the time children are in second or third grade, they often orchestrate different characteristics of stories from their cultures and write stories that have themes or central ideas. They learn to *chain*, or link events to one another, and they learn to *center*, or unify those events with a theme or focus (Applebee, 1978). Stories of older children may include dialogue between and among characters and an expanded time frame. Endings to their stories give a feeling of "wrapping up" rather than just stopping. Third-grader Jillian's story and picture in Figure 6.3 illustrate this level of narrative:

Freddy the Balloon

There was once a hot air balloon named Freddy. Freddy lived in Hawaii, but no one liked Freddy and his friends because he had nothing to weight him down. Everyone was scared to use him. One day the mayor said, "These balloons have to go!" Freddy cried "I want to be used, not thrown away!" But it didn't help. He was sent to New York, split up from his friends and gone forever. Ten years later, he was found by a wise man. "We can make use of this thing," he said. "All we need are some bags of sand." Freddy was

FIGURE 6.3   Jillian's Freddy the Balloon Drawing

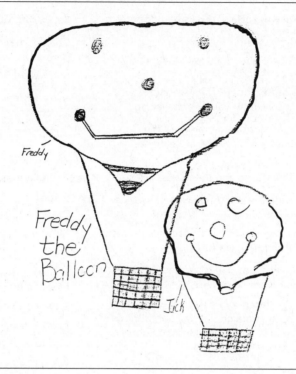

so excited he jumped. He went up, up, up. The only person who ever saw him after that was his friend Jack, while he was flying.

It is said that he landed on the moon, and if you look close, you can see him smiling at night. It is also said that when anyone tries to touch or harm a balloon, Freddy zaps them back in time, never to return.

Figure 6.4 summarizes traditional story elements, gives examples of books, and suggests activities to develop young children's understandings of literary elements.

Expository Text

Kostelnik (1991) offers a useful structure for thinking about the real-world information of expository texts. In order for students to understand it, they need to master certain terminology *(terms)*, acquire accurate basic concepts *(facts)*, and discover underlying concepts *(principles)*. If, for instance, children are learning about houses and homes, they might acquire new terms such as *habitat*. They might learn facts, such as that people and animals both need shelter, and principles, such as that the types of

FIGURE 6.4   Traditional Story Elements

Setting: WHERE does the story happen?

Activities

- Make a mural of the setting or a scenery/backdrop.

  Suggested book: The Napping House as it goes from napping to waking

- Create shoebox dioramas of the settings.

  *Suggested book: The mouse hole home of *The Mouse and the Motorcycle*

- Change the setting of a story, such as an urban version of a farm story.

  Suggested book: Old MacDonald Had an Apartment House

- Imagine what would happen if the environment changed.

  *Suggested book: What if there was a blizzard at the end of Raymond Briggs's *Snowman* instead of sunshine to melt the snow?

Characters: WHO is in the story?

Activities

- Do a character contrast that compares good/bad characters.

  Suggested book: Mufaro's Beautiful Daughters

- Transform a character.

  *Suggested book: Make *Noisy Nora* quiet

- Create colorful masks for each character.

  Suggested book: Who's in Rabbit's House?

Plot: WHAT happens in the story? What events occur?

Activities

- Make a story map of a character's travels.

  Suggested book: Anno's Journey

- Change the story sequence by writing a prequel or sequel.

  Suggested book: Jumanji

- Make a diagram of the characters' actions.

  Suggested book: Over in the Meadow

Theme: WHY was this story written? What is the main message?

Activities

- Change the moral of the story in a folktale or fable.

  Suggested book: The Foolish Frog

- Try to represent the theme through music or art.

  Suggested book: Barn Dance!

- Make a "tall tale" into a "small tale" that tells about ordinary deeds.

  Suggested book: Swamp Angel

Style: HOW is the story written? How does the author use language?

Activities

- Try to follow the author's lead and imitate the author's style.

  Suggested book: A Story, a Story

- List key words that contributed to the author's style.

  Suggested book: The Wall

- Find another author with a similar style.

  Suggested books: Compare Margaret Wise Brown and Charlotte Zolotow, James Stevenson and Steven Kellogg homes people construct are affected by the climate, available materials, and cultural traditions.

In terms of a developmental sequence, you need only look to children's literature to see the progression. The youngest children's information book is a series of labels under a category, such as farm animals. As children's thinking matures, their information books supply a few interesting facts about the topic around a central theme.

The most sophisticated understanding emerges when children get the underlying principles. As described by McGee and Morrow (2005), "Information books explain rather than merely describe phenomena of the social, physical, or natural world" (p. 59).

When sharing information books, it is important for teachers to define key terms, to make comments that show how ideas are interconnected, to use words and phrases that point out relationships ("because," "that is why . . ."), to recap information periodically ("So, the steps in the process are . . ."), and to invite children to explain and retell while using the new vocabulary they have acquired.

Here is a recommended procedure for interactive read-alouds of information books with English language learners:

1. Segment the book into sections.
2. Introduce the text and three new vocabulary words prior to reading each section.
3. Draw children's attention to each of the three vocabulary words by supplying a definition, pointing out something in the picture, or dramatizing/pantomiming.
4. Ask three questions: two that require recall and one that is inferential.
5. Reread the section of the text, and emphasize the vocabulary words.
6. Encourage the children to demonstrate their comprehension by recalling elements of the book, connecting with their experiences, or explaining vocabulary in their own words (Hickman, Pollard-Durodola, & Vaughn, 2004).

Teacher Concerns and Basic Strategies

Infants and Toddlers
Caregivers who share books effectively with infants and toddlers use the pictures as the basis for interaction with a child and relate the story to the child's experiences (Bus, 2001). They make the story all about the child—saying, for instance, "Look, the baby's in a carseat. You ride in a carseat. Where did you go today?" Survey the class to see who has experience reading to an infant or toddler. Were they successful? Did they use these practices?

Some teachers question the use of expository text with young children. As first-grade teacher Gemma stated:

> I'm used to reading stories aloud, and I'm not convinced that children will be interested in books that are just full of information.

When thinking about types of books for students, consider not just your past experiences and personal preferences but the interests of all of your students. The same child who does not pay attention to a fairy tale may surprise you by giving her or his full attention to a book about building a tree house, for example. Gender may influence the book choices of elementary teachers, and because the vast majority of elementary teachers are female, books that hold greater interest for boys are some-times overlooked.

Head Start teacher Tekerra wondered, "What is the point of learning to tell a story if you already have the book?"

The original way of sharing stories was to tell them. Advocates of storytelling therefore argue that young children need to experience the direct sharing of stories because it is part of their cultural backgrounds. Learning to tell a story to young children is not such a difficult task (Bauer, 1983, 1987, 1993; Sawyer, 1998). Actually, you probably already know several stories well enough to tell rather than read them.

Sometimes those stories are traditional ones that you have heard many times—stories such as "Goldilocks and the Three Bears," "Little Red Riding Hood," and "The Three Little Pigs." Folksongs that tell stories, such as "Six Little Ducks" and narrative poems such as "The House That Jack Built" also are appropriate.

Recordings by storytellers can also be very helpful in learning a story. You can listen while traveling or as you straighten up your classroom after school. Watching videos of storytellers in action, attending a storyteller's live performance, participating in a storytelling workshop, or asking the local librarian to tell stories to your class are all good ways to get started with storytelling.

There are several factors to consider when sharing stories:

- *Appropriateness.* Choose a story that appeals to you and your listeners. Match the story with the conceptual level of the audience.
- *Quality.* A story should be worth the time that you will have to invest to learn it. It should have a compact, action-filled plot with a clear sequence of events; provide a clear underlying theme; present well-defined characters and memorable dialogue; use language effectively (e.g., repeat colorful phrases, use alliteration and rhyme); and build to a satisfying conclusion (Glazer & Giorgis, 2008; Ollila & Mayfield, 1992).
- *Presentation.* Plan to capture the children's interest immediately. Figure out if the story needs to be adapted in any way. Pace your telling by changing the tempo when appropriate and using pauses effectively. Experiment with the tone and pitch of your voice, and use facial expressions and hand gestures for dramatic effect.
- *Participation.* Consider where the children might chime in (e.g., "I'm not afraid") or where you might ask a question ("So do you think that Henny Penny should trust the fox?").
- *Practice.* Know the story and practice telling it until there is no chance of forgetting it.

Of course, children can function as the storytellers as they retell and enact familiar tales.

PEARSON
myeducationkit

Go to the Assignments and Activities section of Chapter 6 in MyEducationKit and complete the activity entitled "Individual Story Time."

Classroom Activities to Support Children's Mastery of Narrative and Expository Texts

Research and Report
Borrow a book on storytelling, listen or watch a recording (audio or video), or attend a live storytelling performance. As you experience the story, make some notes on how the performer made the story memorable. Which strategies could you add to your repertoire?

PEARSON myeducationkit™

Go to the Assignments and Activities section of Chapter 6 in MyEducationKit and complete the activity entitled "Group Story Time."

Effective teachers balance children's literacy "diets" by using both narrative and expository texts, as shown in the activities that follow.

Interviews and Stories   After a teacher told the Hans Christian Andersen story "The Ugly Duckling" to a small group of first-graders, she interviewed them "in character":

Teacher: Mother Duck, are you worried about your baby duckling?

Maria: I felt mad, but I wasn't worried.

Teacher: Ugly Duckling, how did you feel after you turned into the beautiful swan?

Urie: I wanted to go back to the barnyard and show everyone that I turned out to be very pretty.

Teacher: After you became a swan, how did the others treat you?

Kirsten: They treated me with respect, and they said they were sorry.

Information books lend themselves to an interview format, as well. For students in the primary grades, conducting interviews with community resource people—such as a musician to share *Zin! Zin! Zin! A Violin* (Moss, 1995) and a Civil War reenactor to share *Pink and Say* (Polacco, 1994) can bring narrative and expository texts together.

Storytelling with Props   Use real or representative objects to introduce a character, underscore a key concept, build suspense, or surprise listeners (Cliatt & Shaw, 1988). Two videotapes by Caroline Feller Bauer (1986, 1997) are excellent examples of traditional and modern storytelling with props. She uses line drawings on the chalkboard to tell *Monkey Face* (Asch, 1977) and a stuffed toy dog to recite "Mother Doesn't Want a Dog," from Judith Viorst's (1982) collection of poems, *If I Were in Charge of the World and Other Worries.*

A collection of real objects can be used to tell Catherine Stock's (1985) *Sophie's Bucket,* a story about a girl's day at the beach. Sophie gets two packages at the beginning of the story: a swimsuit and a plastic bucket and shovel. While she is at the beach, she plays in the sand, looks at the seaweed, finds a starfish, watches a pink crab, and saves some seawater in a jar. Each of these objects can be introduced at the appropriate time as the story is shared with young children. Factual books about sea life can also be shared to complement the story.

Television Program   An information book can be converted into an educational program format—a cooking show to go with a cookbook for children, a demonstration to go with a "how-to" book of magic tricks, and so forth.

Pocket Stories   The teacher can introduce story characters as they enter the story by using an apron with pockets. Most adults are familiar with the counting song that begins "There were 10 in the bed and the little one said, 'Roll over!' " This story song can be shared with children using paper or small toys. The characters from Merle Peek's (1981) illustrated picture book version can be used to create the 10 characters in the story, and 10 pockets can serve as a "headboard" for the bed. At the beginning, each character should be positioned inside a pocket; each is then removed when "they all rolled over and one fell out." Pocket stories can also be used with photographs of a real sequence (e.g., from egg to chick) or with real objects (e.g., different types of plants, shells, or rocks).

Draw and Tell/Fold and Cut   Some stories, such as Paul Zelinsky's (1981) *The Maid, the Mouse, and the Odd-Shaped House*, can be drawn as the story is told. Other stories can be illustrated by the teller's paper cutouts of simple objects, such as a jack-o'-lantern used to tell a story about a pumpkin (see Hart, 1987). These stories can be combined with information books such as *From Seed to Pumpkin* (Pfeffer, 2004).

Presentations   After third-graders met a retired racing greyhound named Cuddles and saw a PowerPoint presentation with facts about this type of dog, they asked thoughtful and surprising questions. One boy asked, "When Cuddles was racing, what was her number?" A girl asked, "Can I look at the tattoos inside her ears?" And another child asked, "Will you show us her family tree online?"

Participatory Telling   Children can participate in storytelling, both through speaking the words and enacting the events (Schwartz & Bone, 1995; Stewig, 1994). *The Fat Cat* (Kent, 1972) or *Fat Cat: A Danish Folktale* (MacDonald, 2001) is a story in which a cat devours everyone he meets on the road until a woodcutter's axe helps them to escape. One interesting way of telling the story is to make a large cardboard face for the cat and attach it to a paint stirrer or ruler. Then pull the stick through a hole cut in the center of an old sheet and have a child stand underneath it. As the teacher tells the story, other children who are playing the characters crawl underneath the sheet, causing the Fat Cat to expand rapidly. When the Woodsman intervenes, the other characters emerge in reverse order until the cat is reduced to his original size. As a grand finale, the children can wrap a strip of sheet around the Fat Cat's "incision."

Three-Dimensional Puppets   Two student teachers created a caterpillar puppet that metamorphoses, just like the one in Eric Carle's (1969) *The Very Hungry Caterpillar*. For the beginning of the story, the student teachers created a large leaf backdrop and wiggled the little finger of an old glove through the center to represent the caterpillar crawling on the leaf. They switched to a larger finger of the glove as the caterpillar grew, and the fully grown caterpillar was made from the hand and wrist portions stitched together and stuffed with polyester fiberfill. For the book's final scene, they made a butterfly from nylon stockings stretched over two metal hangers and decorated with brightly colored fabric scraps. As the "chrysalis" wriggled and dropped off the stage, the butterfly first appeared with the wire in the hangers bent; then the hangers were expanded fully and the butterfly appeared to flutter out from underneath the stage. (In this book, the chrysalis is incorrectly labeled as a *cocoon*. Moths, not butterflies, make cocoons.) So it is a great opportunity to read information books about butterflies or actually have them emerge from their chrysalises in the classroom.

Dressing the Part In Arnold Lobel's (1980) *Fables*, the story "The Bear and the Crow" is about a vain and foolish bear who tries to impress others with his finery. On the way into town, the bear meets a crow, who tells him that his attire is completely out of fashion. Librarian Paige Price tells the fable to children by dressing herself in the latest style, just as the crow recommends: with a frying pan on her head, paper bags on her feet, and a bedsheet wrapped around her middle. When the bear arrives in town, he is the object of ridicule, and as he runs home, he meets the crow again. "'Crow, you did not tell me the truth!' cried the bear. 'I told you many things,' said the Crow, as he flew out of the tree, 'but never once did I tell you that I was telling the truth!'" (p. 16).* Even though the message of a fable can be too abstract for young children, making it concrete through ridiculous attire enables even preschoolers to understand the moral of the story: "When the need is strong, some people will believe anything."

Poster and Flannelboard Cutouts *Jennie's Hat* (Keats, 1966) can be built by the storyteller at the flannelboard with pieces of brightly colored felt. Some other good choices for the flannelboard are Charles Shaw's (1947) classic *It Looked Like Spilt Milk* and the folktales "The Three Billy Goats Gruff" and "Little Red Riding Hood." (Use Dick Bruna's [1966] version of the latter story for the patterns.)

Storytelling with Toys The classic story *The Mitten* (Brett, 1989) is another good one to tell with props. The basic theme is found in many cultures: that there is not always room for one more. The story begins when a mitten is left in the forest and a series of different animals crawl inside to get warm. Eventually, the mitten bursts at the seams, and all the animals go back into the forest. To tell the story with toys, cut out a giant mitten from fabric and tack the edges together with a temporary adhesive, such as a gluestick. Then collect small, stuffed toys to represent the forest animals and squeeze them inside until the mitten comes apart at the story's conclusion.

Pam Conrad's (1989) *The Tub People* is an imaginative picture book about the adventures of the pudgy, miniature plastic figures that are often used as tub toys by children. You might set up the water play area with similar toys and invite the children to create original narratives about the toys, perhaps concluding with a video that shows the further adventures of the tub people.

Integrated Approaches   Melissa Renck, a children's librarian, planned a preschool story hour with a camping theme that included storytelling, story reading, singing, and watching a film. First she rolled up brown construction-paper into log shapes and decorated them with streaming orange and yellow crepe paper "flames." When the children arrived, they were seated in a circle around the "campfire." The librarian started the session by assessing the children's prior knowledge with questions such as "What is camping?" "Have any of you ever been camping?" and "What are some of the things you do when you camp out?"

Next, she read the book *Bailey Goes Camping* (Henkes, 1985). Bailey is the littlest bunny in the family, and his older brother and sister get to go camping while he has to stay home. With the help of his parents, Bailey gets to go on a simulated camping trip. He has hot dogs for lunch, goes (teddy) bear hunting, lives in a tent (a blanket over a clothesline), goes swimming and fishing (in the bathtub), tells ghost stories (to his parents), and toasts marshmallows (on the stove).

After the story, the children sang "The Bear Went Over the Mountain." Then the librarian read *Sophie's Knapsack* (Stock, 1988) while unpacking a real knapsack filled with the items from the story. Next, they did the echo chant "Going on a Ghost Hunt," an adaptation of "Going on a Bear Hunt" (Folktellers, 1994). After the librarian told them a ghost story, *Thump, Thump, Thump!* (Rockwell, 1981), the children were anxious to participate in telling stories around the "campfire." Sean told his own version of *A Dark, Dark Tale* (Brown, 1981), while Yolanda shared an embellished version of Mercer Mayer's (1976) *There's a Nightmare in My Closet*. Three-year-old Frank said, "I have one!" and told this one-sentence "scary story," complete with a quavering voice and menacing gestures: "Once there was monster, and he would scratch little children." Other books on camping were made available for borrowing including those with a simple text (e.g., *Maisy Goes Camping*, Cousins, 2009), realistic books with more text (e.g., *When We Go Camping*, Ruurs, 2004), and camping poems (*Toasting Marshmallows*, George, 2001).

The session concluded with sharing the animal crackers that were in the knapsack. This activity can be tied in nicely with expository text by using actual photographs of a camping trip and writing a story to accompany them.

Sensory Experiences with Things in Narrative and Expository Texts   After sharing a book, children can smell, taste, hear, see, and touch what was portrayed in the story. A group of 5-year-olds, for example, made fried bananas after hearing the Philippine folktale *A Crocodile's Tale* (Aruego, 1972), about a monkey who gets a ride across the river to some banana trees by outsmarting a crocodile. Likewise, after hearing the story *Too Many Tamales* (Soto, 1993), second-graders made tamales with the guidance of some parent volunteers (who were very experienced tamale makers) and then created an illustrated book of instructions.

Creative Dramatics Based on Nonfiction Narratives   After hearing a true account of someone's personal experience, children can invent spontaneous dialogue, replay the story with a different cast, create the original or a different setting, and evaluate their efforts. After listening to a reading of *Rosa Parks* (Greenfield, 1973) or *The Story of Ruby Bridges* (Coles, 1995), children can enact the scenes that affected them most deeply. See McCaslin (2006) for more creative dramatics ideas.

Special Storyteller's Objects   Many teachers use a decorated stick or stone to signify whose turn it is to speak and share a story. Only the person who is holding the object is permitted to talk. Others in the group are expected to be attentive listeners. Storytelling sticks or stones are particularly useful when the children are composing a story together. Someone begins the story with one line and then passes the stone to someone else to continue, repeating until the story is finished.

Dialogue Improvisation   One way to teach children how to speak and write the dialogue in stories is to begin with books that have a simple question-and-answer format, such as *Who Is Tapping at My Window?* (Demming, 1988) or *Baby Bear, Baby Bear What Do You See?* (Martin, 2007). After children have had a variety of these experiences with dialogue, they can begin to improvise spoken dialogue or create print versions of dialogue based on picture books.

Conclusion

Knowing the components of both narrative and expository texts is part of being fully literate. Contemporary society is teeming with information, which can be overwhelming at times. Children need guidance as they navigate the Internet and try to decide which sources are credible and which are not. They need to learn how to follow written instructions as well as write them for others. The trend in society is for consumers to manage situations for themselves—to set up their own computers, pump and pay for gasoline, scan their own groceries, manage their own banking transactions. All of this requires the ability to understand information. Moreover, many of tomorrow's children will no doubt be responsible for developing the instructions and designing the procedures that others are to follow in this push toward increased consumer self-sufficiency.

At the opposite end of the spectrum, stories are an ancient "cultural activity through which people participate in complex societies and in which social categories—like age, gender, social class, and ethnicity—matter. Well-known stories are continually articulated anew, as people use them to make some point about the social world they share with others" (Dyson, 1993, p. 393). Through the symbols in stories, children discover answers to these timeless questions: What are people like? Why are they like that? What do they need? What makes them do what they do? (Lukens, 2006).

Storytelling is so fundamental to human existence that common sense might even be conceptualized as "our storehouse of narrative structures" (Shafer, 1981). Narratives are basic in human life because "the world we know is the world we make in words, and all we have after years of work and struggle is the story" (Rouse, 1978, p. 187). When teachers support children's abilities with narrative and expository texts, they simultaneously prepare them to grapple with the information overload of the twenty-first century and connect them with the timeless appeal of stories.

PEARSON myeducationkit To check your comprehension on the content covered in this chapter, go to the MyEducationKit for your book and complete the Study Plan for Chapter 6. Here you will be able to take a chapter quiz and receive feedback on your answers.

Research-Based Literacy Strategies

Storytelling with Digital Technologies

Digital technologies may enhance storytelling in children. Simple and widely available technologies, such as digital photographs, can be the basis for creating a story based on an experience (Bond & Wasik, 2009; Good, 2005–2006). Likewise, children can create a script to accompany a video of a field trip, musical performance, or other event in which the entire class participated. Increasingly, children are using technology—including 2D and 3D—to produce and share digital narratives (Madej, 2003) such as the PBS Kids Share a Story program at http://pbskids .org/sharestory. As computer software for creating stories becomes increasingly sophisticated, children can create characters and physically manipulate the stories (Zhou, 2008). More interactive approaches have appeal for young children who tend to be physically active and captivated by powerful images.

Captioned Video

Many television programs and most DVDs now offer the option of viewing the film with or without captions. (To learn about the different captioning systems and how they work, visit www.robson .org/capfaq/overview.html.) The captions make film more accessible to children with hearing impairments, who can read the captions to understand the visual material (Lewis & Jackson, 2001). Captioned video also provides a print version of oral language so that children viewing can follow along visually as words are pronounced, and English language learners can watch films in their first language as captions translate it into a second language (or vice versa). Teachers use captioned video effectively when they prepare children for viewing the film by building background knowledge, generating interest, making predictions, and so forth. To view tips on how to make the most of captioned video, read the article by Koskinen, Wilson, Gambrell, and Neuman (1993) posted at www.edc.org/FSC/NCIP/ASL_Capvocab .html.

Graphic Organizers

A graphic organizer is a chart or diagram that is used to make thinking more visible. Also referred to as a concept maps or webs, graphic organizers structure information and arrange important aspects of a concept or topic into a visual pattern that is labeled with words (Birbili, 2006; Parks & Black, 1992). The most common graphic organizers are concept maps (with a main vocabulary word/idea and details radiating out from the center), sequence charts (that show a process in step-by-step fashion), compare/ contrast diagrams (such as the Venn diagram), and cause-and-effect diagrams. There is a large body of research that supports using graphic organizers to support comprehension and integrate subject areas (Harvey & Goudvis, 2007; Isenberg & Jalongo, 2009; Yopp & Yopp, 2006). Graphic organizers are most effective when they are consistent (teachers select a few models and use them often), when they are coherent (deal with a limited number of concepts and clearly label the interrelationships among them), and creative (teachers use them at the beginning, middle and end of a lesson; use them for homework/review; pair pictures with words; use them across subject areas; and incorporate them into partner or cooperative group work) (Baxendell, 2003; Nyberg, 1996). Visit the Enchanted Learning website for numerous examples of diagrams (http://members.enchantedlearning.com).

Links with Literature
Folktales

What Is a Folktale?

Folktales are a large body of literature consisting of short stories that reflect the oral storytelling traditions of the masses in various cultures, countries, and eras. Some examples of folktales that are commonly told in the United States would be "The Three Bears," "Little Red Riding Hood," or "The Magic Fish."

What Are the Characteristics of Folktales?

Folktales are particularly well suited to fostering adult/child interaction because these stories tend to focus attention on the relations among reality, beliefs, actions, and motives (Ratner & Olver, 1998). Folktales are also a resource for multicultural education because they are passed from one place to another across time, countries, and cultures (Norton, 2008; Temple, Martinez, Yokota, & Naylor, 2001).

Many folktales attempt to explain why some characteristic of animals or nature exists, like the black iridescence of a crow's feathers and its raspy call in the Native American tale *Rainbow Crow* (Van Laan, 1989) or its Mayan counterpart, *Cuckoo/Cucu'* (Ehlert, 1997). These tales are called *pourquoi* (pronounced poor-QUAH) tales after the French word for "why." Other common features of folktales include patterned openings and endings ("once upon a time . . ." "they lived happily ever after"), a quick presentation of the problem, uncomplicated characters, fast-paced plots, and punishment for villains (Glazer & Giorgis, 2008).

Why Use Folktales?

1. Folktales represent high-quality literature because their form and language have been perfected over time.

2. Folktales have few digressions and build to a satisfying conclusion.
3. Folktales stimulate children's imaginations and foster enjoyment.
4. Folktales often reveal motives and address ethical questions.
5. Folktales preserve each culture's traditions and, at the same time expand children's multicultural and global awareness (Glazer & Giorgis, 2008; Viguers, 1974).

Folktale Retellings

Retellings are a good check on comprehension of a story (Brown & Cambourne, 1990). Follow this procedure for analyzing a child's retelling:

1. Work with a young child between the ages of 3 and 8 who knows you well enough and/or has sufficient confidence to speak with you and share a story.
2. Invite the child to tell you the story that he or she knows and likes.
3. Record the child's retelling of the story.
4. After the story is finished, interview the child with these questions:

   Who told you this story?
   What do you like about this story?
   How did you learn to tell this story? What did you do?
   Do you know some other stories? Which ones?
   Do you like to hear stories? Why or why not?

Names to Know

Alma Flor Ada, Jim Aylesworth, Jan Brett, Marcia Brown, Joseph Bruchac, Demi, Tomie dePaola, Ed

Emberley, Paul Galdone, Betsy Hearne, Rachel Isadora, Steven Kellogg, Nancy Laan, Julius Lester, Margaret Read MacDonald, James Marshall, Jerry Pinkney, Daniel San Souci, Judy Sierra, Uri Shulevitz, Peter Sis, Diane Stanley, Simms Taback, Jane Yolen, Ed Young, and Margot Zemach.

A Sampler of Recently Published Folktales for Young Children

Chicken Little (Emberley, 2009); *Henny Penny* (French, 2007); *Goldilocks and the Three Bears* (Aylesworth, 2003); *Town Mouse Country Mouse* (Brett, 2003); *The Three Little Pigs* (Kellogg, 2003); *The Bremen Town Musicians* (illus. Lai, 2007); *The Fisherman and His Wife* (Isadora, 2008); *This Is the House That Jack Built* (Tabback, 2004); *Martina the Beautiful Cockroach: A Cuban Folktale* (Deedy, 2007).

ELLs
Vocabulary Development

It is widely recognized that, both for adults and children, the concept of a word develops gradually and is constructed over time as they amass additional experience (Nelson, 2007). Young children's vocabulary learning appears to follow the same basic sequence (but not at the same rate) for L1 and L2. When monolingual English-speaking children begin formal reading instruction they typically bring along a vocabulary of 5,000 to 7,000 words in English (Biemiller & Slonim, 2001). Thus, the vocabulary gap between an ELL who is completely new to English and monolingual peers can be enormous; it also can persist. Hutchinson and colleagues' (2003) study of 43 ELLs found that the vocabulary gap did not narrow significantly over a 3-year period.

The speed with which children recognize and understand words is also at issue. Fernald, Perfors, and Marchman (2006) ask not just whether some children have larger vocabularies, but why. Quantitative research often uses rapid naming of pictured items as the way to assess vocabulary—a practice that tends to ignore the cultural context and the source of observed differences in vocabulary. If some children have more opportunities to use L2 both outside and inside school, then their greater vocabularies and comprehension of spoken language in L2 may be attributable to practice rather than to differences in capacity for or willingness to become proficient in L2. When the English vocabulary used in the home is very limited, children's receptive and expressive vocabulary is affected. In order for children to become fluent readers and writers, they need to have an active vocabulary that supports their understanding of the words they encounter at school. Ordinary talk is often inadequate for developing vocabulary; picture books provide visual as well as verbal information, making them a particularly useful tool for expanding vocabulary of English language learners. Listening comprehension is critical to school success and vocabulary is a subset of that ability (August, Carlo, Dressler, & Snow, 2005; Gersten et al., 2007).

One limitation in many studies of ELLs' vocabulary learning is that there is no effort to differentiate between ELLs with language disabilities or disorders and their ELL peers, a practice that tends to confound more generalized language problems with second-language learning issues (Genesee, Lindholm-Leary, Saunders, & Christian, 2005; Lovett et al., 2008).

When teaching vocabulary, realize that, although children learn about 400 new words per year, more than four or five in a lesson can be overwhelming, particularly for English language learners. It usually takes at least 8 to 10 encounters with a word before students know it and even more practice when it is a new language, so repetition of the word in various contexts is essential. When deciding which words to teach, prefer those that cannot be easily depicted with an illustration and words that offer a conceptual challenge, such as *brave, confusing, kind*.

How Do I ...
Teach with Information Books?

Teachers of young children tend to read story-books aloud much more often than informational texts (Dreher, 2003; C. B. Smith, 2003a). Reading information books aloud invites children to engage in meaning-making efforts, model comprehension strategies, and use interactive approaches (Smolkin & Donovan, 2000).

Selection of Information Books: The 5 As

In choosing information books, consider

1. Authority of the author
2. Accuracy of the content
3. Appropriateness of the book for children
4. Artistry of the language
5. Aesthetic or artistic appeal of the book's overall appearance

For tips on science books to read aloud, visit the American Library Association's website (www.ala.org/ala/booklinksbucket/readaloudscience.htm).

Preview and Predictions

Show children the cover and then ask questions such as the following:

- What kind of pictures are these?
- What kind of book is this?
- How do you know?
- What do you expect to find out in this book?

Examples of good choices for preview and predictions include *On Earth* (Karas, 2005); *Elephants Can Paint Too!* (Arnold, 2005); *Working Like a Dog* (Gorrell, 2003); *Cowboys: Roundup on an American Ranch* (Anderson, 1996); *My Brother, My Sister* (Rosenberg, 1991); *Flute's Journey: The Life of a Wood Thrush* (Cherry, 1997); *Anna's Athabaskan Summer* (Griese, 1995); *A Visit to the Zoo* (Aliki, 1997); *Black? White! Day? Night! A Book of Opposites* (Seeger, 2006); *Stars beneath Your Bed: The Story of Dust* (Sayre, 2005); *I Fall Down* (Cobb, 2005).

Reading

Read the story together and then ask questions such as these:

- What do the pictures tell me?
- Are there any special kinds of pictures (close-ups, diagrams, maps) that help me to understand?
- Are there some new words that I didn't know before?

Examples of books to read and discuss together include: *You Can't See Your Bones with Binoculars: A Guide to Your 206 Bones* (Ziefert, 2004); *The Magic Schoolbus inside a Hurricane* (Cole, 1996); *Siesta* (Guy, 2005); *Castle* (Macaulay, 1977); *Are Trees Alive?* (Miller, 2003); *Beaks!* (Collard, 2003); *If You Decide to Go to the Moon* (McNulty, 2005).

Comparing

Show the children a pair of books—one a storybook, the other a factual information book—and then ask questions such as these:

- How are these two books different (size, shape, topic, purpose of text, purpose of illustrations)?
- Do you read an information book like this the same way as a storybook? Why? Why not?
- Can you think of another pair of books—one that is real and the other, pretend?

Examples of good comparison books include, for preschoolers, *Clifford, the Small Red Puppy* (Bridwell, 1961) versus *My Puppy Is Born* (Cole, 1991) or, for children in primary grades, *If Dogs Ruled the World* (McNulty, 2003) and *Stella Unleashed! Notes from the Doghouse* (Ashman, 2008) contrasted with *Sled Dogs* (Haskins, 2007) and *Medical Detective Dogs* (Ruffin, 2008).

Activities with Information Books

- Write a book about how something is made and use digital photos or drawings to illustrate it with books such as *Riki's Birdhouse* (Wellington, 2009); *How Is a Crayon Made?* (Charles, 1988); and

Food Creations: From Hot Dogs to Ice Cream Cones (Ball, 2007) to model the writing style.

• Use computer software that pairs fiction and nonfiction books such as Pair-It Books, from Steck-Vaughn (www.steck-vaughn.com).

• Do an author study of a writer with many nonfiction books, such as Aliki, George Ancona, Claire Cherry, Ruth Heller, Margy Burns Knight, Ann Morris, Jim Arnosky, Arthur Dorros, Gail Gibbons, Barbara Brenner, Walter Dean Myers, Anne Rockwell, or Millicent Selsam

• Use the information book *I'm Dirty!* (McMullan, 2007) to review the parts of speech.

• Create a class alphabet book with factual information, such as *The Ocean Alphabet Book* (Palotta, 1986) or *The Yukky Reptile Alphabet Book* (Palotta, 1989).

• Create a "big book" that documents growth using a book that shows an animal's development, such as *How Kittens Grow* (Selsam, 1992), or that offers interesting facts, such as *Polar Bears* (Markle, 2005).

• Make a factual book with moving parts or realia (real objects), such as a book on recycling that demonstrates how throw-away materials can be recycled into art.

• Make an "all about" book, such as *How Big Is It? A BIG Book All About BIGNESS* (Hillman, 2008).

• In conjunction with a mathematics unit on measurement, create an actual-size book, using *Prehistoric Actual Size* (Jenkins, 2005) as a model.

• Share a book that chronicles history on a topic of interest to children, such as *From Rags to Riches: A History of Girls' Clothing in America* (Sillis, 2005).

• Compose and illustrate a humorous step-by-step expository picture book with the class using a book such as *Laura Numeroff's 10-Step Guide to Living with Your Monster* (Numeroff, 2003) as an example.

• For older students, combine fact and fiction by producing a story that includes both, using *Lady Liberty: A Biography* (Rappaport, 2008) as inspiration.

Adaptations

Children with attention-deficit hyperactivity disorder (ADHD) often experience difficulty with expository texts and may find it challenging to comprehend and recall the information, make inferences, and monitor their comprehension of instructions (McInnes et al., 2003). Additional practice with information books can offer much needed support in understanding nonnarrative texts and provide concrete examples for children to follow when composing expository texts. Many teachers may find, as Camp (2000) reports, that reading fiction and nonfiction texts on the same topic and combining these readings with interactive class strategies (such as Venn diagrams, K-W-L, DRTA, webbing, and activating prior knowledge) serve to boost students' understanding and enjoyment, help teach content material, and ease students into reading content-area textbooks in later elementary years.

Resources: Dreher (2003); Duke (2003); Hall & Sabey (2007); Heller (2006); Kletzien & Dreher (2004); Kobrin (1988); Kobrin (1995); Moss (2002); Ranker (2009); Read, Reutzel, & Fawson (2008); C. B. Smith (2003); Smolkin & Donovan (2000); Stead (2002); Stephens (2008); Webster (2009).

PEARSON myeducationkit™ Now go to Chapter 6 in the MyEducationKit (www.MyEducationKit.com) for your book, where you can:

■ Find Chapter Objectives.

■ Complete Assignments and Activities that can help you more deeply understand the chapter content.

■ Extend knowledge with content-specific Web Links.

■ Check your comprehension on the content covered in the chapter by going to the Study Plan. Here you will be able to take a chapter quiz, receive feedback on your answers, and then access resources that will enhance your understanding of chapter content.

chapter seven

Fostering Growth in Emergent Literacy

Michael Newman/PhotoEdit

FACT FILE on Emergent Literacy

• Reading was promoted during ancient Greek times by having children trace the alphabet with a stylus. In 1678, children were taught the alphabet through the use of a *hornbook:* a small single page on a wooden frame protected by a sheet of animal horn. The *New England Primer*, the text used in most schools from 1727 to 1830, taught children to read using rhymes, two-letter syllables, and pictures. A German educator named Basedow, who lived during the 1700s, taught children their alphabet letters by making them out of gingerbread (Putnam, 1995).

- In 1985, a national report on young children's learning, *Becoming a Nation of Readers*, summarized the situation this way: "The more elements of good parenting, good teaching, and good schooling children experience, the greater the likelihood that they will achieve their potential as readers" (Anderson, Hiebert, Scott, & Wilkinson, 1985, p. 117). Recent research supports this claim (Bennett-Armistead, Duke, & Moses, 2006; Collins & Svenson, 2008; Dickinson & Neuman, 2006; Israel, 2008).

- A study by Reyes and Azuara (2008) of bilingual preschool children found that young children are able to develop emergent literacy skills in two languages simultaneously.

- For children who have hearing loss, developing certain emergent literacy skills poses unique challenges. In a study conducted by Easterbrooks, Lederberg, Miller, Bergeron, and Connor (2008), preschool-age children with hearing loss, deafness, or speech perception difficulties made progress similar to peers in letter recognition and writing but not in phonological awareness skills.

- The acquisition of several specific skills in early childhood has been linked to successful literacy development during the school years: phonological awareness, phonological memory, and rapid automatized naming (RAN) (Anthony, Williams, McDonald, & Francis, 2007).

- The early childhood years are a critical time for young children to learn early emergent skills because by the time a child reaches second grade, basic reading instruction tends to diminish while expectations for independent reading ability in different content areas increases (Kainz & Vernon-Feagans, 2007).

- Upon entry into kindergarten, two out of three children know the letters of the alphabet, while only one out of three know the letter/sound relationships at the beginnings of words, and about one in five know the letter/sound relationships at the ends of words. Very few kindergartners can read single words or words in sentences (National Center for Education Statistics, 2003).

- Reading aloud to young children is a major way of supporting literacy development. Children who are exposed to books early and often become aware that printed words have sounds, and they recognize that print carries meaning (Rashid, Morris, & Sevcik, 2005).

- Several studies have found that young children's motivation to read tends to be high and relatively unaffected by sociocultural status; however, there are significant differences in the purposes that parents and families set for reading. When families approach learning to read as a skill and a necessity, rather than as a source of enjoyment, it can exert a negative effect on children's motivation to read (Baker & Scher, 2002; Sonnenschein, Baker, Serpell, & Schmidt, 2000).

- Most experts agree that preventing reading difficulties is more successful and cost effective than attempting to remediate them (Coyne, Kame'enui, & Harn, 2004; Snow, Burns, & Griffin, 1998; Torgesen, 2002). Based on findings such as these, the early years have become the focus in efforts to prevent reading difficulties (Erickson & Hatton, 2007; Hyson, 2008; Johnston, McDonnell, & Hawken, 2008).

- The National Institute for Literacy suggests that emergent literacy is best supported when teachers build on children's spoken language by talking and listening, teaching children about print and books, emphasizing the sounds of spoken language (i.e., *phonological awareness*), teaching about the letters of the alphabet, and reading books aloud (Armbruster, Lehr, & Osborn, 2003, p. 9).
- Because over 99 percent of U.S. families own a television set, efforts have been made to use television to foster literacy growth in young children. *Sesame Street* and *Between the Lions* are examples of programs designed to support emergent literacy (Linebarger, Kosanic, Greenwood, & Doku, 2004).

Did any of this information surprise you? If so, what? Why? How will you use this knowledge to educate and care for the very young?

What Is Emergent Literacy?

PEARSON
myeducationkit™

Go to the Assignments and Activities section of Chapter 7 in MyEducationKit and complete the activity entitled "Transitions."

Historically, there has been a difference of opinion about when children actually begin the process of learning to read. Perhaps you have heard people speak about *reading readiness* and thought that this was current terminology. Actually, this is an echo from the past; reading readiness is a concept from the 1940s.

In the 1960s, Marie Clay challenged the view that real reading started when children were in formal school settings and reading from their textbooks. She argued that this view disregarded all of the important milestones that occurred before children could read independently (Clay, 1975). For example, perhaps the biggest breakthrough in learning to read is realizing that all of those marks on paper mean something (Erickson & Hatton, 2007). At first, children do not know how an adult performs this almost magical feat of reading a picture book in the same way each time. Young children appear to assume that it is the pictures that are being read, not the words. This is reflected in their earliest attempts to pretend to read, in which they study the illustrations and tell the story while sprinkling in some words and phrases that they remember from repeated readings of the book.

Emergent literacy has been defined as the "reading and writing knowledge and behavior of children who are not yet conventionally literate" (Justice & Kaderavek, 2002, p. 8). Reading emerges as children do the following:

- Acquire oral language by exploring its meaning, noticing its structure (e.g., word order), and experimenting with its sounds (called *phonological awareness*).
- Ascribe meaning to the symbols around them (e.g., a stop sign, a food label, a fast-food restaurant billboard).
- Attempt to produce symbols, signs, and letters.

FIGURE 7.1   Emergent Literacy Behaviors

Children begin to:

1. Demonstrate the ability to understand an oral message by listening and responding appropriately.
2. Pretend to read favorite books, poems, songs, and chants based on familiarity with the text.
3. Use a combination of drawing and writing to communicate, and are capable of reading their own writing, even if no one else can.
4. Learn to "track print" by pointing to the words using left-right and top-bottom conventions.
5. Know critical jargon related to reading and can identify such things as the first word in a sentence, one letter, the first letter in a word, the longest word, and so on.
6. Recognize familiar words, including their own names, names of family members and friends, environmental print (signs, labels), and specific words from favorite books, poems, and songs.
7. Notice if words sound alike or rhyme and engage in spontaneous language play.
8. Name most letters and match words that begin with common initial sounds.
9. Learn what it means to read by making the connections among spoken language, print, and conceptual understanding.
10. Think about their own processes of interacting with print and ways of reflecting on language.

Sources: Allington & Walmsley, 2007; Dickinson & Snow, 1987; Torrance & Olson, 1985.

- Mimic adult literacy behaviors, such as pretending to read the newspaper or writing a check.
- Repeat processes until they are clearer and more refined, such as mastering an action song with all of the accompanying motions.
- Begin to connect speech sounds to print patterns, such as saying "Y-e-s spells *yes*, and n-o spells *no*" (Braunger & Lewis, 2005).

Figure 7.1 summarizes emergent literacy behaviors.

Collaboration with Families and Professionals

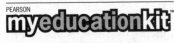

PEARSON

Go to the Assignments and Activities section of Chapter 7 in MyEducationKit and complete the activity entitled "Engaging Families."

Caitlin is a kindergarten teacher in a small rural school. Several of her students come from homes in which reading aloud from picture books is not part of the experience. She wonders how these children, who have been categorized as "unready" for school, are going to succeed, and she knows that a major part of her evaluation as a new teacher will depend on her students' test performance. Some of the teachers are pushing for a readiness test that would

Standards in Education
Review the standards, Learning to Read and Write, that were developed by NAEYC and IRA, particularly Part 4 that provides a continuum of children's development in early reading (www.naeyc.org/about/positions/psread0.asp).

keep these students out of school for another year. This seems unreasonable to Caitlin. If her colleagues truly believe that the home environment is not supporting literacy, why would they postpone the child's opportunity to acquire literacy skills at school?

As a first step, Caitlin decides to talk with children and survey families about their literacy activities at home. The results surprise her. Although the families may not be reading bedtime stories, both the kindergartners and their families report other activities that surely do support literacy. One family, for example, has accepted responsibility for producing the weekly bulletin for their church, and they are teaching their daughter to assist them. In another family, the father is a motorcycle mechanic. He looks at motorcycle magazines and websites with his son, who now knows the names of many different types of bikes. An extended family, which includes the grandparents living right next door, gets together several times a week to sing and play musical instruments; they report that their daughter has begun to recognize the right sheet music for each selection.

Caitlin decides to share her findings in a very positive way with her colleagues. She also works with the school librarian to select several picture books that might be of interest to each of these children and families—books about publishing, motorcycles, and the joys of music. When the children make their reading choices, they are excited to discover books related to their interests and eager to show them to their families. Caitlin attaches a brief note to each book that makes it clear she read the particular family's responses to her survey and considered this in her recommendation. She also encourages the family to share the book with the child and let her know how they all liked it.

Contributions and Consequences

- *Contributions of the teacher:* How did Caitlin's approach respect each family's individual differences and unique way of supporting their kindergarten child's growth in literacy?
- *Contributions of the family:* What provision was made for families to get involved?
- *Contributions of other professionals:* How did professional collaboration support this teacher's efforts?
- *Consequences of collaboration:* What might have happened if Caitlin had decided to go along with some of her colleagues and treat children without extensive prior book experience as a threat to her continued employment?

Overview of Emergent Reading Development

Brandon, age 5, has the story of "The Three Little Pigs" on his lap. As he turns the pages, he invents text to go with each picture. Notice how his personal experience with the game of Hide and Seek affects his rendition of the wolf's words:

Go to the Assignments and Activities section of Chapter 7 in MyEducationKit and complete the activity entitled "Homework."

Three little pigs were going away from their mom, and one was lively, one was happy, and one was smart. The pigs went away, and two little pigs found a man and asked him for sticks to build a house, and one asked for straw to build a house. The one was smart, and he didn't want sticks or straw. He asked the man to give him bricks to build a house. The mean, bad wolf said, "Come out, come out wherever you are" and "If you don't come out, I'll huff and puff and blow your house down."

Brandon's rendition of "The Three Little Pigs" raises many questions about reading, including how it is defined, when it begins, how children learn to read, and the best ways to ensure that they do.

As young children learn to read, they typically go through several stages in emergent and early reading (Doake, 1986; Holdaway, 1979; Snow & Ninio, 1986; Sulzby, 1985). Figure 7.2 recommends ways that parents can support emergent literacy.

FIGURE 7.2   Ways Parents and Families Can Support Emergent Literacy

General Guidelines

- Adults identify, explain, and draw children's attention to forms and functions of literacy.
- Adults relate the story to the child's experiences.
- Children are encouraged to state their interpretations aloud to themselves, their peers, and adults and to ask adults questions for further information or clarification.
- Adults give children feedback about their interpretations of literacy, clarify their confusions, elaborate on explanations, and provide models of the conventional uses and forms.

Specific Pointers

- Provide interesting reading materials suited to the child's level in the home.
- Read for pleasure, rather than quizzing the child.
- Let children see you enjoying reading.
- Take an interest in the reading the child brings home from school or the library.
- Give the child a good place to play, read, and use art materials.
- Plan a quiet time at home when the television is turned off.
- Provide literacy materials for the child that belong to him or her.
- Conceal your anxieties about the child's reading problems.
- Read at least some of what the child reads and then discuss it.
- Avoid criticizing or making comparisons among siblings.
- Let the child know that his or her accomplishments are appreciated, and express confidence in the child's abilities.
- Understand that reading ability affects performance in every subject area, not just reading.
- Realize that a child's "don't care" attitude is often a "do care very much" feeling and that it may be best to allow the child to use this as a safety valve.

Sources: Bond, Tinker, Wasson, & Wasson, 1994; Hiebert & Raphael, 1998.

PEARSON

myeducationkit™

Go to the Assignments and Activities section of Chapter 7 in MyEducationKit and complete the activity entitled "Reading to Toddlers."

Brain and Language
Working memory is the cognitive ability that enables the learner to hold task-relevant information in mind while striving to understand print. Children with ADHD have deficits in working memory that often become barriers in learning to read. These children continue to need visual supports (e.g., diagrams, illustrations, graphic organizers) when processing new or complex information at school (McInnes, Humphries, Hogg-Johnson, & Tannock, 2003). What else could you do to support the working memory of young children?

Throughout the overview of these stages that follows, the assumption is that children have experienced books at home. If for some reason parents/families have not provided this support, the sequence for their child might be similar but on a different timetable.

You will also notice that the ages of the children in the examples do not follow a neat chronological order.

Understanding What a Book Is

At this stage, usually during late infancy and toddlerhood, children are differentiating between books and toys. They look at books briefly and stop when something interests them. Bright, clear, simple pictures of familiar objects are appealing to children at this stage. The following observation of Johnna's behavior illustrates how the typical toddler enjoys a book:

> When I asked 2-year-old Johnna to show me how Mommy reads, she moved her hand across the page of *Rock-a-Bye Baby* and pretended to read the words. She also made her voice go higher and lower, although no recognizable words came out. She used expressive jargon.
>
> When I asked her to show me how Johnna reads, she did the same thing. When I handed her a book, she took it and opened it up. At first, it was upside down, but when she saw a picture of the baby, she turned the book right side up. She seemed to devote most of her time to those pages that depicted action. Pages that just had an inanimate object (like an apple) on them were passed by.
>
> Like many other toddlers I have observed, Johnna did not move systematically through the book from front to back. She just opened to a page, looked at it, and then opened to another page, which could have been any number of pages before or after the last picture.

Because children are just starting to try to control the book physically, they need numerous opportunities to observe adults operating books. They also need durable books constructed of cardboard, cloth, or plastic that they can access themselves.

Understanding How a Book Works

At approximately 2 to 3 years of age, the child begins to learn how a book works. Such things as holding it right side up, turning the pages, and treating it differently from other possessions are some of the accomplishments of this stage (Snow & Ninio, 1986). Children's book use during this phase can best be described as "point-say-connect." They point to a pictured object and then (often in response to the parent's questions) say the object's name. Usually, after naming a pictured object, they relate the picture to their own experience.

The following dialogue between Hua (33 months old) and his mother illustrates this behavior:

> **Mother:** Who is this? (Pointing to a boy.)
>
> **Hua:** Hua.
>
> **Mother:** Who is this? (Pointing to a girl and a dog.)
>
> **Hua:** Renee! (his sister). Coco! (the family dog). (Notices a picture of a bee.) Buzz-Buzzzz! Makes honey. Bee stings me, it hurts.

Older toddlers also enjoy stories with simple plots, such as *Ten, Nine, Eight* (Bang, 1983), and lyrical language, as used in the bedtime story *Where Does the Brown Bear Go?* (Weiss, 1990).

Becoming a Listener and Participant

As children begin the preschool years, they learn more about the listener's role and realize that the focal point of book-sharing sessions is the book. This stage often involves considerable talking about the book. This adult/child dialogue frequently consists of commentary designed to help the child understand the story, the child's remarks relating the story to personal experience, and questions from the child to clarify concepts.

Children at this stage often seek to hear the same story again and again and will repeat certain words or phrases if an adult encourages them. Although adults may grow tired of young children's requests to hear the same story again and again, there is ample research to suggest that revisiting a story until every word is familiar is an important step in learning to read. Figure 7.3 summarizes these research findings.

By now, most children have learned how to control books physically and can look at books independently. They may rehearse familiar favorites aloud, using the pictures as cues. Mandy, a 39-month-old, reads *Hand, Hand, Fingers, Thumb* (Perkins, 1969) by commenting on each picture and interspersing some of the words she remembers:

> Finger, finger, thumb, One thumb drumming on a drum. Hand, hand, drumming on a drum. Dum-di-di, Dum, dum, dum. Blow your nose. Shake hands. Bye-bye.

Inventing Stories to Go with Illustrations

Children who have shared books with caring adults come to clearly associate pleasure with literature, have several favorites, and look for more good stories to add to their repertoire of familiar books. As a result, they strive to "gain independent access to books" (Doake, 1986). They can tell a story in a way that sounds more like book language, and these retellings usually contain some actual words and phrases from the text.

Here is Jessica, a 42-month-old, reading her favorite book, Dr. Seuss's (1954) *Horton Hears a Who*. Notice how her emergent reading is more booklike than Mandy's or Hua's:

> He was in the pool when he was in the jungle, and it was a jungle and Horton heared a Who. The speck was too little to see with him's eyes. "I had a very, very trouble." He was going to jump in that pool, but the elephant said, "No, I gotta save my friend." So, he went running fast to save his friend, and he knew where his friend was going. He was going in the pool, so he got in the water and got the speck out.

FIGURE 7.3 The Value of Repeated Read-Alouds

General Findings

Reading aloud has a positive influence on the following factors:

- Listening comprehension and vocabulary growth
- Reading strategies and competence
- Motivation to read, especially for children who are not yet reading independently or who are reluctant to read
- Interest in and appreciation of literature
- Understanding of different types of texts
- Knowledge of different literary styles and writing abilities

Specific Finding

Interactions between the adult reader and the child change with repeated readings; children actually learn how to talk about the story and initiate more talk over time. The familiarity that comes with repeated reading enables children to reenact stories or attempt to read them on their own.

Implications

Adult readers should encourage children to say more about the story by skillfully using various types of questions:

- What is this?
- What happened next?
- Why did _____ happen?
- Now that _____, what do you think will happen next?
- How are these things alike? Different? How did you decide?
- Did you ever do what _____ in the story did?
- What is good/bad about _____? Why did you like _____?

Specific Finding

With repeated readings, children reveal greater insight about aspects of the story. They also tend to move away from superficial comments and tend to ask more sophisticated questions about word or story meaning and cause/effect relationships. This depth of understanding tends to appear most frequently after the third reading.

Implications

Instead of always seeking to find a brand-new book to share, children should be invited to revisit favorite stories again and again as often as they wish. Ways to achieve this in the classroom include the following:

- Storytimes that include special requests from children to read favorite books
- Participation in library storytimes and borrowing favorite books
- Volunteers who will read aloud to one or more children
- Recordings of favorite books
- Bookpack programs that circulate favorite stories and extension activities
- Flannelboard figures, toys, and dramatic play props that encourage children to retell favorite stories

Sources: Dickinson & Neuman, 2006; Fields, Groth, & Spangler, 2007; Kaderavek & Justice, 2005; Ratner & Olver, 1998; Roser & Martinez, 1995; Yaden, 1988.

At this stage, the focus remains on meaning and context, rather than on the features of print.

The experiences of two children, Anna and Scott, illustrate the role of *prior knowledge* involved in learning to read. When 5-year-old Anna hears the music that accompanies the daily drawing of the state lottery, she rushes into the living room, plops down in front of the television set, and says, "2, oooh, 4, 7." When it is over, she gets up and says, "I love that show," and then she resumes playing outdoors. For Anna, the lottery is like *Sesame Street.* She has no concept of gambling, but she sees that adults are enthused about it and responds to it based on her prior experience with television viewing. Anna may use the word *lottery* and look forward to the program, but she does not understand how a game of chance operates. Seven-year-old Scott, on the other hand, has a more sophisticated concept of how a lottery works because he was a winner. Figure 7.4 presents the story he typed on the computer and the picture his friend Blair drew to go along with it.

FIGURE 7.4   Scott's Lottery Story

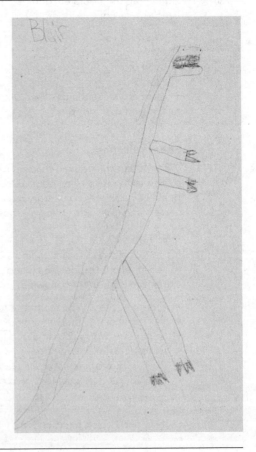

I won a ticket to dinusr world
I won it because I had the same
nubrs on my ticket as the ticket
the man had. me and my mom
and dad and sisdr went on a jet
my sisdr said the cars look so
little. Then we wor ther frist we
saw brotosois then we saw tardtl
then we saw stagasois then we saw
tri sau tops and then we saw it, tryanasres

Sometimes you can actually see children's prior knowledge at work as they try to read. Nikki, age 5, is trying to read *The Gingerbread Man* (Schmidt, 1985). In the original text, the old woman says, "Now watch the oven, and when you can smell the gingerbread, call me. But do not open the oven door."* Notice how this emergent reader calls on her experience with baking to retell the story:

> One day, there was an old man and a little boy and an old woman. One day, she said that she would make him a gingerbread man. And so, she made it. And she said, "Well, when this dings, when this timer dings, you don't open it—just call me." So she left. Then he smelled and he smelled it, and so he opened it a little bit and saw it to see if it smelled like it was. So the gingerbread ran out, and the little boy tried to catch him. He tried to close the door as fast as he could, but the gingerbread was too fast.

In Nikki's retelling, the oven is equipped with a bell that tells the little boy when the food is ready, just like her oven at home. She has incorporated the oven timer into her retelling because it is part of her *schema* (or framework of knowledge) for making cookies. If she had never seen an oven, Nikki's retelling undoubtedly would be different.

Figure 7.5 is a summary of the developmental continuum in children's reading.

Teacher Concerns and Basic Strategies

Go to the Assignments and Activities section of Chapter 7 in MyEducationKit and complete the activity entitled "Literacy in the Environment."

Infants and Toddlers
Between 1 and 2 years of age, most children go through a dramatic burst in naming activity (Goswami, 2001). Usually, the first words that the child recognizes are those that have personal significance, such as family names, labels of familiar foods, and fast-food restaurant signs (Morrow, 2001; Nelson, 2007). What activities can you think of that would build on such knowledge in toddlers?

Learning to read is more challenging than most adults can recall. The Appendix of this chapter provides a simulation that students and parents/families can use to regain some insight into what is required.

What concerns do teachers have about children's developing literacy? As Kate noted:

> The pressure from parents and families in this affluent suburb is *on*. They expect their child to learn to read almost immediately upon entrance into our private preschool. If that doesn't happen, they pull their child out of the program. Our very survival as an institution is dependent upon pushing young children to read. Most adults are successful businesspeople and take the approach of "It worked for me."

Pressuring children to learn how to read is not effective, and neither is expecting all children to progress in the same way. Teachers should help parents understand what does and does not support children's emergent reading (see Figure 7.6 on p. 160).

Teachers may also need to review their own understanding of emergent literacy and how to assess it. Jennifer, a student teacher, said:

---

*Reprinted by permission of Scholastic.

Note: This list is intended to be illustrative, not exhaustive. Children at any grade level will function at a variety of phases along the reading/writing continuum.

Awareness and Exploration: Goals for Preschool

Children explore their environment and build the foundations for learning to read and write.

Children Can

- Enjoy listening to and discussing storybooks.
- Understand that print carries a message.
- Engage in reading and writing attempts.
- Identify labels and signs in their environment.
- Participate in rhyming games.
- Identify some letters and make some letter/sound matches.
- Use known letters or approximations of letters to represent written language (especially meaningful words like their names and phrases such as "I love you").

What Teachers Do

- Share books with children, including big books, and model reading behaviors.
- Talk about letters by names and sounds.
- Establish a literacy-rich environment.
- Reread favorite stories.
- Engage children in language games.
- Promote literacy-related play activities.
- Encourage children to experiment with writing.

What Parents and Family Members Can Do

- Talk with children, engage them in conversation, give names of things, show interest in what a child says.
- Read and reread stories with predictable texts to children.
- Encourage children to recount experiences and describe ideas and events that are important to them.
- Visit the library regularly.
- Provide opportunities for children to draw and print using markers, crayons, and pencils.

Experimental Reading and Writing: Goals for Kindergarten

Children develop basic concepts of print and begin to engage in and experiment with reading and writing.

Kindergartners Can

- Enjoy being read to and themselves retell simple narrative stories or informational texts.
- Use descriptive language to explain and explore.
- Recognize letters and letter/sound matches.

FIGURE 7.5 Continued

- Show familiarity with rhyming and beginning sounds.
- Understand left-to-right and top-to-bottom orientation and familiar concepts of print.
- Match spoken words with written ones.
- Begin to write letters of the alphabet and some high-frequency words.

What Teachers Do

- Encourage children to talk about reading and writing experiences.
- Provide many opportunities for children to explore and identify sound/symbol relationships in meaningful contexts.
- Help children to segment spoken words into individual sounds and blend the sounds into whole words (for example, by slowly writing a word and saying its sound).
- Frequently read interesting and conceptually rich stories to children.
- Provide daily opportunities for children to write.
- Help children build a sight vocabulary.
- Create a literacy-rich environment for children to engage independently in reading and writing.

What Parents and Family Members Can Do

- Daily, read and reread narrative and informational stories to children.
- Encourage children's attempts at reading and writing.
- Allow children to participate in activities that involve writing and reading (for example, cooking, making grocery lists).
- Play games that involve specific directions (such as Simon Says).
- Have conversations with children during mealtimes and throughout the day.

Source: International Reading Association and the National Association for the Education of Young Children. Learning to read and write: Developmentally appropriate practices for young children. *Reading Teacher: A Journal of the International Reading Association, 52*(2), pp. 200–201. Copyright 1998 by the International Reading Association. Reproduced with permission of the International Reading Association via Copyright Clearance Center.

I just found out that I will be assigned to teaching kindergarten, and I'm not quite sure what to expect from 5-year-olds.

One way to do a quick evaluation of the abilities of typically developing children is to refer to a checklist, such as the one in Figure 7.7 (on p. 161).

Geoff, a child-care provider, said:

I am responsible for meeting with a group of parents to answer their questions about early reading. What should I expect?

It is important to anticipate some of the questions that parents and families might ask and to provide the answers in a format that is easy to distribute. Figure 7.8 (on pp. 162–164) is a sample flyer with frequently asked questions and answers that can be distributed to parents and families.

FIGURE 7.6 Helps and Hindrances in Emergent Reading: A Review of the Research

Helps

- Making time for reading and learning
- Providing texts of all kinds and rich resources for learning to read
- Having knowledgeable and supportive teachers
- Providing appropriate instruction in skills and strategies
- Demonstrating how readers, writers, and texts work
- Working with other readers, both novice and expert
- Offering recognition and support of children's reading processes

Hindrances

- Emphasizing only phonics
- Drilling on isolated letters or sounds
- Teaching letters and words one at a time
- Insisting on absolute correctness
- Making perfect oral reading the goal of instruction
- Focusing on skills to the neglect of interpretation and comprehension
- Constant use of workbooks and worksheets
- Assigning children to fixed groups (e.g., high, medium, low)
- Blind adherence to a basal (textbook) program

Source: Braunger & Lewis, 2005.

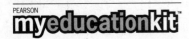

Classroom Activities to Support Emergent Reading

Go to the Assignments and Activities section of Chapter 7 in MyEducationKit and complete the activity entitled "Names and Games."

The abilities discussed throughout this chapter should provide general guideposts for the reading activities that you design.

Environmental Print Book   Create a collection of letters and labels and anything else that children can read; then paste them on sheets of paper and insert them in plastic page protectors. Assemble the pages all of the children have made into a three-ring binder. Try creating a simple story into which environmental print such as toys, cartoons, and restaurant or food logos can be inserted, such as "Once upon a time, a _____ went _____. When she got _____ she decided she wanted to eat _____. After she ate, she saw her friend _____. They played with _____. They had fun!" (Enz, Prior, Gerard, & Han, 2008).

Guided Imagery   Visualization can be used to build prior knowledge (Moline, 1995; Mundell, 1987). Begin with a few warm-up activities, such as inviting children to mentally create images in preparation for sharing a book—for example, asking them to

| FIGURE 7.7 | What Most 5-Year-Olds Can Do with Language: A Checklist |

Check off each task the child can do to conduct a quick assessment of language abilities.

Spoken Language

☐ Understands and follows oral (or spoken) directions

☐ Uses new words and longer sentences when he or she speaks

☐ Recognizes the beginning sounds of words and sounds that rhyme

☐ Listens carefully when books are read aloud

Reading

☐ Shows interest in books and reading

☐ Tries to read, calls attention to self, and shows pride ("See, I can read this book!")

☐ Follows the series of events in some stories

☐ Connects what happens in books with real life and experiences

☐ Asks questions and makes comments that reflect an understanding of the book being read

Print and Letters

☐ Knows the difference between print (words) and pictures and knows that print is what you read

☐ Recognizes environmental print on signs, television, boxes, and many other places

☐ Understands that writing has a lot of different purposes (for example, maps show where something is located, lists can be used for grocery shopping, directions can tell how to put something together)

☐ Knows that each letter in the alphabet has a name

☐ Recognizes at least 10 letters in the alphabet, especially the ones in his or her own name

☐ "Writes," or scribbles, messages

Source: Adapted from Armbruster, Lehr, & Osborn, 2003.

picture a jungle before sharing Nancy Tafuri's (1988) *Jungle Walk*. After each child sees a jungle in his or her "mind's eye," begin to compare/contrast children's descriptions, emphasizing that there are no right or wrong images. Next, lead into the book. On the first page, the boy has just finished reading a book and is switching off the light to go to sleep. You might say something such as "I wonder what he was reading. Hmm. It says *Jungles of the World* on his book. Close your eyes and imagine what sorts of things he may have seen in the book he was reading." Before the children view the entire book, ask them to hypothesize about the story. Then, after they have shared the book, invite the children to compose a group story to go along with the pictures and read it aloud

FIGURE 7.8	Sample Flyer: Questions Parents Commonly Ask about Young Children's .Reading Behavior

I've heard that it is important to read to your child. Why?

Children can develop the knowledge, skills, attitudes, and values of proficient readers by listening to literature. Numerous research studies have concluded that reading aloud to children increases their reading achievement scores, listening and speaking abilities, letter and symbol recognition, ability to use more complex sentences, ability to understand language, concept development, and positive attitudes toward reading.

When should I begin reading to my child?

Your child started on the road to reading the day that you first held your newborn in your arms and sang a lullaby, bounced your baby on your knee in time to a nursery rhyme, or encouraged your toddler to point to pictures in a book and name them. Literature for the very young is not limited to books. Newborns have fully developed hearing and can listen to a lullaby; lullabies are literature. Babies delight in play rhymes like "This Little Piggy"; poetry is literature. Toddlers enjoy "point and say" with simple books; cardboard and cloth books with simple pictures are literature. Preschoolers delight in simple stories told aloud, such as "The Three Bears"; storytelling is literature. Literature is more than a quiet reading of a storybook with your child on your lap. Even the youngest child can begin to associate enjoyment with literature.

Doesn't a child have to be ready to read?

It is common to say that the child must be *ready* to read. But the concept of reading readiness is outdated, mainly because it denies all of the preparation that leads up to reading. Learning to walk is a good analogy. Adults don't sit around waiting for the child to take those first steps; rather, adults lead, support, and coax the child. The same strategies apply to learning to read.

Is it a good idea to try to teach my child to read before he or she starts school?

If you interviewed parents whose children learned to read early, most of them would say, "I never really *taught* him; we just shared stories together and he sort of picked up reading on his own." A relaxed, informal introduction is just what the young child needs. Children need to be invited into the world of literature, not dragged. Sometimes parents try too hard and make reading drudgery. A better strategy is to adopt the same tolerant attitude toward language learning that we have about children's initial singing efforts. We don't panic when young children sing off-key or assume that they are doing irreparable damage to their musical development. Rather, we allow them to experiment, enjoy, and learn.

Why does my child ask me to read and then keep interrupting?

When children listen to a story, they are in on-the-job-training as readers. Reading is the process of deriving meaning from print, and your child's questions show that he or she is working to make sense out of the book. The best story-sharing sessions include playful discussions of the book. In fact, as much as 80 percent of the talk that takes place when a skillful adult reads a picture book to a child could be described as commentary about the

FIGURE 7.8 Continued

pictures or text. Try to follow the child's lead instead of putting her on the spot through constant quizzing. You might show how to think out loud, saying something like, "Hmm. I wonder what the puppy will do now . . ." Another way to talk about books is to merely comment, saying, for instance, "It looks like nobody recognizes Harry now that he is all dirty." Both the adult and the child should leave the session with a feeling of satisfaction.

How do I choose books my child will like?

Although there are books that have delighted children for decades, it is sometimes difficult to predict which books children will really love. One thing is certain: With thousands of new books for children published annually, there is no good reason to stick with a book that does not interest your child. Try borrowing a selection of books from the library with some help from a children's librarian and then letting your child choose. Consult with your child's caregiver or teacher about books that seem to be appealing or lists of recommended books. Apply some basic selection criteria of your own, such as, Does the content or level seem appropriate for my child? Has the book been well endorsed by families (e.g., earned a Parents' Choice Award)? Do the pictures complement the story? Would I enjoy sharing this book with my child? Does the book appear to be a high-quality product (good illustrations, print quality, skillful use of language)? The clear sign that a book has been well received by your child is the request "Read it again!"

Why does my child ask to hear the same book over and over again?

According to Picture Book Studio U.S.A. (1985):

> A picture book of real substance is enjoyed again and again. It is like visiting a favorite vacation spot. No matter how well you know it, going back is always a delight. It is a calm secure place with no real surprises, but a constant supply of good times nevertheless. All the memories are sweet, all the best views and secret places are recalled and anticipated, and the very familiarity is a comfort and a rest. (p. 2)

Even though adults may grow weary of rereading the same book, that repetition leads to a major breakthrough. After children memorize all of the words in a story, they can use familiarity to gain insights about the reading process. When a child protests if an adult misreads a passage or tries to abbreviate the text, it is a sign that the child is learning to read. Although adults sometimes scoff at memorization and say it is not real reading, memorization is a step in the process of learning to read.

My child already knows his letters and numbers. Doesn't this mean he is ready to read?

When children first recite the alphabet or sing "The Alphabet Song," those sounds often have little meaning for them. If we listen carefully, we can even hear that children have memorized chunks of sound. The sequence *l-m-n-o-p*, for instance, is sung as if it were a word, *elemenopea*, rather than individual letters. Behaviors like these should tell adults that the child needs to amass more meaningful experiences with language. Where reading is concerned, activities such as reading and discussing books together; making writing materials accessible; encouraging children to make marks on paper; and providing creative play materials such as blocks, clay, sand, and water will all contribute

(continued)

FIGURE 7.8 Continued

to the child's ability to attribute meaning to those abstract symbols called letters and words. After all, interpreting symbols is what reading is all about.

When should I stop reading to my child?

Most parents think that they should stop reading aloud to a child as soon as that child is reading independently. Actually, hearing a challenging story read aloud by a fluent adult reader is both pleasurable and instructive for children who are already reading. The time to stop reading to a child is when he or she says, "That's okay, I'd rather read it by myself." Even after the child does say this, it is much more satisfying to be able to talk about a book with someone else who read and enjoyed it. So parents should continue to read some of the books that their children recommend to them. You may be surprised to see just how wonderful some of these stories are. *Sarah, Plain and Tall*, for example, was a Hallmark Hall of Fame special that became one of the most beloved films made for television. It was based on a children's book by Patricia MacLachlan.

Source: Adapted from Jalongo, 1992.

together. Later, the children can create their own stories. Each child might then select a favorite story that he or she would read before bedtime and then draw, write, and/or dictate a story about how that reading might become part of a fantastic dream.

Family Literacy Projects   Research suggests that parents and families exert a powerful influence on emergent reading. One problem in some households is the lack of access to reading materials, particularly those of interest to children (Krashen, 2004). Solutions include working with the school and public libraries to loan books; getting a business to sponsor a bookmobile; starting a used book exchange at school; asking churches, synagogues, and mosques for donations; collecting bonus points from book clubs to create a lending library; and asking seniors to staff the projects. Another problem is parents' and families' lack of skill in reading to their child. They make "beginner's mistakes," such as turning the experience into a lesson, correcting the child's errors, or selecting inappropriate materials, including books that are too long or difficult. Some appropriate responses might include providing a Saturday workshop for parents to train them in reading aloud; creating a video library of outstanding guest readers and circulating the tapes to parents; instituting a bookpack program; making read-alouds part of the home visiting program to model reading for parents; getting volunteers (e.g., Future Teachers of America from high school or college students majoring in education) to read to children in their homes; and sponsoring a "read-in" at the mall using "big books" so that anyone can stop, sit, and listen to a great story.

Literacy-Related Play   Children's active participation is a key to supporting literacy growth (McVicker, 2007). Repeated readings of children's books, accompanied by

Research and Report

Children with dyslexia usually have difficulty linking letters with sounds, blending sounds together, or judging whether two words rhyme; after they begin reading, their decoding often is slow and inaccurate and their spelling, poor. Children with dyslexia also tend to have difficulty with remembering material that they appeared to have mastered previously. Find out more about this condition from the International Dyslexia Association (www.interdys .org/FAQ.htm#). How would you respond to a family's concerns about dyslexia?

toys and literacy props, are ways to enrich and extend young children's understandings of picture books (Saracho & Spodek, 2006; Welsch, 2008). For example, after watching an episode of the television program *Martha Speaks* called "Shelter Blues" (available at the PBS website) and reading books about shelter dogs, including *Buddy Unchained* (Bix, 2002), *"Let's Get a Pup!" Said Kate* (Graham, 2003), and *The Stray Dog* (Simont, 2000), children were supplied with a stuffed toy dog, collar, leash, bed/ basket, plastic bowl, dog toy, dog brush, and a cardboard box "dog house" so that they could dramatize various scenes from these books, retell the story, or invent stories of their own. Activities such as these focused on picture books build a bridge between play and language and provide varied opportunities for children to demonstrate their learning. There have been similar findings for learning scientific concepts and vocabulary through repeated read-alouds and related activities (Leong, 2008).

Conclusion

Rather than wait for children to be ready for formal reading instruction, families and early childhood educators need to provide young children with extensive experiences with print. It is not enough to teach children skills. Many children learn to decode words but acquire a lifelong distaste for reading in the process. Reading programs are effective only when they help children to become fluent readers and convince them that learning to read is well worth the effort.

myeducationkit To check your comprehension on the content covered in this chapter, go to the MyEducationKit for your book and complete the Study Plan for Chapter 7. Here you will be able to take a chapter quiz and receive feedback on your answers.

 ## Research-Based Literacy Strategies

Word Walls and E-Sorts

A *word wall* is a display of a large collection of words that appear frequently or relate to thematic units and content-area study (Mackey & White, 2004, p. 31). The main purpose is to build a sight-word repertoire—something that is essential to fluent decoding (Lonigan, 2005). To view many examples,

go to www.edhelper.com and type in "word walls." Many classrooms have word walls with different purposes—for example, Words We Know (*yes, no, stop, I, Mom, love, cat, dog*); Zoo Words (*food, veterinarian, giraffe, lion, tiger*); the *-ack* Word Family (*back, crack, pack, tack, track, sack, stack,* etc.); the *-ing* Suffix (*reading, walking, writing,* etc.); and Words We Know in Spanish (*hola, adios, taco, gato, uno, rojo*).

The effectiveness of word walls depends on how they are used. Experts recommend building these displays with children over time, referring to them often as an instructional resource, and practicing reading the words in an interactive way with the children (Lapp, Flood, Moore, & Nichols, 2005).

Other word wall activities include combining the words on the wall with pictures to accommodate not-yet-readers, sorting the words using various criteria, alphabetizing them, using the words in journal writing, putting them into sentences, and so forth. Working with the words in this way gives children *receptive* vocabulary practice (aural input and visual memory used in reading) that is linked with *expressive* language—speaking and writing. Children can also use digital desktop publishing to create their own electronic word sorts ("e-sorts") and share them with others (Zucker & Invernizzi, 2008). For tips on teaching with a word wall, visit Teachnet.com at www.teachnet.com/lesson/langarts/wordwall062599.html. A streaming video from the Bureau of Education and Research of an experienced teacher using various types of word walls with her young students is available by clicking on "See preview" at www.ber.org/video/wwe.cfm.

"Talking" Reading Support Programs

Since the invention of the tape recorder, recorded books have been used in beginning reading and reading tutorial programs. The book/cassette tape, in which the child was signaled to turn the page at the sound of the bell, was the forerunner of today's "talking" reading support programs. And while book/tape sets continue to be used, computer narration of text is becoming more commonplace.

As Bergman (2005) explains, "talking" books are a reading-while-listening tool for teaching graphophonemic awareness, word recognition, fluency, and pronunciation. Advantages of talking books, such as the *Living Books* produced by Broderbund on CD-ROM, over book/cassette tapes include text and pictures with student self-selected digitized speech, second-language versions, the option

of playing instructional games, and various special effects.

One important issue in using these materials effectively is the rate at which the text is read. Most recorded texts are read at a rate much faster than that of the child who is just learning to read. Bergman (2005) found that the average reading rate of a group of first-grade participants was 53 words per minute, yet the rate of narration in two sample stories was 90 to 120 words per minute. If the narration moves too quickly, the child will become frustrated and much of the benefit of the practice will be lost. Bergman found that allowing the reader to control the rate at which the text was read resulted in the greatest gains for children who were struggling with reading. Not only did they show a significant improvement in reading comprehension and accuracy (though not in speed), but they also had a more positive attitude toward working with the talking books.

Many of these talking reading support programs are a boon to English language learners because the texts often are recorded in second-language versions. Computer-assisted instruction is also valuable in improving phonological awareness in young language learners. It helps them learn to discriminate and sequence the sounds in words, which improves their word-reading ability (Holum & Gahala, 2001, p. 5).

Project Listen is an advanced computerized reading "tutor" that "listens" as the child reads and "talks" when she or he makes a mistake, gets stuck, or clicks for help. To view a video explaining how it works, go to www.cs.cmu.edu/%7Elisten. Examples of commercial talking reading support programs that you may encounter in the schools are Wiggleworks, KidTalk, KidWorks Deluxe, ULTimate Reader, and Acceleread. To find out about the latest in talking books, consult *Publishers Weekly Multimedia Directory* and the *Storybook Software* listings.

Dialogic Reading

Reading aloud to children is more effective when it is interactive (DeBruin-Parecki, 2009; McGee & Schickendanz, 2007; Mol, Bus, DeJong, &

Smeets, 2008; Santoro, Chard, Howard, & Baker, 2008). In dialogic or interactive reading, teachers read, reread, and discuss books with small groups of children (Fisher, Flood, Lapp, & Frey, 2004). Over a decade of research supports that this style of sharing read-alouds with children has a positive impact on emergent literacy skills, particularly oral language (Morgan & Meier, 2008). Teachers incor-

porate strategic questioning in dialogic reading that invites children's responses; they also select books with strong emotional content to engage the learners. For numerous suggestions on ways to begin using dialogic reading, incorporate social-emotional learning, and involve families, see Doyle and Bramwell (2006).

 ## Links with Literature
Big Books and Shared Reading

What Is a Shared Book Experience?

As you lead children into literacy, you will want to model the reading process for them. A widely accepted practice is called the shared book experience (Hay & Fielding-Barnsley, 2007; Holdaway, 1979). It consists of using poster-sized "big books" that have some element of predictability, such as pictures, repetition, rhythm, rhyme, or patterns (like the days of the week, numbers 1–10, a familiar song) to support the beginning reader's efforts to make sense out of the text. These oversized versions of picture books for children are large enough that children can see both the text and the illustrations in a group setting.

Why Use Big Books?

Big books support emergent reading by

- Building on the child's oral language and visual literacy skills.
- Modeling for children what enthusiastic and competent readers can do so that children gain insight into the reading process and are motivated to read.
- Working with entire stories rather than moving from letters to words to sentences. The children's confidence is built as they begin to imitate what fluent readers do.
- Enabling each child to participate at his or her level (e.g., some will rely mainly on pictures, others on memory, still others on print), thereby building self-esteem as a reader.

- Integrating all of the language arts—listening, speaking, reading, and writing—as children make initial attempts to read. Rather than starting with what children do not know, this approach builds on familiarity and enjoyment.
- Emphasizing the social and collaborative aspects of language learning as children read in unison in the group and then work in smaller groups or with a partner afterwards.
- Increasing children's recall of the story and building an understanding of text structures.
- Drawing children's attention to print and practicing skills in context.
- Helping parents and families to see their child functioning competently in beginning reading (Wood, Rawlings, & Ozturk, 2003).

How to Share Big Books

Consider the following suggestions when sharing big books:

1. Read the book aloud first.
2. Read the book while pointing to each word.
3. Have children join in while you read the book.
4. Have the children dramatize the story or parts of the story.
5. At the next reading, read all but the last word on each page and have the children supply the word. This helps teach the concept of what a "word" is.
6. At the next reading, arbitrarily leave out certain words and have the students tell you the words.

7. Write the story on an overhead, blackboard, or handout so that the children can read it from a "different source."
8. Point out the concept of letters, words, and phrases as you reread the text with the children. (For example, What is the third letter on this page? What is the fourth word on this page?)
9. Record the story for use at the listening center.
10. Give small groups of children a copy of one page of text from the book and have them create their own illustration for it.
11. Guide the children in creating an original group story that follows the same basic pattern as the big book (Fisher & Medvic, 2000)

Some Sources for Published Big Books

Big books that are ready-made typically have a card-stock cover and are approximately 17 × 22 inches.

They usually cost somewhere between $20 and $30. Blank big books that are already stapled together and ready for use are also available. Companies such as Scholastic Books, The Wright Group, and Harcourt Brace Jovanovich publish a wide variety of big books. It is also possible to convert a book that the children particularly enjoy into an oversized book on a printer that can print on larger paper. Teachers sometimes make their own big books on poster board but this can be an expensive and time-consuming alternative.

ELLs
Oral Language Skills as Predictors of Literacy

Listening comprehension, defined as the young child's ability to understand what he or she hears, is highly predictive of overall academic achievement. Children with listening comprehension difficulties face serious learning challenges and are much more likely to fall behind their peers as they progress through school (Field, 2001; Mendelsohn & Rubin, 1995). There is extensive documentation that oral language skills of listening and speaking—both in L1 and L2—are linked to literacy with print; however, this should not be oversimplified (see Geva & Yaghoub-Zadeh, 2006; Proctor, August, Carlo, & Snow, 2006, for a discussion). Oral language and written language are fundamentally different. This can best be demonstrated by two recurrent findings; first, even though most young children without disabilities learn to speak or listen, not all become fluent readers and writers (Schultz, 2003), and second, oral language deficits and reading problems frequently co-occur (Bishop & Snowling, 2004).

Nevertheless, although single-grade-level studies have mixed results, the longitudinal research suggests that oral language skills are highly effective predictors of later reading skill in English. In a longitudinal study of 249 Spanish-speaking ELLs, Lindsey, Manis, and Bailey (2003) found that oral language variables—even more than word identification—predicted reading comprehension in first grade. Nakamoto, Lindsey, and Manis (2008) studied 282 Spanish-speaking ELLS in first through third grades and concluded that facility with oral language (both in L1 and L2) was a significant predictor of reading achievement in sixth grade. There is also support for cross-language transfer between L1 and L2, particularly in the area of phonological awareness (see Manis, Lindsey, & Bailey, 2004, for a review). The more similar L1 and L2 are in terms of alphabet and phonetics, the greater the potential for transfer; some research suggests that cross-language transfer is greater for ELLs who have Italian or Spanish as L1 and are trying to learn English (D'Angiulli, Siegel, & Serra, 2000; Lindsey, Manis, & Bailey, 2003).

How Do I ...

Introduce New Words to Children?

Studies estimate that of 100 unfamiliar words met in reading, between 5 and 15 of them will be learned (Beck, McKeown, & Kucan, 2002). In order to attain the goal of 10,000 words in 6 years, the child has to learn an average of 2,000 words a year, 38 words per week, and 5 to 6 words per day (Byrnes & Wasik, 2009, p. 107). For words that are not quickly understood through pictures or demonstration, children need several repetitions in different contexts in order to gradually build their understanding of a word (Baumann, Kame'enui, & Ash, 2003; Stahl, 2003). Children can acquire new vocabulary by listening to their teachers read aloud. Reading aloud is particularly effective at expanding vocabulary when teachers use interactive reading strategies (Bradham & Brown, 2002).

Begin with Letters and Sounds

Be certain that the child knows the letter sounds necessary to figure out the word. Explain to the child that you are going to teach the sounds of some letters. Only teach the most common sound of each letter. (The sound of *b* is very short; it is not "buh.") Write the letter clearly on a piece of paper. Teach the sound of the letter using the following model: "Watch. When I touch under the letter, I'll say the sound." Demonstrate how to say the sound. Touch under the letter and make the sound. Say, "Do it with me." Have the child practice with you several times, as you touch under the letter. Have the child say the sound alone when you touch under the letter. Review or repeat any steps if necessary. Let the child take a turn at saying a word slowly and guessing the word.

Practice the New Sound

Write the new letter sound and several known letters clearly on a piece of paper. Tell the student to say the sound of a letter when you touch under it. Have the student say the new sound first, and then go back and forth between previously learned sounds and the new sound. Keep going back to the new sound many times. If the student forgets a sound or answers incorrectly, go back and teach the sounds.

Teaching a New Word

After the child has mastered a small number of letters, begin teaching words. Select these words carefully; they should be phonetic. Even if a word seems easy because it is common, such as *there*, or short, such as *was*, don't use it unless it makes the common sounds. It is best to simply memorize these words as sight words because they are not phonetic (i.e., spelled the same way that they sound). After selecting the word, model how to sound it out. Touch under each letter and sound out the word in a smooth, connected way, with no breaks between the sounds.

Investigate Word-Teaching Programs

One program that directly teaches words is called Word Building. This activity provides a chain of words that differ by a single written letter, or *grapheme*, at the beginning, middle, or end of the word. After creating an initial word from letter cards, the child is given instructions to change a particular letter card (e.g., "Take away *t* and put *p* in its place") and then read the newly formed word. The new grapheme card in each trial is highlighted to focus the child's attention on different positions in the word form by holding constant the other letters from the previous word. After each transformation, the child decodes the new word, which looks and sounds similar to the previously decoded word. The Word Building approach builds on the child's prior knowledge and arranges the word-reading tasks from simple to complex—for instance, simple consonant/vowel/consonant (CVC) words (*pin*), to words that have silent *e* (*pine*), words with vowel digraphs (e.g., *ee, ai, oa, ow, oy*), and words with *r*-controlled vowels (e.g., *star*). The final four units involve changes in vowel sounds in different phonetic environments (i.e., changes in vowel pronunciation when a vowel is followed by an *r*).

Research has identified several strategies that help to build young children's vocabularies, including (1) selecting important words to teach, (2) providing "student friendly" definitions, (3) teaching the word in different contexts, and (4) repeated encounters with the word (Beck, McKeown, & Kucan, 2008; Wasik & Bond, 2009). Think about how you can incorporate these strategies into your everyday interactions with students.

References: Beck, McKeown, & Kucan (2002); Carnine, Silbert, Kame'enui, & Tarver (2004); Denton, Parker, & Jasbrouck (2003).

PEARSON **myeducationkit**™   Now go to Chapter 7 in the MyEducationKit (**www.MyEducationKit** .com) for your book, where you can:

- Find Chapter Objectives.
- Complete Assignments and Activities that can help you more deeply understand the chapter content.
- Extend knowledge with content-specific Web Links.
- Check your comprehension on the content covered in the chapter by going to the Study Plan. Here you will be able to take a chapter quiz, receive feedback on your answers, and then access resources that will enhance your understanding of chapter content.

APPENDIX 7.1

Mel and Tod: A Learning-to-Read Simulation for Adults

Mel and Tod
A Reading Simulation

Mary Renck Jalongo

How to Use This Simulation

1. Cover the right side of the page. Go over the vocabulary first but do so quickly.
2. Go through the pages, one at a time, asking individual students to try to read the page *independently*. No fair looking back at the vocabulary, looking ahead at the answers, or getting help from other students!
3. If a few people caught on quickly and you didn't, how did that feel? Were you embarrassed if you could not accurately decipher the page?

Vocabulary

ө	I	⊓¥	so
±µ€	Mel	ÇШөⷀ	this
Ç¥ß	Tod	€µÇ'⊓	let's
€¥¥≠	look	ÐҤЪ	run
£¥±µ	come	⊓Ωөß	said
ΩÇ	at	ШΩnµ	have
Ω±	am		

Ç¥ß Tod   ±µ€ Mel

"€µÇ'⊓   ÐҤЪ, ±µ€!"
⊓Ωөß Ç¥ß.

"Let's run, Mel!" said Tod.

"Look at this, Tod."

"I am first, so I win!"

"This is what we can do next!"

ÇШ µ   µ Ƅß
THE   END

Another Source of Confusion: The Terminology Used to Talk about Reading

Literacy researcher Elizabeth Sulzby contends that readers can become overwhelmed and hopelessly confused, not only by the task of interpreting the symbols of reading but also by the barrage of unfamiliar terminology that teachers use to talk about reading. Imagine that you are a child in a classroom and your teacher presents the following lesson.

"Today we are going to learn some new freeples. All of these freeples have the €l schmak. Here's the first freeple:

€¥ ¥≠ Let's schmak it out. Who can use this freeple in a lunchpatter? How about the next word: €µ¢⊓? Now, look at this freeple: €µ Does it have the schmak? Right, it does. But the € schmak in all the end of the freeple.

This is all very confusing unless the learner figures out that:

- freeple = word
- € = l
- schmak = sound
- lunchpatter = sentence

Reflections on the Simulation

- What strategies did you use as you tried to figure out the text of Mel and Tod? What are some of the skills involved in reading?

- How did you feel when you could not decipher the symbols or understand the teacher's talk?

- Have you ever listened to a young reader and thought to yourself, "Come on, you know this word—it's easy." Has this simulation caused you to rethink this? How? Why?

- Most children learn to talk without direct instruction. Why is learning to read a different type of challenge? In other words, what do children need to be able to do to succeed in reading?

- What is the apparent value of practice and repeated readings of the same text?

- Imagine that, day after day, you arrived at school and were expected to read another story that contained several new words. What might be the cumulative effect on your attitudes toward reading, school, and self-concept?

chapter eight

Supporting Early and Independent Reading

Lindfors Photography

FACT FILE on Early and Independent Reading

• Reading textbooks produced in the United States during the 1800s combined alphabetic and phonic methods (e.g., the *Webb Readers, Noah Webster's Blue Back Speller*) (Putnam, 1995). *Basal readers,* or controlled-vocabulary textbooks (e.g., "Look. Look. See the dog."), were introduced in the late 1940s. The most popular basal series was *Fun with Dick and Jane.* Supplemented with workbooks and other instructional materials, it was used in many schools well into the 1970s.

• An international reading skills study conducted in 2001 indicated that U.S. fourth-grade students had higher reading literacy scores than 23 out of 34 countries with Sweden, the Netherlands, and England's students scoring significantly higher than U.S. students (Lemke & Gonzales, 2006).

- According to the National Early Literacy Panel Report (2008), the skills children acquire between 3 and 5 years of age are a determinant of how well they will be able to read as they enter the school-age years. In 2000, the National Reading Panel (NRP) conducted an extensive review of studies on reading. Their conclusion was that balanced approaches that combine literature with direct instruction in phonics are preferred for early reading instruction.

- The acquisition of reading skills is more than a cognitive process. Research suggests that children with strong self-regulatory and social skills become more competent readers by age 14 (Smith, Borkowski, & Whitman, 2008).

- At the start of kindergarten, 26 percent of children who were read to by family members three or more times per week knew all of the letters of the alphabet whereas 14 percent of students who were read to less frequently knew the alphabet (National Education Association, 2007). Students from homes with more than 10 children's books had reading test scores 86 points higher than those of students with 10 or fewer books in the home (NEA, 2007).

- According to the National Center for Education Statistics (2005), by the spring of grade 3, almost all children (95 percent or more) could identify ending sounds, common sight words, and words in context in reading.

- Despite having normal intelligence and adequate educational and socioeconomic opportunities, between 3 and 10 percent of school-age children fail to learn to read efficiently (Heath & Hogben, 2004).

- The No Child Left Behind (NCLB) Act of 2002 included a $900-million national initiative called "Reading First" that was designed to improve the reading of kindergarten through third-grade students. Federal funding is tied to schools' implementation of "evidence-based methods of reading instruction" (National Early Literacy Panel, 2009).

- Children are expected to recognize and understand more than 80,000 words by the end of third grade (at age 8 or 9) (Byrnes & Wasik, 2009). About one-third of students cannot read adequately at the end of fourth grade (National Center for Education Statistics, 2007).

- Reading independently and understanding what was read relies on verbal and visual/spatial working memory, each of which makes unique contributions to different aspects of comprehension (McInnes, Humphries, Hogg-Johnson, & Tannock, 2003).

- Just because children learn how to sound out words, it does not mean that they understand them. Children may show impressive gains in decoding skills without corresponding improvement in their comprehension of written passages on reading tests (Perfetti, 2007).

- Research indicates that the acquisition of reading skills and motivation to read are inter-related, which suggests to those who work with struggling readers that emphasis on motiva-tional strategies may be helpful in improving reading performance (Morgan & Fuchs, 2007).
- Approximately 15 percent of the total population of the United States are dyslexic, meaning that they experience severe difficulties in learning to read. The fact that a child is dyslexic, however, does not necessarily mean that he or she cannot use oral language capably (Cruger, 2005). Dyslexia is a problem with the mental processing of print, not with verbal communication or intelligence (Katzir, Youngsuk, Wolf, O'Brien, Kennedy, Lovett, et al., 2006).

Did any of this information surprise you? If so, what? Why? How will you use this knowledge to educate and care for the very young?

What Is Early and Independent Reading?

PEARSON
myeducationkit™

Go to the Assignments and Activities section of Chapter 8 in MyEducationKit and complete the activity entitled "Journals."

PEARSON
myeducationkit™

Go to the Assignments and Activities section of Chapter 8 in MyEducationKit and complete the activity entitled "Reading for Understanding."

When people think about young children's reading, they usu-ally think of *materials* such as books, papers, and workbooks; *settings* such as the classroom, the library, or a parent's lap; and *behaviors* such as decoding words, reading aloud in reading groups, or reading independently. Although all of these factors are undeniably associated with reading, they do not adequately define the process of learning to read because reading is much more than deciphering print like the bar-code scanner at the grocery store.

Marie Clay (1992), a leading researcher in children's read-ing, defines *reading* as

a message-getting, problem-solving activity which increases in power and flexibility the more it is practiced. . . . Lan-guage and visual perception responses are purposefully directed by the reader in some integrated way to the problem of extracting meaning from cues in a text, in sequence, so that the reader brings a maximum of understanding to the author's message. (p. 6)

Thus, learning to read is the process of bringing meaning to a text in order to get meaning from it. According to Kathryn H. Au (1993), *literacy* can be defined as

the ability and the willingness to use reading and writing to construct meaning from printed text, in ways which meet the requirements of a particular social context. (p. 20)

Figure 8.1 provides an overview of how our definitions and expectations for literacy have changed over the years. As this historical perspective indicates, we have ever-increasing expectations for reading ability.

FIGURE 8.1 Historical Overview of Definitions for Literacy

Era	Definition
1600s–1700s	*Signature literacy*—the ability to read and write one's own name.
	Sociohistorical Context: In order to conduct business, a person had to be able to "make his mark"—not necessarily be able to write his entire name but at least make some marking to represent a signature. In the 1600s in England, convicted felons could request "benefit of clergy." By demonstrating the ability to read at least one Bible verse, criminals could get a lesser sentence, such as being branded rather than being put to death.
Mid 1800s	*Recitational literacy*—the ability to orally recite a memorized text.
	Sociohistorical Context: One of the major purposes of literacy was to learn religious doctrine. In the colonial United States, the materials used for literacy instruction had a heavy moralistic tone. When children learned the alphabet, for example, the letter I was accompanied by the words "The Idle fool is whipt at school."
Early 1900s	*Decoding/analytic literacy*—the ability to read previously unseen text; what we now refer to as *basic literacy.*
	Sociohistorical Context: With the advent of the Industrial Revolution, many more people, including the recently immigrated, needed to be put into productive employment. The 1900 U.S. Census determined literacy with a yes/no question: "Can you read and write?" The 1930 U.S. Census definition of *literacy* was extended to those who did not speak English: "Any person 10 years of age or older who can read as well as write in any language."
Mid 1900s	*Test-based literacy*—the ability to pass a reading test.
	Sociohistorical Context: During World War II, the criterion for induction into the U.S. Army was based on the ability to pass an examination written on a fourth-grade level. By 1950, the UNESCO definition for *literacy* focused on the ability to perform a reading task: "A person is literate who can with understanding both read and write a short, simple statement on his everyday life."
Late 1900s	*Educational attainment of literacies*—those who successfully completed a particular number of years of school were considered to be literate; the definition of literacy is expanded beyond literacy with print.
	Sociohistorical Context: The 1960 U.S. Census defined as *literate* "[a]ny person 25 years of age or older who has some formal schooling." The 1962 UNESCO definition of *literacy* was broadened to include other areas of the curriculum: "Literacy is the possession by an individual of the essential knowledge and skills which enable him or her to engage in all

(continued)

FIGURE 8.1   Continued

of those activities required for effective functioning in his or her group and community and whose attainments in reading, writing, and arithmetic make it possible for him or her to use these skills toward his or her own and the community's development." The 1988 UNESCO definition: "Functional illiteracy is the inability to use reading and writing with facility in daily life. Widespread illiteracy severely hampers economic and social development. It is also a gross violation of the basic human right to learn, know, and communicate."

There has been a well-documented shift from a literal decoding model of reading to one of reading as a strategic process in which readers construct meaning by interacting with the text. They use not only what is in the text (words and their meanings) but what they bring to the text (their knowledge and experiences) to construct meaning. In addition, the interactions among teacher and students, the purposes set for reading, and the contexts for reading and development influence reading and comprehension.

Early 2000s   *Critical/translation literacy*—the ability to summarize, analyze, and evaluate texts; to use literacy to make inferences, think critically, and solve problems; increased international concern about the social and political consequences of illiteracy.

Sociohistorical Context: In a rapidly changing information society, where most workers deal with knowledge or provide human services, workers need to reason effectively, to commit to lifelong learning, and to master the skills of collaboration. The National Literacy Act of 1991 defined *literacy* as "an individual's ability to read, write, and speak in English and compute and solve problems at levels of proficiency necessary to function on the job and in society to achieve one's goals, and to develop one's knowledge and potential" (National Council of Teachers of English and the International Reading Association, 1996, p. 4). Being literate in contemporary society means being active, critical, and creative users, not only of print and spoken language but also of the visual language of film and television, commercial and political advertising, photography, and more (NCTE and IRA, 1996, p. 5).

Source: Newman & Beverstock, 1990.

How is this sophisticated form of reading behavior achieved? Most experts agree that it is the complex interaction of four types of variables:

1. The reader's background, prior experiences with print, observations of expert readers, knowledge about the subject matter, and previous opportunities to talk about reading material with responsive readers (Smith, 2006)

2. The reader's purposes, which reflect her or his values, attitudes, interests, motivation, and persistence (see Turner, 1997)

3. The interactive systems within the reader, including her or his developmental level, acuity of perceptual systems, cognitive-processing abilities, verbal/linguistic intelligence, and ability to connect understandings of pictures (visual literacy) and print

4. Environmental influences, including the reader's independent access to books, distractions from reading, time allotted for reading and related literacy activities, adults' expectations for literacy growth, peers' valuing of reading, and opportunities to engage in conversations with adults and peers based on relevant pieces of print (Nielsen & Monson, 1996)

When we ask a child to read, what is it exactly that we expect him or her to do? As the National Reading Panel explains, there are five key aspects of early and independent reading skills (adapted from the National Reading Panel, 2000):

1. *Phonemic awareness*, defined as the ability to hear and identify sounds in spoken words. A child with phonemic awareness can detect the smallest units of sound in words *(phonemes)* and the corresponding smallest written units of language *(graphemes)*.

2. *Phonics*, defined as a working knowledge of the rules that govern language and how to put together and break apart words, particularly unfamiliar words. Children who use phonics have learned the relationship between the letters of written language and the sounds of spoken language. *Phonics instruction* teaches students how to use letter/sound relationships to read and spell words (see Bear, Invernizzi, Templeton, & Johnston, 2007; Cunningham, 2008).

3. *Fluency*, defined as a level of automaticity in mentally processing print that enables a reader to move through a passage of text at a steady and satisfying pace. Children who are fluent readers have the capacity to read text accurately and quickly.

4. *Vocabulary*, defined as the words students must know to communicate effectively. A child with an adequate vocabulary knows a sufficient number of words to make sense out of print as he or she decodes it.

5. *Comprehension*, defined as the ability to understand and gain meaning from what has been read. When a child is reading, he or she is deriving meaning from printed text.

What Children Need to Become Readers

As described by Mackey and White (2004), "Reading is ubiquitous. We live, work, and play in a world that is saturated with print, words, books, and ideas. Learning to read, then, is a necessity" (p. 30).

Specifically, children learning to read need the following:

- Time for reading and learning
- Access to texts of all kinds and rich resources for learning to read
- Interactions with other readers, both novice and expert
- Effective instruction in skills and strategies suited to their developmental levels
- Demonstrations of how readers, writers, and texts work
- Awareness of their own reading process (adapted from Braunger & Lewis, 2005)

Collaboration with Families and Professionals

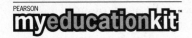

Go to the Assignments and Activities section of Chapter 8 in MyEducationKit and complete the activity entitled "The Whole Child."

Two new students, Mitchell and Jeannie, moved into the district in January and were assigned to Ms. Liebman's first-grade class. Mitchell seemed very mature and adultlike in his speech. He appeared to be capable of concentrating, persisting at a task until it was completed, and generally functioning at a level far beyond that of his peers. Ms. Liebman discovered that he could read anything in the room, including a page from a teacher's manual lying on her desk! She recognized that Mitchell would need learning experiences that differed from those of many of his peers.

When Mitchell was tested by the school psychologist, he scored in the "genius" range. After a meeting attended by Mitchell's family, the teacher, the school psychologist, and the teacher responsible for the gifted program, several approaches were proposed. They agreed that because Mitchell's giftedness was primarily in the language area, he would read material at his reading level three times per week with a sixth-grade buddy and two times per week with a senior citizen who volunteered at the school. About this, Mitchell's mother said, "I am so relieved that Mitchell will get the level of work that he needs. We were so worried that he would end up getting bored or would be treated like a misfit brainiac instead of a little boy who learned to read early."

Jeannie, the other new child in Ms. Liebman's class, was already struggling with her schoolwork. After Ms. Liebman noticed Jeannie rubbing her eyes, squinting, and holding papers and books close to her face, she requested a vision screening. It turned out that Jeannie did need corrective lenses for nearsightedness.

The school principal called a meeting with Jeannie's mother, stepfather, social worker, and teacher. Although Jeannie's parents were very willing to approve an eye examination and wanted to get glasses for her, Jeannie's father was permanently disabled and her large family relied on her mother's minimum wage job salary as their sole source of income. The local chapter of the Lion's Club worked with an optometrist, and Jeannie was fitted with glasses.

Yet even after Jeannie's vision was corrected, some of her difficulties with reading persisted. After further evaluation, Jeannie was referred to Reading Recovery, an early intervention program developed by Marie Clay (1992). It provides children with 30 minutes a day of individual tutoring with a specially trained teacher for 12 to 16 weeks. Jeannie's parents have this to say about the support services provided to their daughter: "It's a good thing that this school is better than our other one. They are really looking out for Jeannie, getting her glasses and special help and all. Nobody in our family is good at reading. At least Jeannie is getting a chance to do her best in school."

Contributions and Consequences

- *Contributions of the teacher:* What role did the teacher play in addressing these families' concerns about reading?
- *Contributions of the family:* How did each family get involved?
- *Contributions of other professionals:* How did professionals in other fields contribute to addressing the needs of these children and families?
- *Consequences of collaboration:* How might this story have ended differently if the adults had never reached consensus?

Overview of Children's Early and Independent Reading Development

This section provides a general developmental sequence for learning to read.

Focus on Print, Meaning, and Story Knowledge

Brain and Language
Whenever neurons fire, a small amount of electrical energy is released that can be measured using EEG (electroencephalogram) technology. Records of this activity suggest that language development advances in spurts rather than as a slow, steady, incremental process (Richmond & Nelson, 2007). These cognitive spurts tend to occur when children have the support of a good teacher or mentor. A video about this research by Kurt Fischer of Harvard is posted at www.uknow.gse.harvard.edu/learning/index.html. What are the implications for educators?

Children gradually realize that the text of a book is what makes it the same book from one reading to the next. As a result, they are convinced that the print needs to be watched and matched somehow to the words of the story. Their word knowledge is developing gradually, as depicted in Figure 8.2, which is an overview of the stages of word knowledge. Children will often self-correct if a word does not fit the context of the book. Amy, a 5-year-old, was reading *A Pocket for Corduroy* (Freeman, 1968), and read "He looked at all the towels and sheets" when the last word actually was *washcloths*. At that point, she corrected herself, saying "No! I mean *washcloths*—a big heap of towels and *washcloths*." When Amy encountered an unfamiliar word, she substituted something that made sense but then realized that the word could not be *sheets* because it began with a *w*, not an *s* and because it was a long word whereas *sheets* is a short word.

Focus on Word Configuration and Sound/Symbol Correspondence

At this stage, children use the letters, words, and sounds they know and try to give a precise word-by-word reading of the book's text. Because children at this stage understand that adults' reading is an exact decoding of the text, they often refuse

---

FIGURE 8.2   Stages in Word Knowledge

1. **Logographic—Words are learned as whole units.**

   Typical age: Preschool

   Recommendations: Draw children's attention to environmental print.

   Sample activity: Make a book out of labels (e.g., cereal box covers, advertising, catalogs) that are familiar to the child.

2. **Alphabetic—Children use individual letters to identify words.**

   Typical age: Kindergarten/first grade

   Recommendations: Focus children's attention on letters.

   Sample activity: Encourage play with the alphabet—alphabet books, blocks, foam or magnetic letters, and so on.

3. **Orthographic—Children begin to see patterns in words.**

   Typical age: Primary grades

   Recommendations: Focus on word families.

   Sample activity: Play games that change just the first letter (e.g., all combined with *b*, *c, f, h, m,* etc.) or group of letters (e.g., *str-, fl-, th-*).

Source: Adapted from Firth, 1985.

---

to pretend read. Sometimes, they focus so strongly on word appearance that the meaning and context are compromised in the process. They may, for example, substitute a familiar word for an unknown word even though it does not make sense in the story context. For example, Vivian, a 6-year-old, came to the word *stripes* in a passage about tigers, but she read it as "stop."

Behaviors like these occur because children are applying whatever word analysis skills they know at the time. They might know about initial, medial, and final consonants; know something about word configuration (length/shape/outline); or know about looking for familiar letters and combinations of letters in the rest of the word. In fact, their attention to print may become so strong that they will sometimes produce nonwords, like second-grader Chaka, who encountered the word *vanilla* on a box of pudding and read it as "vanlah."

Sulzby (1985) believes that this is a very important transition for the young reader. It often occurs in the midst of formal reading lessons during kindergarten or in the primary grades. If children are exposed to a barrage of letters, sounds, sight words, and rules at the wrong time, it may undermine their confidence and confuse them. As children work through this awkward stage in learning to read, adults may mistakenly assume that they are regressing because they relied on memory previously and seemed more fluent before. Actually, children are orchestrating everything they know about reading and books (Doake, 1986).

FIGURE 8.3 Sixteen Alternatives to "Just Sound It Out"

Some things to say when children are trying to figure out a new word include the following:

"Tell me about what you've read so far."

"Start right here and try again."

"Look at the picture. What word might make sense? Remember, it starts with ____."

"You thought the word might be _____. Look here. Could that word be spelled this way?"

"The word rhymes with _____."

"I noticed that you are stuck. Is it a word you can't figure out?"

"Is the word that you are having trouble with a big word you haven't seen before or a little word that you forgot?"

"Try reading it again; only this time, try to slow down."

"Oh, I think you know this one. It's a lot like _____."

"See what the sentence says without that word."

"Can you put in a word that makes sense?"

"Show me which part is giving you trouble."

"Did you ask your reading partner?"

"Read the next couple of sentences to see if you can figure it out."

"Could the word be _____?"

"Look at all the letters *before the vowel*. What sound does *str-* make? Now look at the rest: *a-w*. Put the two together."

Coordinating Knowledge of Print and Story

For some children, this stage occurs in first or second grade; for others, it occurs much later. Children begin to coordinate all of the experience they have amassed in interacting with print. They are learning to use all the sources of information available to a reader—phonics, syntax, semantics, and pragmatics—at the appropriate time.

When confronted with new words, adults often instruct children to sound them out, yet many words in the English language are not phonetic, in other words, not spelled the way that they sound. Rather than rely entirely on sound/symbol correspondence, children need to be encouraged to build a repertoire of strategies. Figure 8.3 suggests varied ways to help children tackle unfamiliar words.

Children at this stage may be found spelling and practicing words over again until they become known. They have better self-correction and, with additional experience, will be on the way to becoming independent readers.

Figure 8.4 is an overview of the stages in early and independent reading and writing.

FIGURE 8.4 Developmental Sequence in Early Reading and Writing

Early Reading and Writing: Goals for First Grade

Children begin to read simple stories and can write about a topic that is meaningful to them.

First Graders Can

- Read and retell familiar stories
- Use strategies (rereading, predicting, questioning, contextualizing) when comprehension breaks down
- Use reading and writing for various purposes on their own initiative
- Orally read with reasonable fluency
- Use letter/sound associations, word parts, and context to identify new words
- Identify an increasing number of words by sight
- Sound out and represent all substantial sounds in spelling a word
- Write about topics that are personally meaningful
- Attempt to use some punctuation and capitalization

What Teachers Do

- Support the development of vocabulary by reading daily to the children, transcribing their language, and selecting materials that expand children's knowledge and language development
- Model strategies and provide practice for identifying unknown words
- Give children opportunities for independent reading and writing practice
- Read, write, and discuss a range of different text types (poems, informational books)
- Introduce new words and teach strategies for learning to spell new words
- Demonstrate and model strategies to use when comprehension breaks down
- Help children build lists of commonly used words from their writing

What Parents and Family Members Can Do

- Talk about favorite storybooks
- Read to children and encourage them to read to you
- Suggest that children write to friends and relatives
- Bring to a parent–teacher conference evidence of what your child can do in writing and reading
- Encourage children to share what they have learned about their writing and reading

Transitional Reading and Writing: Goals for Second Grade

Children begin to read more fluently and write various text forms using simple and more complex sentences.

Second Graders Can

- Read with greater fluency
- Use strategies more efficiently (rereading, questioning, and so on) when comprehension breaks down
- Use word identification strategies with greater facility to unlock unknown words
- Identify an increasing number of words by sight
- Write about a range of topics to suit different audiences
- Use common letter patterns and critical features to spell words
- Punctuate simple sentences correctly and proofread their own work
- Spend time reading daily and use reading to research topics

What Teachers Do

- Create a climate that fosters analytic, evaluative, and reflective thinking
- Teach children to write in multiple forms (stories, information, poems)
- Ensure that children read a range of texts for a variety of purposes

FIGURE 8.4 Continued

- Teach revising, editing, and proofreading skills
- Teach strategies for spelling new and difficult words
- Model enjoyment of reading

What Parents and Family Members Can Do

- Continue to read to children and encourage them to read to you
- Engage children in activities that require reading and writing
- Become involved in school activities
- Show children your interest in their learning by displaying their written work
- Visit the library regularly
- Support your child's specific hobby or interest with reading materials and references

Independent and Productive Reading and Writing: Goals for Third Grade

Children continue to extend and refine their reading and writing to suit varying purposes and audiences.

Third Graders Can

- Read fluently and enjoy reading
- Use a range of strategies when drawing meaning from the text
- Use word identification strategies appropriately and automatically when encountering unknown words
- Recognize and discuss elements of different text structures
- Make critical connections between texts
- Write expressively in many different forms (stories, poems, reports)
- Use a rich variety of vocabulary and sentences appropriate to text forms
- Revise and edit their own writing during and after composing
- Spell words correctly in final writing drafts

What Teachers Do

- Provide opportunities daily for children to read, examine, and critically evaluate narrative and expository texts
- Continue to create a climate that fosters critical reading and personal response
- Teach children to examine ideas in texts
- Encourage children to use writing as a tool for thinking and learning
- Extend children's knowledge of the correct use of writing conventions
- Emphasize the importance of correct spelling in finished written products
- Create a climate that engages all children as a community of literacy learners

What Parents and Family Members Can Do

- Continue to support children's learning and interest by visiting the library and bookstores with them
- Find ways to highlight children's progress in reading and writing
- Stay in regular contact with your child's teachers about activities and progress in reading and writing
- Encourage children to use and enjoy print for many purposes (such as recipes, directions, games, and sports)
- Build a love of language in all its forms and engage children in conversation

Source: International Reading Association and the National Association for the Education of Young Children. Learning to read and write: Developmentally appropriate practices for young children. *Reading Teacher: A Journal of the International Reading Association, 52*(2), pp. 200–201. Copyright 1998 by the International Reading Association. Reproduced with permission of the International Reading Association via Copyright Clearance Center.

Teacher Concerns and Basic Strategies

Infants and Toddlers
The act of looking at a picture book engages all areas of the brain, as the child uses motor skills to pick up a book and turn the pages, vision to look at the words and pictures, reasoning to interpret the meanings of the words, and gestures or speech to respond to the pictures (Sorgen, 1999). How might looking at a book with just a few cardboard pages and simple pictures build the very young child's ability to read later on?

PEARSON
myeducationkit™

Go to the Assignments and Activities section of Chapter 8 in MyEducationKit and complete the activity entitled "Hermit Crab Story."

Being able to motivate students is an important teaching skill. As Mariska said:

> There are some children in my third-grade class who are disinterested in reading. I can't seem to get them motivated at all, and I am constantly reminding them to pay attention or complete their work.

Motivation is essential to engagement in reading during a literacy event (Jalongo, 2007). Engagement in the task of reading depends on the following elements:

- Children must see themselves as readers and be seen as readers by those around them.
- Children need to regard the reading task as personally meaningful.
- Reading must be perceived as a low-risk activity and accomplishable task by the child.
- Children who are learning to read must have the opportunity to bond with other readers.
- Children need attainable challenges that they can master and experience success with (Cambourne, 1995; Lonigan, 2005).

Figure 8.5 is an overview of some of the motivational issues associated with reading.

Classroom Activities to Support Early and Independent Reading

Basal Reading Series   The basal reading program is far and away the most popular and widely used method of teaching reading, with 85 percent of U.S. classrooms relying on the reading books, workbooks, and practice sheets that are produced by various publishers. Most elementary schools use the particular series adopted by the school or the district from kindergarten through sixth grade.

PEARSON
myeducationkit™

Go to the Assignments and Activities section of Chapter 8 in MyEducationKit and complete the activity entitled "A Language Experience Approach."

In concept, these basal materials are supposed to be basic—a sequential set of resource materials that the teacher

FIGURE 8.5 Research on the Motivation to Read: The Questions Children Ask Themselves

Question: What is reading?

- Classic studies of young children have concluded that emergent readers have incomplete understandings about what it means to become literate (e.g., Bissex, 1980).

- At first, children tend to focus on observable behaviors of adults, such as turning pages and commenting on the illustrations. They believe that when they imitate these behaviors (e.g., a toddler who turns the pages of a newspaper and talks), they are reading (Strommen & Maters, 1997).

- Next, children begin to realize that reading somehow involves relying on the information in the book to produce a sequenced, meaningful, and fixed account. At first, they may think that this is based on the illustrations alone; later, they realize it is the words that are used. Children typically begin to realize that reading involves decoding (e.g., "doing letters") and may expect to learn to read those letters by magic (Strommen & Maters, 1997).

- Even after children acquire significant skills, they often remain unclear about the relationships between those skills and learning to read. Children eventually realize that reading involves interpreting text and learn to use the multiple strategies necessary in becoming fluent readers (Strommen & Maters, 1997).

Implications for Instruction

- Model the reading process using enlarged texts ("big books").

- Let children glimpse your own thinking as a reader by using a think-aloud strategy (e.g., "Let's see, this word can't be jump—no *j*. It has three letters, starts with an *h*, and is something the rabbit is doing . . .").

- Convince children, parents, and families that memorizing a favorite book is learning to read (even if it is not actually deciphering words).

- Interview children periodically to get a glimpse of their understandings about reading (Hudson-Ross, Cleary, & Casey, 1993).

- Particularly for older children who are reluctant to read, try asking them to tell a story called "The child who did not like reading" (Davis, 2007).

- Create situations that challenge children's assumptions. For instance, if a child thinks that reading is memorizing, ask the child to write something; then have a reader demonstrate how he or she can read it without ever seeing it before.

Question: Can I do this task?

- Generally speaking, people will not undertake a task unless they believe they have *at least* a 50 percent chance of success.

- Children's reading motivation is affected by children's general beliefs about their competence.

- Children's prior patterns of success and failure in their attempts to read affect their willingness to persist at the task of learning to read (Wigfield & McCann, 1996/1997).

(continued)

FIGURE 8.5   Continued

Implications for Instruction

- Structure situations for success so that children do not lose confidence in themselves as readers and become confused about the purposes for reading (Sulzby, 1985).
- Use open-ended tasks that offer children meaningful choices, graduated challenges, control over their own learning, and opportunities for collaboration, and encourage them to examine the consequences of their strategies and efforts.
- Be cautious about using terms that are confusing to beginning readers (e.g., *word, sentence, letter, beginning sound,* etc.) (Strommen & Maters, 1997).
- Use predictable books, shared book experiences, language experience stories, easy readers, and multitextual approaches to increase children's chances of success.
- Caution parents and families about discussing children's reading difficulties in front of them or being harshly critical of early reading efforts.

Question: Do I want to do this task, and why?

- Generally speaking, extrinsic reinforcement can motivate people, but the effect may disappear when the rewards are no longer given or have lost their appeal (Kohn, 1996).
- A growing body of evidence suggests that teachers need to build situational interest in learning tasks by planning motivating activities (Jalongo, 2007).

Implications for Instruction

- Conduct an interest inventory periodically to get a sense of children's interests and curiosities.
- Provide a wide array of high-interest reading materials on various topics.
- Consider how much the definition of *reading* has been affected by the contemporary child's multimedia environment (Levy, 2009).
- Recommend books to children based on your knowledge of their favorite topics, authors, and illustrators.
- Model enthusiasm for books and authors.
- Try to extend children's literary preferences through the use of film, computer software, audio, and other media.
- Expand children's familiarity with different literary genres.

For further information on supporting young children's disposition to learn, see Wilford (2008).

draws on to plan for effective reading instruction. But in fact, most basal programs include so much material that if teachers follow them religiously, they will have little time for anything else. In some instances, the reading selections, the types of questions, the reading curriculum, and even what counts as reading are all determined by the basal reading program.

Buddy Reading   Children's reading to each other in pairs is a strategy for supporting independent reading (Friedland & Truesdell, 2004). It is best to vary the teams. Sometimes, a skilled reader is paired with a less skilled one. At other times, children at about the same reading level use an "I read a page, you read a page" turn-taking strategy, or you might try some teams in which children share a book in two languages with each reading the text in his or her native language. To clarify their roles, consider giving children cards with pictures that help them remember to either "read" (a picture of lips) or "listen" (a picture of an ear). These cards help to remind children about their particular roles; the picture of an ear reinforces the idea that the child holding it is not supposed to talk, while the picture of the lips reinforces the idea that the child holding it is supposed to do the reading aloud (Zaslow & Martinez-Beck, 2006).

Interviews on Reading   Try getting a glimpse of children's understanding and motivation for reading by conducting interviews. This will help you to get a clearer idea of how children understand what is expected of them (see Figure 8.5). First-graders, for example, have defined *reading* in a variety of ways. "Something you do when you look at books." "It's words with letters." "It's another way of telling you something, but no sound." When asked why people read, another first-grader said, "So they will know how to read when they get older. Big people read long letters and different papers. If they did not read, then nobody would have any newspapers, and who would read me a story at night?" Another said that people read "To learn. For information."

Bookmarks and Pointers   Children sometimes have difficulty keeping their place while reading, so materials that help them to follow along in the book can be helpful. Bookmarks or 6-inch rulers can be used to underline each line of text. When working with a group and a big book or chart, try making a device that will focus attention. One student teacher used an old rubber glove, stuffed it with fiberfill, and inserted a dowel rod inside, all secured with glue and a rubber band. She then added a gaudy plastic ring and red fake fingernails and used it as a pointer. Another way to highlight words is to construct a "word window" from a bright piece of cardboard with the center cut out.

Asking Good Questions   Experts emphasize the importance of asking questions in the reading process (Raths, Wassermann, Jonas, & Rothstein, 1986) for these specific purposes:

- *Observing/gathering and organizing data.* Children are encouraged to look carefully and describe what they see. They use observational data to support their ideas and try to organize what they have observed.
- *Comparing and classifying.* Children look for similarities and differences and relate new information and ideas to what they already know. The teacher reminds children of previous learning that will help them solve the current problem.
- *Summarizing and interpreting.* Children recap what they know so far and explain things from their own points of view.
- *Identifying assumptions/suggesting hypotheses.* Children are asked to make educated guesses about the assumptions they have made.
- *Imagining and creating.* Children are encouraged to use visualization, or create mental images that will help them solve the problem.

Language Experience Approach   The *language experience approach*, or LEA (Van Allen, 1976), begins with a concrete experience that is used to produce a story dictated by the children, which is then transcribed by the teacher as reading material. The LEA is designed to make children aware of the conventions of print, encourage social interactions among children, involve children in practical uses of written language, and build on children's familiarity with spoken language to move into reading. When working with a group, the teacher can select a shared experience with cultural relevance (e.g., making an ethnic food for snack, learning a simple game from another culture). Each child suggests a sentence that results in a simple, sequential story, which the teacher writes on a wall chart. Sentences contributed to the chart story are labeled with the child's name to show her or his contribution. The concrete experience helps to make the words more understandable because they are used in context and focus on children's home cultures (Carasquillo & Rodriguez, 2002). Reading activities based on the LEA story chart include:

- Cutting the story into sentence strips and having the children reassemble it in sequence.
- Covering key words with self-adhesive notes and rereading the sentences, asking children to fill in the missing words.
- Making a small version of the story for a child to take home and read.
- Exchanging LEA charts with another class and asking the other class to respond to what your class wrote.
- Drawing attention to certain features (such as rhyming words or punctuation) with highlight markers or highlight tape (transparent fluorescent tape).
- Using a series of commercially produced pictures, digital photographs, or children's drawings to create a common experience and produce a class big book.

Blocks of Time for Reading   Schedule a time when children can read or, if they are not yet reading, choose books to look at. Be certain to model your own enthusiasm by reading during this time. Schoolwide programs such as SSR (sustained silent reading) and DEAR (Drop Everything and Read)—in which everyone in the building, including the support staff, reads—have been successful in emphasizing the importance of reading.

Conclusion

The Center for the Improvement of Early Reading Achievement (2001) issued this statement about effective instruction:

> Primary-level instruction that supports successful reading acquisition is consistent, well-designed, and focused. Teachers lead lessons where children receive systematic word recognition instruction on common, consistent letter-sound relationships and important but often unpredictable high-frequency words, such as *the* and *what*. Teachers ensure that children become adept at monitoring the accuracy of their reading as well their understanding of texts through instruction in strategies such as predicting, inferencing, clarifying misunderstandings, and summarizing. Instructional activities that promote growth in word recognition and comprehension include repeated reading of text, guided reading and writing, strategy lessons, reading aloud with feedback, and conversations about texts children have read.

When you teach, bear in mind that the most important goals of programs designed to promote early and independent reading are twofold: to foster young children's ability to make sense out of print and to motivate them to want to read.

---

myeducationkit To check your comprehension on the content covered in this chapter, go to the MyEducationKit for your book and complete the Study Plan for Chapter 8. Here you will be able to take a chapter quiz and receive feedback on your answers.

 ## Research-Based Literacy Strategies

Free Voluntary Reading

Free voluntary reading (FVR) refers to the independent practice children acquire by reading books during their free time (Allington & McGill-Franzen, 2003; Padak & Rasinski, 2007). FVR is the foundation of language education as well as the best predictor of comprehension, vocabulary, and reading speed. In addition, FVR exerts a positive influence on writing style, spelling, and grammatical development. The chance of learning a word from a single exposure is between 5 and 20 percent, which means that children need to encounter words repeatedly in order to build a sight vocabulary and become fluent readers (Krashen, 2004). They may actually need to encounter nearly 1 million words per year to make 1,000 of them part of their active vocabulary. How, then, can you get children to engage in FVR? Notable strategies include (1) directly encouraging children to read by recommending the right type of reading materials to them, (2) offering opportunities for peers to talk about and recommend books to one another, (3) providing book displays and modeling the appropriate use of materials, and (4) increasing children's access to books that are matched to their reading levels. Ways to provide wide opportunities for voluntary reading include the following:

• Schedule at least one block of structured sustained silent reading (SSR) for students each day. Have children document what they read, and give them opportunities to talk about what they have read. In terms of time, 15 minutes is usually appropriate for kindergartners, with gradual increases in time as students' abilities and attention spans develop.

• Model your own pleasure reading during sustained SSR. Resist the urge to use this time to work with students, correct papers, and so forth.

• Provide a varied collection of print materials in your classroom: library, personal, and student-written books; newspapers (community, city, regional); magazines (for children, community based); brochures and pamphlets of interest to the children in your room; and menus and other such environmental print.

• Provide an opportunity for each child to acquire a library card. Many public libraries have programs that work closely with the public schools to make their services accessible to all children.

A free source for easy readers is Reading A-Z, which can be found at www.readinga-z.com/newfiles/tour/tour7.html.

Readers' Theater

Readers' Theater (RT) is "a text that is expressively and dramatically read aloud by two or more readers." The emphasis is on reading out loud and creating pictures of what's happening in the minds of the listeners (Kirkland & Patterson, 2005). In Readers' Theater, children do not need to wear costumes or pantomime. This is not a play; it is a reading performance. RT gives children practice in reading aloud and reading expressively.

Most RT activities begin with a script that is color coded. Each reader gets a copy of the script with just his or her part highlighted so that the children do not lose their places while reading. Teachers and students can create their own RT scripts, use books of prepared RT scripts—such as the series by Susan Barchers—or go to online sources, such as Aaron Shepard's RT (www.aaronshep.com/rt/index .html) for numerous ready-to-print-and-use scripts. Often, picture books are adapted into RT scripts by teachers, which is easier if the book includes quite a bit of dialogue already, such as *Owl Babies* (Waddell, 1996).

Teachers can accommodate different levels of reading ability in students by carefully selecting the parts to be read in Readers' Theater. The narrator's role, for example, is often the most difficult to read. The teacher could read this part or ask a child who is advanced in reading to be the narrator. Conversely, some characters may have just a couple of lines or a repeated phrase. Reading such parts is achievable, with practice, for children who are struggling with reading or who are English language learners. A wide array of online resources for Readers' Theater are available online at http://literacyconnections .com/ReadersTheater.html and www.teachingheart .net/readerstheater.htm.

Repeated Oral Reading and Scaffolded Silent Reading (ScSR)

Repeated interactive read-alouds, a systematic method of reading aloud, allow teachers to scaffold children's understanding of the book being read, model strategies for making inferences and explanations, and teach vocabulary and concepts. A storybook is read three times in slightly different ways in order to increase the amount and quality of children's analytical talk. During the first reading, teachers introduce the story's problem, insert comments, ask a few key questions, and finally ask a "why" question calling for extended explanation. This is accompanied by elaborations on a few key vocabulary words. The second reading of the text capitalizes on children's growing comprehension of the story by providing enriched vocabulary explanations and asking additional inference and explanation questions. The third time the story is read, children are guided in reconstructing the story, which requires them to recount information as well as provide explanations and commentary (McGee & Schickendanz, 2007). Quantitative and qualitative results from a year-long study in a third-grade class suggest that repeated oral reading and scaffolded silent reading can be used to make children's silent reading practice more focused and effective (Reutzel, Jones, Fawson, & Smith, 2008).

Links with Literature

Easy Readers and Learning to Read

When children are just beginning to read, it is often helpful to give them books that are predictable and likely to reward their reading efforts with success. Like the big books that are predictable, easy readers are intended to build children's confidence as readers. Of course, some easy readers are of higher quality than others.

Books for Beginning Readers

General Characteristics

1. Predictable connections between pictures and print so that struggling readers can search illustrations for answers
2. Wide spacing, large print, few words per page, and short sentences that do not discourage the beginner
3. Controlled vocabularies that use commonly known high-frequency nouns, verbs, adjectives, and adverbs
4. Literal language rather than symbolic language use (e.g., limited use of idioms and metaphors)
5. Structures that make the text more predictable (e.g., question-and-answer, rhyme, days of the week, repetition of phrases)

Easy Readers and Predictable Books, Classic and New

The Adventures of Max and Pinky, Best Buds (Eaton, 2008); *Brown Bear, Brown Bear, What Do You See?* (Martin, 1967); *Car Wash* (Steen & Steen, 2001); *Dog and Bear: Two Friends, Three Stories* (Seeger, 2007); *The First Day of Winter* (Fleming, 2006); *First the Egg* (Seeger, 2007); *Go Dog Go* (Eastman, 1961); *Green Eggs and Ham* (Seuss, 1960); *Hop on Pop* (Seuss, 1963); *How Do Dinosaurs Say Goodnight?* (Yolen & Teague, 2000); *Mommies Say Shhh!* (Polacco,

2005); *My Beak, Your Beak* (Walsh, 2002); *My Friend Is Sad: An Elephant and Piggie Book* (Willems, 2007); *Oh, Look* (Polacco, 2004); *One Fish, Two Fish, Red Fish, Blue Fish* (Seuss, 1960); *Orange Pear Apple Bear* (Gravett, 2007); *Put Me in the Zoo* (Lopshire, 1960); *Someone Bigger* (Emmett, 2005); *Thank You Bear* (Foley, 2007); *This Is the Teacher* (Greene, 2005).

Easy Readers: Series

Aladdin Paperbacks Ready-to-Read

Bantam/Bank Street Ready-to-Read

HarperCollins: My First I Can Read Series, Fancy Nancy Series

Harper Trophy I Can Read Books

Houghton Mifflin: The Sheep Series (Shaw, 1995)

Puffin Easy-to-Read

Random House Step into Reading

Scholastic Hello Reader

School Zone Start to Read

The Wright Group (The Story Box and Sunshine at Home)

Recommended Resources for Locating Easy Readers

Gunning, T. G. (2007). *Creating literacy instruction for all students.* Boston: Allyn & Bacon.

Riggle, J., Molnar, L. M., & Barston, B. (2007). *Beyond picture books: Subject access to best books for beginning readers* (3rd ed.). Englewood, CO: Libraries Unlimited.

A Sampler of Children's Books about Learning to Read and Using the Library

Amber on the Mountain (Johnston, 1994). A young girl who lives in a remote rural area discovers how reading and writing can establish and maintain friendships.

Anno's Twice Told Tales (Grimm, Grimm, & Anno, 1993). A fox child's pretend reading of a book including two fairy tales is contrasted with the actual text read by his father in this book that helps children to understand real reading.

Aunt Chip and the Great Triple Creek Dam Affair (Polacco, 1996). A town consumed by television closes the library and begins to use books for many purposes other than reading, including plugging up the dam. Then a child learns to read and revolutionizes the town's thinking.

The Bee Tree (Polacco, 1993). After Mary Ellen grows tired of reading, her grandfather suggests that they go on a hunt for bees. They are accompanied by many interesting characters until they find the honey, return home to celebrate, and rediscover the joys of reading.

But Excuse Me That Is My Book (Child, 2007). In this book from the Charlie and Lola series, Lola is dismayed when her favorite book is not on the shelf—and is being borrowed by someone else!

Come Back, Jack! (Anholt & Anholt, 1994). A young girl who doesn't like books watches her brother quite literally get lost in a book by disappearing into a fantasy world of nursery rhymes.

The Day of Ahmed's Secret (Heide & Gilliland, 1990). Readers follow Ahmed through the marketplace in Cairo as he makes his way home. His secret? He has learned how to read!

Dream Peddler (Haley, 1993). Based on the true story of a poor peddler from the 1700s, John Chapman, who became so well known for bringing books to the people that they were named after him: "chapbooks." Even after becoming a successful businessman, he continued to share the power of literature with others.

Good Books! Good Times! (Hopkins, 1990). A collection of 14 poems about reading and books.

Harriet Reads Signs and More Signs (Maestro & Maestro, 1981). A humorous story about reading environmental print.

Hey! I'm Reading! A How-To-Read Book for Beginners (Miles, 1995). Watercolor illustrations and an upbeat text reassure emergent readers that they can learn to read.

I Can Read Signs. I Can Read Symbols (Hoban, 1983). A colorful reminder of all the things that children have learned to read in their environments, even before formal reading instruction begins.

I Like Books (Browne, 1989). A chimpanzee character talks about all the different kinds of books he reads and loves.

I Took My Frog to the Library (Kimmel, 1990). An imaginative and funny story about the consequences of allowing a host of unusual pets to accompany a young child to the library.

Just Juice (Hesse, 1999). Juice, a 9-year-old girl, learns to appreciate the value of literacy as she watches her unemployed father's struggle to prevent losing their home.

Library Lil (Williams, 1997). A larger-than-life librarian convinces everyone to read when the electricity goes out. Humorous illustrations by Steven Kellogg make the tall tale come alive.

Library Mouse (Kirk, 2007). A little mouse who lives at the library and loves books decides to become an author and leave his creations out for others to pick up and read.

More Than Anything Else (Brady, 1995). Booker T. Washington's desperate wish to learn to read as a child is finally fulfilled.

Mr. George Baker (Hest, 2005). A young child and an elderly neighbor share a common goal: learning to read.

Olaf Reads (Lexau, 1961). An initially reluctant reader begins to see the advantages of "breaking the code."

Please Bury Me in the Library (Lewis, 2005). A collection of silly poems about reading and the library.

Poppleton (Rylant, 1997). An easy reader about a pig who spends Mondays at the library and experiences a range of emotions in response to the books he finds there.

Reading Is Everywhere (Wright Group, 1988). This predictable book helps children see opportunities to read in the environment.

Richard Wright and the Library Card (Miller, 1999). In this story about racial discrimination, a famous African American novelist from Tennessee is not permitted access to the Memphis Public Library to read the books he has written and published.

Running the Road to ABC (Lauture, 1996). Six Haitian children travel through the beautiful countryside to their school where they learn letters, sounds, and words that will enable them to become readers.

The Signmaker's Assistant (Arnold, 1992). A young boy's silly signs wreak havoc in the community in this humorous book about the function of signs.

Something Queer at the Library (Levy, 1977). A hilarious read-aloud mystery about contemporary children who get locked in the library and have to problem solve their way out.

Thank You, Mr. Falker (Polacco, 1998). A popular children's author tells how an understanding teacher helps a child who still cannot read in fifth grade.

Tomás and the Library Lady (Mora, 1992). The child of migrant farm workers finds a refuge and intellectual stimulation at the library in this true childhood story of Tomás Rivera, the famous writer.

The Wednesday Surprise (Bunting, 1989). A child surprises the family by teaching her grandmother how to read.

When Will I Read? (Cohen, 1977). The classic question is answered in this book about first-grader Jim's experiences in school.

You Read to Me, I'll Read to You (Ciardi, 1982). Short, funny poems written at a first-grade level invite an adult and child to read together.

You Read to Me, I'll Read to You: Very Short Stories to Read Together (Hoberman, 2002). Part of a series of books designed for reading by two people—some parts are read individually while others are read in unison.

Online Resource: Washburn-Moses (2006).

ELLs
The Literacy Achievement Gap

The literacy achievement gap refers to the disparity in academic achievement between different groups (Teale, Paciga, & Hoffman, 2007). Statistically speaking, overall rates of literacy achievement for Spanish-speaking children are not as high as that of their white, middle-class peers (Foster & Miller, 2007). Lower achievement in literacy also is linked to educational attainment, defined as the number of years students stay in school. When children struggle with literacy, they are less likely to finish high school or pursue higher education. The reasons for this are complicated because children who speak Spanish as a first language tend to be from low-income backgrounds and frequently are learning the language of instruction in U.S. schools—English. As a first step, early childhood educators need to recognize that the source of bias against young Spanish-speaking children in the United States often has more to do with the socioeconomic status of their family than with English proficiency (Laosa & Ainsworth, 2007; Saracho & Spodek, in press). International comparisons are helpful in making this point. In Canada, for example, most ELLs are middle class (such as children learning French and English in the province of Quebec) and attitudes about bilingual education generally have a more positive "enrichment" approach (Lovett et al., 2008). In Britain, children from Pakistan and Bangladesh who are learning English tend to struggle academically, particularly with respect to literacy in English, and views of second-language learning are less positive (Genesee, Lindholm-Leary, Saunders,

& Christian, 2007; Hutchinson, Whiteley, Smith, & Connors, 2003). Such international trends suggest that it is not the task of learning the mainstream language alone that creates a challenge; rather, the issues of English language learning are clouded by larger social issues and factors that put children at risk, such as poor nutrition, inadequate housing, and other health and safety considerations (Freeman & Freeman, 2002; Garcia, 2008).

In response, educators need to implement the essential principles of programs that have been successful in supporting not only second language learning but also children living in poverty: (1) focusing on children in the lowest quintiles for services, (2) timing interventions in ways that match learners' developmental levels, (3) increasing the intensity of support programs, (4) providing ongoing professional training, (5) coordinating services with other agencies, (6) investing time in creating more opportunities for children to learn, and (7) carefully monitoring and evaluating attainment of programmatic goals (Neuman, 2009). An important goal is to reduce the number of children identified as learning disabled in reading in the later years of elementary school (Foster & Miller, 2007; Magnuson & Waldfogel, 2005).

How Do I ...
Teach a Guided Reading Lesson?

At one time, it was common for teachers in the primary grades to meet with each of three reading groups (high, medium, low) to introduce the new vocabulary and then send students back to their seats to read silently and do workbook pages. That practice has been challenged by researchers who argue that it labels children and does not provide enough support and monitoring of individual progress (Morrow, 2001). Also, providing struggling readers with texts that are matched to their reading levels is a critical variable in promoting vocabulary growth (Allington & Walmsley, 2007; Swanborn & de Glopper, 2002).

1. *Select the text.* Choose a book that offers a moderate challenge to the children's thinking and one that is worthy of in-depth analysis.

2. *Introduce the text to students.* This includes mentioning title and author; confirming students' prior knowledge; inviting students to recall related books; supplying information and explaining vocabulary that is critical to the gist of the story; probing for students' knowledge of key words; enriching understanding of key words; prompting students to interpret illustrations; defining the central problem, plot, or purpose of the book; inviting personal responses to the book; drawing attention to illustrations in ways that support comprehension of literary devices; elaborating on the meaning of the text; explaining how print and language signal the use of literary devices; drawing attention to an important character or event; encouraging students to say new words; elaborating on information essential for comprehension; and promoting active reading of the text.

3. *Reading the text.* Teacher observes a small group of readers at the reading table as they read aloud, confers with them briefly, and takes notes on their progress.

4. *Discussing and revisiting the text.* Students use the book as evidence to support their ideas and read aloud a particular passage.

5. *Extending understanding.* The teacher fills in a chart as children discuss the book's structure, events, characters, plot, and so on.

6. *Word work.* The teacher writes key words, one at a time, and supports the children in "solving" each one. Each word is erased as it is figured out and a new one is written.

For more on guided reading, see Fountas and Pinnell (1996), Mackey and White (2004), and Schwartz (2005). Fisher (2008) recommends a system for keeping track of a student's response history. See also Cunningham's Four Blocks model at www.wfu.edu/~cunningh/fourblocks/block1.html and Hurst's guided reading strategies with children's literature at www.carolhurst.com/profsubjects/reading/guided.html.

PEARSON myeducationkit™ Now go to Chapter 8 in the MyEducationKit (**www.MyEducationKit.com**) for your book, where you can:

- Find Chapter Objectives.
- Complete Assignments and Activities that can help you more deeply understand the chapter content.
- Extend knowledge with content-specific Web Links.
- Check your comprehension on the content covered in the chapter by going to the Study Plan. Here you will be able to take a chapter quiz, receive feedback on your answers, and then access resources that will enhance your understanding of chapter content.

chapter nine

Leading Young Children to Literature

Annie Pickert/Pearson Education

FACT FILE on Children's Literature

- Prior to the 1600s, no books were published specifically for children. An alphabet book called *Orbis Pictus: The World in Pictures*, written by John Comenius in 1657, was the first. To this day, the National Council of Teachers of English sponsors an annual Orbis Pictus Award for Outstanding Nonfiction for Children. According to the Cooperative Children's Book Center, approximately 5,000 to 5,500 children's books are published each year.

- Many of the early books written for children were used to teach a moral or lesson. In 1744, John Newbery published *A Pretty Little Pocket-Book*, which was the first children's book published with the idea of reading for pleasure in mind. Today, the Newbery Medal is one of the most prestigious awards given for excellence in children's picture books.

• The early mass-produced picture books, such as Wanda Gág's (1928) classic *Millions of Cats,* contained black-and-white ink sketches. Technological advances in photography, printing, and producing books in unusual formats (e.g., with moving parts) have made today's books for children more brilliantly colored, lavishly illustrated, and interactive than ever before (Lima & Lima, 2008).

• It was not until 1962 that a picture book depicting a minority character earned one of the most prestigious picture book awards, the Caldecott Medal. That book was *The Snowy Day,* by Ezra Jack Keats, and it is now a classic.

• The human brain appears to "run" on narratives, or stories (Bruer, 1993; Michael & Sengers, 2003; Newman, 2005). Human beings tend to recall information better when it is presented in story form; therefore, narratives are an important route to supporting young children's literacy (Lehman, 2007; Sipe, 2008) and their reading abilities (Evers, Lang, & Smith, 2009; Meier, 2009).

• The main influences on home storybook reading appear to be (1) educational beliefs, (2) views of the purposes for reading, (3) approaches to sharing (e.g., didactic versus interactive), and (4) parents' own literacy practices (Bus, 2001).

• In a study of families with incomes below the poverty line, only 40 percent of children less than 5 years of age owned 10 or more books, and only 39 percent of the families mentioned reading aloud as a favorite activity or reported sharing books at bedtime (High, LaGasse, Becker, Ahlgren, & Gardner, 2000).

• Carefully chosen children's literature can help children through transitional stages and to build bridges to learning new concepts; therefore, teachers and families should work closely together when selecting literature for young children (Zeece, Harris, & Hayes, 2006).

Did any of this information surprise you? If so, what? Why? How will you use this knowledge to educate and care for the very young?

What Is Literature for Young Children?

Suppose that someone describes a marvelous gift for a child that:

• Is relatively inexpensive and durable
• Does not require an electrical outlet or batteries
• Captures a child's attention and sustains interest over an extended period of time
• Has a positive effect on the child's ability to listen, speak, read, and write

There is such a gift! That gift is literature.

PEARSON
myeducationkit™

Go to the Assignments and Activities section of Chapter 9 in MyEducationKit and complete the activity entitled "What is Literature?"

Literature may be defined as the imaginative shaping of life and thought into the forms and structures of language (Huck, Kiefer, Hepler, & Hickman, 2003). Literature in early childhood education is not limited to books but is a general term that also includes songs, rhymes, and all types of stories, poems, and plays—even the literary material that is shared with the very young through the spoken word, such as traditional lullabies sung to an infant or nursery rhymes recited for a 3-year-old. Of course, societies that value literacy tend to write, illustrate, and publish all of these products in various formats. The focus of this chapter will be on the print versions of children's literature.

If you have not had much opportunity to browse through top-quality children's books at the library or in a bookstore, you will be dazzled, both by the variety and the production quality of contemporary children's books. As a start, you may want to evaluate your prior experiences with children's books using the self-assessment checklist in Figure 9.1.

Collaboration with Families and Professionals

Standards in Education
The American Library Association defines high-quality books as "of especially commendable quality, books that exhibit venturesome creativity, and books of fiction, information, poetry and pictures . . . that reflect and encourage children's interests in exemplary ways." To view booklists that reflect these standards, visit www.ala.org and click on Notable Children's Books.

After Maria sent a letter to parents and families, inviting them to read to the toddlers in her child-care facility, only two parents, both mothers, volunteered. At first, Maria was inclined to criticize the families or assume that scheduling was the major problem. But when she talked with the families about it informally, she was surprised to hear parents make comments such as "I didn't think you could read to them that early," "My son won't sit still long enough to hear a story," and "Angela doesn't read books; she destroys them."

First, Maria located information on why books are important for infants and toddlers (see Links with Literature, Chapter 3). Then she developed a brochure in English and Spanish that explained why and how to share books with toddlers and provided a list of helpful resources. Maria also worked with the video production students at the community college to film some adults reading to toddlers and she wrote the voiceover that became the basis for an instructional video. The purpose of the project was to teach parents how to share books with the very young by modeling the process for them. Finally, Maria worked with the librarian to distribute lists of books suitable for babies and met with the library board to persuade them to expand the collection of books for babies.

After family members saw the recording and used the books successfully at home with their toddlers, 15 of them, including several fathers, agreed to contribute to the lending library by making a video at home or at school. In telling about this project, Maria said, "Now that I have convinced families that books are appropriate for toddlers, I use their videos with families who are new to the program. Reading to toddlers is catching on!"

FIGURE 9.1 Memories of Children's Literature: A Self-Assessment

What were some of your favorite nursery rhymes, stories, books, and authors as a young child? Even if you cannot recall a specific title or author's name, try to describe a favorite piece of literature from your early years. If you have a different ethnic or cultural background, take this opportunity to educate others about literature from your background.

Which of these classic and popular storybook characters do you remember? Check any that are familiar.

☐ *Clifford* (the big red dog)
☐ *The Little Engine That Could* (a circus train)
☐ *Frances* (a little badger and family)
☐ *The Berenstain Bears* (a contemporary bear family)
☐ *Swimmy and Frederick* (a fish and a mouse who are individualists)
☐ *Horton* (who hears a Who and hatches an egg)
☐ *Rosie* (a chicken who takes a farmyard walk)
☐ *The Little Red Hen* (who bakes some bread)
☐ *Wilbur and Charlotte* (a pig and his spider friend)
☐ *Pinkerton* (a Great Dane who always wreaks havoc)
☐ *Goldilocks* (who wrecks the Three Bears' home)
☐ *Winnie the Pooh and Tigger* (Christopher Robin's toys)
☐ *Madeline* (a little French girl)
☐ *Curious George* (a mischievous monkey)
☐ *Ferdinand* (a bull from Spain who is a pacifist)
☐ *Petunia* (a silly goose)
☐ *Harold* (who writes his way out of trouble with a purple crayon)
☐ *The Hungry Caterpillar* (who eats his way through foods)
☐ *The Grinch* (who steals Christmas)
☐ *Millions of Cats* (who walk through the town)

☐ *The Ugly Duckling* (who turns out to be a swan)
☐ *Sal* (who meets a bear while collecting blueberries)
☐ *The Velveteen Rabbit* (who is a discarded toy)
☐ *Rapunzel* (who lets down her golden hair)
☐ *The Gingerbread Man* (who runs away from everyone but the fox)
☐ *Harry the Dirty Dog* (who is unrecognizable to his owners)
☐ *The Peddler* (who has caps for sale and trouble with monkeys)
☐ *Chicken Little* (who thought the sky was falling)
☐ *Ducklings* (who stop city traffic)
☐ *Little Red Riding Hood* (who meets the wolf on her way to Grandma's house)
☐ *Ralph S. Mouse* (who gets a motorcycle)
☐ *Sylvester* (who finds a magic pebble)
☐ *Strega Nona* (who has a magic pasta pot)
☐ *The Three Little Kittens* (who lost their mittens)
☐ *Jack* (who climbs the beanstalk)
☐ *Mr. Rabbit* (who helps to select the perfect present)
☐ *Alexander* (who has a terrible day and who used to be rich)
☐ *Peter Rabbit* (who goes into Mr. McGregor's garden and loses his new coat)
☐ *The Beauty* (who married the Beast)
☐ *Max* (who wears his wolf suit and travels to see Wild Things)
☐ *Three Little Pigs* (who have houses to build and a wolf to fend off)
☐ *James* (who encounters a giant peach)
☐ *Ira* (who sleeps over)
☐ *The Three Billy Goats* (who had trouble with a troll)
☐ *The Snowman* (who can fly to the North Pole)
☐ *Mary* (who had a little lamb)
☐ *Amelia Bedelia* (who has trouble with language)

Contributions and Consequences

- *Contributions of the teacher:* What role did the teacher play in making this project successful?
- *Contributions of the family:* How did the families support the project after they understood it?
- *Contributions of other professionals:* How did professionals in other fields contribute to addressing the needs of the child and family?
- *Consequences of collaboration:* How might this story have ended differently if the adults had not collaborated with one another?

Overview of Children's Literature

Reasons for Using Literature

Brain and Language
Neuroscience suggests that each learning experience prepares the mind for future learning and that repeated exposure to a thought, idea, or experience enhances memory and recall of it (Jensen, 2006). Using this research as a basis, formulate a response to the parent who says, "I get so tired of reading the same stories over and over again."

Children's literature is the ideal learning medium for the young child because it stimulates the intellect as well as the imagination. Quality children's books share the following qualities:

- *Begin with enjoyment.* They use language in surprising and satisfying ways and teach children to associate pleasure with literacy events.
- *Provide a language scaffold.* Books hold a sample of language constant so that children can return to it again and again, building more meaning with each encounter.
- *Extend experience.* Literature simultaneously affirms what children already know and extends beyond what they know.
- *Provide support for readers.* When adults share a book with a child, they provide a role model of the literate adult in action—a model that the child can emulate.
- *Increase vocabulary, comprehension, and thinking skills.* Picture books introduce new words in meaningful contexts, supply children with pictorial clues, and give them the opportunity to ask questions and explore answers.
- *Develop insight.* Through literature, children get to glimpse the inner workings of characters' minds and gain perspective on personal feelings and motives.
- *Stimulate imagination.* Literature can transport children into the world of fantasy and imagination and then invite them in.
- *Build self-image and transmit social values.* Literature shows children what it means to be human and function as a member of a richly diverse social group (Harris, 1997). Books foster multicultural and multiethnic education when they communicate the universality of human emotions.

• *Match developmental levels.* The picture book builds first on children's knowledge of pictures and oral language and then gradually moves their attention to written language, thereby extending their competence.

• *Focus attention and build interest.* Reading books to young children early and often appears to stimulate an enduring interest in books and literacy. Children's interest is as much a prerequisite as a consequence of book reading. In order to enjoy and appreciate books, children often need help and guidance from more competent readers.

• *Enrich vocabulary and thinking skills.* Reading books goes beyond the here and now to deal with the past and future, as well. The language used in stories often differs from that used in children's everyday verbal interactions.

Ways of Using Literature

If you picture a successful story-sharing session in your mind's eye, it will no doubt include children gathered around the reader, enthralled by the book he or she is presenting. The realization of this ideal is not a happy accident; it is the outgrowth of careful planning. Actually, there are several issues involved in planning how to use literature, including book quality, selection, genres, and presentation.

Quality

Which books are better than others? Why?

Good picture books are more than cute. As early childhood educator James Hymes (1971) once said, think of *cute* as a one-word insult, taken to mean that something is childish rather than childlike. Children's book author Joan Aiken (1982) offers this description of a good book for young children: "Good books for children are never perfunctory, dull, meaningless or trivial; they do not contain a hidden sales message, do not moralize or preach, and do not speak condescendingly to children" (p. 31).

PEARSON
myeducationkit™

Go to the Assignments and Activities section of Chapter 9 in MyEducationKit and complete the activity entitled "Literature to Learn Social Skills."

Even in a small library, however, there are hundreds of picture books from which to choose. How do you begin? One way is to consult the resources in Chapter 1 for locating quality books on pages 22–23.

When evaluating the illustrations in children's books, look for illustrations that are "understandable, evoke emotional identification and intense emotional response, that allow room for the exercise of the reader's own imagination, that provide the reader with a new, wholesome and vital way of looking at the world and life" (Ciancolo, 1984, p. 847). The five basic elements of art are line, color, texture, shape, and arrangement or composition. In a picture book, each of these elements should be used in a way that complements the story. An artist may draw delicate sketch marks or bold black outlines (line); use soft chalk pastels or bright primary hues (color); create surfaces that are smooth and lustrous or rough and almost three-dimensional (texture); produce shapes that are distinct or that are subtle and impressionistic (shape); and confine pictures to a portion of one page or span two pages with one picture (arrangement or composition). Teaching children to view the illustrations is part of the total experience with picture books.

Selection

Which books are best suited to which child or group of children?

One of the challenges in using literature is matching a book to a child or group of children. As a start, take a look at the suggestions for choosing books based on the developmental characteristics of children in Figure 9.2.

Another way to target the level of a book is to look for a recommended age group printed directly on the book by the publisher. Seek out the opinions of resource people—librarians, faculty, experienced teachers. Also refer to periodicals that review and discuss children's books, such as *Booklinks, School Library Journal, Young Children, Childhood Education,* and *Early Childhood Education Journal.*

Eventually, you will gain confidence in your own professional judgment, just like Chris, a student teacher, who is at the library looking for a copy of "The Three Little Pigs." She locates several different versions. The first follows the old folktale closely: The wolf eats two of the little pigs, and the third pig avenges his brothers (Zemach, 1988). The second is a humorous rendition of the story in which the pigs' mother saves the day and the wolf has a change of heart (Kellogg, 1997). Chris decides that children would need to know the original story well to appreciate the humor of this version. In a Caldecott-winning version by David Weisner (2001), *The Three Pigs,* the animals are transformed as they take flight from the classic tale and storybook frame; Chris decides to use this one after the children are familiar with the traditional version.

Yet another version includes a fox who is outsmarted by the pigs' big sister, Hamlet, in an Appalachian version of the story (Hooks, 1989). Hamlet is the only one of the three who remembers the three things her Mama told her:

> One: Watch out for that mean, tricky old drooly-mouth fox. Two: Build myself a safe, strong house out of rocks. Three: Come home and visit my dear, sweet mama every Sunday.

A variant of the tale by James Marshall (1989) includes witty dialogue such as this:

> "I know," said the little pig. "I'll buy your straw and build a house." "That's not a good idea," said the Man. "Mind your own business, thank you," said the little pig.

There is also a bilingual version by Lowell (2009). *The Three Little Havelinas/Los Tres Pequeños Jabalíes* will be a great resource for Spanish-speaking students. Finally, Chris reads Scieszka's (1989) *The True Story of the 3 Little Pigs! by A. Wolf,* which is a completely different tale told from the wolf's perspective. The wolf protests that he is innocent and misunderstood. The collapse of the first house, he says, was an accident caused by a sneeze:

> That whole darn straw house fell down. And right in the middle of the pile of straw was the first little pig—dead as a doornail. He had been home the whole time. It seemed like

FIGURE 9.2 Choosing Appropriate Books for Young Children

0–2 Years

Developmental characteristics: Exploring the world through sensory input and motor activity (Piaget); dealing with issues of building basic trust (Erikson); fascinated by good/bad behavior and rewards/punishment (Kohlberg).

Appropriate books: Those that are accessible, durable, familiar, colorful, and interactive.

2–4 Years

Developmental characteristics: Continuing to interact with the environment and to acquire basic concepts; age of imagination where the line between fantasy and reality is not sharply drawn (Piaget); dealing with issues of autonomy and asserting self (Erikson); generally eager to please others (Kohlberg).

Appropriate books: Those that are brief and have simple plots with satisfying endings; rhythm, rhyme, and repetition; and consequences of behavior.

4–7 Years

Developmental characteristics: Performing basic mental operations (Piaget); dealing with issues of acquiring competence and new skills that lead to a sense of accomplishment (Erikson); tend to look at behavior from the perspective of conforming to role expectations for "good girls and boys" (Kohlberg).

Appropriate books: Those that have imagination, fantasy, humor such as slapstick, and incongruity; also folktales, predictable books, and information books.

7–9 Years

Developmental characteristics: Beginning to understand time; emerging understanding of more abstract ideas (e.g., justice, courage) and social constructs (e.g., prejudice) (Piaget); seeking to break free from adult domination and function more independently (Erikson); may begin to explore rules, laws, and respect for authority as a means of maintaining an orderly society (Kohlberg).

Appropriate books: Those with high fantasy and adventure and that explore past and future worlds. Are intrigued by mysteries and problem solving and identify strongly with characters. Enjoy nonfiction, biography, and adventure.

a shame to leave a perfectly good ham dinner there in the straw so I ate it up. Think of it as a cheeseburger just lying there.

Based on her knowledge of child development and of picture books, Chris decides that the first version is best suited for preschoolers because it is a simple, straightforward, and familiar story. She chooses the Marshall version for kindergarten or first grade because the children know the story well enough to appreciate the humor. She decides that the Appalachian version would be perfect for storytelling and makes plans to learn the story so that she can use it with a mixed-age group of children with whom she has volunteered to work at the community center. The bilingual version will be a great support for the dual-language learners, and Chris arranges with a native speaker of Spanish to make a recorded version to accompany the book. Finally, she decides that the satire of the fourth version is best suited to older children and checks out the book for her roommate, who is student teaching in third grade.

Genres

Which types of books are generally appropriate for the very young?

In a true picture book, both the words and illustrations are equally important, and both are read (Shulevitz, 1989). *Nursery rhymes* are picture books for the very young that place special emphasis on the lyrical quality of language, including rhythm, rhyme, and cadence. The nursery rhymes can be traditional, such as Mother Goose, or they may be contemporary rhymes written in the style of nursery rhymes.

PEARSON
myeducationkit™

Go to the Assignments and Activities section of Chapter 9 in MyEducationKit and complete the activity entitled "Books and Brain Development."

A retired teacher who has volunteered to work with infants and toddlers at a day-care center has discovered the importance of nursery rhymes such as "This Little Piggy" and "Rock a Bye Baby." She uses these traditional rhymes while cuddling, rocking, and singing to the babies. She knows that they are listening carefully because they stop to look at her intently or to vocalize (coo, gurgle, babble) when they hear their favorites, such as baby Angela's response to the rollicking rhyme of the picture book *Baby Danced the Polka* (Beaumont, 2004).

Poetry books for older children sometimes contain a single illustrated poem. Other poems, called *narrative poems*, tell a story. In addition to books of individual poems and songs, there are also illustrated collections of poetry and music (see Chapter 5, Links with Literature).

Folktales are traditional tales that were originally told, rather than published and read (see Chapter 6). A good example of a folktale is the story of *The Gingerbread Boy* (Galdone, 1975). It is a story with a long history and many variants. In one of the old published versions of the folktale, the gingerbread boy isn't a cookie at all; he is a pancake (Power, 1969).

Mr. Hanson, a prekindergarten public school teacher, remembers a family story about his great-great-grandfather's first day of school, during which the children heard the story of the pancake in a one-room schoolhouse in rural Colorado. The children had cut out circles of paper to represent the pancake, but a gust of wind blew Great-Great-Grandfather's across the prairie—an event that not only upset him but also made the possibility of a personified pancake seem more real.

The story of the gingerbread boy has been passed down through the generations by word of mouth but also in picture book form. During Mr. Hanson's unit on the gingerbread boy, the children ground fresh ginger and made gingerbread following a rebus recipe; then they decorated their gingerbread people with icing and raisins.

Back in the classroom, while they waited for the gingerbread to bake, they listened to Rowena Bennett's poem "The Gingerbread Man" (1988).

Afterward, the children enacted the story using paper plate masks. When the children returned to the school cafeteria to take their gingerbread people out of the oven, they were introduced to the cook, who said that they must have run away. They met the janitor in the hallway and asked him if he had seen their gingerbread. He said he had seen trays of gingerbread while cleaning the floor and suggested that they report the incident to the principal. The children went to the office and met the school secretary, who then introduced them to the principal. He greeted them and said that he had spotted their gingerbread people moving down the hallway and advised them to check back in their classroom. After the children returned from meeting school personnel and touring the building, they found their gingerbread creations and milk waiting for them at their seats.

Legends and myths are traditional stories that try to explain events in the natural world and significant happenings in supernatural ways. Legends are magical explanations about the origins of the things in our world. Two stories retold and illustrated by Tomie dePaola are examples of legends that have been handed down from generation to generation. *The Legend of the Indian Paintbrush* (1987) is a Native American story that accounts for the blooming of desert flowers, and *The Legend of the Poinsettia* (1994) is a Mexican legend that explains the origins of the popular Christmas flower.

Myths are traditional forms of literature that attempt to explain the creation of the world and other significant events. Rosemary Wells's (1998a) *Max and Ruby in Pandora's Box* is a book of myths for young children.

Fairy tales are high fantasy stories that have been passed down through several generations. They often involve royalty and contain many familiar themes, including ordeals that must be endured in pursuit of a goal and a triumphant return home, ferocious and deceitful beasts, magical objects, the fulfillment of wishes, goodness disguised as ugliness, and good triumphing over evil (Bettelheim, 1976).

A junior high school English teacher and a second-grade teacher collaborated on a fairy tales project. The project began with the second-graders hearing many different fairy tales. Some were familiar favorites that originated with the Brothers Grimm (such as "Beauty and the Beast") and Hans Christian Andersen (such as "The Nightingale"). Some were fairy tales from other lands, such as Carol Carrick's (1990) *Aladdin and His Wonderful Lamp,* and some were so-called fractured fairy tales, such as *Sleeping Ugly* (Yolen, 1981), a collection by Jon Scieszka (1992) called *The Stinky Cheese Man and Other Fairly Stupid Tales,* and the Texas version of "The Princess and the Pea," *The Cowboy and the Black-Eyed Pea* (Johnston, 1992). Of all the fairy tales they heard, the second-graders liked *Mufaro's Beautiful Daughters* (Steptoe, 1987) the best. The teacher's challenge to his junior high students was to make that fairy tale come alive for the second-graders, which they did with great relish. They created African costumes and lush jungle scenery, and then developed a script from the book.

Books for infants and toddlers introduce children to literature for the first time. As described in Chapter 3, books suited for the youngest children usually have the most minimal text; often the words are more like labels or captions for the pictures. When plot exists in books for babies, it often consists of a single event within the child's daily experience, such as taking a bath. And because the typical toddler is just learning how to manage a book, durability is important. These books are often referred to as *board books* because they have pages made of cardboard that are easier for the child to grasp. Participation books (also called *pop-up books* or *toy books*) involve the child in some sort of direct physical interaction with the book. Some of these books have textured surfaces for the child to feel, cut-out pages, flaps to lift, and so forth (see Chapter 1), such as *Where Does Maisy Live?* (Cousins, 2000) or *Peek-a-Moo* (Cimarusti, 1998).

Concept books teach one basic idea: colors, shapes, letters, numbers, opposites, and so forth. Children's book editor Ellen Roberts (1984) says that concept books are almost like commercials for ideas.

Information books (also called *expository texts*) are nonfiction and might be thought of as a child's version of an article in *National Geographic* (Roberts, 1984). They focus on real people, places, and things. Information books are nonfiction or factual explanations about the world and how things live and function (see Chapter 6).

Illustrated storybooks and chapter books have much more text and far fewer pictures. Often, these books are intended for children who are learning to read independently or for adults to read aloud to groups of children. A good example of an illustrated storybook is E. B. White's classic (1953) *Charlotte's Web*, with sketches by Garth Williams. Teachers in the primary grades often read chapter books, one chapter per day, right after the students return from lunch.

Song picture books are illustrated versions of songs, such as Glen Rounds's (1989) boldly illustrated version of *Old MacDonald Had a Farm*. As explained in Chapter 4, even nonreaders who know the song are capable of unison reading a chart of the song's lyrics. Therefore, song picture books are not only aesthetic objects but also tools for initial reading instruction.

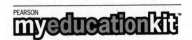

Go to the Assignments and Activities section of Chapter 9 in MyEducationKit and complete the activity entitled "Whole Group Story Time."

Presentation

How should books be shared with young children? Before reading any book to a child or children, the teacher should be thoroughly familiar with it and be able to read it skillfully. Figure 9.3 offers suggestions for reading aloud expressively.

After that initial preparation, the adult's role during a story has four dimensions (Cochran-Smith, 1986).

1. *Informer/mediator.* The adult negotiates the meaning of a story with a child by making brief comments that show the child how the book is related to his or her experience ("Look, she has a little brother just like you") or brings his or her experience to bear upon the story ("Remember when we went to the zoo?").

2. *Co-respondent.* In this role, the adult shares personal reactions and invites responses from the child (Roser & Martinez, 1995). The adult could say, "Hmm. That dog Ralph certainly seems interested in Benny's birthday cake. I wonder what will

FIGURE 9.3 How to Read Aloud Expressively

1. Relax and speak clearly.
2. Project from your diaphragm, with breath support.
3. Vary your phrasing by paying attention to punctuation and the emotions expressed.
4. Vary pace as the action indicates.
5. Vary volume for effect.
6. Read with feeling.
7. Seat the audience so everyone can see.
8. Hold the book so that the pictures face out toward the audience constantly.
9. Familiarize yourself with the material in advance so you can make eye contact with your listeners and only glance at the pages occasionally.
10. Pause at the end to give listeners a chance to think the book over and savor the ending.

For additional information on reading aloud to children, see Shedd (2008).

happen next?" (Rice, 1993). When children are familiar with the book, they tend to participate in discussions about it and control the discussions more (Bus, 2001).

3. *Monitor.* In the role of monitor, the adult recaps the child's understanding of a story and provides additional information as needed ("It looks like the good witch knows some magic, too").

4. *Director.* When the adult introduces a story, paces the narrative, and announces the conclusion, she or he is functioning as a director. Studies show that the frequency and quality of shared book experiences is affected by the interactive experiences that children share with adults in general and that parents' interaction styles frequently are influenced by their experiences as children (Bus, 2001).

There are two basic ways of using these four roles to share a picture book with children: individually and in a group. When a teacher is responsible for an entire class, it is easy to overlook the option of sharing stories one to one, yet this is often the best way to invite the child with limited book experience into the world of literature. Opportunities for individual story sharing can be accomplished in many ways, such as finding volunteer readers among parents and grandparents, high school and college volunteers, cross-age tutors from the elementary school, and peers. To help guest readers learn how to share literature effectively, follow the guidelines in Figure 9.4.

When sharing literature with a group, most teachers find that it is easier to attract and maintain children's interest if they plan a storytime program, rather than just read book after book. Dee, a college student who is enrolled in an early literacy methods course, planned a very successful storytime program for the small group of preschoolers in a private nursery school where she has volunteered to get some additional teaching experience.

It is fall and the children are intrigued by the squirrels that scamper through the large oak trees in the fenced-in yard behind their school. At circle time, Dee asks the

---

FIGURE 9.4   Reading Tips for Guest Readers

Selecting

- Look over the book before reading it to the child.
- Read the book yourself before reading it aloud. This way you will be able to find something that you and the child will both enjoy.
- Include the child when you visit the library. Let the child pick out books.
- If the book turns out to be tedious instead of interesting, forget the print and just make up a story to go with the pictures, or make another selection.

Previewing

- Talk about the book with the child before reading it. One way to do this is to read the title and talk about the picture on the cover.
- You may want to look through some of the pictures and comment on them before beginning to read.
- Try to connect the book with something familiar to the child.

Timing

- Find a time when children are ready to stop whatever they are doing and ready to enjoy a change of pace.
- Establish a regular time when you plan to read.
- If the children become restless, either stop your reading or conclude the story quickly and move on.

Reading

- Use an expressive voice, facial expressions, and gestures to make the story come alive.
- Try using the voices that you think the characters in the book might use.
- Model enthusiasm for reading so that children will look forward to reading.

Inviting Participation

- Encourage children to participate in the reading experience. Let them point to pictures and name objects that they recognize.
- Let children ask questions and guess what might happen next.
- Explain words that they might not understand.
- Rather than quizzing, try asking questions that have no right or wrong answers, such as "What would you do?" or "Why?"
- If children are already reading, let them read words or parts of the book to you.

Revisiting

- Talk about the book and go back to look at the children's favorite pictures.
- Talk about what happened in the story and how the characters felt.
- If the children ask for the same story to be read over and over again, take it as a compliment! You did a great job of reading.

Sources: Berger, 2007; Halsall & Green, 1995.

children about the squirrels. "I wish they'd let us catch 'em," says Chuckie. "I want to touch one," adds Earlene wistfully, "but they run away when you get close, just like the birds."

Dee says, "I noticed how much you like the squirrels, so today, I've brought some things that will let us look at squirrels very closely. First, here is a book with photographs in it. My favorite is this one; it shows the babies all snuggled up in their nest." The children examine the pictures carefully, commenting on what they see. "I also brought a squirrel, but this one is not alive. It died and someone took its skin and stuffed it, like a stuffed toy. I borrowed this squirrel from my science teacher at college. Have any of you seen animals that used to be alive?" Sean says, "My dad has a buck's head. My mom won't let him hang it in the living room, so he put it in the basement." Colleen adds, "Wolves. I saw them at the museum."

Dee continues: "Here is the squirrel that used to be alive. You can touch it if you want to." The children stroke the squirrel's body, tentatively at first and then with more confidence. "How'd they do its eyes?" Tamika asks. "They're made out of glass, sort of like marbles," Dee responds. "I like the tail," says Chaka. "It's fluffy."

Dee continues, saying, "Now, look at the cover of this book. Here is another animal that is related to the squirrel. How is this chipmunk like a squirrel? How is it different?" She writes the children's ideas on a chart and then leads into the story with "If you were as small as a chipmunk or a squirrel, you could do all kinds of things that you can't do now. This book, *Chipmunk's Song*, was written by Joanne Ryder (1987). It is a pretend story about a child who shrinks down to the size of a chipmunk and gets to play with him in his home under the ground." The children listen to the story and discuss it. Then Dee further develops the concept of hibernation through other books such as *Under the Snow* (Stewart, 2009) and *Do Not Disturb* (Packlam, 1989). The final activity is to talk about the fact that other animals, such as bears, hibernate or sleep during the winter. Dee concludes with *Bear Wants More!* (Wilson, 2003), the story of a bear that is very hungry after a long winter's nap. Children join in on the refrain "But bear wants more!" each time it is repeated.

> **Infants and Toddlers**
> The collective findings of almost 30 studies showed that early reading experiences provided by caregivers correlated with children's language growth and later reading achievement (Bus & van IJzendoorn, 1999). How would you use such findings to encourage parents and families to share books with infants and toddlers?

As Dee's story session illustrates, sharing literature in the classroom is not pulling a book off the shelf at random and reading it aloud without any prior preparation. The remainder of this chapter provides a wide array of suggestions for making literature come alive in your teaching.

Teacher Concerns and Basic Strategies

Ruth is a first-grade teacher in her third year of teaching in a remote rural area. Although she has always scheduled a storytime for read-alouds, she has not explored

Research and Report
Locate several different versions
of the same story for children and
check them out from the library.
Compare/contrast the different
interpretations of the story. Which
ones would you use with children
at different developmental levels?
Why?

PEARSON
myeducationkit™

Go to the Assignments and Activities
section of Chapter 9 in MyEducationKit
and complete the activity entitled
"Knowing What Inspires Children."

other uses of children's literature, other than the pieces of literature in the school district's basal reading series. Ruth says:

> I was one of the few teachers under the age of 45 until the kindergarten and second-grade teachers retired last year. Now that I have two colleagues who are very skilled and enthusiastic about literature, I want to do more. I realize that there is so much to learn.

As you think about using literature in your classroom, you, too, will realize how much there is to learn. Not only do you need to know about books, but you also need to know how to use them more effectively and make them an integral part of the curriculum (McGee, 2007). Figure 9.5 offers some recommendations for using literature more effectively. As you read them, think back to Dee's story session on the squirrels and how her strategies reflected an understanding of these basic principles.

FIGURE 9.5   Recommendations for Using Literature More Effectively

Do less introducing of books that demand information from children.

Do more inviting into the literature experience that encourages children to explore possibilities.

Do less insisting that children memorize bits of information and reminding them of what they have left out.

Do more starting with children's initial impressions and moving them to fuller, deeper understandings.

Do less talking and following your own agenda and dealing in absolutes when discussing literature.

Do more listening and following the children's lead by picking up on what they say and encouraging them to form their own hunches, wonderings, and well-formed interpretations.

Do less superficial and hasty discussion that leaves little room for questioning, probing, and enriched understandings.

Do more relevant and relaxed conversation that elicits responses from children, asks for clarification, invites participation, and models how to speak and listen in respectful and mature ways.

Source: Adapted from Langer (1994).

Classroom Activities to Support Responses to Literature

Go to the Assignments and Activities section of Chapter 9 in MyEducationKit and complete the activity entitled "Identifying with Characters."

The following activities engage children in literature.

Author/Illustrator Profile To get children in the primary grades started with basic research skills, give them a format to follow for a presentation on a favorite author or illustrator:

1. Choose an author, illustrator, or author/illustrator whose work you admire.
2. Collect interesting information (e.g., birthdate/place, childhood, books, and interesting facts; videos or filmstrips; photos downloaded from websites; materials gathered from book clubs, such as letters to the class; book jackets from the librarian; and so forth).
3. Read several books by the author.
4. Create a display—an interactive bulletin board, diorama, trifold poster, mobile, brochure, or computer-generated materials—that will persuade others to appreciate your author.
5. Consider other activities focused on books and their authors, such as converting old book jackets into jigsaw puzzles, setting up a book exchange, or creating a matching game with book authors and reduced-size color copies of the covers of their books.

Booktalks A *booktalk* is like a commercial for a particular book. Unlike a report, a booktalk does not tell the entire story. Rather, it is more like the movie previews we see on television to advertise a newly released film. It gives just enough information to intrigue the audience. Also, unlike a book report, a booktalk should be short—about 3 minutes at the most. Booktalks attract attention to high-quality books and increase children's motivation to read, build their interest in listening to a story that will be read aloud, encourage older children to read longer or more challenging books, and introduce children to the best authors for their reading levels. To view a wide variety of expertly delivered booktalks, visit the Scholastic website at http://teacher.scholastic.com/products/tradebooks/booktalks.htm; for guidelines and examples, see the American Library Association's site (www.ala.org/ala/mgrps/divs/yalsa/profdev/booktalking.cfm) and Nancy Keane's website titled Booktalks—Quick and Simple (http://nancykeane.com/booktalks/tips.htm). Print resources on booktalks include the series by Caroline Feller Bauer and Joni Bodart.

Author/Illustrator Study Learning about authors and illustrators can occur through real, live interactions through video link or online. The purpose of author visits is to give budding writers and illustrators an opportunity to see how professionals work and live. It is also possible for the teacher to plan an *author talk*, in which she or he shares a few pieces of information about the writer or artist that will be of interest to young children. In introducing the classic children's books by Robert McCloskey (1941), for example, the teacher could talk about how he brought real ducklings into his house and watched them swim in the bathtub before he drew the pictures for *Make Way for Ducklings*. To begin, just type the name of the children's book author or illustrator into your browser; most of the well-known ones have their own home page or website, such as Gail Gibbons (www.gailgibbons.com) or Jan Brett (www.janbrett .com). For online resources on various authors from the American Library Association, check out www.teachingbooks.net. A good print resource is Miller (2004). To see an example of an exceptionally thorough author/illustrator study of Eric Carle, visit the Scholastic site at www2.scholastic.com/browse/article.jsp?id=3234.

Book Characters Day   As an alternative to Halloween, plan a day when teachers and students dress in costumes related to books and story characters. Sponsor a read-a-thon, in which books are shared throughout the month by guests who read aloud their favorite books while in the costume of a story character.

Make a Mural   Use a large sheet of paper to create a mural that celebrates and commemorates an author's birthday, National Book Week, or some other literacy event, such as a special program at the library.

Multicultural Book Days   At the beginning of the year, invite every child and family to find a picture book that is connected in some way with their family history or culture. It might be a story about a foster family, extended family, adoptive family, or blended family formed by remarriage. Work with the school and public libraries to prepare a list of recommended books and to create book displays that feature all kinds of families. Then provide opportunities for every child's and family's book to be read to the class.

Literature-Based Prop Box   Combining books with other materials—such as dramatic play props, music, and literacy tools—gives children a chance to incorporate their story experiences into their dramatic play experiences. For more ways to integrate children's play and other areas of the curriculum with children's books, see Baker and Schiffer (2007) and Miller (2004).

Conclusion

Literature is the imaginative transformation of experience and ideas into language. Literature for young children includes rhymes and songs as well as stories, poems, and plays. One cornerstone of contemporary children's literature is the picture book, a blend of pictorial art and language. There are many thousands of picture books and many different genres within the classification of picture book. The teacher's role in promoting picture books includes being knowledgeable about children's literature, selecting books carefully, presenting books effectively, building a literature-based curriculum, and assessing children's responses to literature.

myeducationkit To check your comprehension on the content covered in this chapter, go to the MyEducationKit for your book and complete the Study Plan for Chapter 9. Here you will be able to take a chapter quiz and receive feedback on your answers.

Research-Based Literacy Strategies

Reading with Companion Animals

A growing body of research documents the positive effects of the human/animal bond on children's development (Jalongo, 2004a; Melson, 2003). When a child reads aloud in front of peers or teachers, evidence suggests that she or he experiences a form of performance anxiety that is responsible for elevating blood pressure (Lynch, 2000). However, when children were asked to read aloud under three conditions (to a peer, to an adult, and to a therapy dog), the presence of a therapy dog lowered blood pressure, slowed heart rate, and reduced other observable signs of anxiety (Friedmann, Thomas, & Eddy, 2000).

In response, some librarians and educators have begun inviting registered, insured, highly trained, and carefully groomed dogs into schools and libraries as a way of motivating children to read. In such a program, the dog's handler serves as the literacy mentor, while the dog functions as the non-judgmental listener. The dogs are referred to as *therapy dogs* because their purpose, unlike service dogs and search-and-rescue animals, is to supply a calming presence and offer stress-reducing benefits.

Therapy dogs are not ordinary household pets; they are trained at a level well beyond basic obedience. Two organizations that test and register these animals are Therapy Dogs International, Inc., and Delta Society. Contact these groups to determine if the program is available in your area. An organization that offers training for the handlers in supporting children's reading is the Reading Education Assistance Dogs® program of Intermountain Therapy Animals (www.therapyanimals.org/read/about.html).

Bilingual Children's Literature and Second-Language Acquisition

When children encounter books in their native or first languages, it is a way of affirming their diversity.

Some types of books for dual-language learners include the following:

1. Those originally published in a language other than English, such as *Russian Poetical Alphabet* (Klekovkin, 2008), that are available in the United States.
2. Those with the complete text in both languages, side-by-side in the same book, such as *Uncle Nacho's Hat/El Sombrero de Tío Nacho* (Rohmer, 1997) or *Platero y Yo* (Jimenez, 2003). Or books that switch between languages such as *My Way/Mi Manera* (Reiser, 2007), *Margaret and Margarita* (Reiser, 1996), or *Say Hola to Spanish Otra Vez (Again!)* (Elya, 1999).
3. Popular U.S. picture books translated into other languages, such as *No Te Sientes Bien, Sam?* (Hest & Riojas, 2007) from *Don't You Feel Well Sam?* (Hest, 2002), *Too Many Tamales* (Soto, 1996) and the Spanish equivalent, *Qué Montón de Tamales* (Soto, 1996), or the French version of *The Very Hungry Caterpillar, La Chenille Qui Fait Des Trous* (Carle, 2002).
4. Books written mainly in English with some interspersed words or phrases in another language such as *I Love Saturdays and Domingos* (Ada, 2004) and *Isla* (Dorros, 1999).

Bilingual books have many uses, such as introducing a new topic, supporting transfer of reading skills from the first language to the second, encouraging independent reading, previewing or reviewing a topic, comparing/contrasting two languages, supporting family literacy, teaching teachers and peers words in students' native languages, and promoting pleasure reading (Ernst-Slavit & Mulhern, 2003).

Joint Attention and Print Referencing

There is a particular style of sharing picture books that is the most effective in building literacy. Research suggests that when families and teachers (1) focus their attention on pictures and print, (2) make story sharing interactive, and (3) make explicit references to print, these three practices yield the best outcomes for literacy (Aram & Levin, 2002; Justice, Kaderavek, Xitao, Sofka, & Hunt, 2009; Rudd, Cain, & Saxon, 2008). These practices

are referred to as "joint attention" and "explicit text referencing." Adults who combine read-alouds with instruction of specific concepts and skills such as letter recognition, letter sounds, and name recognition activities assist children in acquiring emergent literacy skills (Fields, Groth, & Spangler, 2007; Gaffney, Ostrosky, & Hemmeter, 2008; Phillips, Norris, & Anderson, 2008) and, interestingly, it is even more effective with children who have less experience with books (Aram & Biron, 2004; Phillips, Norris, & Anderson, 2008; Rudd, Cain, & Saxon, 2008; Sylva, Scott, Totsika, Ereky-Stevens, & Crook, 2008). Recent research indicates that both verbal and nonverbal means of drawing young children's attention to print exert a positive influence on children's emergent literacy skills (Justice, Pullen, & Pence, 2008).

Links with Literature

Literature Circles

What Is a Literature Circle?

Discussion is a major way for children to respond to what they read from narrative and expository (informational) texts. A literature circle is a small group of children who (1) choose a book, (2) make decisions concerning the reading and sharing of the text, and (3) function as the facilitators of the discussion. The children's literature used as the basis for these discussions varies with the age level of the students and the specific objectives of the curriculum (Daniels, 2002). With preschool or kindergarten, the basis for the literature discussion group is often a picture book read aloud. For children in the primary grades, the reading material might be a poem, a picture book that children have selected to read, or a chapter book read aloud in class by the teacher or chosen by a small group of interested students.

Why Use Literature Circles?

Literature discussion groups have three purposes: (1) to encourage children to connect with literature, (2) to promote higher-order thinking skills, and

(3) to meet the goals of cooperative learning. The book discussion process typically includes the following phases:

- Previewing the story and making predictions based on the title, cover illustrations, and so forth
- Reading and wondering as the group reads the story and shares their thoughts about it
- Responding to the story briefly through talk, drawing, or short written responses
- Reflecting as the group discusses their short responses
- Extending responses as children draw, write, or use other forms of creative expression to show how the literature has affected them
- Looking back to review what the total group has learned from their experiences with the story (adapted from Dugan, 1997)

How Is a Literature Circle Conducted?

The basic principles of literature circles include the following characteristics:

- They consist of small groups (4–6 members).
- All students have heard or read the text.

- The literature chosen for discussion is often selected by the children.
- All members of the group facilitate the sharing process.
- All members of the group have equal status, equal voice, and shared responsibility during the discussions.

The process used in literature circles is modeled and directed by the teacher at first. Later, as children gain experience with discussions focused on a piece of literature, they assume greater responsibility for managing literature circles. For younger children or children with limited experiences in literature discussion, just 10 to 15 minutes may be sufficient at first. As children gain confidence and competence in interacting with books, more time can be allocated.

Good questions are the key to literature circles. Ideally, questions should be open-ended, with a wide range of acceptable answers possible from individual students.

Suggested Questions for Literature Circles

What do you think? (asked after reading the book)

How do you think _____ felt when _____?

Why did _____ feel that way? How can you tell?

If you could talk to anyone in this story, whom would it be? Why? What would you say to him or her?

What else could _____ have done?

Is there anyone in this book who reminds you of yourself? Who? Why?

Would you change anything about this story? What? How would you change it? If you were writing a sequel to this story, what would you have happen next? If you were writing a prequel, what would you have happen earlier?

If you could talk to the author of this story, what would say or ask?

What was the best part of the story? Why?

Additional Resources

For more information on literature circles, see Literature Circles.com at www.cdli.ca/CITE/lang_lit_circles.htm.

ELLs
Comprehensible Input

Learners of a new language need "comprehensible input," or an understanding of what they hear (Krashen, 2003). An initial step in making language understandable is ensuring that children hear the message, so teachers need first to attend to characteristics of the classroom as a listening environment. On any given day, about a third of first-graders are not hearing normally due to allergies, background noise, tinnitus (caused by medications), ear infections, and so forth (Crandell, Flexer, & Smaldino, 2004). Such situations further compound the listening difficulties of young ELLs, so clinicians in the speech/hearing/language field endorse sound amplification systems to make the speaker's voice audible above classroom noise (Cole & Flexer, 2007). Even simple changes, such as investing in chair glides to reduce background noise during classroom transitions, can make a difference.

The next step toward promoting comprehensible input is to combine what Bruner (2004) refers to as the enactive mode (physical activity and gesture) and the iconic mode (real objects, photographs, drawings) with the symbolic mode (words and other symbols). The enactive mode engages the learners in actually doing something in order to connect it with language (e.g., a fingerplay or action song). The iconic mode uses concrete objects (e.g., fruit or plastic replicas of fruit) or pictorial representations of objects (e.g., photographs, clip art) to support vocabulary growth and make the language that is heard understandable. Deliberately linking the enactive, iconic, and symbolic modes in lessons also serves to differentiate instruction because all children can participate at some level in the activity (Rothenberg & Fisher, 2007).

The learner's experience with linguistic components is yet another consideration. A child who begins school without previous English language experience will be in the company of peers with a 4- to 5-year advantage (Hutchinson, Whiteley, Smith, & Connors, 2003). Children in classrooms are expected to engage in academic tasks that require more focused and persistent meaning-making efforts, and this places high demands on the young child (Field, 2001; Lund, 1991; Vandergrift, 2006). Take, for example, the common situation of listening to a picture book read aloud. As case study research describes, young children may come from a culture that emphasizes oral communication and have very little experience with books; they also may lack the prior knowledge to make sense out of what they hear and therefore show little interest in the stories that are shared (Gallas, 1994, 1997). A picture storybook read aloud requires maintaining sustained listening, filtering out distractions, drawing on background knowledge, and using metacognitive strategies (Lundsteen, 1993). To support listening development, story sharing for ELLs evidently needs to be more engaging and interactive. In Cabrera and Martinez's (2001) study of the story comprehension of a group of students in their second year of a bilingual program, two simplified stories were presented, but the second one was accompanied by gestures, repetition, and comprehension checks. The second, more concrete and engaging way of presenting the story significantly improved comprehension in L2.

How Do I ...

Create a Book Guide?

Select an award-winning picture book published in the past 5 years. Include complete bibliographic information on the book along with the following:

- A book synopsis
- A powerful introduction/motivation for the book
- Critical thinking/discussion questions
- Child-centered, open-ended questions that encourage responses from children
- Extension activities that connect the book with other subject areas in the curriculum
- A chart or web of the bookguide

Story Summary

In this tale by Keiko Kasza (1987), *The Wolf's Chicken Stew*, a perpetually hungry wolf finds a chicken for supper but decides that she needs to be fattened up first. He is busy cooking away in his kitchen and secretly leaves food on her porch every night. First, he brings 100 pancakes, then deposits 100 doughnuts, and finally delivers a 100-pound cake. But when he goes to get Mrs. Chicken and prepare the stew, he is surprised by 100 thankful chicks who rush out the door and smother him with kisses. After all these accolades and a dinner prepared by Mrs. Chicken, he gives up on the idea of chicken stew. As the wolf walks home, he thinks to himself, "Aw shucks, maybe tomorrow I'll bake the little critters a hundred scrumptious cookies."

Introduction

Show children clip art pictures of pairs of animals—a cat and a mouse, a bird and a worm, a lion and a gazelle, a wolf and a rabbit, and a fox and a chicken. Ask them what they know about these animals and whether or not they usually get along. Develop the idea of a predator—an animal that hunts other animals for food. Then say, "We are going to read a story today about a wolf and some chickens. Let's look at the cover. What do you notice? The name of this story is *The Wolf's Chicken Stew*. What predictions do you have about this story?" Write each child's name and his or her prediction. Then say, "I am going read the book to you now and, as I do, I want you to listen carefully to see if the wolf and the chickens are going to be friends—or not." After you have read a portion of the story and the plot appears to be changing, pause and

The baby chicks jumped all over the wolf and gave him a hundred kisses.

"Oh, thank you, Uncle Wolf! You're the best cook in the world!"

ask the children if they want to revise or change their predictions.*

Mathematics

• In the story, Uncle Wolf makes 100 of everything. How much is 100? Read *From One to One Hundred* (Sloat, 1995) and *One Hundred Hungry Ants* (Pinczes, 1999). Small groups of children make chick, egg, pancake, and cookie stamps out of styrofoam. Use a stamp pad with tempera paint so that each group can create 10 pages of 10 items each. Cut apart for one-to-one correspondence.

• Make 100 simple chick finger puppets out of yellow construction paper. Ask children to figure out how many each child will need to make to get 100 if people use all ten of their fingers.

Science

• Find out more about real wolves. Why are some people afraid of them? Compare photographs, realistic drawings of wolves such as those in Trina Schart Hyman's (1983) *Little Red Riding Hood,* and cartoon-type drawings like Allard's (1977) in *It's So Nice to Have a Wolf around the House.*

• What relationships exist between wolves and the family dog? Read *The First Dog* by Jan Brett (1988).

Literature

• Read a picture book version of an Aesop's fable, *The Boy Who Cried Wolf* (Hennessey, 2006). Compare it to the fractured fairy tale of *The Wolf Who Cried Boy* (Hartman, 2002). Find classics about hungry wolves and foxes pursuing birds, such as *Chicken Little* (Kellogg, 1985) or *Squawk to the Moon, Little Goose* (Preston, 1974).

• Share another wolf story with a happy ending, *Wolf's Coming* (Kulka, 2007).

• Read other books by the same author, such as *The Pigs' Picnic* (Kasza, 1988) and *When the Elephant Walks* (Kasza, 1990). Are there any similarities among them?

• Read other stories about predators such as *Feathers for Lunch* (Ehlert, 1990a) or *Wolf's Favor* (Testa, 1986).

Music, Art, and Drama

• Play the song "De Colores" by Raffi (1985), a song about baby chicks, and then share the picture book by Diaz (2008), *De Colores: Of Colors.*

• Share and discuss a book about vibrant colors, *Spicy Hot Colors* (Shahan, 2007), and invite children to create artwork using that color palette in their responses to the story.

• Listen to the traditional recording of "Peter and the Wolf" and then look at the picture book version by Voight (1980). Then compare it with *Peter and the Wolf Play Jazz* (Van Ronk, 1990).

• Make ears and a tail for the wolf. Enact scenes from the story. Dramatize the story with finger puppets. Have children enact some of the scenes that are not depicted in the book, such as how the hen and chickens react to having all the goodies dropped on their doorstep.

• What do chickens like to eat? Design a cake especially for chickens. What would you put inside of it? How would you decorate it?

• Read and sing along with Peter Spier's (1961) *The Fox Went Out on a Chilly Night.*

• Imagine that you are one of the grateful chicks and you want to make or buy something very special for Uncle Wolf. What would it be? Remember, he is a wolf. Think about what he might like that is different from what people like. Draw a picture of your present.

• The book showed just a little bit of the wolf's house and the chicken's house. Design a diorama that shows what their houses might look like. Remember, the houses need to be especially designed for the hen and her chicks and for the wolf.

Cooking

• Make pancakes using a rebus recipe. Use the wordless book by Tomie dePaola (1978), *Pancakes for Breakfast*, to review the steps in making pancakes. After you have enjoyed your pancakes, read another story about hungry animals and pancakes, such as *The Story of Little Babaji* (Bannerman, 1997).

• Bake chocolate chip cookies. Count out 5 chocolate chips for each cookie. How many cookies will it take to use 100 chocolate chips?

Writing

• Use the wordless book *Bobo's Dream* (Alexander, 1970) to create a group story about the dreams of a dog; then read *Fox's Dream* (Tejima, 1985) and invite children to develop their own stories about the dreams of different animals.

• Have children dictate, write, or create a rebus recipe for some of the wolf's treats, such as the 100-pound cake.

• Have children work with a partner to chart the plot of the story or make a story map that shows the wolf's travels. For children who are inexperienced with making these maps, try giving them a blank chart to fill in with pictures or words.

Critical Thinking

• What if one of the wolf's friends decided to eat his new chicken friends? What could he say or do to change their minds? How could he help his "nieces" and "nephews"?

• Write a group story that is a prequel (and explains how the wolf grew up to be so nice) or a sequel (that tells what happens after the chicks grow up).

PEARSON **myeducationkit**™   Now go to Chapter 9 in the MyEducationKit (**www.MyEducationKit .com**) for your book, where you can:

■ Find Chapter Objectives.

■ Complete Assignments and Activities that can help you more deeply understand the chapter content.

■ Extend knowledge with content-specific Web Links.

■ Check your comprehension on the content covered in the chapter by going to the Study Plan. Here you will be able to take a chapter quiz, receive feedback on your answers, and then access resources that will enhance your understanding of chapter content.

chapter ten

Drawing and Writing to Communicate

Annie Pickert/Pearson Education

FACT FILE on Drawing and Writing

• Preschool children tend to rely on drawings or drawing-like devices to support their emergent writing (Baghban, 2007b; Mayer, 2007). They also recognize drawing as drawing before they recognize writing as writing, which suggests that drawing is the primary representational/communicative system (Levin & Bus, 2003).

• Learning to write is a developmental process. By the age of 3 when children draw a picture, the scribbles they use to represent their names are distinctively different from those they make to represent a picture (Haney, 2002).

- Throughout history, left-handedness was considered to be a defect and many different instructional and coercive techniques have been used to convert left-handedness to right-handedness (Martin & Porac, 2007); however, left-handedness does not automatically mean poor handwriting skills and allowing children to use their dominant hand when writing is more developmentally appropriate (Bonoti, Vlachos, & Metallidou, 2005).

- In an Israeli study of 3- to 5-year-olds from low-income backgrounds, children who were actively involved in joint writing activities outperformed those who participated in a traditional early childhood program and those who participated in a program that emphasized reading only (phonological awareness, word writing, orthographic awareness, and letter knowledge) (Aram & Biron, 2004).

- Learning to write is a social process. Children first create various shapes and symbols to represent meaning, which eventually become letters and words. It is important that teachers and families respect emergent writing (Kissel, 2008a, b) as a precursor to formal writing so that children learn to love the writing process later on in the primary grades (Martin & Thacker, 2009).

- Elementary school-age children spend about 30 to 60 percent of the schoolday involved in tasks that require handwriting or other fine motor skills; thus, those children who struggle with handwriting are at a greater risk of academic problems and lowered self-esteem (Feder & Majnemer, 2007).

- There is a learning disability called written-language disorder in which children are unable to write properly; boys are two to three times more likely to have this condition (Katrusic, 2009).

- Research suggests that children who are deaf may learn written communication in advance of hearing peers because writing is a way of communicating with those who are not proficient in sign language systems, such as American Sign Language or finger spelling (Ruiz, 1995).

- Invented spelling refers to the child's attempts to represent oral language in written form (e.g., *hpy* for *happy, strz* for *stars*) and it is an essential part of learning to spell words correctly (Ouellette & Senechal, 2008). Attempting to spell and getting feedback on correct spelling is more intellectually challenging for students than tracing or copying correctly spelled words (Richgels, 2008).

- A study of the writing of over 100 young Spanish–English bilingual children concluded that they sometimes write the same letters in both languages (but read them differently) or combine both languages in one sentence or paragraph to convey their message. Teachers of bilingual children should provide them with many opportunities to write in both languages and view bilingualism as a strength (Rubin & Carlan, 2005).

Did any of this information surprise you? If so, what? Why? How will you use this knowledge to educate and care for the very young?

What Is the Relationship between Drawing and Writing?

PEARSON

myeducationkit™

Go to the Assignments and Activities section of Chapter 10 in MyEducationKit and complete the activity entitled "Family Ties."

Three kindergarten children are playing restaurant in a socio-dramatic play center that they helped to create. Their drawings of hamburgers, french fries, beverages, and sweets are on the wall. A sign that reads "McDonald's" is posted over the door, which has been cut out of a refrigerator box. The children are using a small table for the counter and a cutout in the side of the box for the drive-through window. Casey is the window clerk, Josh is the manager, and Amanda is the cook:

Casey: A bus is coming through! (Writes furiously on order pad.) We need 30 burgers, 50 fries, 20 Big Macs, and 70 Cokes.

Josh: Well, do it, but they'll have to wait.

Amanda: (Rolls her eyes and wipes her forehead.) I think I'm quitting, Josh.

Josh: You can't quit! Just keep makin' those hamburgers.

By envisioning these three 5-year-olds at play, we can see how they use one thing to represent another. They are learning how to think symbolically and how to use pictorial and written symbols to represent their ideas (Schickedanz & Casbergue, 2004).

Particularly for young children, drawing and writing go together, because both are ways of expressing ideas and feelings. The drawings of young children usually emphasize the communication of ideas rather than the production of pleasing visual images (Hipple, 1985), so many experts look at both drawing and writing as composing processes (Baghban, 2007; Narey, 2008). Drawing and writing are equally important ways of expressing ideas (see www.wiu.edu/thecenter/articles/draw1.html).

Jeremy, age 4, is a good example. He had a funny dream about a monster last night, and as he illustrates the dream (see Figure 10.1), he discusses it with his teacher:

Jeremy: I had a dream about a monster.

Teacher: Were you afraid?

Jeremy: No, 'cause we be'ed friends. We played cards.

Teacher: Let's make a picture of the monster.

Jeremy: Okay (while drawing).

Jeremy: Here is the big, fat monster's belly. This is his head. Here's his feet and his hair. There's his great, great big ears.

Teacher: Where are you?

Jeremy: I'm right down here by the table. We played cards here. See the cards? These is monster cards. You have man cards.

Teacher: What else did you do?

Jeremy: We drank pop in glasses.

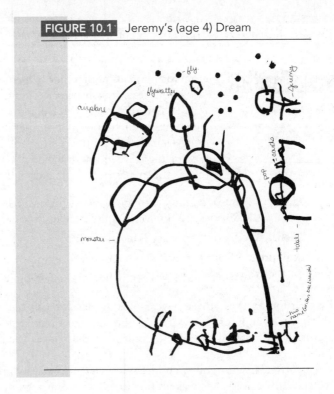

FIGURE 10.1   Jeremy's (age 4) Dream

Teacher: Did you do anything else?

Jeremy: We setted on a rocking chair.

Jeremy can re-create his dream by drawing it *and* talking about it. His words can be written down first by an adult and eventually by Jeremy himself.

Whether it occurs at home (Levin & Bus, 2003) or school, pictorial signs (drawing) and graphic signs (writing) share several important attributes:

Drawing and writing involve some of the same psychomotor skills. Both involve the fine-motor skill of holding a writing implement and making marks on a paper. Ask a 2-year-old to draw, and she will scribble; ask her to write, and she will scribble. Drawing and writing share the same basic psychomotor skills.

Victoria, age 6, is excited about using a new box of crayons "with the points still on." For this special occasion, she decides to write and draw about her pet dog. Notice in her drawing (Figure 10.2) that she uses her skills in handling a crayon to communicate in both graphic and pictorial images. Here's how she describes her drawing:

Victoria: This is Softy; he's my dog and he's a Pekingese. He's really fluffy, and he gets so hot in the summer, you should see his coat. I'll draw a picture because I can't tell ya. (She scribbles with a crayon all over the page and then prints the word *hot* on top.) His coat looks big, even bigger than that. Long,

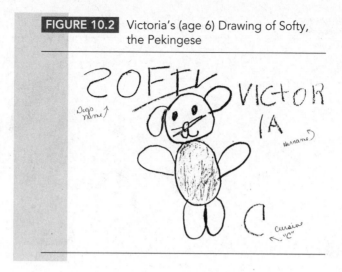

FIGURE 10.2 Victoria's (age 6) Drawing of Softy, the Pekingese

long, longer than my hair! I'll write my name. Here's my cursive *C*. I like to draw Softy standing up because I give him a walking lesson every day.

Drawing and writing depend on similar cognitive abilities. Beth, a 4-year-old, is a good example of the think/draw/write connection. She has decided to draw pictures of familiar objects and make a corresponding list of the words for all the objects. Clay (1975) has referred to this behavior as spontaneously taking inventory of knowledge. Figure 10.3 (p. 226) shows how Beth represented her thinking.

Drawing and writing are both expressive arts. Even very young children recognize the expressive power of words and pictures. Alyssa, who has just had her third birthday, is asked by an interviewer if she can write and draw (see Figure 10.4 on p. 227). Alyssa points to the *A* in the lower-left-hand corner and says, "There, that's Alyssa."

Next, she draws a rectangular shape and puts several dots on it. She points to it and puts her fingers to her mouth, saying, "Yum! See, this is a banana." Both drawing and writing are forms of self-expression.

Drawing and writing are both developmental. Both follow a basic, general pattern that is affected by the individual child's rate and style of development. In other words, both writing and drawing are tools that reflect the child's level of understanding about the world. Figure 10.5 (p. 228) is an overview of the relationships among the child's level of understanding, drawing, and writing.

Drawing and writing are both purposeful. There are four shared purposes for teaching writing and art (Mosenthal, 1983):

1. *Practical.* Written and graphic symbols provide a way to pass on cultural norms and function in society.
2. *Cognitive developmental.* Both drawing and writing are used to promote intellectual growth and lifelong learning.

FIGURE 10.3   Beth (age 4) Takes Spontaneous Inventory of Her Knowledge

FIGURE 10.4 Alyssa's Drawing and Writing

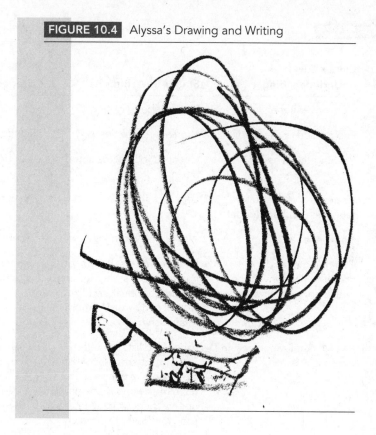

3. *Emancipatory.* Art and literacy offer ways of enhancing self-expression and promoting equal opportunity.
4. *Self-concept enhancing.* Both composing processes develop the child's sense of autonomy and self-worth.

Preschooler Samantha's invention of a personified pumpkin illustrates all four of these purposes. She uses self-guiding speech as she draws and writes (see Figure 10.6 on p. 229):

Samantha: I'm gonna draw a pumpkin . . . make his hair blue and kinda green. Gonna write his name, Sam. He needs a lot of feet because he has to go to a pumpkin meeting. He has to walk. He can walk on his head. Here's my name. My mom taught me how to write it.

Samantha has learned the practical value of drawing and writing and their place in the culture. If we observed her with the other 4-year-olds in her nursery school, we would see how her drawing, writing, and the discussions surrounding them enable her to participate more fully in that social circle. Other children are intrigued by

FIGURE 10.5   Relationships among Understanding, Drawing, and Writing

Child's Level of Understanding	Stages in Writing	Stages in Drawing
Nonconventional	Prealphabetic writing	Nonrepresentational art
Exploration of the medium	Nonlinear scribbles	Random scribbling
Refining the form	Linear scribbles, repeated designs	Controlled scribbles
Awareness of the cultural relevance of the symbol	Letterlike forms	Naming of scribbles
Conventional	Alphabetic writing	Representational art
Beginning of understanding the conventions in drawing and writing	Random letters, letters, or numbers in a string; letters or numbers clustered like words; early word/symbol relationships	Early representational attempts
Overgeneralization of rule hypothesis	Labels and lists, invented spelling, letters of inconsistent size/shape; then moves to uniform size and shape and upper- and lowercase letters used randomly; experiments with cursive writing	Preschematic drawing
Formal structure	Upper- and lowercase letters used correctly; standard spelling	Schematic drawing

Sources: Brittain (1979); Fields, Groth, & Spangler (2007); Lamme (1984).

Samantha's drawing and writing; they ask her questions, comment on her efforts, and sometimes ask her advice on especially challenging projects they have undertaken. The cognitive developmental value of drawing and writing is evident in her composing processes, too. Samantha reasons that an object that is round and has feet on every surface could move very quickly. She also has some ideas about meetings: that they involve travel and require participation.

Additionally, if we could see the expression of pride on Samantha's face as she completes her drawing and writes her name all by herself, it would be clear that these newly acquired abilities in language and art have enhanced her self-concept. Figure 10.7 summarizes how children use drawing for self-expression.

FIGURE 10.6 Samantha's (age 4) Personified Pumpkin

Collaboration with Families and Professionals

Mr. Dettwiler has been teaching in a rural elementary school for 2 years. Ever since he arrived, the other teachers have advised him that he is wasting his time trying to convince certain families to participate in planned school events. But Mr.

FIGURE 10.7 How Drawing Contributes to Self-Expression and Writing

1. *Filling in.* Before children can represent all of their ideas in words, pictures provide much of the context that they cannot provide in written words.
2. *Warming up.* Through drawing, children are able to begin thinking about what they want to write. Drawing can serve as a prewriting activity.
3. *Planning with.* Children can use drawing to organize their thinking and remind them of what they want to write about.
4. *Elaborating on.* Children can use a drawing or a series of drawings that stimulate writing and motivate them to produce more involved stories.
5. *Talking about.* Drawing can serve as a prop for discussions and dramatizations, not only of what is pictured but also of what is written as text.
6. *Evaluating with.* Children can evaluate the relative sensibleness of the drawings and writings they have produced in terms of whether what they have depicted would occur in the real world or belong to the realm of fantasy.

Sources: Adapted from Dyson (1988) and Salinger (1995).

Standards in Education
The National Council of Teachers of English discusses their position on writing in the brochure *NCTE Writing Initiative: What We Know about Writing: Early Literacy,* posted at www.ncte.org/library/ NCTEFiles/Resources/Positions/ wrtgearlyltcybrochure.pdf. Discuss the implications of this document for the writing curriculum.

PEARSON myeducationkit™

Go to the Assignments and Activities section of Chapter 10 in MyEducationKit and complete the activity entitled "Collaborations."

PEARSON myeducationkit™

Go to the Assignments and Activities section of Chapter 10 in MyEducationKit and complete the activity entitled "First-Hand Experiences."

Dettwiler knows that many of the families that have been identified as uncooperative and disinterested confront obstacles that other families do not. Included among the parents and families who have not attended school functions are the 20 percent of the school population who are transient workers, those who had bad experiences themselves as children in schools, and those who lack the material resources (e.g., reliable transportation, money for a babysitter, appropriate clothing) to come onsite for a face-to-face meeting with the teacher.

Mr. Dettwiler knows that a popular meeting place in the small town is the bank parking lot, where pickup trucks gather on the weekends in late summer and early fall as farmers in the surrounding communities try to make money by selling fresh produce. He does some reading about integrating the arts into the curriculum and then enlists the help of two colleagues: the music specialist and the art teacher. Together, they plan a display of children's work and a musical performance for a Saturday morning.

To make the most of this event, the teachers coordinate their efforts with the building principal and the bank manager. The bank contributes a large tent to be set up on the grounds, thereby enabling the children to perform and have their artwork and writing displayed, even if the weather does not cooperate. Other charitable organizations, such as the university honor society, and community organizations, such as the Jaycees, will be there to sell popcorn and soft drinks. Activities such as the vision screening sponsored by the Association for the Prevention of Blindness and the Well Baby Clinic will be represented with information booths. The all-school event is planned for the time that the produce sale usually wraps up, which is about 11:30 A.M.

About their first annual Harvest Celebration and Information Fair, Mr. Dettwiler says, "It was a huge success. Parents and families who felt alienated from the school saw that we were sincere about reaching out. They accessed the information, and they were pleased and proud about their children's work."

Contributions and Consequences

- *Contributions of the teacher:* What role did the teacher play in supporting the children's drawing and writing efforts?
- *Contributions of the family:* How did parents and families support the children's drawing and writing efforts?
- *Contributions of other professionals:* How did professionals in other fields participate?

• *Consequences of collaboration:* How might this story have ended differently if the adults had not collaborated?

Overview of Children's Drawing and Writing Development

Brain and Language
Neuroscience suggests that the brain has the most intense response to simple, concrete, strong images and symbols (Rushton & Larkin, 2001). What are the implications of these findings for children's efforts to represent what they know through drawing and writing?

PEARSON
myeducationkit™

Go to the Assignments and Activities section of Chapter 10 in MyEducationKit and complete the activity entitled "Self-Portrait."

Notice how these children of different ages show more sophisticated understandings about writing with additional experience:

Jason (age 4):   It's marks on paper.

Desmond (5):   Writing is putting down words and letters.

Camille (7):   It's something we learn to do so we can write Grandma a thank you note for the birthday gift. It's something the teacher gives us plus or minus on. And Dad writes Mom a note when he has to tell her something and she's not there.

Children gave these responses to the question "Why do people write?"

Raquel (age 5):   To work. My mom is a secretary and my daddy has to read to drive—he has to read the signs.

Yukiko (8):   So someone can write a letter instead of calling on the phone.

Neneh (7):   To let people know things. You write so you can keep it.

Brian (8):   So when they don't talk, they have something to say. People write to show their ideas.

A general sequence for writing development (Lamme, 1984) and art development (Brittain, 1979) has been used to design the developmental sequence discussed here.

Prealphabetic Writing and Nonrepresentational Drawing

The initial stages in writing are called *prealphabetic*, meaning that no real letters are recognizable. The corollary to this stage in drawing is *nonrepresentational*, meaning that what the child draws does not look like the object. Even at the scribble stage, children's efforts reveal much about their emerging concepts of communication through symbols.

Random Scribbling   The first scribbles of toddlers appear random and disordered but are composed of definite lines made with simple movements. This is a first step for all children in developing their ability to control the marking tool and to put marks only where they want to. Chris, a 17-month-old, made the random scribbles in Figure 10.8.

Controlled Scribbling   Most 3-year-olds have more control over the writing implement than toddlers do. As a result, they stay on the paper more, and their scribbles

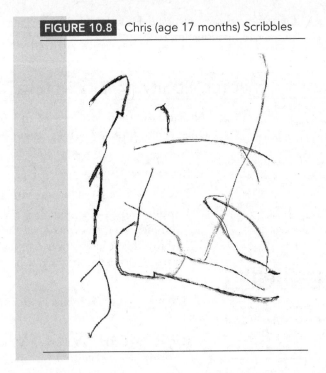

FIGURE 10.8   Chris (age 17 months) Scribbles

acquire definite placement patterns. Later in this stage, their scribbles become more linear (see Figure 10.9).

Naming of Scribbling   Four-year-olds often begin to label or explain their scribbles and see the relationship between the marks on paper and ideas, objects, and words. Katie, a 3-year-old, made the scribbles in Figure 10.10. About the scribble in the upper-left-hand corner, she explained, "It says 'hello;'" about the second, she said, "It's a picture of Kirsty" (a dog).

Alphabetic Writing and Representational Drawing

At this stage, children's drawings gradually begin to look more like the objects being portrayed, and their writing becomes more readable.

Early Representational Drawing, Mock Letters, and Letters   Usually, the drawings of 4-year-olds represent people or objects that have particular significance. Each drawing is portrayed as a separate entity. Victor, a 4-year-old, used words to guide his drawing efforts and switched from a crayon to a pencil when he wrote his name on the paper (see Figure 10.11 on p. 234). As he explained:

> **Victor:**   I'm making a horse. Horse, shoe, horse, shoe. That's how you make a tail—in and back out. I'm making a fox after this. This isn't a horse. Now it's

FIGURE 10.9 Controlled Scribbles

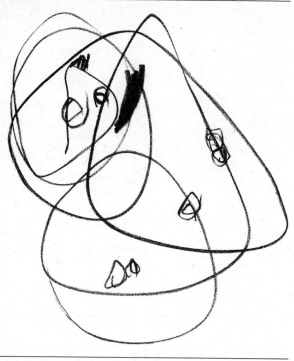

FIGURE 10.10 Naming of Scribbling

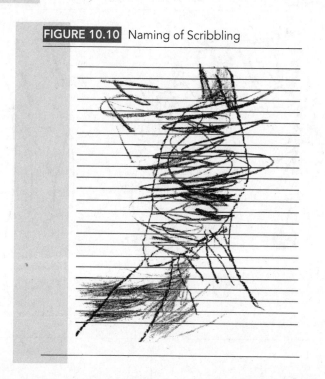

FIGURE 10.11 Victor (age 4) Draws and Writes

FIGURE 10.12 Mandi's (age 3½) Drawing and Writing

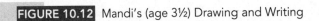

"A little girl in a pretty necklace."

FIGURE 10.13 Mock Letters and Letters

"It says 'Aunt Donna.'"

FIGURE 10.14 Elizabeth's (age 5) Letters and Numbers in a String

a bird. I'll draw a horse down there where I put the dot. (He starts to draw the fox.) Yellow is my favorite color, my favorite color in the United States.

In writing, the child at this stage produces mock letters—repeated designs and shapes that have some features of print. Three-and-a-half-year-old Mandi used early representational drawing and letterlike forms to print her name (see Figure 10.12):

Teacher: Do you know how to draw? Show me how you draw.

Mandi: Me can jaw (draw) eyes, noss, mouse. I give her a pitty (pretty) necklace. She has lots and lots of hairs. She's a little, little girls. She can go to school.

Teacher: Do you know how to write? Show me how you write.

Mandi: I know how to do all the days. Me sometimes wites the biggest letters. Mommy taughts me tos. I been witing since I was one. I can wite like Mommy. I do weal good. I can write; I can wite the best than anyone. *D* is the biggest witer (letter). And make some dots. I have a dot (referring to the dot over the *i* in her name). Mandi. Done!

Children may begin to write letters and numbers randomly or arrange them in a string. Jenny, a 3-year-old, wrote the letterlike shapes and letters in Figure 10.13. Elizabeth, age 5, wrote the letters and numbers in a string in Figure 10.14.

Preschematic Drawing and Semiconventional Alphabetic Writing The majority of 5-year-olds have gained the fine-motor skills to plan their drawings a bit more. Children experiment with drawing until they develop their own style of representing people. Geometric shapes often show up in pictures.

In writing, letters and numbers are often clustered like words, and letters of inconsistent size are common, as illustrated by Figure 10.15. Gradually, children begin to make the connection between letters and sounds and attempt to spell words based on their understandings about language at the time. Even though many of these invented or temporary spellings of words do not conform to the spellings in the dictionary, children's writing becomes easier for others to read as they gain more experience (Scharer & Zutell, 2003).

FIGURE 10.15 Clustered Letters and Numbers of Inconsistent Size

Schematic Drawing and Conventional Writing As children enter the primary grades, they often produce detailed, precise drawings that reflect careful observation and planning. In writing, the child begins to make letters of uniform size, to reverse letters and numbers less, to experiment with cursive writing, and to use upper- and lowercase letters correctly.

As 8-year-old David draws and writes, he adjusts his drawing and writing to the audience. The audience is his cousin, Leigh Ann, who is studying to be a teacher. David begins by displaying what he knows, assuming that this is what a teacher will like. He uses a combination of spoken and written words to imagine a situation that will entertain Leigh Ann (see Figure 10.16):

David: I am going to make some shapes. I know how to spell *circle*. I know more shapes: diamond, stop sign, and ummmm, what else? (He looks around the room.) Aha! Here is another shape (the oval-shaped knob on the stereo). All the shapes on the bottom are the same color because they are different shapes. (David sits and thinks, looking straight ahead with his chin resting on his hands.) I think I'll draw a tree. I'm good at trees. Here is the ground. Here is me; I have pants on. I'll put you beside me. You are bigger than me. I'll spell

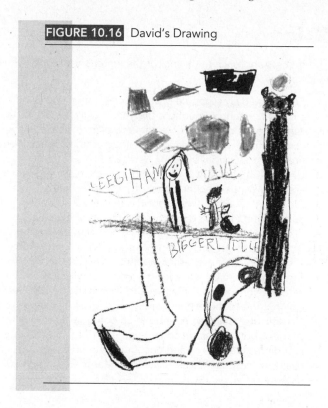

FIGURE 10.16 David's Drawing

bigger under you and *little* under me. My hair is sticking up funny—it just got a little tangled in the tree. I was climbing the tree. Your hair got tangled, too! I need a pen to write my words.

In elementary school, most children's knowledge of composition, spelling, and handwriting becomes increasingly conventional. But children do not learn to write conventionally just by having someone *tell* them about writing; they learn to write by *doing* (Feder & Majnemer, 2007). One of the major means of instruction in written composition was developed by Donald Graves (1994) and it is called a *process approach to writing* or *writer's workshop* (Capello, 2006; Martin & Thacker, 2009). Figure 10.17 explains the principles of this strategy and supplies some recent resources.

Another helpful way of thinking about the teaching of written composition is called the Six Traits Model. In an update of the model, a seventh trait was added. Figure 10.18 (on p. 239) is an overview of these characteristics and picture books that illustrate each attribute of effective writing.

Teaching Handwriting

If you talk to some older people who are left-handed, you will find that it was once common practice to try and "break" children of this "bad habit." Today, we know that

FIGURE 10.17   Principles of the Process Approach to Writing and Writer's Workshop

The *process approach to writing,* or the *writer's workshop* (Graves, 1994), highlights the following principles:

1. *Time.* The daily schedule provides time for writing (Moutray & Snell, 2003) as well as a plan for writing throughout the year (Calkins, 2003; Parsons, 2005). In the writer's workshop, students are given time to plan, revise, and eventually publish/share their compositions, rather than being expected to produce them within a predetermined time period (Cappello, 2006).
2. *Choice.* Children get to choose drawing and writing topics, rather than have them assigned by the teacher (Love, Burns, & Buell, 2007).
3. *Modeling.* Children have opportunities to see other writers in action and hear them talk about their writing processes (Schulze, 2006).
4. *Response.* Children get to share writing with peers, families, and others in the school and larger community (Kissel, 2009b). Regular conferences with teachers are essential to success (Calkins, Hartman, & White, 2005).
5. *Structure.* Children learn the routines that will support them in their drawing and writing efforts, such as maintaining a portfolio of their best work. Teachers help children to see the connections among all of the language arts (Schulze, 2006).
6. *Community.* Children operate in an enthusiastic community of composers who produce both drawing and writing. This social interaction stimulates their thinking, recognizes their effort, and encourages them to seek new drawing and writing challenges (Cleaveland & Ray, 2004; Martin & Thacker, 2009).

being left-handed is related to brain functioning and that it is useless, even detrimental, to force children to become right-handed.

In the United States, it is customary to begin formal handwriting instruction with *manuscript* (printing) in kindergarten and first grade. *Cursive* (handwriting) is typically introduced in second grade. Figure 10.19 (on p. 240) shows sample alphabets in manuscript and cursive. The rationale for beginning with manuscript rather than cursive writing is based on the following principles:

1. Printing requires two basic hand movements: straight lines and circles (or portions of circles).
2. Printing is more like the typing that children encounter when they are reading.
3. Manuscript is more legible than cursive writing, so adults can decipher children's initial writing efforts more readily.

Paper placement, or the way that the paper is positioned on the desk, needs to be considered when children are handwriting. When children are printing, the paper should be straight up and down on the desk because printing is straight rather than slanted. If the children are doing cursive writing, however, the paper should be slanted in the direction opposite to the hand with which the child writes. This means that when you are looking over the shoulder of a right-handed child, the paper should be

FIGURE 10.18 Seven Traits of Effective Writing and Related Children's Books

Ideas: the content of the piece of writing—the heart of the message.

Knuffle Bunny: A Cautionary Tale (Willems, 2004); *Jamberry* (Degan, 1995); *I Love You the Purplest* (Joosse, 1996); *Not a Box* (Portis, 2006); *The Rainbow Fish* (Pfister, 1992); *The Story of Ferdinand* (rev. ed., Leaf, 2000); *Nothing Ever Happens on 90th Street* (Schotter, 1999); *The Secret Knowledge of Grown-Ups* (Wisniewski, 2001)

Organization: the internal structure of the piece of writing.

Verdi (Cannon, 1997); *The Important Book* (Brown, 1990); *If You Give a Mouse a Cookie* (Numeroff, 1985); *The Napping House* (Wood, 1991); *The Story Blanket* (Wolf & Savitz, 2009).

Voice: the soul of the piece; the characteristics that make the writer's style individual and that convey thoughts and feelings through words.

My Friend Rabbit (Rohmann, 2007); *Kitten's First Full Moon* (Henkes, 2004); *Voices in the Park* (Browne, 2001); *Oh, How I Wish I Could Read!* (Gile, 1995); *Alexander and the Terrible, Horrible, No Good, Very Bad Day* (Viorst, 1987); *Kiss! Kiss! Yuck! Yuck!* (Mewburn, 2008); *A Story with Pictures* (Kanninen, 2007)

Word Choice: selecting just the right word; using language that moves and enlightens the reader.

Miss Alaineus: A Vocabulary Disaster (Frasier, 2007); *Max's Words* (Banks, 2006); *The Boy Who Cried Wolf* (Hartman, 2002); *Hairy, Scary and Ordinary: What Is an Adjective?* (Cleary, 2001); *Calling the Doves: El Canto de las Palomas* (Herrera, 2001); *Bark Park* (Ruelle, 2008)

Sentence Fluency: the flow of the language, the sound of word patterns—the way the writing plays to the ear, not just to the eye.

Llama, Llama Red Pajama (Dewdney, 2005); *The Sign of the Seahorse* (Base, 1992); *Guess How Much I Love You?* (McBratney, 1994); *Chicka Chicka Boom Boom* (anniversary ed., Martin & Archambault, 2009); *The Little Engine That Could* (rev. ed., Piper, 1990); *Tikki Tikk Tembo* (rev. ed., Mosel, 2007)

Conventions: precision and correctness—the extent to which the writer uses grammar and mechanics appropriately.

Punctuation Takes a Vacation (Pulver, 2004); *Nouns and Verbs Have a Field Day* (Pulver, 2007); *Eats, Shoots & Leaves: Why, Commas Really Do Make a Difference!* (Truss, 2006); *Alphie the Apostrophe* (Donohue, 2006)

Presentation: the overall impression created by the work—the ways in which the whole is more than the sum of its parts.

Polar Express (anniversary ed., Van Allsburg, 2005); *Owl Moon* (anniversary ed., Yolen, 2007); *Night in the Country* (Rylant, 1991); *Cloud Dance* (Locker, 2003); *Grandfather's Journey* (Say, 1993)

Sources: Culham (2005); Paquette (2007); Spandel (2008).

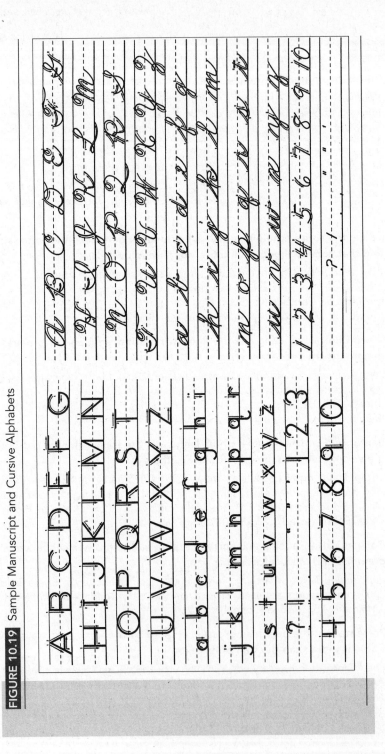

FIGURE 10.19 Sample Manuscript and Cursive Alphabets

slanted slightly to the left. When you are looking over the shoulder of a left-handed child, the paper should be slanted to the right. If you fail to position the paper properly for a left-handed child, she or he will compensate by hooking her or his hand around, and the result will be a less comfortable and fluid style of writing.

Although large-group instruction in handwriting is the most common strategy, it is not the best strategy. Giving individualized feedback and working with small groups of children with similar writing needs are both more effective than large-group instruction (Koenke, 1988). The teacher should demonstrate how to form letters and encourage the children to compare their letter formation with his or her model. Children master handwriting better when they actually form letters than when they trace, copy, or write in the air (Mayer, 2007).

Teacher Concerns and Basic Strategies

Infants and Toddlers

Some children as young as 2 years of age are able to distinguish between scribble writing and scribble drawing. They may separate them on the page and point to which is the picture and which is the story (Morrow, 2001). How would you go about supporting the efforts of all young children to "make their mark"? What materials would you provide? What adaptations would you make for children with disabilities?

PEARSON
myeducationkit™

Go to the Assignments and Activities section of Chapter 10 in MyEducationKit and complete the activity entitled "Creating a Puppet."

When you are working with young children who are learning to use the two major sign systems of drawing and writing, keep the following points in mind:

Be aware of children's purposes. Your careful planning does not include planning the child's response. If you preselect the topic and format (such as asking children to copy a thank you note from the chalkboard), then everyone's work will look the same. Allow children to use multiple symbol systems to accomplish something they care about; respect children's culture and perspectives (Dyson, 2003, 2007, 2008a, b; Staton, 1982). Give them time to draft both their drawing and writing.

Be sensitive in responding to children's efforts. Giving children the time to discover a satisfying form is important (Kissell, 2008a). As teachers, we must resist the right/wrong mentality that discourages young children from trying out their ideas (Dyson, 2006, 2008a; Dyson & Smitherman, 2009). Children are well aware that they are making errors in language. In fact, one kindergarten teacher distributed red pencils to her students and asked them to circle every word that might be spelled incorrectly. Most of them were able to do this, even if they could not provide the correct spellings. We must try to remember that children are still learning.

Plan a varied curriculum. Any teacher who is bored by students' work is giving them boring work to do. If children are encouraged to experiment with drawing and writing, their work will be a fascinating documentary of their interests, skills, and hypotheses about how language works. A community that values children's drawing and writing will find teachers and children using symbols together—making lists, creating posters, designing murals, writing stories on charts, creating original song picture books, corresponding with others, and so forth (see Armington, 1997). The audience for children's work should be varied, too. Instead of drawing and writing only for the teacher, children should have opportunities to share their work with classmates, parents, children in other classes and grade levels, administrators and other school personnel, and visitors to the classroom, to name a few.

Make activities concrete and functional.   Written language is more abstract than oral language because it is removed from the immediate context. Therefore, when children are first making the transition from oral to written language, their writing should be tied to their experiences. Young children need to talk about their writing, to draw pictures to accompany their writing, and to enact the stories they create.

Provide opportunities for excellence.   Drawing and writing activities should provide feedback from real, live audiences to the writers and give them opportunities to revise and revise again until they are satisfied with the outcome. Children should be encouraged to make their finished written products beautiful—for example, creating books with fabric covers or laminated pages and keeping them in the classroom library.

Classroom Activities to Support Children's Drawing and Writing

Research and Report
Volunteer tutors—defined as individuals who do not have professional teaching credentials but focus on supporting children's literacy—can exert a powerful and positive impact on children's reading. Twenty-one empirical studies have concluded that "students who work with volunteer tutors are likely to earn higher scores on assessments related to letters and words, oral fluency, and writing as compared to peers who are not tutored" (Ritter, Barnett, Denny, & Albin, 2009, p. 20). Learn more about volunteer tutors and how you might become one or include them in your classroom (Chagnon, 2004; Craft Al-Hazza & Gupta, 2006; Denton, Parker, & Jasbrouck, 2003).

The drawing and writing activities we plan for young children should be open-ended, providing many different responses, rather than a single correct response. Classroom walls decorated with rows of nearly identical papers, neatly colored in the designated hues, and accompanied by carefully copied proverbs or poems are (or should be) a thing of the past. Such practices simply do not reflect current theory and research about how children construct their knowledge of pictorial and graphic symbols. Some recommended activities are described in the following sections.

Fingerpainting/Writing   Teachers sometimes think that materials such as fingerpaint and clay are strictly for art class, but these materials offer excellent ways of supporting children's early writing and drawing efforts. Fingerpainting enables very young children to explore making marks on paper because it does not require managing a writing implement. It frees the child to practice the types of finger, hand, and arm movements made later during writing. For a different texture and feel, try a plastic dishpan partially filled with colored sand or cornmeal. Children can use the sand to make simple graphic symbols and change them at will.

"Magic Slates" "Magic slates" can be created for use with kindergarten or primary-grade children by using heavyweight, self-sealing sandwich bags and condiments. Just press the air out of the bag, put in a few tablespoons of ketchup or mustard, and glue the opening shut with waterproof glue. (Be sure to tell the children that they should not use sharp objects to make their marks.) The children can place the bag on a flat surface, smooth out the surface with the palm of a hand, and use an index finger to write or make pictures. To obliterate the marks they have made, all they need to do is smooth out the bag again. The "slates" also have a cool, smooth, and interesting feel. They will keep for quite a while if they are refrigerated at night.

Creating Writing and Drawing Materials As an alternative to drawing and writing with pencils or crayons, children can create different types of writing implements. For very young children, who are just learning to make marks on paper, you can make multi- or single-color "crayon circles" out of recycled crayons by following this procedure:

1. Preheat the oven to 300°F.
2. Remove the paper wrappers from pieces of broken crayons.
3. Place the crayons in the cups of an old muffin tin, filling each cup about half full.
4. Turn off the oven and put the muffin tin inside.
5. When cool, remove the crayons from the muffin tin, and let children use them to draw and write.

Paint Rollers A writing implement that is especially useful when making large posters or signs is a discarded plastic roll-on deodorant bottle filled with a thin mixture of tempera paint. After prying out the roller balls of several bottles with a knife, fill them with different colors of paint, and then snap the rollers back on; let the children use them when they want to create big, bold lines. Refillable paint markers with sponge tips are commercially available as well. These writing tools can be particularly satisfying for the toddler or 3-year-old who is just learning how to make marks on paper.

Colored Pencils Second- or third-graders might enjoy experimenting with the special effects of double lines. All they need to do is fasten two pencils together side by side with a rubber band and hold them so that both pencil tips touch the paper. This creates a double line that is particularly useful for creating lovely handwriting for homemade greeting cards and so on. Many different types of markers are also available with triple tips, zigzag tips, and calligraphy tips that can be used by children who are already writing.

Words and Pictures in Different Formats Vary the type of writing paper available to children by contacting a local print shop and getting their scrap paper. Children can recycle computer paper and create huge letters, messages, murals, or comic strips.

As children begin to write more conventionally and draw more representationally, they might try creating murals or timelines related to a subject of study. Large rolls of shelf paper can be positioned on two wooden dowels and pulled through a box with a "screen" cutout to share a story with a larger audience.

Callouts   Introduce the concept of a cartoon "bubble" that encapsulates the character's speech by making a paper cutout of a favorite cartoon character and posting a new and interesting message in the bubble each day. Other conventions of cartoons, such as frames, can be introduced by using separate cards for individual scenes or by using the callout shapes on a word-processing program.

A Writer's Briefcase   Use an old briefcase or suitcase as a container for a collection of writing papers and implements that can be checked out by a child and carried home at night or over the weekend (Wrobleski, 1990). Materials that stimulate writing—such as pictures of story characters (commercially available as story cards or blocks) and copies of pictures of storybook characters read about in school—may also be included.

Question-and-Answer Books   Books with a predictable format can be used as models for writing. In a kindergarten class, children heard *The Very Busy Spider* (Carle, 1989), which contains dialogue such as the following:

> "Moo moo!" said the cow. "Want to eat some grass?" The spider didn't answer. She was very busy spinning her web.

Five-year-old Michael invented and dictated the following episodes using the book as a model:

The Very Busy Spider

> "Queep Queep," said the fox. "Want to come and bark at some dogs?" But the spider didn't answer. She was too busy spinning her web.

Bill Martin, Jr.'s (1978) *Brown Bear, Brown Bear What Do You See?* has been translated into many different languages, such as the Urdu/English version (Brown, 2004). Six-year-old Marlea wrote this in response to the book:

> Brown horse, brown horse, what do you see? I see a black cow looking at me. Black cow, black cow, what do you see? I see a red bird looking at me. Red bird, red bird, what do you see? I see a person looking at me. Person, person what do you see? I see my mother looking at me.

Cumulative Stories   Share literature in which characters are added one at a time and the ever-growing list of characters is recapped after each addition. In one first-grade class, the children had learned the cumulative song "Today Is Monday," which mentions a different food for each day of the week. The children had been studying the food pyramid, so they created their own version of the song with favorite nutritious foods and made seven posters to accompany their song. Each day, as they got ready to leave for the bus, the children would sing one child's version of the tune, such as this one:

FIGURE 10.20 Simple Alphabet Books

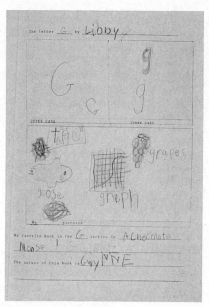

Today is Monday, today is Monday. Monday, rizcakz (rice cakes). All you hungry children, come and eat it up!

Picture books that use a cumulative format include *Bear Snores On* (Wilson, 2003), *Mushroom in the Rain* (Ginsburg, 1987), and *The Mitten* (Brett, 1989).

Designing an Abecedarius   After children have looked at many different illustrators' versions of an abecedarius (an alphabet book), challenge them to create alphabet books of their own using the cursive writing they have learned. The variety in children's responses to this is amazing. One child glued a three-dimensional object on every page. Another used yarn to stitch each letter. Another created a type of robot for each letter of the alphabet. Some examples of simple alphabet books created by children are shown in Figure 10.20.

Interviews   Conducting interviews is a good way to develop writing skills (Haley & Hobson, 1980). Children need to write to contact the interviewees, to formulate their questions, to summarize what they have learned, and to thank the interviewees afterward. At a country school in a small town, a half-grown bear came into the schoolyard and rummaged through a few trash cans before it was shot with a tranquilizer gun by the game warden. The elementary schoolchildren had seen the bear, and they were bursting with questions. They interviewed the game warden, asking questions like these:

Does it hurt the bear when you shoot it to put it to sleep?

How long before he wakes up again?

What will happen to him now?

Would he hurt you if he was awake?

As a grand finale to the interview, the children had the opportunity to look at the sedated bear, sprawled out in the back of the game warden's station wagon. Afterward, some students wanted to find out more about bears and wrote reports, some wrote letters to relatives and enclosed the story and photographs that appeared in the newspaper, and some composed original stories and poems about bears.

Dialogue or Response Journals   Another highly motivating composition activity is the use of dialogue or response journals in which the child writes on a regular basis about self-selected topics. Teachers and peers can then respond to passages the child wants to share. Try the following procedure (Hipple, 1985):

1. Staple together five pieces of paper (one page each for Monday through Friday) to make one journal. Make a journal for each child, and put it into his or her mailbox every Monday.
2. Devote 30 minutes per day to journal writing. Encourage children to talk quietly throughout this time period. Meet with several children each day and function as a listener ("Tell me what you have written," "How's the writing going, Koji?") or take dictation, if a child wishes.
3. Notify two children a day in advance that they will be sharing their work with the class. The other children should practice giving positive feedback and posing open-ended questions (not just "What?" but "How?" and "Why?").
4. Make the dialogue journal interactive, meaning that not only the teacher but also the child's peers respond to what the child has written.

For more interactive writing strategies, see Neumann (2007); Patterson, Schaller, and Clemens (2008); and Zygouris-Coe, Wiggins, and Smith (2004).

3–2–1   The 3–2–1 strategy requires students to summarize key ideas from a text they have listened to or read independently (Zygouris-Coe, Wiggins, & Smith, 2004). First, students write about three things they discovered. Next, they write about two things they found interesting. Last, they write one question they still have. In this way, writing becomes a tool for assessing listening or reading comprehension.

Conclusion

Drawing and writing are distinctive but related abilities in young children. Those who initiate children into the world of graphic and pictorial symbols should remember that their experiences with drawing and writing will resonate throughout life.

As a teacher of young children, you play an important role in introducing them to the communicative power of pictures and words. If you make those early experiences challenging, stimulating, and satisfying, you will contribute greatly to the children's ability to master the multiple symbol systems of modern society.

PEARSON
myeducationkit To check your comprehension on the content covered in this chapter, go to the MyEducationKit for your book and complete the Study Plan for Chapter 10. Here you will be able to take a chapter quiz and receive feedback on your answers.

Research-Based Literacy Strategies

"Talking" Drawings

The "Talking" drawings (McConnell, 1993) strategy enables children to combine their prior knowledge with the new information they have learned from an expository text. Begin by sharing numerous examples of diagrams that are labeled with words (Paquette, Fello, & Jalongo, 2007). Science books, social studies books, information books, and www.enchantedlearning.com are good sources for diagrams. Next, select a short text on a topic of relevance that can be read aloud or read by the children. Before the book or passage is shared, ask children to work with a partner to create a labeled drawing that represents their prior knowledge of the topic. Then share the text and, after children listen or read the material, have them return to their drawings and redraw or revise, adding all of the new terminology and features they now know about. When this was done with a passage on the octopus, for example, children's prelearning drawings were like cartoons. After hearing about the octopus, however, their drawings were much more detailed and showed the suction cup surfaces of the tentacles and their written labels included the new vocabulary (Paquette, Fello, & Jalongo, 2007). By evaluating the "before" and "after" drawings, the teacher quickly can identify advances in students' reading and listening comprehension for a particular topic.

Multimedia Composing

In *multimedia composing*, children combine writing with visual and aural multimedia in their school projects by using various software programs (Kara-Soteriou, Zawilinski, & Henry, 2007). The advantage of multimedia is that it results in complex, multilayered compositions that simultaneously support children's growth in drawing and writing. Children can combine widely available technologies and software (e.g., digital photography, PowerPoint) to construct digital stories and improve their literacy with print. The use of graphic organizers, such as those produced with Kidspiration, can be a tool for monitoring students' learning outcomes in relation to information and communications technologies. Some of the software being used in the schools that support children's multimedia composing include The Amazing Writing Machine (Broderbund), Crayola Makes a Masterpiece (IBM), HyperStudio (Knowledge Adventure), Write Outloud and Co-Writer (Don Johnston Company), and Kid Works Deluxe and Writing Blaster (Knowledge Adventure).

Gender Influences on Children's Drawing and Writing

There is little question that the gender messages sent both by the popular media (Genishi & Dyson, 2009) and by children's peers influence their drawing and writing (Coates, 2002). We know, for example, that children tend to prefer a hero/heroine of their own sex in their stories and that some storylines with gender-stereotyped roles find their way into children's books as well as into their original compositions (Yeoman, 1999). Males and females tend to process visuospatial information differently; males may engage regions that are associated with a visuomotor network, whereas females use the area of the brain that processes spatial attention and draws on working memory (Clements-Stephens, Rimrodt, & Cutting, 2009).

Some of the observed differences in boys' and girls' writing and drawing are as follows:

- The characters in elementary schoolchildren's creative writing tend to fit stereotypic gender roles, with boys being more active and girls more dependent (Trepanier-Street & Romatowski, 1999).
- Primary-school-aged girls tend to write longer, more complex texts than same-age boys and use a wider range of verbs and adjectives (Kanaris, 1999).
- Girls tend to draw stylized images of houses, children, and flowers on each piece of their writing, no matter how varied the topic (Millard & Marsh, 2001).

- The narrative writing style of girls is distinctive from that of boys and tends to emulate the style of their mothers in terms of length, cohesion, elaboration, coherence, and provision of content (Peterson & Roberts, 2003).
- Boys often draw to portray key events and actions in their work and use their drawings to enhance their written text (Millard & Marsh, 2001).

The research makes two major recommendations: (1) Combine drawing with writing to get primary-grade students to produce more words and better stories overall (Norris, Mokhtari, & Reichard, 2002), and (2) get children—particularly the boys—to dramatize stories so that they are more receptive to nontraditional gender roles (Rice, 2002).

Links with Literature

Picture Books to Inspire Drawing and Writing

There is a wealth of information about leading young children to produce original picture books and for introducing them to the work of authors and artists. The following resources offer ideas for teachers.

Writing, Bookmaking, and Publishing Resources

Brewster, J. (1997). Teaching young children to make picture books. *Early Childhood Education Journal, 25*(2), 113–118.

Capello, M. (2006). Under construction: Voice and identity development in writing workshop. *Language Arts, 83*(6), 482–491.

Chapman, G., & Robson, P. (1995). *Making shaped books.* Brookfield, CT: Millbrook Press.

Cummings, P. (1992, 1995). *Talking with artists* and *Talking with artists II.* New York: Simon & Schuster.

Ives, R. (2009). *Paper engineering and pop-ups for dummies.* New York: For Dummies.

Johnson, P. (1992). *A book of one's own: Developing literacy through making books.* Portsmouth, NH: Heinemann.

Johnson, P. (1993). *Literacy through the book arts.* Portsmouth, NH: Heinemann.

Johnson, P. (1997). *Pictures and words together.* Portsmouth, NH: Heinemann.

Kissel, B. T. (2009). Beyond the page: Peers influence prekindergarten writing through image, movement, and talk. *Childhood Education, 85*(3), 160–166.

Levin, I., & Bus, A. G. (2003). How is emergent writing based on drawing? Analyses of children's products and their sorting by children and mothers. *Developmental Psychology, 39*, 891–905.

Love, A., Burns, M. S., & Buell, M. J. (2007). Writing: Empowering literacy. *Young Children, 62*(1), 12–19.

Moutray, C. L., & Snell., C. A. (2003). Three teachers' quest: Providing daily writing activities for kindergartners. *Young Children, 58*(2), 24–28.

Nemmeth, K. (2009). *Many languages, one classroom: Tips and techniques for teaching English language learners in preschool.* Beltsville, MD: Gryphon House.

Ray, K., & Glover, M. (2008). *Already ready: Nurturing writers in preschool and kindergarten.* Portsmouth, NH: Heinemann.

Schickedanz, J. A., & Casbergue, R. M. (2004). *Writing in preschool: Learning to orchestrate meaning and marks.* Newark, DE: International Reading Association. Available from NAEYC.

Schulze, A. C. (2006). *Helping children become readers through writing: A guide to writing workshop in kindergarten.* Newark, DE: International Reading Association.

Shagoury, R. (2009). Nurturing writing development in multilingual classrooms. *Young Children, 64*(2), 52–57.

Society of Illustrators. (1993). *The very best of children's book illustration.* Cincinnati, OH: North Light Books.

Swain, G. (1995). *Bookworks: Making books by hand.* Minneapolis, MN: Carolrhoda.

Tunks, K. W., & Giles, R. M. (2007). *Write now! Publishing with young authors, preK–grade 2.* Portsmouth, NH: Heinemann.

Tunks, K. W., & Giles, R. M. (2009). Writing their words: Strategies for supporting young authors. *Young Children, 64*(1), 22–25.

Nonprint Media

Get to know Lois Ehlert [video]. (1994). New York: Harcourt.

Sampler of Children's Books and Activities to Inspire Children's Drawing and Writing

T = Toddler, Pre-K = Prekindergarten,
K = Kindergarten, P = Primary

Amelia Writes Again (Moss, 1995); *Amelia Hits the Road* (Moss, 1996); *Amelia's Notebook* (Moss, 1997). (P). Three books that demonstrate how to produce a sketchbook-type journal. Use them to introduce the idea of a personal journal that includes drawings as well as writing.

Are You My Mother? (2nd ed.). (Eastman, 1993). (Pre-K/K). This classic uses patterned dialogue as a baby animal searches for its mother. The familiar story is just right for homemade books that follow a similar question-and-answer format and could be written for younger children by children in the primary grades.

The Art Lesson. (dePaola, 1989). (P). (Big book). Young artist Tommy grows up in a family of artists and understands that art is more than following directions or copying. Try a class book titled "Art is . . ."

Behind the Mask: A Book about Prepositions. (Heller, 1995). (K/P). Gloriously illustrated prepositions that will beckon children to produce their own books of prepositions. See other Heller books about nouns and adjectives. Create original books about the parts of speech and other conventions of print, such as punctuation marks.

Ben Franklin's Almanac: Being a True Account of the Good Gentleman's Life. (Fleming, 2003). (P). Introduce children to the concept of a historical journal with this book; consider pairing it with *Our Eleanor: A Scrapbook Look at Eleanor Roosevelt's Remarkable Life* (Fleming, 2005) and asking children to research and create a journal about a famous person they admire.

The Big Bug Book. (Facklam, 1998). (All ages). This book compares insects to objects that are familiar to children so that they can get a sense of relative sizes. Knowing that a mother and her son created the book together can be used to inspire children to engage in collaborative drawing/writing projects with family and friends.

A Birthday Basket for Tia. (Mora, 1992). (T, Pre-K). This story about Cecilia's filling a basket with treasured objects that remind her of someone she loves invites children to write and draw about the baskets they might create for someone they care about deeply.

Brava, Strega Nona! (dePaola, 2008). (Pre-K/K/P). Fans of the magical Italian grandma and her stories of magic will be fascinated by this pop-up book and encouraged to make books with moving parts.

Captain Abdul's Pirate School. (McNaughton, 1994). (K/P). In this humorous story related through a child's illustrated diary, a father sends his son to pirate school to toughen him up. Ask students to think about what sort of zany schools they could imagine. After some brainstorming about how these schools would differ from regular schools, put children into small groups to produce a picture book about each one.

Chester. (Watt, 2009). (K/P). An author/illustrator produces a story about a mouse only to have Chester, her cat, take over the work, red marker in hand. A humorous way to discuss creative differences of writing/drawing teams.

Counting Kisses. (Katz, 2003). (T/Pre-K). A story of a gentle bedtime ritual, this book can lead to children's stories about their ways of getting relaxed and ready to go to sleep. Combine this with *Time for Bed* (Fox, 1997), *Ten, Nine, Eight* (Bang, 1991), and the classic *Good Night, Moon* (Brown, 1991) to spark a discussion from toddlers.

Diary of a Fly. (Cronin, 2007). (P). A humorous look at life from a fly's perspective. Combine with *Diary of a Worm* (Cronin, 2003) and *Diary of a Spider* (Cronin, 2005) to prompt other imaginary diaries from the perspective of unusual characters.

Dog Diaries: Secret Writings of the WOOF Society. (Byars, Duffey, & Myers, 2008). (P). A group of dog writers unite to publish their work and prove that they can do more than respond to the commands of human beings.

The Dot. (Reynolds, 2003). (Pre-K/K/P). What to do when you can't think of what to draw? This book advises children to "just make a mark" and get the process started. Pair it with *Ish* (Reynolds, 2004) by the same author and *Begin at the Beginning* (Schwartz, 2005) to encourage discussions about making art.

Emma. (Kesselman, 1980). (K/P). Based on a true story, this is an account of a woman who begins a painting career in her seventies out of a desire to represent her village the way she remembers it. A nice follow-up to a field trip or other shared experience where each child illustrates who or what made an impression.

Forest Tracks. (Duffy, 1996). (Pre-K/K/P). A puzzle book that asks readers to guess which animals made the tracks that they see, after which they can find the answer on a subsequent double-page spread. What other puzzle books can children imagine?

The Graphic Alphabet. (Pelletier, 1996). (All ages). An inventive alphabet book that just might encourage children to follow this author/illustrator's lead and create their own graphic alphabet or an alphabet book with other imaginative formats.

Grandma Calls Me Beautiful. (Joosse, 2008). (Pre-K/K). Use this touching story of a Hawaiian grandma and her grandchild to inspire original stories about beloved family members.

Hands. (Ehlert, 1997). (K/P). This beautiful book, fashioned in the shape of a glove, talks about all the things that can be made by hands. Creative use of photo collages, shaped pages, and page flaps will interest children in using similar techniques in their books. Other books by Ehlert with exceptionally imaginative formats are *Nuts to You!* (with squirrel in his hollow tree) and *Snowballs*, a book that stretches children's imaginations about what a snowman could look like and what found materials might be used for decoration. Make books using found objects after reading these by Ehlert.

The History of Making Books. (Krensky, 1996). (P). From monks creating illuminated texts to children using computers, this book tells the story of bookmaking so that children can see how authorship began. A good introduction to a book about an author or an author visit.

How to Make Super Pop-Ups. (Irvine, 2009). (P). To provide a challenge for children with good mechanical skills, try this book of instructions on making moving parts that can be included in children's original books. See other books on the same topic, such as *Easy to Make Pop-Ups* (Irvine, 2005) and *Making Books That Fly, Fold, Wrap, Hide, Pop Up, Twist & Turn* (Diehn, 2009).

If . . . (Perry, 1995). (P). A book that leads children to consider things they have not seen previously and then uses imaginative illustrations to show what the surprising proposition would look like. The book concludes by inviting them to use their imaginations to write and draw their own versions of the book.

In Flight with David McPhail: A Creative Autobiography. (McPhail, 1996). (P). This book in Heinemann's Creative Sparks series introduces children to a picture book author/illustrator's creative processes. Use this series to teach beginning research skills and to create author profiles that can be stored on a computer.

I Went Walking. (Williams, 1989). (Pre-K/K). The simple question-and-answer structure of "I went walking . . ." and "What did you see?" makes this "big book" a natural for similar stories invented by children. Another book with a similar format is *Let's Go Visiting* (Williams, 2000).

I Wish I Were a Butterfly. (Howe, 1987). (Pre-K/K/P). Imagining all the things you might do as a different creature opens up new possibilities for composing a class book. Each child can contribute a page about the animal he or she would most like to be and why.

Jorah's Journal. (Caseley, 1997). (P). Jorah, the new girl at school, uses journal writing as a way of expressing her emotions as well as a way of fulfilling her teacher's requirements. A good introduction to interactive journals.

Just Look. (Hoban, 1996). (Pre-K/K/P). A visual guessing-game book with cut-out holes invites children to experiment with new book formats in their own bookmaking. Relate this book to Eric Carle's *The Very Hungry Caterpillar*, and then give children the challenge of designing a book that uses cutouts.

Keepers. (Watts, 1997). (P). After a 7-year-old spends his money on a baseball glove instead of a present, he decides to make a very special book for his grandmother, who is the keeper of the family stories.

The Kissing Hand. (Penn, 2007). (Pre-K/K/P). This book about the fears associated with starting school is sure to inspire other stories about the worries associated with doing something new and becoming more independent.

The Letters Are Lost. (Ernst, 1996). (Pre-K/K/P). An alphabet mystery book that invites children to search for alphabet blocks that have disappeared. Children will be intrigued by this new twist on an alphabet book and might begin thinking about a sequel called *The Numbers Are Lost* or another sort of book with the answers hidden in the pictures.

Library Lion. (Knudsen, 2006). (Pre-K/K). Imagine what would happen if a lion loved to read and started frequenting the library—he still has to follow the rules! But, in an emergency, even roaring is allowed. Pair this story with other books about animals eager to participate in school activities such as *Book! Book! Book!* (Bruss, 2001) or *Don't Let the Pigeon Drive the Bus!* (Willems, 2003).

The Little Painter of Sabana Grande. (Markun, 1993). (Pre-K/K/P). Based on a true story, a child learns to mix paints from plants and then uses them to decorate the family's adobe house in the absence of a canvas. A great introduction to using sidewalk chalk out on the surface of the playground to draw/write a story.

Love to Langston. (Medina, 2002). (K/P). The life of the famous African American poet from Harlem, Langston Hughes, written in verse for children.

Lucy's Picture. (Moon, 1995). (Pre-K). What sort of picture would Lucy's blind grandfather appreciate? In trying to answer that question, Lucy decides that a flat painting won't do and creates a textured collage instead. Children will be interested in the idea of making art as presents with the recipient in mind.

Matthew's Dream. (Lionni, 1991). (P). A trip to an art museum inspires a little mouse to become a painter when he grows up. Try using this book as an introduction to a museum visit on video, on the Internet, or in person.

Mouse's Scrapbook. (Cartlidge, 1995). (Pre-K/K/P). A mouse's scrapbook, complete with photos, notes, mementos, and captions. This imaginative book begs the question "What kinds of scrapbooks might other animals keep?"

My Grandma, My Pen Pal. (Koutsky, 2003). (K/P). A scrapbook-like remembrance of the correspondence between a granddaughter and her grandmother and a special bond maintained through writing.

Only Opal: The Diary of a Young Girl. (Whiteley, 1994). (P). Actual excerpts from the diary of a young girl who moves to Oregon with her family. Use this book to introduce students to the idea of day-by-day writing and historical journals.

Open Wide: Tooth School Inside. (Keller, 2003). (K/P). A school for teeth?! This zany book, illustrated in the style of children's drawings, encourages students to look at a topic from a completely different and wildly imaginative point of view.

The Painter. (Catalanotto, 1995). (Pre-K/K/P). A young child whose father is a painter gets to work in his studio at the end of the day, where she uses the opportunity to produce a painting of her own. Consider using this book to introduce children to the lives of artists and to prepare them for a visit from an artist, such as a children's picture book author/illustrator.

Pictures from Our Vacation. (Perkins, 2007). (K/P). When two children attempt to chronicle their family's cross-country road trip with notebooks, hand-drawn maps, photos from instant cameras, and captions, they discover that the best memories often defy description. Multiple perspectives, thought bubbles, and the realities of a long journey make this book a standout.

Rebus Riot. (Christensen, 1997). (P). Clever rebus rhymes will invite children to try their hand at combining pictures and words.

Round Trip. (Jonas, 1983). (P). Children and adults are fascinated by the design of a book that can be read backward and forward and just might be inspired to write a circular story or poem of their own.

Sholom's Treasure: How Sholom Aleichem Became a Writer. (Silverman, 2005). (K/P). The life of a famous Yiddish storyteller, one of 12 children living in poverty, who did not allow the many challenges he faced to dissuade him from becoming a writer.

The Squiggle. (Schaefer, 1996). (P). A child goes for a walk in the park, finds a red ribbon, and uses it to stimulate her imagination. Illustrated in Chinese brush painting style, this book will invite children to think about all the different shapes a piece of ribbon can suggest or perhaps try their hand at brush painting techniques.

Stringbean's Trip to the Shining Sea. (Williams, 1988). (K/P). A cross-country trek, chronicled through postcards as Stringbean sets out to see the ocean. Use this book to introduce story maps.

Su Dongpo: Chinese Genius. (Demi, 2006). (P). A gloriously illustrated account of one of China's most respected and multitalented individuals from the eleventh century.

Three Days on a River in a Red Canoe. (Williams, 1981). (K/P). A child's travel journal chronicling a summer vacation with his aunt and mother. This book includes postcards, sketches, and even a camping recipe. Ask each child to choose a place he or she would like to visit and, after investigating it through books, films, the Internet, or software, produce an imaginary travel journal.

Under My Nose. (Ehlert, 1996). (P). A favorite children's book author/illustrator introduces children to her creative processes, particularly the use of collage. Try making a class collage to go along with a theme (e.g., families, growing things, etc.).

The Way I Feel . . . Sometimes. (DeRegniers, 1998). (K/P). Humorous cartoons depict different ways of dealing with powerful emotions. A good book to spark similar good news/bad news stories such as Remy Charlip's (1993) *Fortunately.*

What Do Illustrators Do? (Christelow, 2007). (K/P). An insider's look at how picture books are illustrated.

Wish You Were Here: Emily's Guide to the 50 States. (Krull, 1997). (P). A grandmother and grandchild keep a diary of their travels throughout the United States. Try using this book to create a similar travel diary for a class field trip.

A Young Painter: The Life and Paintings of Want Yani— China's Extraordinary Young Artist. (Zehshun & Low, 1991). (P). A profile of a child artist, chronicling her works from age 3 to 6. This book also introduces children to Chinese brush painting as a technique. Use it to inspire books that depict their personal progress as writers or artists.

Online Resources

Telling Stories with Pictures: The Art of Children's Book Illustration

    www.decordova.org/decordova/exhibit/1997/stories/
    Default.htm

Exhibits of the artwork of children's book illustrators.

Writing Fix

    www.writingfix.com

Advice on writing for children of all ages.

Make Beliefs Comix

    www.makebeliefscomix.com

Children can create their own comic strips in Spanish and English.

National Center for Children's Illustrated Literature

    www.nccil.org

Exhibits of the work of children's book illustrators.

Scholastic

    www.scholastic.com

A great resource for information on authors and illustrators.

ELLs

Metacognitive Strategies

A metacognitive strategy is a way of "thinking about thinking" with an eye toward understanding what each of us needs in order to learn (Goh & Taib, 2006). Metacognitive strategies often are categorized by when they occur—before, during, or after an encounter with a written text. For ELLs, these activities focus on listening comprehension if they are not yet reading or, if they are, a text that is in their L1 or a text that is written in both L1 and L2.

Before the Text

To integrate metacognitive strategies *before*, educators need to devote time and thought when planning learning activities. A clear purpose for the lesson must be identified—and shared—with the learners. Some "before the text" drawing and writing activities include recording (or asking children to write) predictions about a story based on the title and cover; filling in a blank K-W-L chart (see Chapter 5) with a partner or small group; taking notes or making a sketch based on a video selected to build prior knowledge; making maps, diagrams, or other graphic materials in preparation for the story (Rothenberg & Fisher, 2007); creating a class pictionary of key terms in the text; or demonstrating and writing the steps in a process (e.g., planting a bean seed) prior to reading about it.

During the Text

To integrate metacognitive strategies *during* children's work with text, the focus should be on monitoring comprehension. Some drawing/writing activities that educators might incorporate as children read include pausing to revise predictions that were made before the story as they listen and gain more information; following a simple map related to the plot sequence of the story; checking off a list of items or characters mentioned in the story; contributing new vocabulary words to a word wall; writing the refrain in a story or song and joining in; or completing a blank graphic organizer that identifies common misconceptions addressed in an expository text or compares/contrasts two story characters.

After the Text

After the text activities help ELLs detect comprehension failures and direct them to try alternative strategies. Some "after the text" drawing and writing activities include creating a group sequel or prequel to a story, working with a partner to depict the sequence in aural text through drawings and/or words, adding to picture dictionaries written and maintained in both languages, summarizing the story plot, or comparing/contrasting two different versions of the same basic folktale.

All of these strategies help learners to become more aware of their thinking processes and provide ways to maximize their learning through drawing and writing.

How Do I ...

Use Dictation and Digital LEAs Effectively?

Children often are capable of composing stories orally before they have the fine motor skills and knowledge of print to produce writing (Gadzikowski, 2007). In these circumstances, a teacher, volunteer, tutor, or technology can be used to produce a written text. Multimedia can also complement the *language experience approach* (LEA), in which children have an experience, dictate stories about it, and use their original stories to practice reading skills (Turnbill, 2003). The LEA may be particularly helpful in reading instruction with English language learners because it begins with what they know—their own experiences (Schulz, 2009). Labbo, Eakle, and Montero (2002) recommend a digital LEA that follows this procedure:

Setting up the Experience

1. The teacher or the teacher and students together select a stimulus experience. (The teacher offers suggestions, scouts out a location, discusses expectations for students, gathers materials, decides the duration of the activity, etc.)
2. The teacher and students make decisions about picture taking:
   Who will direct photographing (when and which activities)?
   What type of photographs will be taken (candid or posed)?
   How many photographs will be taken?

Photographing the Experience

3. The children engage in the stimulus activity.
4. The teacher photographs the children engaging in the stimulus activity using a digital camera.

Composing a Multimedia Story or Photo Essay

5. The children use digital photographs to prepare for composing by doing the following:
   Importing photos into creativity software
   Viewing photographs and recalling the stimulus experience
   Discussing and selecting photographs that may best tell the story
   Arranging photographs in sequence or on a story board

6. The children compose a story about the stimulus experience:
   The teacher types student dictation for each photograph (or a student types with teacher support).
   The teacher (or computer voice synthesizer, if available) reads the text.
   The children decide if ideas are stated appropriately; if not, revisions are made onscreen and on the spot.
   As an optional extension, the children can add multimedia effects to enhance the story (music, sound effects, animation).
   The children may also record their voices reading the story.

Engaging in Follow-Up Activities

7. The children interact with the story for additional literacy learning:
   Multimedia interactions—They may read chorally with the multimedia story onscreen, echo read, listen to the story read aloud by different voice synthesizer characters, and so on.

The teacher may make a printout for each student to encourage reading at the word level and to promote fluency.

The LEA stories may be saved on the computer or in print form for review or as reading practice materials. A variety of computer-generated drawings produced by young children are posted at www.readingonline.org/electronic/elec_index .asp?HREF=kindergarten/index.html.

PEARSON myeducationkit™   Now go to Chapter 10 in the MyEducationKit (**www.MyEducationKit .com**) for your book, where you can:

- Find Chapter Objectives.
- Complete Assignments and Activities that can help you more deeply understand the chapter content.
- Extend knowledge with content-specific Web Links.
- Check your comprehension on the content covered in the chapter by going to the Study Plan. Here you will be able to take a chapter quiz, receive feedback on your answers, and then access resources that will enhance your understanding of chapter content.

chapter eleven

Understanding Media Influences and Applying Technology

Annie Pickert/Pearson Education

FACT FILE on Media Influences and Technology

• The average American child spends more time watching television than pursuing any other activity, except sleeping (American Academy of Pediatrics, 2001). A typical child watches on average 28 hours of television per week (American Psychological Association, 2005). During the summer months, children's television viewing increases by 150 percent (Smart Television Alliance, 2009).

• Although television watching is not considered to be a suitable pastime for children under the age of 2 years, 59 percent of children have started watching TV by the age of 6 months (Ofcom, 2008).

- Over 99 percent of U.S. families own a television set so efforts have been made to use television to foster growth in young children. *Sesame Street, Between the Lions, Martha Speaks,* and *Reading Rainbow* are examples of programs designed to support early emergent literacy (Linebarger, Kosanic, Greenwood, & Doku, 2004; Moses, 2009).

- Twenty-seven percent of 5- and 6-year-old children use a computer for about 50 minutes per day (Vandewater et al., 2007). When the amount of time children devote to watching television is combined with other types of "screen time"—computers, games, etc.—it can be excessive.

- Whereas children's out-of-school literacy practices may tend to emphasize quickly processing fleeting visual images, formal schooling often requires children to concentrate on stationary print (Knobel & Lankshear, 2003; Marsh, Brooks, Hughes, Ritchie, & Roberts, 2005). Some suggest that reading instruction in school could benefit from incorporating the visual training aspects, appeal, and individualization of computer games (Compton-Lilly, 2007).

- Studies of computer use in classrooms suggest that it is motivating and engaging for most children (Baron, 2005). Moreover, when used effectively, it can help children with learning disabilities to stay on task (Spooner, 2004; Stephen & Plowman, 2003). Learning at the computer appears to be most effective when it is combined with teacher instruction and opportunities for peer interaction (Lau, Higgins, Gelfer, Hong, & Miller, 2005; Walton-Hadlock, 2008).

- Nearly all U.S. schools have access to the Internet; the percentage of instructional rooms with access increased from 51 percent in 1998 to 94 percent in 2005 (U.S. Department of Education, 2007).

- Both boys' and girls' primary Internet activities are communicating with friends and downloading music—usually done while multitasking.

- In 2000, Congress passed the Children's Internet Protection Act (CIPA). This federal law states that school districts must protect students from harmful materials—such as pornography and obscene language—to be eligible for federal E-rate money, which can subsidize up to 90 percent of school's telecommunications and technology costs (Phelps Deily, 2009, p. 19).

- Brief but consistent computer-based reading lessons that supplement rather than replace conventional reading instruction can enhance reading achievement (Holum & Gahala, 2001; Tracey & Young, 2007).

Did any of this information surprise you? If so, what? Why? How will you use this knowledge to educate and care for the very young?

What Are the Media and What Is Media Literacy?

PEARSON

myeducationkit™

Go to the Assignments and Activities section of Chapter 11 in MyEducationKit and complete the activity entitled "Describing the Water Cycle."

Without question, the communication environment has changed dramatically in recent years. Each time new media are introduced into a culture, they exert an undeniable influence on the behavior of that culture's children (Genishi & Dyson, 2009). When the communication environment changes due to technological advances (e.g., the printing press, the Internet), the effects are felt in three ways. First, technology changes our interests (what we think about); second, it changes the symbols and tools we use (what we think with); and third, it alters the nature of our communities (how we interact) (Innis, 1951).

The *mass media* include a wide variety of images, symbols, and messages. Young children are inundated with messages from the popular media, defined as television, radio, advertising, the Internet, and print materials, such as magazines and newspapers. These messages tend to shape what children know, think, and do. To illustrate, consider the situation of Claire, a 5-year-old. Her family is home to Hobbes, a new designer cat that is bred to look like a miniature tiger. As the kindergartner explains, "Mommy named him Hobbes, you know, like the cartoon *Calvin and Hobbes.* If you want to see pictures of what he looks like, just Google Toygers—t-o-y-g-e-r-s. He's a boy but he can't have babies; 'cause he's been neutralized." In this brief comment, Claire has touched upon three major types of popular media: the newspaper, the Internet, and television (she was familiar with a commercial in which a spray "neutralizes odors" and substituted it for the less familiar word *neutered*). As Claire's experience illustrates, children can sound surprisingly sophisticated about their high-tech society and, at the same time, charmingly naïve.

The mass media also affect how children think about things and the ways that they approach problems, extending even to what they consider to be possible. A student teacher in a third-grade classroom made a "computer" out of a milk carton to review with her students some facts on health and safety. She cut a slot in the top of the milk carton and inserted small cards with a question on one side and answer on the other into the slot. Inside the milk carton, she put a piece of cardboard that flipped the card over, so that when it came out a second slot in the bottom, the answer was on top. Unfortunately, on her way to school, the piece of cardboard in the center had become dislodged and her "computer" wouldn't work. As the student teacher tried to figure out what to do, one child suggested, "Why don't you plug it in?" and another child remarked, in all seriousness, "You don't plug it in; it runs on batteries. Maybe you left it on and the batteries ran out." Clearly, these children expected everything in the world to operate using electrical power.

The media can influence children's lives in profound ways, affecting what they talk about, wish for, act like, and believe in (Strasburger, Wilson, & Jordan, 2009). Companies realize this and use powerful images to grab attention, sell products, and promote their ideas on billboards, in stores, on product wrappers, in newspapers and magazines, on television and radio, and in movies.

What exactly are the implications of pervasive media? In cognitive terms, it has been argued that living in today's channel-surfing, sound bite world tends to make us reluctant to pursue difficult problems and to be impatient for solutions, thereby exerting a negative effect on motivation, persistence, and concentration—all of which are important in learning to listen, speak, read, and write effectively.

Increasingly, early childhood educators are asking themselves what *literacy* means in contemporary society (Comber, 2003; Quintero, 2009; Vasquez, 2003). The traditional areas of the language arts—listening, speaking, reading, and writing—need to be augmented with other elements, including visual literacy, critical thinking, and media literacy (Williams, 2007). Today's children are "digital natives"; they have never known a time without technology. By age 2, over 70 percent of children turn the TV set on by themselves; by age 3, 45 percent can use a mouse to point and click; by age 6, 34 percent of children are looking at websites on their own (See www.digitalbeginnings.shef.ac.uk/final-report.htm.) Children need a curriculum that can enable them to navigate and interpret the messages and images in which they are immersed (Pailliotet, Semali, Rodenberg, Giles, & Macaul, 2000). The greatest challenge is not finding information; that can be accomplished by the touch of a button. The real challenges are (1) how to manage the constant stream of information that saturates society, (2) how to assess the quality of that information and its sources, and (3) how to "critically read and write with and across varied symbol systems" (Semali & Pailliotet, 1999, p. 6). Figure 11.1 gives an overview of different types of media literacy.

Developmentally speaking, differentiating between real and pretend or interpreting the motives of others would pose a cognitive challenge to many young children. What they can do, however, is to think more concretely about these problems. As a starting point, they can ask such questions as, "Who is telling this story?" "What is it that you see and hear?" "Is it true?" "How do you know?" To illustrate how this approach might operate, have children think about a commercial for a heavily advertised doll or action figure. They can figure out that somebody who wants people to buy the toy is responsible for the commercial. Through experience, they may be able to point out misleading elements that they see and hear (such as the fact that you have to buy all of the items that appear in the commercial separately or that they have to be assembled or require batteries). At this point, they can begin discussing their disappointments with toys and realizing that not everything is as it appears—an important media literacy concept. Figure 11.2 (on p. 260) summarizes the basic concepts of media literacy as it affects early childhood education.

The Center for Media Literacy (2007) identifies five key questions that children (and adults) need to consider as they interact with the media:

Go to the Assignments and Activities
section of Chapter 11 in MyEducationKit
and complete the activity entitled
"A WebQuest Dinosaur Activity."

1. Who created this message?
2. What creative techniques are used to attract my attention?
3. How might different people understand this message differently?

FIGURE 11.1 Media Literacies: Definitions and Questions

Definitions

- *Media literacy.* The ability to communicate competently in all media forms—print and electronic—as well as access, understand, analyze, and evaluate the images, words, and sounds found in contemporary culture.
- *Information literacy.* The ability to access and use information, analyze content, work with ideas, synthesize thought, and communicate results.
- *Digital literacy.* The ability to attain deeper understanding of content by using data-analysis tools and accelerated learning processes enabled by technology.
- *New literacy.* The ability to solve genuine problems within a deluge of information and its transfer in the digital age.
- *Computer literacy.* The ability to accurately and effectively use computer tools such as word processors, spreadsheets, databases, and presentation and graphic software.
- *Computer-technology literacy.* The ability to manipulate the hardware that is the understructure of technology systems.
- *Critical literacy.* The ability to look at the meanings and purposes of written texts, visual applications, and spoken words to question the attitudes, values, and beliefs behind them. The goal is development of critical thinking to discern meaning from an array of multimedia, visual imagery, and virtual environments, as well as written text.

Questions about Technology and Literacy Instruction

- *Research.* What empirical evidence exists to confirm that new technologies can be effective in support of literacy instruction? What technologies actually improve literacy programs? What technologies have little or no effect? Are any technologies, in fact, harmful to the development of successful literacy instruction?
- *Practice.* Precisely which technologies, to date, are being used successfully to support literacy instruction? What technologies hold promise for the future? How are teachers integrating them into literacy instruction?
- *Professional development.* How has professional development in literacy-based contexts been influenced by the advent of educational technology? What skills do teachers need for integrating technology into literacy instruction?

For You to Do

- Review work in the United Kingdom on media literacy at www.ofcom.org/uk.
- Get free resources and watch a 6-minute video about media literacy at the Center for Media Literacy website (www.medialit.org/reading_room/article709.html).

Source: Adapted from Holum & Gahala, 2001.

4. What values, lifestyles, and points of view are represented in, or omitted from, this message?
5. Why is this message being sent?

See www.medialit.org/pdf/mlk/02_5KQ_ClassroomGuide.pdf for details on these questions and free lesson plans.

FIGURE 11.2   Basic Tenets of Media Literacy in Early Childhood

- *Access.* Children are capable of using media and new technologies to receive and send information. They should not be denied access based on socioeconomic status or geographic location.

How do the media shape a child's self-image and sense of power to influence the media?

- *Analysis.* Children strive to make sense of the media messages that they encounter. They use visual literacy skills to analyze the forms of these messages, reflect on the functions of these messages, consider the intent of communication as well as the consequences, and think about the meaning of the media in their lives and their communities.

How do the media affect children's literacy—the way they view, listen, speak, read, write, discuss, and perceive the worlds of work, study, leisure, and family?

- *Evaluation.* Children render judgments about the media that are based on aesthetic elements, practical issues, and value systems.

How do the media influence power structures, civic participation, and forms of social interaction?

- *Production.* Children create messages using a variety of media as a way of participating in shaping the information culture in which they live.

What opportunities do children have to influence the media?

Sources: Megee (1997); Semali and Hammett (1999); Share, Jolls, and Thoman (2007).

As these questions suggest, media literacy calls on learners to evaluate the media, an approach that is referred to as *critical literacy* (Chafel, Flint, Hammel, & Pomeroy, 2007; Comber & Simpson, 2001). Critical literacy is based on the theories of Bakhtin (1981). In a nutshell, Bakhtin regarded literacy as a powerful social dynamic influenced by context that is used to construct a sense of self, exerting a powerful influence on participation in communities (Nichols, 2007). Ultimately, literacy determines who has power and whose story gets told (Genishi & Dyson, 2009; Semali & Hammett, 1999; Vasquez, 2000).

This may sound rather theoretical until it is applied to a child's experience. When Lori was 4, she became fascinated with the Disney film *The Little Mermaid*. She watched the DVD so many times that she had it virtually memorized. She also owned a picture book about Ariel, a CD with the soundtrack, a T-shirt with images and words, a lunchbox, several plastic figures of the characters collected from a fast-food restaurant that she used to retell and reinvent the story, a Little Mermaid doll with clothing, a plastic necklace featuring the main character, and a Halloween costume. Yet it could be argued that her level of literacy about *The Little Mermaid* was seriously lacking. Lori did not know the original story by Hans Christian Andersen, that it differed from the one with which she was familiar (the mermaid dies at the end), that Andersen had written another story she owned ("The Ugly Duckling"), and that a statue of the Little Mermaid stands in the harbor in Copenhagen, Denmark, as a national tribute to the author.

In sum, Lori's knowledge was limited to popular culture, and in fact, she insisted that anything that deviated from her mass media knowledge was wrong. So popular culture texts extensively promote one small part of the many things that can be known, often in the interest of selling a product. As a result, they may have a limiting or distorting effect on children's knowledge.

Collaboration with Families and Professionals

Brain and Language

Neuroimaging technology shows which areas of the brain are activated during various activities. Complex cognitive processes stimulate brain activity in areas throughout the brain (Jensen, 2006). Some advocates of intensive phonics have claimed that brain activity is evidence of effectiveness; however, as Strauss and Altwerger (2007) point out, neuroimaging does not demonstrate the connection between decoding and meaning making while reading. What do you think?

PEARSON
myeducationkit™

Go to the Assignments and Activities section of Chapter 11 in MyEducationKit and complete the activity entitled "Learning About Shapes."

When 4-year-old April arrived at her Head Start class, she was terrified of something. She crawled underneath a table and screamed whenever an adult approached her. The teachers were mystified by this behavior pattern until they spoke with April's mother, a 19-year-old single parent. She said that she could offer no explanation for April's fears, but during the conversation, she mentioned that she liked to watch horror movies. April's mother further explained that she was afraid to watch the films by herself and asked her daughter to watch with her. "Do you think that's a bad idea?" she asked.

About this, April's teacher said:

At first, I was angry that April's mother did not realize this was inappropriate and had shaken her daughter's sense of trust. Evidently, April had learned from these horrible movies that it is a mean and scary world out there, where adults jump out and injure you at every turn. But then I began to think about the fact that April's mom is very young and may not have anyone to turn to for advice. She seemed to suspect that there could be a link between April's fears and those terrifying movies, or she would not have mentioned it. I also kept in mind that my first responsibility was to April. If I did not establish a trusting relationship with her mom, then I would not be in a position to improve the situation for April. I told April's mother that her instincts were right—that it was not a good idea for April to watch these movies because they were too frightening for a young child. I urged her to stop right away.

Gradually, April adjusted to school and learned that it was a place for learning where the adults could be trusted. April's mom was warmly invited to join the parent meetings, and she became a responsible parent volunteer in the classroom as the Head Start personnel worked with her.

Contributions and Consequences

- *Contributions of the teacher:* What was your initial response to this situation? How did the teacher's response differ from your own?
- *Contributions of the family:* How did the parent participate in finding a solution?

- *Contributions of other professionals:* How did the work of other professionals make a contribution to resolving this issue?
- *Consequences of collaboration:* How might this story have ended differently if the adults had simply blamed one another and refused to work together?

As you read the guidelines on media and technology that follow, relate them to April's situation.

Teacher Concerns and Basic Strategies

For decades, teachers have been concerned about the programming to which children are exposed. When television was first introduced in the 1950s, parents and educators had numerous concerns. They asked: Will TV fulfill its educational promise of being "a window on the world"? Will it draw children away from more valuable pursuits? What effects will it have on the family and interpersonal relationships? Will it cause children to expect constant entertainment? Will it shorten their attention spans? Will it adversely affect their intellectual development? Their creativity and imagination? Will it ruin their eyes?

Today's media are far more sophisticated and integrated into family life than those big wooden boxes with the tiny black-and-white screens. Yet such concerns are still commonplace among teachers. As Figure 11.3 explains, American parents do not compare well with those in other countries when it comes to controlling television.

La Toya, a kindergarten teacher, said, "I wonder if the media sometimes 'undo' what adults try to teach about race, ethnicity, gender roles, and compassion for others."

The popular media often do perpetuate stereotypes. When a 4-year-old child was asked what his mother would do now that she had earned her doctorate (actually, a Ph.D.), the boy replied, "I don't know—I don't think she can be a doctor, I think she has to be a nurse." The child's answer had been shaped by his babysitter's daily habit of watching soap operas in which the men were the doctors and the women, the nurses. Usually, the villains in children's programming are of indeterminate (but not Caucasian) race, are old women, speak English with an accent, and/or do not have families. Viewing these messages for many hours can exert a strong influence over what children expect and accept as "normal."

Although we may be well aware of the race and gender "isms," there are other types of stereotyping and prejudice that are everywhere in the media. Overweight individuals, for example, are portrayed as eating constantly or consuming huge portions of food. Most comedies include at least one sight gag to reinforce the message that those who are overweight deserve to be ridiculed. It is not surprising, then, that overweight children are a primary target for teasing and bullying.

Infants and Toddlers
The American Academy of Pediatrics issued a statement that at no point in childhood should children spend more than 2 hours a day in front of any screen, and children under 2 should watch no TV. Their concern centers on a possible link between excessive television watching and attentional difficulties later on. In response to this research, some children's shows, like *Blue's Clues*, avoid rapid pace, repeat key points, and actively involve children.

FIGURE 11.3 Children and Television in the United States

Consider these data on time spent watching television versus time spent in school:

	Television	School
Approximate hours per day	6–7	5–6
Days per week	7	5
Approximate weeks per year	52	30

- *Excessive and inappropriate viewing.* American children watch programs intended for teenagers and adults most of the time (Tomopoulos, Valdez, Dreyer, Fierman, Berkule, Kuhn, & Mendelsohn, 2009). Many American children have television sets in their bedrooms where they watch television programs that are not suited for them. Excessive viewing affects children's ability to sustain attention; exposes them to sex, drugs, and violence; increases sedentary behavior; encourages them to make poor food choices; and influences them to be consumers who think that buying things brings happiness (National Institute on Media and the Family, 2009).
- *Teaching about media literacy.* The United States produces and consumes more television programming than any other country, yet it lags behind in national efforts to teach about the media. In comparison with other nations, notably Canada and Great Britain, the United States teaches children less about who is communicating, for what purpose, with what effect, and on behalf of which individuals.
- *Television advertising.* American children see approximately 20,000 TV commercials per year, or about 1 hour of commercials for every 5 hours of commercial television watching. The United States is the only country that permits advertising toys, games, and food directly to children. In 1984, the Federal Communications Commission stopped regulating children's television.
- *Marketing to young children.* The U.S. advertising industry considers children to be full-fledged consumers by age 3, even though research shows that children younger than 6 do not understand that the purpose of advertising is to sell a product.
- *Support for public television.* The United States spends $1 per person per year on public television, while Japan spends $17, Canada $32, and Great Britain $37. Throughout Europe, Asia, and Latin America, some nations devote 12 to 15 percent of their broadcast schedule to educational programming for children. The United States devotes only about 1 percent to such programming.

For You to Do:

- Visit the Media Education Foundations website (www.mediaeducationfoundation.org) to locate teaching materials, resources for parents/families, and a chart of free streaming videos. Watch leading early childhood experts discussing "Consuming Kids: The Commercialization of Childhood."
- Consult the resources available at the Media Literacy Clearinghouse (http://medialit.med.sc.edu) for use in communication with families.

Sources: Bergin and Bergin (in press); Center for Media Education (2009); Erwin and Morton (2008); Levin (1999); Megee (1997); Moses (2009).

Martina, a child-care provider, wondered, "How strong is the connection between what children watch and what they do? I've read about the concerns with children imitating aggressive behavior, but what about other behaviors?"

It is true that children often imitate what they see in the media. A preschool teacher was surprised to overhear three girls begging one of their classmates to "play *Emeril Live* again!" The boy would stand at the wooden stove, manipulate the various plastic food replicas around, then add imaginary spices with a flourish and call out, "BAM!" Many would think that this conveys a positive message—namely, that men can prepare food as well as women. Yet at other times, children may mimic other, less socially acceptable, behavior. Jarrett, for example, was an avid fan of the Pirates of the Caribbean videos and decided to use a stick as a sword out on the playground. In the process, he disrupted the play of several other children and struck another child, so the teacher had to intervene to stop the swashbuckling.

Without a doubt, the popular media affect children's perceptions, not only of others but also of themselves. A first step is to accept the fact that the media are not "neutral"; rather, they are a potent and pervasive influence on children. Therefore, the best approach is to monitor—and sometimes prohibit—the messages allowed into children's homes and schools, hearts and minds. Figure 11.4 offers a set of guidelines for families on the responsible use of the media.

 ## Classroom Activities to Support Media Literacy

Media literacy should teach children to access, decode, analyze, evaluate, and produce communication in a variety of forms with a variety of functions and purposes (Robinson, 1996). For young children, understanding the media needs to begin with *visual literacy*, or the interpretation of images that they see. Those images might occur in a television program or commercial, on a billboard, on a website, in a video game, and so forth. Realize, however, that sometimes, "seeing is believing," and children's ideas may be resistant to change (Chang, 2000; Yates, 2000).

Developmentally effective media literacy activities for young children are discussed in this section. Figure 11.5 (on p. 267) highlights some general recommendations for integrating technology.

Media Mentor   Find a person who works in the field of media, such as a website designer, a children's book illustrator, a product/packaging designer, or a college student who has assembled an artist's portfolio. Ask this person to share items from his or her work that will be interesting and appropriate for young children.

FIGURE 11.4   Recommendations to Families on Responsible Use of the Media

- *Time.* Make a deliberate effort to control the media. Limit the total amount of "screen time" that children spend with the media to 1 to 2 hours a day for older children. Talk with children to plan what those hours will be, realizing that some difficult decisions will be necessary.
- *Use.* Avoid turning media into an "electronic babysitter;" television watching is not a suitable activity for children under age 2. Do not make the mistake of believing that videos or television programs are a satisfactory substitute for real, live interaction with your child about high-quality picture books. Remember that part of what makes a vacation memorable is conversation about a shared experience, not the video game or DVD that they were watching.
- *Access.* Move the media away from the center of family life. Avoid leaving the TV set or radio on constantly, as this tends to interfere with conversation. Turn off the television, radio, or computer during meals or at other times when the family is together. Make your child's bedroom a media-free zone, because many children watch inappropriate programs late at night when they are not supervised.
- *Modeling.* Be a good example of responsible media use. Show your child how you control and plan media choices, rather than aimlessly channel or Internet surf. Excessive "screen time" from a very early age can contribute to attentional problems (Christakis, Zimmerman, DiGiuseppe, & McCarty, 2004). Counteract some of the inappropriate media that children experience with materials designed specifically for them that can be borrowed from the library, such as Scholastic/Weston Woods DVDs that encourage children to respect diversity: *Do Unto Otters* (Laurie Kellar), *Emily's First 100 Days of School* (Rosemary Wells), *Max's Words* (Kate Banks), and *Wallace's Lists* (Barbara Bottner).
- *Appropriateness.* Just because a program has cartoon characters, that does not mean it is harmless or suitable for young children. In fact, there is more violence in cartoons than in any other type of program. Remember that, particularly for children with developmental delays, the ability to differentiate between fantasy and reality also may take more time to emerge (Erwin & Morton, 2008). Seek out television programs that have been developed by educators to promote young children's learning, such as *Caillou.*
- *Discussion.* Raise questions about what your child has seen, heard, or read. Point out exaggerated or false claims in advertising, and remind children of their disappointments with various heavily advertised toys. Talk about stereotypes, addressing what they are, and how they can affect attitudes. Help children differentiate between fantasy and reality, and discuss misconceptions that might be promoted in the media (e.g., that people can easily do dangerous stunts without being harmed).
- *Options.* Plan for the next electrical power outage or television set breakdown with a packet of interesting games, stories, and activities, so that children see there are alternatives to the popular media.

Additional Resources on Controlling Television to Share with Parents/Families

Smart Television Alliance (www.smarttelevisionalliance.org)

A group of nonprofit organizations committed to controlling the influence of TV on children, this site evaluates and recommends children's programs for different age groups, suggests ways of controlling TV, and provides the latest statistics on problems associated with excessive TV viewing.

(continued)

FIGURE 11.4   Continued

Center for Screen Time Awareness (www.screentime.org)
Advocates a "TV-Turnoff Week" and parental control over children's screen time with computers, television, and games. Provides suggestions for instituting a TV-free week in homes.

Center on Media and Child Health, Children's Hospital Boston (www.cmch.tv/research/searchcitations.asp)
Provides the latest research findings on the effects of the media on children's health.

The Henry J. Kaiser Family Foundation (www.kff.org/entmedia/upload/7638.pdf)
Produces an annual survey on parents, children, and media.

Product Evaluation   Collect three examples of a product: one that clearly is inferior, one that is typical, and one that is outstanding. For instance, you might bring in a broken toy car, one that barely rolls, and one that operates very smoothly. For a more detailed example of product evaluation in a third-grade language arts classroom, see Sinclair's (1996) lesson on holiday season toy advertising. Talk with children about what makes a product good or bad. Ask them to cite examples of experiences with toys that were disappointing.

Information Literacy   Children in the primary grades can learn to use the Internet to research questions with immediate relevance. Jukes, Dosaj, and Macdonald (2000) describe the five A's that can be used to address information needs: (1) *asking* key questions, (2) *accessing* relevant data, (3) *analyzing* the acquired data, (4) *applying* the data to the task, and (5) *assessing* both the result and the process.

Purposes of Advertising   Ask children to bring in toy or food advertisements that captured their attention (Moore & Lutz, 2000). Invite them to reflect on four factors: (1) what they found appealing, attractive, or convincing; (2) what the advertisement actually says or claims; (3) what it suggests or appears to say; and (4) what it leaves out. Try a similar approach for familiar phrases and slogans from commercials. After each child has shared a particular advertisement, discuss differences in people's reactions and why one person reacts negatively to an ad that someone else finds captivating.

Exploding the Stereotype   Vigil and Robinson (1997) conducted a 2-week integrated unit entitled "The Big Bad Wolf and Stereotype and Bias in the Media," which was designed to develop the critical viewing/thinking skills of children in the primary grades. Children were asked to think about how wolves are portrayed in children's literature, using questions like these to guide them in detecting stereotypes:

FIGURE 11.5 Research-Based Recommendations for Using Technology to Promote Language Development and Literacy

- *Consider the environment.* Locate computers in the classroom, rather than in a lab. Set up stations with seating for two or three children, based on research suggesting that young children prefer to work collaboratively with peers at the computer (National Association for the Education of Young Children [NAEYC], 1996b).
- *Consider the learners.* The Internet makes a major contribution when it allows children to participate in new communities, such as the community of writers. Check into a program such as Word Central (Merriam Webster, 2001) that enables children to hear new vocabulary words pronounced and to build their own dictionaries (www.wordcentral.com).
- *Evaluate multicultural aspects.* When children are given a chance to link immediately to the work of other children throughout the world and locate pen pals, the Internet begins to fulfill its promise of broadening horizons. Check out sites such as Web Kids' Village (www.ks-connection.org/village/village.html).
- *Support oral language.* Observational studies of young children suggest that while working at the computer, they initiate interactions frequently, exhibit high levels of spoken communication, and engage in frequent turn-taking and other types of cooperation (NAEYC, 1996b). Teach children to talk quietly at the computer.
- *Begin concretely with live lessons.* Before children work with simulations at the computer, give them experiences with concrete materials and hands-on activities. If, for example, children are making a script for a play, have them work in groups and sketch out their plan; then have them move to the computer and use word processing for ease in making corrections and producing multiple copies. Or, if they first construct puppets out of paper and found materials, later experiments using software to invent puppets will have more meaning for them.
- *Choose quality software.* Prefer software that allows for interaction, rather than emphasizing drill; software should be more than an expensive electronic workbook. Select software that represents some real advantages over the paper format and allows children to use their creativity, such as Inspiration 8, which makes it possible to create all types of flowcharts and mind maps.
- *Integrate technology into the curriculum.* Choose software that extends and complements curriculum content and spans different subject areas (Edwards & Willis, 2000).
- *Promote equity.* Be aware of the "digital divide" that gives greater access to high-income families and that emphasizes computer use for boys over girls. Realize that technology is not a reward for high-achieving or obedient children but a tool for everyone.
- *Exercise caution.* When using the Internet, always preview and monitor the sites visited by children. Look into the school's policies and ways of blocking pornography and other offensive and inappropriate material.

Are the wolves in stories real or pretend?

Have you ever seen a real wolf in a book, on television, in a video, or at a zoo? How do real wolves act and look? Do they try to trick people or attack them?

What do you know about the relationship between wolves and dogs?

Sounds/Images/Verbal Information   All media messages rely on sounds, images, and verbal information to convey a message. In a movie such as *Babe, the Gallant Pig*, the sounds consist of the characteristic sounds made by the various barnyard animals and their voices, instrumental music, and the whistles and commands of the farmer who owns the border collies. An example of a visual image is the litter of puppies bounding out of the barn. Textual information is presented in written form as well as through written symbols. Use large paper on a roll, such as newsprint, to make three posters: one with a clip-art image of an ear, one with an eye, and one with a mouth. Before viewing a high-quality film, let children know that they will be working in groups to draw or write about the sounds, images, and verbal information they experience.

Constructing Literacy Materials   Have children use the computer to make literacy materials for use in play, such as signs for their pretend grocery store, a menu for their restaurant, a poster for their theater, placards for their zoo of stuffed toys, or a picture book. Word processing, clip art, and print-shop software can be used to explore shapes, make pictures, and paint, draw, or otherwise illustrate a wide array of literacy materials.

Multiple Storybook Literacy   Choose a high-quality children's television program based on a picture book such as *Arthur* or *Curious George*. Compare the book with an episode from the program using a Venn diagram. Visit the www.pbskids.org website to review other activities based on the books. Ask children to identify some recurring themes. See The Center for Media Literacy for resources (www.medialit.org).

Instant Video Revisiting   Use a small video camera to record and then narrate everyday school activities. The newer, smaller units enable you to preview a film clip and see it instantly. Video cameras with fold-out screens allow children to watch their activities immediately after they happen and to discuss them with a teacher—what Forman (1999) refers to as *instant video revisiting* (IVR).

Assistive Technology   When children with special needs bring assistive technology into the classroom, the other students are naturally curious, wondering why it is used and how it works. A competent teacher builds on this curiosity and uses it to promote the goals of inclusion. You might, for example, create a scheduled time when each child in the class gets to meet with the child using the assistive technology and have an opportunity to see it demonstrated. For more on assistive technology see Judge, 2006 and Mistrett, 2004, and for ways to assess it, see Parette, Blum, and Boeckmann, 2009.

Virtual Field Trip   Use a virtual field trip on the Internet as the basis for writing a group story. For example, you can take a virtual field trip to Brazil at www.vivabrazil.com.

Intergenerational Project   Seniors are sometimes very interested in accessing the information on the Internet but approach computer use with some trepidation. Young children can be the best coaches because they are nonthreatening and can explain procedures in a straightforward manner. For more on intergenerational projects, see www.kidscare.org.

Conclusion

By age 70, the average American adult will have devoted 7 years of life or more to television viewing (American Academy of Pediatrics, 2001). When these hours are combined with those logged in front of a computer, it should cause us to question whether media-based activities merit the investment of such a significant part of a human being's lifespan. If, for example, every American contributed just 20 percent of the time spent watching television to some form of community service, how might society be transformed?

These are the kinds of questions with which contemporary educators have to wrestle. We need to keep technology in perspective. Technology is a tool, and it can be used to support learning. It can also be a sales pitch, a purveyor of stereotypes, and a passive activity that contributes to obesity (Blass et al., 2006) and reinforces solitary activities that interfere with social relationships and personal growth. Above all, more and better technology is not a panacea for solving complex social problems and magically enabling children to become literate.

Reasonable educators neither unquestioningly accept all of the claims that technology makes nor steadfastly resist technological innovations. Thoughtful teachers take a step back, reflect on the implications for student learning, and critically examine what is offered, always remaining a bit skeptical. In other words, they not only teach critical literacy and media literacy, but also practice it themselves.

It is far easier to place an order for hardware or software and get connected to the Internet than it is to give children personal attention, to be good teachers and parents, and to collaborate for community support of educational aims. Ultimately, our goal as early childhood teachers of the language arts is to teach students not merely to read words but, as Paulo Freire (1970) asserts, to read the *world* and be empowered to change it for the better.

PEARSON
myeducationkit To check your comprehension on the content covered in this chapter, go to the MyEducationKit for your book and complete the Study Plan for Chapter 11. Here you will be able to take a chapter quiz and receive feedback on your answers.

Research-Based Literacy Strategies

Educational Television and Literacy

Over the years, research has consistently found that merely sitting children down in front of a TV is inadequate to improve their literacy skills, particularly for those children who are at high risk of experiencing literacy challenges (Moses, 2009). Why?

Children need to be moderately familiar with print in order to pay attention to it on television and find it interesting and moderately challenging. If print is relatively unfamiliar, children will find it confusing and complicated and therefore disregard it (Linebarger, Kosanic, Greenwood, & Doku, 2004). At the opposite end of the spectrum, children who have extensive experience with print and are already well on their way to becoming fluent readers may not evidence much improvement either. Actually, children who are in the middle—the emerging readers with some print exposure—are the ones most likely to benefit from television programs that reinforce literacy with print (Linebarger et al., 2004). To learn more about the effects of television on children's learning, see Fisch (2004).

Online Publishing of Children's Drawing and Writing

Technology is a natural medium for enabling children to publish their work and share it with a larger, perhaps even international, audience. Going public with children's writing is a way to build students' self-esteem, increase their sense of satisfaction with writing, and motivate them to refine their writing skills (C. B. Smith, 2003; Karchmer, 2001). When posting work online, it is particularly important to keep the child's direct contact information confidential to protect against Internet stalkers and other types of unwanted contact.

The publishing process might begin with desktop publishing—using a word-processing program to format the text, lay it out in a way that is pleasing to the eye, and insert illustrative material. More advanced students can use the spell-check and grammar-check functions of the word-processing program to edit. The online publishing option offers special opportunities for English language learners because they may be capable of publishing and reading in their first language and then translating a text into English.

A reputable site for publishing children's work is Kids' Space (www.kids-space.org). Students can view drawings and writings of children from different cultures and age groups and correspond with these child authors and illustrators through adults. Most of the work is done by children of at least 5 or 6 years of age. Children who are particularly advanced in literacy may find it interesting to interact with similarly advanced students. More information for teachers can be found at Publishing with Students (www.publishingstudents.com).

Internet-Based Communication and E-Pals

E-pals communicate via e-mail. The e-pals may be other children, college students studying to become teachers, adults in personal care homes, or experts on particular topics of study who have agreed to answer children's questions (Shandomo, 2009). Getting a personalized, genuine response to writing (or a scanned drawing) can be a motivator that demonstrates the real power of writing and helps children see why it is worth the effort. E-pals have been used very successfully with young children, both with and without disabilities (Salmon & Akaran, 2005; Stanford & Siders, 2001). One of the most well-known resources for beginning electronic correspondence with other children worldwide is ePALS (www.epals.com). This site supports 132 languages and has hosted 4.6 million students and teachers from 191 countries, with over 104,000 classroom profiles. Teachers can request up to 35 student accounts for free as well as correspond with other teachers at the ePALS Classroom Exchange. English language learners have the option of corresponding in eight different languages. To see an ePALS project in action, go to the home page at www.epals.com and click on the "Video" button. For more information on young children as e-learners, see Donohue, Fox, and Torrence (2007).

 ## Links with Literature

Literacy Websites

Why Use Literacy Websites?

Literacy websites provide materials that any family can access, either on a home computer or at the public library. Major categories include (1) children's stories and related activities or games, (2) literacy resources for families, (3) websites that complement educational programs for children, and (4) literacy websites for teachers.

Early Literacy Websites for Teachers, Parents, and Children

For Children

Aesop's Fables
   www.aesopfables.com

American Folklore
   www.americanfolklore.net

Candlelight Stories
http://candlelightstories.com

Children's Storybooks Online
www.magickeys.com/books

Circle of Stories
www.pbs.org/circleofstories

Funschool
http://funschool.com

Great Web Sites for Kids
www.ala.org/greatsites

StoryDog
www.storydog.com

Webbing into Literacy
http://curry.edschool.virginia.edu/go/wil/home.html

World Wide School
www.worldwideschool.org

Parent/Family and Teacher Resources

The Center for Early Literacy
www.ume.maine.edu/~cel

Citations on Early Literacy
www.indiana.edu/~eric_rec/ieo/bibs/earlylit.html

Colorín Colorado
www.colorincolorado.org/homepage.php

Early Language and Literacy
www.parentbookstore.com/earlylit.htm

Early Literacy Activities in the Home
http://nces.ed.gov/pubs/ce

Early Literacy—Beginning Reading
www.sccoe.k12.ca.us/earlylit.htm

Education Place—Houghton Mifflin features a "Kids Clubhouse," a "Teacher's Center," and a "Parent's Place"
www.eduplace.com

Helping Children to Read
www.studyweb.com/grammar/read/childread.htm

Lee y Serás (Read and You Will Be)
http://leeyseras.net/site/main.html

Literacy Connections
www.literacyconnections.com

Literacy Resources on Line
www.mcrel.org/resources/literacy/litonline.html

Project Read Literacy Network
www.golden.net/~projread/Tips.html

ELLs
Environmental Print

Environmental print refers to all of the print material—letters, numbers, logos, universal symbols—that exists in the natural settings that young children experience. It includes labels of all types (e.g., food packaging, toys, logos), various kinds of signs (e.g., billboards, for restaurants, in stores and other buildings, directional signs on roadways). Activities that focus on environmental print offer particular advantages for young ELLs.

1. The children have prior experience with the materials (Aldridge, Kirkland, & Kuby, 2002). For example, children can create a collage of the labels from their favorite breakfast foods.

2. The materials are free or inexpensive. For example, children can do a letter search through print

materials to find all of the different type styles—lower- and uppercase, fonts, colors—in which a particular letter appears. Then, using the special effects capabilities of a word-processing program, children can, for example, choose the letter that begins their names and experiment with many different styles and colors.

3. The materials are readily accessible. Children sitting in class no doubt have many different types of print on their possessions—labels on their clothes, sizes on their shoes, logos on a t-shirt, and so forth. Teachers can discuss the purposes of these forms of environmental print with the students to build the idea that print conveys meaning, such as laundering instructions for clothing or helping to locate the correct size of shoe at the store.

4. Environmental print changes with the context. A walk through the school building will introduce children to many types of signs—in the cafeteria, at the library, in the main office—and images that convey meaning, such as the restroom signs, no smoking signs, and so forth. Some ELLs shop in stores that include labels in their first language or in two languages—yet another opportunity to learn if teachers take the time to coach parents about how to make the most of such opportunities.

For more on environmental print see Xu and Rutledge, 2003. A sample lesson on environmental print is posted at www.readwritethink.org/lessons/lessom_view.asp?id=3.

How Do I ...
Integrate Technology to Support Diverse Learners?

For All Students

• The programs that most teachers have on their computers at home and at school—such as Microsoft PowerPoint (Parette, Hourcade, Boeckmann, & Blum, 2008) or other widely available programs such as Symbols 2000 (Parette, Boeckmann, & Hourcade, 2008) and Clicker 5 (Parette, Hourcade, Dinelli, & Boeckmann, 2009) can be used to develop instructional materials for young children.

• Make a listening center using a cassette player, commercially prepared audiotapes, an audio splitter, and headphones.

• Use a scanner and desktop publishing software to produce a class newspaper that includes children's drawings and writings (Sahn & Reichel, 2008).

• If your school has an overhead projector, electronic whiteboard, or Elmo projector, this technology can be integrated through the schoolday to share children's work, engage students in literacy lessons, and foster critical thinking (Solvie, 2007).

• Identify award-winning computer software and evaluate it using the Software Evaluation Instrument posted at www.childrenssoftware.com/rating.html#inst.

• Create a virtual reality environment for children to explore (see Patera, Draper, & Naef, 2008, on a use of Magic Cottage).

• Use computer software to support young children's reading and composing, such as My First Incredible, Amazing Dictionary; Destination: Neighborhood; Discis Book; Hyperstudio; Kidspiration; Intellitalk; and Kid Pix Studio.

• Create your own recorded library by encouraging parent/family members to read a book aloud or teach a simple children's game from their culture and record it on audio or video.

• Evaluate a website for children using Kathy Schrock's criteria posted at http://school.discoveryeducation.com/schrockguide/eval.html.

• Make your own audio using Microsoft Movie Maker, Audacity, or Apple iMovie; these can be burned on CDs, copied to MP3 players, or even uploaded to a website as a podcast so that anyone with a computer and Internet connection can access them.

• Some Internet sites that are free sources for audio books include Aesop's Fables, Online Collection, All Free Online Children's Books, and Kids' Corner at Wired for Books.

• Use collections of photographs, such as those found at Microsoft Office Online or www.babyanimalz.com, as a resource in making class books. Be sure to check the content of the site before using it with children.

For Children Who Are Deaf or Hard of Hearing

• Use prerecorded videos that include an American Sign Language (ASL) interpretation of picture books or songs, such as the YouTube video of children signing the words to the song "Change a Heart, Change the World" (www.youtube.com/watch?v=TPTMv0bBe4o).

• Locate someone in the community that has an IBM system called SiSi (Say It Sign It) that automatically converts the spoken word into sign language, which is then signed by an animated digital character or avatar. Share this with the children.

• Make a video that teaches some basic signs from American Sign Language. Ask college students from the sign language group to sign a children's story or song. Use a digital video camera to create your own "sign-along" recordings of picture books, poems, songs, presentations by guest speakers, or documentaries of field trips.

• Use computer clip art to introduce the concept being signed and signing flashcards to show how to form each sign; then have a child who knows ASL demonstrate.

English Language Learners

• Make a video about the schedule and the curriculum on tape or DVD in the child's first language.

• Use wordless books to prompt original storytelling that is recorded in various languages, which can then be sent home with an accompanying typed text for the child to share (Jalongo, Dragich, Conrad, & Zhang, 2002).

• Invite parents to tell a children's story from their culture in their home language. Record it and add illustrations using clip art with software such as Dreamweaver Deluxe.

• Use audiobooks so that children can follow along in the printed texts, thereby building fluency and expanding vocabulary.

• Work with high school or college students to make recordings of books read aloud in two different languages so that dual-language learners can hear the story both in L1 and L2.

Children with Attentional Problems

• Make an audio recording of a big book that includes an audible signal for when to turn the page, such as a bell. Put the child in charge of turning the pages, using a pointer, and of leading the discussion before and after the book.

• For children with attention deficits, recorded books typically include other audible "extras" that promote active listening such as music, sound effects, or interviews with authors (Mediatore, 2003).

• Use a digital camera to obtain sequential photographs of a significant event that the child experienced at school. Have the child dictate a story to accompany the photographs that is recorded and placed at the listening center for all to enjoy and the child to revisit.

• Play music softly in the background; this may calm and focus children with special needs, thereby enhancing learning (Črnčec, Wilson, & Prior, 2006).

Children Who Are Visually Impaired or Blind

• Make your own audio recordings of picture books in which you read the story expressively, being sure to narrate the pictures as well.

• Create original books in Braille using a portable embosser. Pages can be assembled into a three-ring binder.

• Use commercially produced audiobooks so that children can experience literature by listening (Holum & Gahala, 2001).

• Share several books with textures to feel, such as DK Publishing's board books. Children who have a visual impairment can work with a partner to create texture books that can be donated to a local child-care center for infants and toddlers to use.

• Explore interventions that use technology to support the literacy growth of young children who are visually impaired or blind (Erickson & Hatton, 2007; Erickson, Hatton, Roy, Fox, & Renne, 2007).

Children New to the Class

• Use desktop publishing software to create a one-page newsletter each week. Maintain them in plastic page protectors in a binder or online. To see how teachers build a class website using templates, visit www.teacherweb.com.

• Create a video tour of the class and an overview of class routines narrated in English, American Sign Language, and other languages spoken by children in the classroom. The video with accompanying narration can be burned onto a CD so that children can share it with parents/families.

• Make a video of each child in the class saying his or her name and holding up a card with his or her first name printed on it. Loan it to the child or give the child an opportunity to view it at school if there is no video equipment in the home.

• Make a class big book using digital photos that documents an important event; use these books to orient newcomers to the class about what has gone on before.

Children Leaving the Class
• Send the child off to the new school with a memory book that recounts his or her accomplishments so that he or she can share it on the first day.

• Create a class book to which every child contributes a page and tells why he or she will miss the classmate.
• Contact the child's new teacher and class and correspond via e-mail.

Source: Adapted from Skouge, Rao, & Boisvert, 2007.

PEARSON myeducationkit™ Now go to Chapter 11 in the MyEducationKit (www.MyEducationKit.com) for your book, where you can:

■ Find Chapter Objectives.

■ Complete Assignments and Activities that can help you more deeply understand the chapter content.

■ Extend knowledge with content-specific Web Links.

■ Check your comprehension on the content covered in the chapter by going to the Study Plan. Here you will be able to take a chapter quiz, receive feedback on your answers, and then access resources that will enhance your understanding of chapter content.

chapter twelve

Designing and Managing a Language Arts Program

Annie Pickert/Pearson Education

FACT FILE on Language Arts Programs

• Two out of three mothers of preschool-age children and three out of four mothers of school-age children are in the labor force (Children's Defense Fund, 2008).

• Nationally, 33 percent of children live in a family where no parent has full-time, year-round employment. Fifty percent of African American families, 51 percent of Native American and Native Alaskan families, and 38 percent of Hispanic American families do not have a parent who is employed full time all year (Annie E. Casey Foundation, 2005).

• High-quality early childhood programs are effective in reducing the number of un-educated, illiterate adults who are overrepresented in the prison population. It costs, on average, 2.8 times as much to keep a prisoner in jail as it does to educate a child in public school (Children's Defense Fund, 2008).

• Head Start is the national federally funded early childhood program for families with low incomes. Only about one-half to two-thirds of the children eligible for Head Start are enrolled (Children's Defense Fund, 2008).

• Research has indicated that when teachers plan activities around students' interests, the children stay engaged in tasks longer and are more intrinsically motivated to learn (Vartuli & Rohs, 2008). There is a strong link between a play-based environment and the development of literacy skills in young children (Saracho & Spodek, 2006).

• Classroom conversations can be limited to teacher directives and one-word responses from children and can fail to compensate for limited opportunities to engage in extended conversation in the home (Barbarin et al., 2006; Gest, Holland-Coviello, Welsh, Eicher-Catt, & Gill, 2006; LaParo & Pianta, 2000; McClelland, Acock, & Morrison, 2006; Wasik, Bond, Hindman, & Jusczyk, 2007).

• Social and emotional relationships in the classroom environment play an important role in children's academic success (Shonkoff & Phillips, 2000). Research has shown that teachers who cultivate positive relationships with and among students expose them to greater literacy learning opportunities (Ostrosky, Gaffney, & Thomas, 2006).

• In a multisite study that observed 141 kindergarten teachers instructing English lan-guage learners during several reading classes, teacher quality variables were related posi-tively to student engagement and negatively to time spent in noninstructional activities (Cirino, Pollard-Durdola, Foorman, Carlson, & Francis, 2007).

• Research findings suggest that when selecting a phonics program, six factors should be considered: (1) time and scheduling, (2) classroom management, (3) student diversity and adaptations, (4) materials provided, including supplementary and home enrichment materials, (5) specific feedback techniques, and (6) practice and review activities (Santi, Menchetti, & Edwards, 2004, p. 196).

• Title I is a multibillion dollar federal education program for elementary and second-ary schools, instituted by the Elementary and Secondary Education Act of 1965 and now encompassed by the No Child Left Behind Act of 2001. Funds under Title I are targeted to high-poverty schools and districts and used to provide educational services to students who are at risk of failing to meet state educational standards (Phelps Deily, 2009).

• In a study by Barton and Coley (2007), one in five students misses three or more days of school a month. Asian American students have the fewest absences. The United States ranked 25th of 45 countries in school attendance.

Did any of this information surprise you? If so, what? Why? How will you use this knowledge to educate and care for the very young?

What Is a Balanced Curriculum?

PEARSON
myeducationkit

Go to the Assignments and Activities section of Chapter 12 in MyEducationKit and complete the activity entitled "A Hands-On Approach to Curriculum."

Schools are expected to provide solutions to many of society's most pervasive problems. When children's literacy learning is at stake, the pressure on schools and programs to supply the answers is particularly intense. Parents and families are convinced, and rightly so, that early literacy experiences set the tone for later experiences. Even the casual observer can watch a young child grow up and see that early childhood is the time of life when language develops rapidly, moving within a few years' time from smiles and gurgles to the conversational ability of the typical first-grader. On these two points— that early experiences in literacy are significant and that early childhood is a critical window of opportunity for language development—families, communities, educators, and other professionals can agree (Copple & Bredekamp, 2009; Gonzalez-Mena & Eyer, 2008; Kostelnik, Soderman, & Whiren, 2007; National Early Childhood Accountability Task Force, 2008).

We all understand that early literacy is important, and we even know why. The perplexing and perennial question that remains is how to go about it. How do we support literacy growth in ways that meet the needs of every young child? As an initial step, teachers need to understand the general characteristics of classrooms that support literacy. An effective literacy program for young children is *language-rich*, which means that the students are immersed in planned opportunities to become more effective listeners, speakers, readers, and writers every day (see Pence, Justice, & Wiggins, 2008). The characteristics of such classrooms are presented in Figure 12.1.

The *curriculum* is the overall plan for promoting children's learning. Based on a Latin term meaning "path" or "road," it includes all of the experiences and activities in an educational program. In order to understand the curriculum fully, it is also necessary to consider the *written curriculum* (documents and standards), the *taught curriculum* (the teacher's interpretation and methodology), and the *tested curriculum* (the instruments used to evaluate children's progress or overall program effectiveness) (Poston, English, Steffy, & Downey, 2008).

Some experts have argued that there is also a so-called *hidden curriculum*, which comprises all of the lessons that children learn about school itself as an organization and as a mirror of society's values. Suppose, for example, that an

PEARSON
myeducationkit

Go to the Assignments and Activities section of Chapter 12 in MyEducationKit and complete the activity entitled "Supporting Literacy and Reggio Emilia."

early childhood teacher is presenting a lesson on letter sounds and decides to focus on the letter *j*. She begins the lesson by saying to her first-graders, "Who can think of some words with the sound of *j*, like the word *jump?*" A child named Paige responds that her name has a "juh" sound but it doesn't have a *j*. The teacher was not expecting that answer and simply moves on, saying, "We are studying the letter *j* now."

It could be argued that the lesson Paige learned from this interaction has very little to do with the curriculum standards or the subject matter. Instead, the child may have learned that being a good student means guessing what is on the teacher's mind or that conformity is the goal of education. Over time, the child might feel disregarded

---

FIGURE 12.1   Classrooms That Support Literacy

Underlying Assumptions

- For almost all children in a literate society, learning to read and write begins very early in life.
- Literacy develops in real-life settings so that the functions of literacy are an integral part of learning.
- All of the language arts develop concurrently.
- Children learn through active engagement, constructing their understanding of how written language works.
- Literacy events—times when children and parents/families interact around print—are fundamental to language learning (Teale & Sulzby, 2003).

General Characteristics

- An abundance of high-quality literacy materials, rather than just a basal series or textbook
- A classroom design that facilitates reading and writing rather than encouraging low-level tasks such as coloring, cutting, and pasting objects; filling in a blank; or drawing a line to or circling the right answer; and so forth
- A variety of grouping strategies, instead of fixed-ability groups, such as top, middle, and low reading groups
- Daily literacy routines, including read-alouds, independent reading and writing, and sharing, rather than a lesson that introduces new vocabulary, briefly discusses a story, and then assigns seatwork
- Varied instructional techniques to meet individual needs, rather than a structured presentation followed by doing workbook pages
- A curriculum that integrates the language arts, rather than isolating them into time slots (e.g., 60 minutes for reading, 30 minutes for language arts or phonics, 20 minutes for handwriting)
- A curriculum that integrates the disciplines through the use of children's literature, rather than designating a discrete time block for mathematics, science, social studies, and so on
- A culturally responsive curriculum, rather than a program that focuses on white, middle-class experiences; Christian holidays; and heavily advertised films, television programs, and books
- Assessment that is used to guide instruction, rather than as a way to sort or label children or compare their achievement to that of peers

---

Source: Adapted from McGee & Richgels, 2007.

and learn to dislike school. Thus, children not only learn content but also rules, both explicit and implicit, about what school is and what it means to become an educated adult. When the concept of curriculum is broadened in this way, it becomes virtually everything that occurs in school. Curriculum, then, is the pathway of education.

FIGURE 12.2 Six C's of Literacy Motivation

- *Choice.* Let the children select high-interest materials.
- *Challenge.* Match materials to the child's reading level, depending on whether she or he is reading independently or with support.
- *Control.* Let the children control the book, such as deciding when to turn the page, when to linger over an illustration, and when to stop and talk.
- *Collaboration.* Approach reading with a "conspiratorial" attitude of "We're in this together; we're going to beat this tough task."
- *Constructive comprehension.* Urge readers to keep making sense out of what they read; pay attention to places where readers might get confused.
- *Consequences.* Demonstrate the positive outcomes of reading, such as having something interesting to talk about, getting useful information, finding answers to questions, and the like.

Sources: Jalongo, 2007; Turner, 1997.

An early literacy program that is committed to developing every child's potential is well balanced, meaning that it focuses "simultaneously on the functions, forms, and conventions of print, with lessons addressing phonemic awareness, knowledge of letters, sound symbol relations, context and syntax clues, syllables, and punctuation" (Morrow, 2001, p. 264). Part of building that interest is fully engaging students. As Brian Cambourne (2001) explains, learners are more likely to become fully engaged under these conditions:

- They believe they are capable of learning or doing whatever is being demonstrated.
- They believe that learning has some potential value, purpose, and use for them.
- They are free from anxiety.
- They are being taught by someone they like, respect, admire, trust, and would like to emulate.

Figure 12.2 identifies six basic principles of motivating students to become literate.

Collaboration with Families and Professionals

Standards in Education
Review the National Council of Teachers of English (NCTE) and International Reading Association *Standards for the English Language Arts* at www.ncte.org/standards.

It is late summer, and Inez has just been hired to teach first grade beginning the last week of August after graduating with honors last May. Instead of feeling relief that she has secured a job, her mind is swirling. She wonders about the questions that were raised at her interview, such as how she plans to reconcile the need to meet the state curriculum standards with her responsibility to meet the individual needs of all children in the

PEARSON
myeducationkit™

Go to the Assignments and Activities
section of Chapter 12 in MyEducationKit
and complete the activity entitled "How
Families Can Nurture the Classroom
Environment."

class. A quick look at the school calendar reveals that parents will be visiting during National Education Week and that there is an open house with parent/teacher conferences next month.

Although Inez's first response is a sense of panic about all that needs to be accomplished, she decides to meet the challenge in a step-by-step fashion. She decides to (1) reflect more deeply on her philosophy of teaching, (2) interact with colleagues she respects, (3) locate resources on working with parents and families, and (4) learn more about the No Child Left Behind Act and its implications for assessment. Inez has to do what is expected by her supervisors yet remain true to her ideals.

At the same time, Inez is busy setting up her classroom. She wants to organize her room around centers, begin building her classroom library, and create a book corner. During her student teaching experience, Inez worked with a teacher who encouraged children to create their own books, and she wants to include this activity in her classroom as well (see Figure 12.3). Inez thinks that it is important to give children choices, so she creates a check-in/check-out procedure at each center by providing a pocket to collect nametags. She also establishes a rule of "No more than five children at a center at one time." In addition, she seeks the advice of a new colleague who has devised a workable system for scheduling individual weekly writing conferences with children. At their grade-level meetings, the teachers discuss aligning the curriculum with academic standards of their state. One of the teachers serves on the state-level early childhood committee and she reports back on what other districts are doing to meet the standards and comply with federal legislation.

About all of this, Inez says, "School hasn't even started yet, and I am working very hard! It will be a busy first year, but I plan to make it a good one."

Contributions and Consequences

- *Contributions of the teacher:* What roles did the teacher play in planning this curriculum?
- *Contributions of the families:* How might talking with parents and families have helped?
- *Contributions of other professionals:* How did the use of professional resources contribute to this teacher's understanding of the curriculum?
- *Consequences of collaboration:* How might this story have ended differently if the teacher had failed to use human and material resources?

According to the Early Childhood and Literacy Development Committee (1985), a high-quality literacy program has the following characteristics:

- Recognizes the central role that parents and families play in early language development
- Enables children to build on their existing knowledge of written and oral language

- Builds positive attitudes in children toward their own emerging literacy abilities
- Promotes meaningful verbal interaction, not only from teacher to child but also from child to teacher and child to child
- Supports the child when confronted by linguistic challenges
- Involves children in meaningful listening, speaking, reading, and writing experiences appropriate to their abilities
- Encourages the child to use language at the most sophisticated level possible
- Uses predictable types of language to build the child's confidence as a learner of language
- Supports the child and family in attaining higher levels of literacy

FIGURE 12.3 Book Making Center

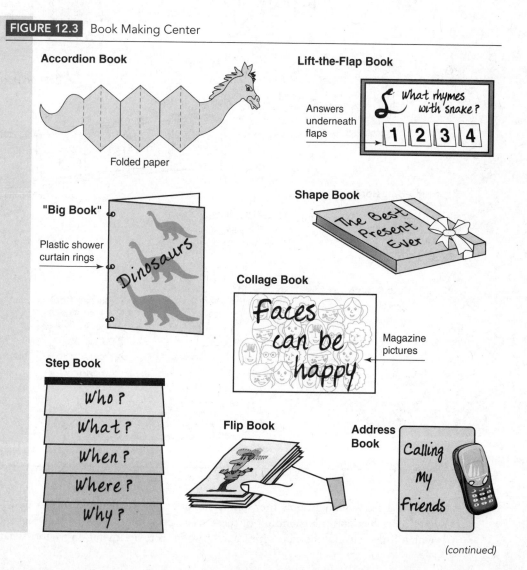

Accordion Book

Folded paper

Lift-the-Flap Book

Answers underneath flaps

What rhymes with snake?

1 2 3 4

"Big Book"

Plastic shower curtain rings

Dinosaurs

Shape Book

The Best Present Ever

Collage Book

Faces can be happy

Magazine pictures

Step Book

Who?
What?
When?
Where?
Why?

Flip Book

Address Book

Calling My Friends

(continued)

FIGURE 12.3 Continued

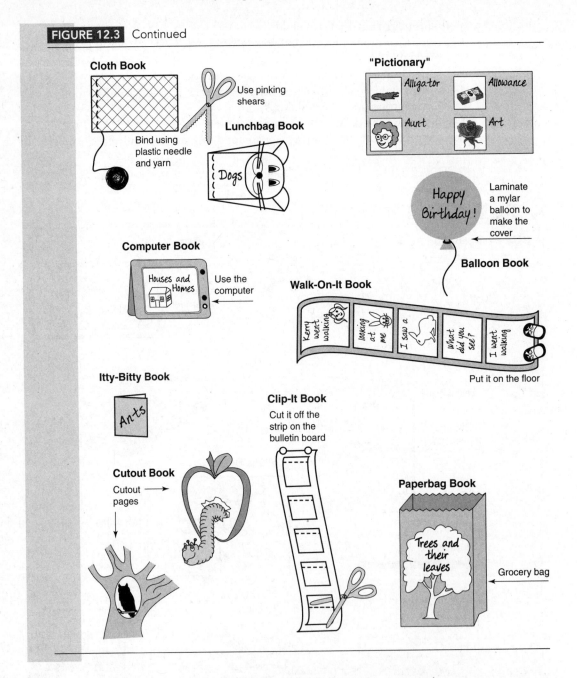

Consider for a moment how Inez's efforts to adjust to the demands of her new teaching job reflect an understanding of these basic principles. Now look at Figure 12.4, which lists early childhood practitioners' responses to an invitation to note what they

Hope to See

flexible schedules • energetic, enthusiastic teacher • toys • blocks • learning centers • a reading center • teachers reading to children—individually, in small groups, in large groups • comfy spots for reading • an assortment of children's literature • "big books" • puppets • flannelboard • print-rich environment • music and art activities • child-authored and -illustrated books • cross-age tutoring • sharing time • many writing opportunities • reading buddies • community involvement (parent volunteers, foster grandparents, guest readers) • sustained silent reading • song, poem, story, and experience charts • an assortment of writing materials • book backpacks • an overhead projector that children can use • all children's work displayed (not just the "good" papers!) • creative play areas • labels and signs • magnetic board and letters/numbers/shapes • CD-ROM and developmentally appropriate software • tape-recorded books • "word walls" of the words children know • print and pictures at children's eye level • children's books throughout the room • an Author's Chair and writing center • children's responses to literature • children collaborating with peers • teachers who act as facilitators of children's learning • teachers who model a passion for language learning • evidence that teachers are sensitive to socioeconomic differences • evidence of parent communication (e.g., bulletin board, lists of recommended books, newsletters, "good news" messages) • time for children to think, read, and write • themes and projects • teachers really listening • children listening to one another • children's work carefully arranged in attractive portfolios • book boxes of recommended trade books for individual children

Hope Not to See

rigid schedules • teachers who have lost their enthusiasm • gender stereotyping (e.g., boys/girls as constant categories) • enforced silence all day • teacher-directed activities dominating throughout day • desks in rows • children being pressured • children showing signs of frustration • teachers who are impatient and pushing children to hurry • piles of worksheets • long lists of "Don'ts" posted as rules • classroom books on shelves only • bulletin boards that are purely decorative (e.g., store-bought holiday decorations everywhere) • computers and software used for drill only • basal readers and textbooks as the only reading material • children's literature turned into a dreary exercise • the teacher sitting in front at the desk • rooms so neat that nothing exciting could be happening • overuse of television, videocassettes, or filmstrips • teachers who insist on absolute correctness • children copying from the board • workbooks for every subject • "star charts" that show who the "good" children are • inflexible ability grouping • teachers rushing through to cover material • rapid-fire questions and answers • tons of patterns to copy and instructions to follow • children's work being disrespected (e.g., thrown in piles or desks) • tests, tests, and more tests • an emphasis on competition • a "closed door" policy classroom • teachers failing to put children first • the names of children who misbehave listed on the board • notes reporting on children's misbehavior going home with children • children's papers evaluated with frowny faces and other negative messages • adults yelling at children • children coloring "in the lines" instead of creating their own drawings • insignificant or tired topics of study (e.g., apples, teddy bears, community helpers) • a stand-in-front-of-the-room type of teaching • a print-deficient environment • absence of opportunities for play

Source: This list was created by graduate students in the early childhood program at Northern Michigan University in Marquette, Michigan, during the summers of 1997 and 1998.

would "hope to see" and "hope not to see" in an early childhood classroom (Carter & Curtis, 1994).

Overview of How Early Childhood Educators Shape the Curriculum

Brain and Language
Neuroscience suggests that these characteristics enhance learning: (1) an attentional mind-set; (2) low to moderate stress; (3) coherent, meaningful tasks; (4) massed practice; (5) learner-controlled feedback; (6) repetition of tasks; (7) overnight rest between learning sessions (Jensen, 2006). How can you apply this in the classroom?

Go to the Assignments and Activities section of Chapter 12 in MyEducationKit and complete the activity entitled "Scaffolding Learning."

How do educators put their ideals into practice? Usually, the process involves five steps: (1) reflecting on your philosophy, (2) arranging the physical environment, (3) grouping for instruction, (4) managing student behavior, and (5) determining the learning experiences that you will provide. Each step will be discussed in the sections that follow.

Reflecting on a Philosophy

The type of language arts curriculum you provide depends, to a considerable extent, on what you believe and value (Villareale, 2009). Too often, teachers fail to take a stand and claim that they are being eclectic—just picking and choosing from whatever comes along in the way of a philosophy, curriculum, or instructional strategy. The problem with this noncommittal approach is that it offers little guidance or direction in a complex and challenging field. Before long, teachers without a philosophy deteriorate into doing things out of habit or expedience, rather than commitment to their ideals. They become less, rather than more, proficient after additional years of experience. Thus, it is far better to be mindful of your goals, values, and beliefs where literacy is concerned. Effective language arts teachers believe that they can exert a positive influence on children's lives despite the complex challenges they confront (Bandura, 1997). Over and over again, research has indicated that the best teachers believe *all* children can learn (Ayers, 2001). They do not blame the school, the family, or the child when learning is difficult. Instead, they do everything in their power to help young language learners reach their full potential.

Arranging the Physical Environment

How a teacher arranges the room, uses equipment, and selects materials all exert an influence on the language arts program (Morrow, 2008). The environment that children experience on a daily basis speaks volumes about the teacher's philosophy, planning, and pedagogical skill. For example, unlike the traditional classroom for older children, which positioned the teacher's desk in the front of the room and students' chairs in neat rows, most early childhood classrooms and programs (other than those for babies) are organized by learning centers. Figure 12.5 shows a sample floorplan for a preschool classroom.

FIGURE 12.5 Sample Floorplan for a Preschool Classroom

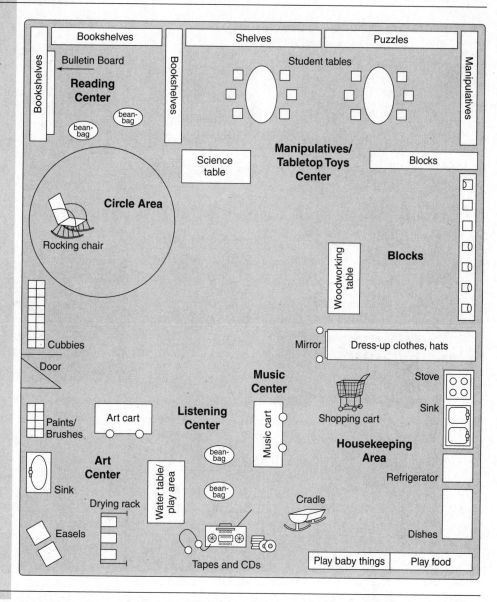

Equipment refers to the larger, more expensive, and relatively permanent items that teachers are likely to use in their teaching. Figure 12.6 (on p. 286) provides some examples of equipment that supports the early childhood language arts.

FIGURE 12.6   Equipment for a Language Arts Classroom

Three-Sided Rolling Book Display

Pocket Chart

Today is my birthday.

Folding Screen

Jumbo Foam Letters

Magnetic Alphabet Board

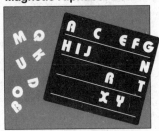

Audiocassette and CD Player

Ee Ff

Cc Dd

Aa Bb

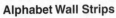

Alphabet Wall Strips

Storytelling Apron

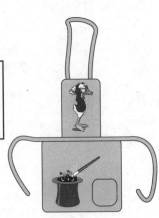

Teacher's Easel

Materials include the things that children use and play with, the consumable items that have to be replaced regularly, such as crayons, markers, and paints. Figure 12.7 includes some examples of materials that are commonly found in language arts programs.

FIGURE 12.7 Literacy Materials for Children

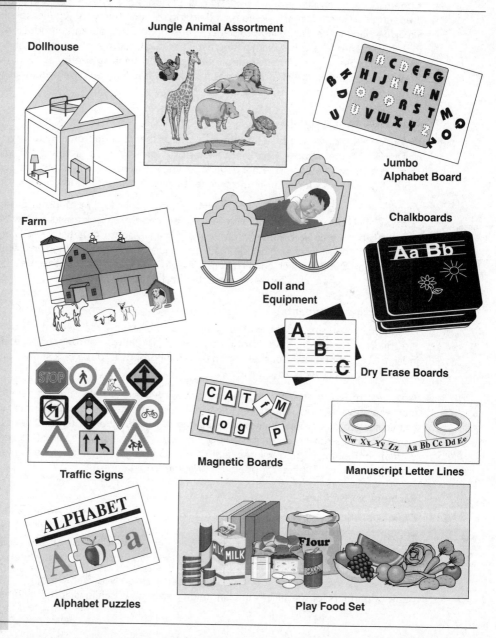

FIGURE 12.8 Grouping for Instruction

Whole-Class Experiences

Definition. The entire class comes together to interact with the teacher and peers. The purpose is to build a sense of community by creating whole-class cohesiveness and, at times, to arrive at consensus.

Activities. community building • morning meetings • read-alouds at story time • singing • poems, chants, and fingerplays • creating class books or stories • planning (e.g., preparing to work in centers, going on a field trip, getting ready for a guest speaker) • making decisions • discussing problems • presenting concepts and introducing topics or themes for study • culminating activities (e.g., authors' teas, presentations for parents, puppet play) • demonstrating reading/writing/thinking strategies • shared book experiences • end-of-the-day gatherings to review what children have accomplished, bringing focus and providing closure

Teacher-Led Small Groups

Definition. The class is divided into flexible groups that change from day to day, depending on the purpose. This is not fixed-ability grouping but grouping that gives all children a chance to work together at various times. The purpose is to provide somewhat more structure and support from the teacher than with student groups.

Activities. groups based on shared interests or work habits (e.g., a dinosaur group, a poetry writing club) • groups with complementary strengths (e.g., artists and writers creating a picture book together) • grouping for minilessons on particular skills or tasks • groups that need teacher-guided practice • groups for sharing reading and writing (e.g., reading clubs in which each child reads from a different text or presents a booktalk, Author's Chair where children read to teacher and peers for feedback)

Small Groups of Students

Definition. These small, flexible groups are monitored by the teacher but led by the children. The purpose is to promote active collaboration, interdependence, and individual accountability. Teachers often use small groups to get a task started and then switch to individual work.

Activities. groups for supported practice that allow peers to help one another • groups that take on various responsibilities (e.g., in a study of pets, one group contacts the animal shelter, one group invites a veterinarian to speak, other groups create pet care instruction books based on their reading) • groups for listening/speaking (e.g., creative drama), for reading (e.g., reading a familiar big book together), and for writing (e.g., reading a Readers' Theater script aloud for audience response)

Partners or "Buddies"

Definition. A child is paired with another child or adult. That partner could be an agemate, a more experienced child in a multigrade classroom, a "big kid" from the upper grades, or an adult volunteer (college student, parent, senior, or other community member). The purpose is to support growth in language through two-way interaction.

Activities. partners to listen to a child read • partners for "you read a page, I'll read a page" • partners for tutoring in the language arts (e.g., if a child is absent and needs to

FIGURE 12.8 Continued

catch up) • partners to build and maintain friendships • bilingual partners (e.g., Spanish-speaking children who help classmates learn a Spanish nursery rhyme)

Individual Experiences

Definition. A child receives individual instruction from the teacher or works independently. The purpose is to focus on language development, one child at a time.

Activities. spontaneous instruction (e.g., teacher circulates around the room, then stops to give a child help) • conferences with children about their work • independent practice (e.g., looking at books, working with writing and drawing materials) • interviews with the child about interests • observations of the child at work • responses to literature • assessment of each child's understanding of a concept (e.g., spelling words)

Source: Gregory & Chapman, 2007.

Grouping for Instruction

Teachers must pay attention to children's ways of knowing, interacting, and working. One part of this is the decisions they make about whether to work with the whole group, small groups, or individual children, as explained in Figure 12.8.

Managing Behavior

Teachers also make decisions about what is acceptable and unacceptable behavior in the classroom. For example, teachers of young children take delight in the fact that the very young are frequently playful, spontaneous, unpredictable, and imaginative as they work to master whatever they are learning. When a preschool teacher held up a picture of some Concord grapes and asked, "What color is this?" a child responded with "graple." Rather than dismiss the child's response, this teacher considered how the child had arrived at his answer. Beginning with knowledge of the color purple and also knowing something about grapes, he put that thinking together to create a new word. So instead of correcting him, the teacher responded with "*Grapes* and the color *purple* do go together." If that teacher had interpreted the curriculum as simply a body of facts to be covered, she might have been annoyed by this young child's surprising answer and could have treated his sincere effort to make sense of language as a distraction, problem, or even deliberate misbehavior. Figure 12.9 offers some general suggestions for managing the early childhood language arts classroom.

Designing Learning Experiences

Planning appropriate language arts activities for young children must begin with understanding children's literacy growth and development. Effective teachers assess

FIGURE 12.9   Guidelines for Classroom Management

   1. *Plan ahead.* In order for children to have a clear idea of what they are to do, the teacher must first have a clear idea. This means troubleshooting to anticipate what will likely be unfamiliar or difficult for the students.

   2. *Communicate clear expectations to children.* When teaching young children, very few assumptions can be made about their prior understanding of classroom procedures. Consider the teacher who announces, "Let's get ready to hear a story." What does this mean to a child inexperienced in the ways of school? Be specific by asking children to stop and listen, to put things away, to go to the carpeted area of the room, and so forth.

   3. *Use modeling and rehearsal.* If you were traveling to an unfamiliar place with a complicated set of directions, which would you prefer: a map or a copilot in your car? Most of us would prefer to have someone show us the way. The same holds true for children who are learning proper classroom procedures. If we want to have individual conferences with young children about their favorite books or their writing, we need to explain the purpose of a conference and rehearse with the children about how to conduct themselves, both during their own conferences and during the conferences of others.

   4. *Practice the necessary procedures, establish routines, and smooth transitions.* Routines are learned through daily practice. Let's suppose that a teacher wants children to return books, records, and toys to the shelf. She can plan the procedures and routines with the children and then rehearse them. Order often breaks down when children are stopping one activity and starting another. However, there are ways to handle these times, called *transitions*, skillfully. Providing a cue, such as singing a work song while putting things away, lighting an electric candle to signal the beginning of a story session, or doing a fingerplay while waiting for the bus to arrive, is an effective way of managing transitions.

   5. *Use encouragement rather than praise.* It is preferable to encourage children (e.g., "I noticed that you worked very hard in your group to write your puppet play") rather than shower them with generalized phrases that say nothing about their effort (e.g., "Very good, everyone").

   6. *Be aware of the total classroom.* Teachers can become so absorbed with the activity at hand that they disregard other classroom activities. One way of avoiding this problem is to be alert and keep moving about the room and monitoring what is going on.

   7. *Gain children's attention before speaking.* If a teacher gets into the habit of "talking over" children's talk or repeating instructions several times, then children will soon learn that there is little to be gained by listening. A classroom mascot/puppet is a good device for capturing children's attention. Using the puppet does not require that the teacher become an amateur ventriloquist. Instead, the mascot "whispers" to the teacher, and the teacher conveys the message to the children. The puppet can be shy and reluctant to come out when the children are noisy. This device for getting children's attention is far more effective than admonishing them to be quiet or turning off the lights for a moment.

   8. *Use voice, movement, and pacing to get and maintain attention.* An expert teacher who senses that attention is waning will change something to regain children's interest, such as in his or her vocal pattern. If a person speaks softly while telling a good story, then listeners will strain to hear every word. Another strategy is to use movement. The teacher can become more animated or invite the children to move. A third way of attracting and maintaining attention is pacing. Teachers can quicken the pace if things

FIGURE 12.9 Continued

are bogging down. They can slow the pace of a lesson or even start over if children are failing to understand.

9. *Limit the amount of information given.* When a teacher overwhelms young children with information, it is difficult for them to decide what is important and where to begin. A good example is teaching children to use the tape recorder. If they are told every operating procedure at once, then they may get the steps out of sequence. But if they go through it one step at a time, they will be more likely to be able to operate equipment themselves. A teacher could further limit the information by teaching children how to play a tape at one session and how to record on the machine at a subsequent session.

10. *Give instructions on a one-to-one basis.* Young children's reactions to instructions are sometimes like their reactions to the rules of a game: They know that these things exist but are not very clear on whether or how they apply to them. Children are far less experienced in seeing themselves as members of a group and being addressed in a general way. Young children may easily misinterpret statements like "Some of you need to put your things away," "Does everyone have crayons?" and "I hope you remembered to put your names on your papers." Probably more often than not, the child's reaction is "I wonder if the teacher means me?" In order to make it clear who is being addressed, the teacher should give instructions on a one-to-one basis whenever possible. If a child is reading to a partner, the teacher might say "Christina, you will be reading this big book together with Amahl. Remember to use the pointer to slide under the words as you say them, just like I do. And Amahl, you say 'okay' when you are ready to go on to the next page. Then it will be your turn to read, and Christina gets to listen and tell you when she's finished looking at the page. Do you have any questions?" Notice that these instructions have a personalized coaching tone, rather than sounding like a vague pronouncement from above. In general, this type of instruction is more likely to have the desired effect.

children's prior knowledge, consider children's interest in the topic under study, and draw on their observations of children's learning processes. No matter how clearly specified the content may be in the state curriculum guidelines or the teacher's manual, teachers have to shape the material and consider factors such as the following:

- What are the key concepts and terminology?
- What is a good way to introduce those concepts and terms?
- What types of questions should be formulated?
- What skills need to be developed?
- Which illustrative examples and connections with prior learning might be best for this group?
- What are some interesting activities that will enable children to apply what they are learning?
- How can all of the language arts—listening, speaking, reading, and writing—be integrated into the lesson?
- How do these learning experiences fit with program goals and state curriculum guidelines?

- How are these learning experiences relevant to the backgrounds of these students and respectful of the larger community?

One way to think about the different components of an early childhood curriculum is to consider how children learn to "translate" from one language art to another, such as from talking to writing or from writing to reading. This process, called *transmediation*, provides young children with the practice they need to become proficient users of multiple symbol systems. When you think about it, most of the activities that we plan for students involve the forms of transmediation in Figure 12.10.

One curriculum-planning task that you may underestimate is coming up with the sometimes large number of activities that are necessary to accomplish a seemingly simple goal, such as learning the letters of the alphabet. Teachers of young children need to be particularly resourceful as they revisit concepts that are foundational in the language arts. To illustrate, Figure 12.11 (on pp. 294–296) suggests different types and levels of activities for teaching the alphabet to young children.

Teacher Concerns and Basic Strategies

Infants and Toddlers
The quality of the overall program and the quality of child-care provider interaction both make a significant contribution to toddlers' language scores (NICHD Early Child Care Research Network, 2000; Ridley, McWilliam, & Oates, 2000). Based on what you have learned thus far, what would you expect to see in a program for infants and toddlers that demonstrates positive caregiving and fosters language stimulation?

PEARSON
myeducationkit

Go to the Assignments and Activities section of Chapter 12 in MyEducationKit and complete the activity entitled "Developmentally Appropriate Environments."

Teachers are often advised to make classroom language activities *functional,* or to use language to communicate in purposeful ways. How, exactly, can this be achieved? Two leading experts on language arts have provided an answer. In 1975, M. A. K. Halliday identified seven functions of language, and in 1982, Ken Goodman elaborated on those language functions to show how they could become the basis for a comprehensive language arts program. In the following list, each of these functions is explained and illustrated.

1. *Instrumental, or "I want," language* is used to satisfy needs or desires. Instrumental language activities include signing up for learning centers, checking out library books, playing store, reading advertising, filling out order blanks, and using a picture menu to select food at a pretend restaurant. One third-grade teacher presented this challenge to students: "Design your dream room using old catalogs. Tell or write about what is in your room and why." In response, 8-year-old Brian created a room with wipe-off wallpaper. "So you can change it whenever you feel like it."

2. *Regulatory, or "Do as I tell you," language* is used to control the behavior of others. Language activities with a regulatory function include creating guidelines for the care of class pets and plants, following directions on the use of classroom materials (such as the computer), and playing

FIGURE 12.10 Transmediation in the Literacy Curriculum

Viewing → Talking

From Viewing to Talking Activities. watching a commercially produced film and discussing it • talking about works of art • commenting on the illustrations in picture books • responding to the drawings of other students • planning and discussing the illustrations for a class "big book" • watching a video of a song, poem, or chant and then singing or speaking it • viewing a video of a class performance and then evaluating it

Viewing → Reading

From Viewing to Reading Activities. watching the movie; then reading the book • looking at a wordless book on a subject; then reading a book with text on the same subject • looking at photographs of an event; then reading about it • looking at art prints; then reading a picture book about the artist's life

Talking → Writing

From Talking to Writing Activities. using voice-recognition software to produce text • having an individual child dictate a story to the teacher, aide, volunteer, or peer • producing language experience stories on chartpaper • working with a partner or small group to produce a piece of writing

Writing → Talking

From Writing to Talking Activities. dramatizing children's original stories • having a child meet with the teacher for a writing conference • working with a partner at the word processor to revise written text • inventing a rap, chant, poem, or story and then reading it aloud • writing and then performing a puppet play

Drawing → Writing

From Drawing to Writing Activities. writing captions for pictures • using the storyboard technique to plan a picture book or video • making schematic diagrams • producing drawings with cartoon "bubble" callouts of dialogue

Reading → Talking

From Reading to Talking Activities. discussing stories read aloud in a large group • participating in literature circles in small groups • engaging children in individual reading conferences with the teacher • presenting booktalks • enacting storybook characters and scenes through dramatic play and creative dramatics

Writing → Reading

From Writing to Reading Activities. reading aloud from the Author's Chair • writing original stories; then making audios or videos of them • leading peers in choral reading of original raps, chants, poems, and stories • producing a class newsletter • corresponding by letter or e-mail

Reading → Writing

From Reading to Writing Activities. composing an original version of a patterned book • converting a favorite story into a Readers' Theater script • responding to a letter or e-mail • writing to an author or illustrator of a book that has been read

FIGURE 12.11 Alphabet Activities

Preschool/Kindergarten

Activity Center

Have children collect labels, boxes, and wrappers of items that they can read. Classify the items into categories (people, places, foods), and paste them, in collage fashion, on the six sides of small cartons. Roll the boxes like large dice, and then have children point to and read words that they know.

Blocks

Create word trains. Have teams of children arrange alphabet blocks using picture/word cards (e.g., a picture of a cup and the blocks for *c, u,* and *p*) as cues. Then put the blocks on a large wooden toy and drive it past the children, asking the rest of the group to read the word. Have the team hold up their picture card as a check for understanding.

Language and Literacy Center

Compare/contrast a wide variety of alphabet books. Then construct a school alphabet book that illustrates objects from *A* to *Z* that are found at home or at school. Make an alphabet rap or chant after listening to *Chicka Chicka Boom Boom* (Archambault & Martin, 1991).

Emergent Writing

Use fingerpaints and large paper for each child to write the first letter of his or her name. Also have children use alphabet letter stamps and a stamp pad to print their names.

Primary Grades

Spelling

Play several spelling games, such as Boggle and Scrabble. Also get children involved in making alphabet flashcards and games for younger students using recycled greeting cards and wrapping paper.

Mathematics

Make picture dictionaries. Give children the challenge of figuring out how many folded pages of four sides they will need to construct a book with 27 letters and a front and back cover. What will they put on the remaining pages (dedication, something about the authors, etc.)?

Reading

Have children share *You Read to Me, I'll Read to You: Very Short Stories to Read Together* (Hoberman, 2001), an easy reader written as a script, with a peer, parent volunteer, or tutor. Make a "word wall" of words that are repeated and words that rhyme in the book.

Handwriting

Make name configuration books. Have each child write his or her name in extra large, thick cursive script. Cut out this white paper and mount it on a different-colored background.

FIGURE 12.11 Continued

Preschool/Kindergarten

Science

Go on a walking field trip. Ask children to find interesting natural objects, and then decide what letter each begins or ends with. Dictate several descriptive words about each object.

Social Studies

Have children construct a book of bright, colorful pictures of familiar objects gathered from magazines. Then ask each family to write the word for each pictured item in their native language during open house.

Media Studies

Make a video about an alphabet letter, such as *S*. Begin with a sign that reads "What begins with *S*?" and then have each child share an object or picture that begins with this letter. At the end, have all children say, in unison, "And these are some things that begin with *S!*" Later in the year, do the same for ending letters.

Technology

Have a classroom volunteer make a banner for each child's name. Post one banner per day, and call out each letter in the name. Use the banners and a pointer to demonstrate how letters are formed.

Primary Grades

Science

Create a field guide for some natural category of objects, such as rocks and minerals, seashells, leaves, flowers, or insects. Work in groups to provide an informative page about each item; alphabetize the pages and compile them into a book.

Social Studies

Use all the resources in the school to make a book in which each page shows the entire alphabet from different languages, including Braille and sign language.

Media Studies

Watch the video of *Thank You, Mr. Falker*, by Patricia Polacco (1998). Simulate a learning disability for the students by smearing petroleum jelly on the lenses of an old pair of sunglasses and asking each child to read a passage while wearing them. Ask why it is very difficult for some children to learn to read.

Technology

Create personalized stationery for each child's initials, and print them as borders on paper. Then have each child use the paper to write a letter.

Recommended Readings on Integrating Curriculum

Evers, Lang, & Smith, 2009; Hurless & Gittings, 2008; Justice, Pence, Bowles, & Wiggins, 2006; Rule, 2001; Schickedanz, 2008; Whitin & Piwko, 2008

(continued)

FIGURE 12.11   Continued

Recent and Recommended Alphabet Books

A Apple Pie (Spirin, 2007)
A Was an Apple (Delessert, 2005)
A Was Once an Apple Pie (Lear, 2005)
ABC NYC: A Book about Seeing New York City (Dugan, 2005)
Alpha Bugs (mini edition): A Pop-up Alphabet (Carter, 2006)
Alphabears: An ABC Book (Hague, 1999)
Alphabet Adventure (Wood & Wood, 2001)
Alphabet House (Wallace, 2005)
Animal Antics: A to Z (Lobel, 2005)
ANTics (Hepworth, 1996)
Around the Alphabet: A New Way to Look at Letters (Williams, 1999)
Bad Kitty (Bruel, 2005)
Black and White Rabbit's ABC (Baker, 1999)
Click, Clack, Quackity Quack: An Alphabetical Adventure (Cronin, 2005)
Found Alphabet (Shindler & Graniczewski, 2005)
In the Leaves (explores 10 Chinese Mandarin characters) (Lee, 2005)
Max's ABC (Wells, 2007)
Me! Me! ABC (Ziefert, 2006)
Miss Bindergarten Celebrates the Last Day of Kindergarten (Slate, 2006)
Now I Eat My ABCs (Abrams, 2004)
Superhero ABC (McLeod, 2006)
The Alphabet Room (Pinto, 2003)
The Bouncing, Dancing, Galloping ABC (Doyle, 2007)
The Construction Alphabet Book (Pallotta, 2006)
The Hidden Alphabet (Seeger, 2003)
The Racecar Alphabet (Floca, 2003)
The Turn-Around, Upside-Down Alphabet Book (Ernst, 2007)
Z Is for Zamboni: A Hockey Alphabet (Napier, 2006)

For more ideas on using alphabet books, see http://nancykeane.com/rl/372.htm.

Follow-the-Leader-type games, such as Simon Says. An example of regulatory language by children was found in a kindergarten block corner, where one student made a sign that read "Do not noc dn this bldn."

3. *Interactional, or "me and you," language* is used to establish and maintain relationships. An example of the interactional function of language is found in groups working together to achieve a common goal, such as making a class get-well card for a classmate in the hospital.

4. *Personal, or "here I come," language* is used to express personal opinions, feelings, and individuality. Activities that stem from the personal function of language include singing songs into which each child's name can be inserted, reading books about self and family, dictating individual stories, identifying with story characters, and assembling family and class photographs that have been captioned by the children. Rhonda, a day-care teacher, used pictures of children's parents at work to help her 3-year-olds adjust to starting school. Each child brought a photograph of his or her parent(s) at work and dictated a caption to go with it. The photos and captions were placed on the bulletin board to remind students where their parents were and that they would return as soon as work was over.

5. *Heuristic, or "tell me why," language* is used to explore and find out. Language activities with a heuristic function include keeping a journal on a class pet, conducting simple science experiments, or keeping a question box in the classroom where children can deposit a question and have it answered. Kareem, a second-grade teacher, invited the local ambulance crew to talk to the children during a unit on safety. They explained the use of a blood pressure cuff for a baby, a soft cast, and an oxygen tank. The children then toured the ambulance and asked other questions about rescue procedures.

6. *Imaginative, or "let's pretend," language* is used to create a world of one's own. Some examples of using language imaginatively are playing dress-up, playing with miniatures (farms, gas stations, etc.), and creating original stories and enacting them. Ms. Goldstein, a teacher in a private nursery school, went to a thrift store and found several old pith helmets that mail carriers wear in the summer. This simple prop led to an imaginative play theme called "Expedition." The children used all of the jungle animal toys already in the classroom, and more were brought in. Children created all sorts of themes—Pursuit and Capture, Daring Rescues, Finding Treasures, Falling in Quicksand—and then dictated stories about their play each day.

7. *Informational, or "something to tell you," language* is used to convey information. Informational uses of language include all types of announcements, message boards, bulletin boards, e-mail, notes to parents and children about upcoming events, class newspapers, a weather board, a community newspaper, web pages, and posters or flyers about events. Leah, a first-grade teacher, had just completed a unit on friendships and wanted to gather information about the good deeds that were occurring in the classroom. In this activity, each child drew the center of a daisy with a stem and leaves but no petals. Each child's petals were formed by a classmate's drawing or writing depicting her or his kindness and helpfulness, such as a petal that read "Brandon shrz hs mrkrs."

Classroom Activities to Support Diverse Language Learners

Through functional language activities, teachers can create a communication environment that supports young children's language growth.

Demonstrations A *demonstration* provides the opportunity to see how something is done and invites the observers to try the task for themselves; as such, it is a tool for engagement (F. Smith, 1983). Think about the many times we are prompted to try something without the slightest bit of direct persuasion. It could be a person, such as an excellent storyteller; a product, such as beautifully arranged flowers; or an artifact, such as a patchwork quilt. A demonstration may be summarized in one question: Can you do _____ if I show you how?

Collections   An article by Plourde (1989) describes a first-grade project on collections. The teacher began by sharing her personal collection of teddy bears. The class discussed the bears' outfits, names, and facial features, as well as their construction and history. Next, the children voted for their favorites, stating reasons for their choices.

Following this introduction to the concept of being a collector, children were put in small groups of three to five and instructed to arrive at a group decision about what to collect during the next two weeks. The teacher ruled out expensive items and suggested things such as rocks, flowers, stamps, stickers, and cloth scraps. Then a note was sent home to the parents, and each group was given a special box in the classroom in which to store their collection. At the end of the second week, each group made a 5- to 10-minute presentation. Other related activities involved interviewing collectors from the local community, using the collections for classification and seriation, brainstorming lists of similarities and differences, guessing games (one object in a total collection was described, and other children had to guess the type of collection), and creating imaginary collections, such as one of extraterrestrials.

Project Approach and Emergent Curriculum   A *project* is an in-depth study or investigation that a group of children undertake on a particular topic or theme (Helm & Katz, 2000). It is a form of emergent curriculum, meaning that it emanates from the children's interests, rather than being completely preplanned by the teacher (Ha, 2009). Usually, the focus of a project is something that the children have an opportunity to observe directly. Examples include a study of construction prompted by a renovation project at school or a study of hot-air balloons at a local fairground that is a walking field trip away from the child-care center. Projects give children rich opportunities to pursue their interests at their own pace and interact with experts in their communities (Carter & Curtis, 2007; Lotherington, Holland, Sotoudeh, & Zentena, 2008). The following websites have numerous examples of project work with children:

www.projectapproach.org

www.mothergooseprograms.org

http://illinoisearlylearning.org/project-approach.htm

www.innovativeteacherproject.org

Conclusion

Literacy researcher Judith Langer (2002) completed a 5-year study of effective schools that were exemplary in promoting children's literacy growth. What would you predict to be the essential conditions for high student achievement in literacy? Interestingly, Langer found six attributes of highly effective schools:

1. Professionalism is valued.
2. Teachers have access to professional development resources.
3. Teachers are encouraged to function as members of professional communities.
4. Teachers participate in meaningful decision making.
5. Teachers care about the curriculum and student learning.
6. Teachers make the commitment to becoming lifelong learners (p. 1).

A high-quality early childhood language arts curriculum builds on what children already know. It invites and welcomes children into literacy. It capitalizes on children's natural curiosity and playfulness. It provides carefully paced experiences matched to children's individual levels of competence. And it does all of these things in an environment that simultaneously supports children and adults, so that all children feel confident enough to take the risks associated with real learning and become self-directed language learners, both now and in the future.

PEARSON myeducationkit To check your comprehension on the content covered in this chapter, go to the MyEducationKit for your book and complete the Study Plan for Chapter 12. Here you will be able to take a chapter quiz and receive feedback on your answers.

Research-Based Literacy Strategies

Design Features of Literacy Environments

Studies of learning environments suggest that the following three design features support literacy (McGee & Morrow, 2005; Roskos & Christie, 2007):

1. *Presence of print*, meaning that it is abundant across the setting, at the children's eye level, attractive and appealing, and presented in a variety of formats
2. *Proximity to the learners*, meaning that literacy should be matched to children both physically (accessible, suited to the children) and psychologically (respectful of children's cultures, linked to their real-life experiences, tied to their interests and preferences)
3. *Productive*, meaning that it nudges children forward in their understanding about becoming literate and teaches them that becoming literate will enable them to accomplish important tasks, find pleasure in literacy activities, and use language as a means of personal expression

All children are provided with opportunities to learn when these conditions are met.

Effective Learning Centers

Learning centers at which children can work on literacy tasks individually or in small groups are an important tool for supporting literacy (Isbell, 2008; Morrow, 2008a; Stuber, 2007).

To establish productive learning centers, consider these questions:

• *Objectives.* What do you hope students will learn? What will they accomplish in the centers? How does this correlate with the curriculum? How will each objective best be accomplished?

• *Grade level.* What grade level or levels is this lesson suited for? Can it be adapted for older or younger students? Can it be modified for students who are more advanced, have disabilities, or are learning English?

• *Number of centers.* Where will the centers be located: in the library and/or the classroom? Can they be easily put away between classes? Will students need any supervision or assistance? Who will help?

• *Length of time for each assignment.* Will students be able to complete all centers in one class period? Will it take two or more classes to complete all centers?

• *Tracking sheet.* How will students know which centers they have completed? Which center do they go to next? Must they do all centers or a specified number of centers?

• *Materials.* Will students be using computer or Internet programs? Will they need consumable materials? What library resources and equipment will they need? Are there enough materials to share?

• *Activities.* Do the activities include a variety of media? Can they be done independently or with a partner? Are a variety of learning styles and intelligences included?

• *Evaluation.* How will students know they have successfully completed the activity? Will they be provided self-check answer keys or a rubric? Who will do the evaluation? (Miller, 2004, pp. 17–18).

Reading Recovery and Tutorial Programs

Based on the work of Marie Clay (1992), Reading Recovery is an intensive one-to-one program that provides intensive tutoring in reading for children, usually during first grade. Its goals are to increase children's reading accuracy, improve their comprehension, and bolster their self-confidence (Reynolds & Wheldall, 2007). In 2007, federal researchers concluded that there were positive effects of students' participation in Reading Recovery across all four of the domains in their review—alphabetics, fluency, comprehension, and general reading achievement (Phelps Deily, 2009).

Generally speaking, effective tutoring programs share these characteristics:

• Appropriate training, mentoring, strategies, and materials for tutors
• Access and opportunity to a wide variety of reading materials that are matched to readers
• Attention to each reader's choices, interests, motivation, general self-esteem, and self-confidence as a literacy learner
• Sufficient time for learners to read with supportive guidance, feedback, and demonstrations from the tutors
• High expectations for success in a supported environment (Morrow, Woo, & Radzin, 2000)

Children who benefit most from one-to-one interventions often have short attention spans and low self-esteem; they also may read below grade level, have limited ability in English, and come from homes where assistance with schoolwork is not available. The following tutorial strategies are recommended:

• Review work learned in the regular classroom program.
• Discuss families, pets, school, and the like to motivate drawing and writing.
• Play structured games to motivate interest in skill acquisition.
• Read stories from classroom materials to provide reinforcement.
• Work with phonics.
• Do both oral and silent reading.
• Expand vocabulary and use context clues to figure out words.
• Predict outcomes in stories.
• Summarize the stories read.
• Use leveled books to provide students with appropriate reading materials.
• Provide high-interest reading materials for the child.
• Encourage children to write and draw in journals each day.
• Conference with the child.
• Keep a list of words to enhance vocabulary development and sight vocabulary.
• Offer support and encouragement (August & Shanahan, 2008; Morrow, Woo, & Radzin, 2000; Pence, Justice, & Wiggins, 2008; Samway, 2006; Uribe & Nathenson-Mejia, 2008; Wilford, 2008).

Links with Literature
Literature-Based Themes

What Is a Literature-Based Theme?

Teaching all of the subject areas through literacy is an effective way of integrating the curriculum (Neuman, Roskos, Wright, & Lenhart, 2007). A literature-based theme uses children's books as the centerpiece of curricular integration (Labbo, Love, Prior, Hubbard, & Ryan, 2006; Vestergaard, 2005). There are many different ways of organizing literature-based themes, such as the following:

- By *literary genre,* for example, a theme on nursery rhymes from different countries
- By a *broad concept* that cuts across subject areas—for example, What is reading?
- Around a *literary motif or theme*, such as the theme of transformations
- By focusing on the works of *a particular author and/or illustrator* of picture books
- Around *different versions or variants* of familiar stories, such as different versions of the town mouse and the country mouse story

Why Use Literature-Based Themes?

Literature-based themes

- Make children's literature an integral part of the total curriculum rather than limiting it to a separate story time.
- Build the teacher's understanding of how to present the material in developmentally appropriate ways.
- Provide a rich resource for information that is more diverse and current than that typically provided in textbooks.
- Build interest in and enjoyment of literature.
- Increase the amount of reading.
- Improve attitudes toward reading and self-concept as readers.
- Yield higher reading achievement.
- Provide greater opportunities for teachers and children to talk about books, recommend books to one another, and share them.

Checklist for a High-Quality Literature-Based Theme

The theme should include the following:

_____ A motivating introduction

_____ Communication with parents about the theme

_____ A large selection of books and time to read them

_____ Opportunities to work in flexible groups

_____ Child-initiated, child-directed activity

_____ Opportunities to learn outside the classroom

_____ Resource people brought into the classroom

_____ Activities to familiarize the children with the author and illustrator

_____ Interactive bulletin board ideas

_____ Learning center activities

_____ Other books, poems, songs, and so on, to extend the theme

_____ Original responses from children

_____ The fine arts as well as the traditional "academic" subjects

_____ A satisfying culminating activity that gives children the chance to share what they have learned with other audience(s)

Additional resources on theme teaching can be found at TeachNet (www.teachnet.org) and On-line-Offline: Themes and Resources (www.rockhill.com).

Sample Theme on Letter Writing for Primary Grades

Deliver the Letter: The Post Office

Song cassette. "Mail Myself to You," Woody Guthrie

In-the-room props. Refrigerator box for post office, large decorated box for mailbox, individual mail slots (e.g., snack food canisters labeled with children's names), open/closed sign for post office, clock face with movable hands, small tablets for receipts, cash register for selling stamps

Literacy materials. Crayons, pencils, pens, envelopes of different sizes, recycled cards and postcards, stickers (for stamps), self-inking stamper (for canceling stamps), scissors, glue, tape, boxes

Dramatic play props. Hat, old blue shirt, totebag for mail carrier of the day

Additional Learning Opportunities

- *Guest speaker.* Invite a postal carrier or card shop owner to talk about his or her job.
- *Letter exchange.* Have children write real letters to one another prior to a holiday; then actually mail them to their homes.
- *Address book.* Create a class address book so that children can correspond with one another.
- *Field trip.* Visit a real post office and look for evidence of the postal system along the way (e.g., mailboxes at each home, drop-off mailboxes on corners, mail trucks).

Picture Books about Letters and Correspondence

Amber on the Mountain. (Johnston, 1994). (P). A girl's motivation to correspond with the friend who taught her to read leads her to learn how to write.

Beethoven Lives Upstairs. (Nichol, 1994). (P). The letters exchanged between a young boy and his uncle between 1822 and 1825 describe the uncle's eccentric neighbor, composer Ludwig van Beethoven.

Bunny Wishes: A Winter's Tale. (Morgan, 2008). (Pre-K/K). Best friend bunnies exchange wish lists and letters that brighten the cold, dreary days of winter.

Dear Annie. (Caseley, 1991). (Pre-K/K). Annie shares a shoebox full of 100 cards and notes from her grandpa at Show-and-Tell in this story that vividly illustrates the value of correspondence.

Dear Bear. (Harrison, 1994). (K/P). A child copes with her fear of bears through a series of letters.

Dear Brother. (Asch, 1992). (P). Two mice who live in the attic discover letters and pictures exchanged between their great-great uncles, one a city mouse and the other a country mouse.

Dear Juno (Pak, 2000). (K/P). A Korean child stays in touch with his grandmother in Seoul through her letters.

Dear Max. (Grindley, 2007). (P). A year's worth of letters between a 9-year-old boy and his favorite author; see also *Bravo, Max!* (Grindley, 2007).

Dear Mrs. LaRue: Letters from Obedience School (Teague, 2002). (P). A humorous story about a dog packed off to canine boot camp who corresponds with his owner to catalog his many complaints.

Dear Oklahoma City. (Ross & Myers, 1996). (P). Real letters and drawings selected from the over 10,000 produced by children in a poignant response to the Oklahoma City bombing. The children's work was shared with rescue workers to give them the inspiration to go on.

Dear Rebecca, Winter Is Here. (George, 1993). (Pre-K/K/P). A grandmother's letter to her grandchild provides a poetic yet factual explanation for the change of seasons.

The Jolly Postman. (Ahlberg & Ahlbert, 1986). (K/P). In this humorous book that contains pages made into envelopes, readers encounter all types of correspondence (e.g., invitation, greeting card, postcard, business letter, etc.) as familiar storybook characters correspond with one another.

La La Rose. (Ichikawa, 2004). (Pre-K/K/P). Use this story of a beloved toy that is lost to inspire children's original stories about lost treasured objects.

Larabee. (Luthardt, 2009). (Pre-K/K). A frisky little dog who belongs to the postal carrier helps to deliver the mail but yearns to receive a letter all his own.

Learning to Swim in Swaziland: A Child's Eye View of a Southern African Country. (Leigh, 1993). (P). An 8-year-old girl stays in touch with her former classmates in New York after her family moves to Africa through a series of letters richly embellished with drawings, photos, and other objects from her new home.

Letters from a Desperate Dog. (Christelow, 2007). (P). A frustrated dog corresponds with a canine columnist for the *Weekly Bone* to get advice about getting along with one human and one cat.

The Long, Long Letter. (Spurr, 1996). (K/P). A windstorm carries a letter from one sister to another.

The Magpie Song. (Anholt, 1996). (P). A city child and her rural grandfather express their love for one another through an exchange of letters.

Mailing May. (Tunnell, 1997). (P). A true story about a financially strapped family from Idaho who send their child through the mail as cargo in 1914 so that her wish to see her grandmother can be fulfilled.

Mouse Letters. (Cartlidge, 1993). (K/P). The rodent occupants of a house send tiny pull-out letters that detail all of their adventures for the little girl who lives there.

Mr. Grigg's Work. (Rylant, 1989). (Pre-K/K). A gentle story about a small-town postmaster who enjoys his work and the services he can provide to neighbors and friends.

Pictures from our Vacation. (Perkins, 2007). (P). An instant camera and ties with extended family make for a memorable family trip.

Postcard Passages. (Joyce, 1995). (P). Inspired by her Great Aunt Gladys's travels as documented in postcards, Susan saves her money so that she can travel too.

Additional Resources: Sipe (2008); West & Cox (2004).

ELLs

Teachers' Cultural Competence

Cultural competence refers to the ability to embrace, understand, and respond in positive ways to people from other cultural and ethnic backgrounds (Gay, 2000). Early childhood educators who approach young ELLs with warmth, acceptance, and a genuine desire to communicate—irrespective of their knowledge level in the child's L1—exert a positive effect on language outcomes for young children (Tabors, 2008). A commitment to children and families, despite the adversity they may face, is the surest way to offer an effective early childhood language arts program (Jalongo & Li, in press). Cultural competence and culturally responsive teaching are evident in early childhood programs with the following features:

• A school environment that is positive and reflects high-quality, respectful and meaningful exchanges between and among children and families, teachers, and administrators

• Teachers who understand second-language development and treat L1 as an asset (rather than a liability) and L2 as enrichment (rather than remediation of deficiencies); teachers with education, continuing professional development, and established competence in implementing best practices of instruction (Gibbons, 2002; Goh & Taib, 2006; Hawkins, 2004)

• Curriculum that is supported by research and developmentally suited for diverse learners, incorporating higher-order thinking skills and aligned with standards and assessment (Copple & Bredekamp, 2009; Crosse, 2007)

• Educators who fully appreciate that no single approach or method is likely to be effective for all ELLs (Epstein, 2007), given the tremendous diversity in their cultural and language backgrounds; levels of proficiency in both L1 and L2; and their beliefs, values, and attitudes about the acquisition of L2 (Genesee, Lindholm-Leary, Saunders, & Christian, 2005; Montecel & Cortez, 2002)

• Ongoing professional training in second-language acquisition for all teachers to serve the culturally and linguistically diverse students in their classrooms (Ellis, 2007; Fillmore & Snow, 2002; Purdy, 2008)

Additional Resources

Espinosa, L. (2008, January). *Challenging common myths about young English language learners* (Policy Brief No. 8). New York: Foundation for Child Development. Available online at www.fcd-us.org/resources/resources_show.htm?doc_id=660789.

National Council of Teachers of English. (2008). *English language learners: A policy research brief produced by the National Council of Teachers of English.* Available online at www.ncte.org/library/NCTEFiles/Resources/Positions/Chron0308PolicyBrief.pdf.

How Do I ...

Write a Standards-Based Lesson Plan with Children's Literature?

The great majority of professional organizations in education have produced standards to guide teachers' practice and each state is required to have academic standards and testing systems in place in order to qualify for federal funding.

1. Review the National Association for the Education of Young Children's Academy for Early Childhood Program Accreditation standards for language development at www.naeyc.org/standards/standard2/standard2D.asp.

2. Review the International Reading Association and National Council of Teachers of English standards at www.readwritethink.org/about standards.html. Remain at this site for steps 4 and 5.

3. Locate the reading and/or language arts standards for your state. Use a common search engine and type the name of your state and the words "Department of Education" or "Office of Education" in the box. After you arrive at your state's Department of Education, search for standards and then for reading or language arts.

Now visit the National Council of Teachers of English and International Reading Association website at www.readwritethink.org/lessons to view a wide range of lesson plans based on award-winning picture books. You can select the grade level and literacy strand; there is also a section of student materials and other web sources. Identify a well-known, high-quality picture book that would be suitable for the developmental levels of the students that you have in mind. Make sure that the book is very well suited for reading aloud to a group; books that have too much text may not sustain young children's attention. Get your instructor's opinion on the book's appropriateness. Read through the book and reflect on the various standards. Identify several that would apply to sharing the book and related activities that you are considering. You can create a custom-tailored list of relevant books at the Database of Award-Winning Children's Literature (www.dawcl.com). To get your thinking started, take a look at some sample lesson plans posted at http://hastings.lexingtonma.org/Library/Yes/lessons.htm.

4. Organize your thoughts chronologically:

   Before reading. What can you do to immediately grab children's attention, introduce the book, and build interest in listening? How can you assess what children already know about the topic of the book? How will you talk about the cover? Might it be useful to take the children on a "picture walk" through the story first? Which vocabulary words are crucial to an understanding of the book? What purpose will you set for their listening? How can you involve the children in making predictions?

   While reading. What comments and questions can you use while reading to guide children's thinking so that they get the point or the gist of the book? How will you draw children's attention to print and vocabulary as you read? Where will you pause and why? How will you encourage children to connect with the book and relate it to their own experiences?

   After reading. How will you determine if your goals for sharing the book were met? What small group or individual activities would extend children's understanding of the book? How will you design these activities so that children at various developmental levels or with different types of disabilities can experience success?

5. Click on Web Resources at the Read/Write/Think site. For more literature-based lessons, check out the following:

   A to Z Teacher Stuff (http://atozteacherstuff.com)
   Book Hive (www.bookhive.org)
   Blue Web'n (www.kn.pacbell.com/wired/bluewebn/search.cfm)
   Carol Hurst's Children's Literature Site (www.carolhurst.com)

PEARSON myeducationkit Now go to Chapter 12 in the MyEducationKit (**www.MyEducationKit** **.com**) for your book, where you can:

- Find Chapter Objectives.
- Complete Assignments and Activities that can help you more deeply understand the chapter content.
- Extend knowledge with content-specific Web Links.
- Check your comprehension on the content covered in the chapter by going to the Study Plan. Here you will be able to take a chapter quiz, receive feedback on your answers, and then access resources that will enhance your understanding of chapter content.

chapter thirteen

Documenting Children's Progress in the Language Arts

Annie Pickert/Pearson Education

FACT FILE on Assessment

• Many of the major concerns of teachers today focus on assessment issues, such as how to reshape the school curriculum to incorporate local, state, and national standards; determine ways to assess each standard; and create a comprehensive assessment system (Carr & Harris, 2001).

• Even though standardized testing as mandated by No Child Left Behind starts in third grade, preschools are under increased pressure to prepare children by placing a greater emphasis on attaining academic skills at an earlier age (Stipek, 2006).

- Although standardized testing is the most common form of assessment utilized today, many educators are promoting the use of assessment practices that take place as the child interacts with familiar adults in the natural classroom setting during routine activities and tasks (Barone & Xu, 2008; DeBruin-Parecki, 2008; Downs & Strand, 2006).

- The most important factor in the successful use of classroom-based assessment strategies is the teacher. Teachers who create comfortable classroom environments will see a more realistic representation of children's abilities when utilizing performance-based assessment strategies (Schappe, 2005).

- In their work with children whose primary language is not English, educators sometimes do not make a distinction between language differences and language disorders. When this occurs, a child may be referred for specialized services that are inappropriate or unnecessary (Espinosa, 2005).

- Gestures play an even more important role in the communication of toddlers than previously understood (Goldin-Meadow & Rowe, 2009; Iverson & Goldin-Meadow, 2005; Nyland, Ferris, & Dunn, 2008). Gestures are particularly significant for English language learners and children with hearing impairments as well. Therefore, researchers recommend assessing speech and gestures separately (Cabrera & Martinez, 2001; Hoskin & Herman, 2001; Nyland, Ferris, & Dunn, 2008).

- Most referrals for intervention services in schools are based on readily observable *expressive* oral language behavior (speaking). However, failing to assess *receptive* oral language (listening comprehension) tends to overlook other children who need support services (Zhang & Tomblin, 2000).

- The National Assessment of Educational Progress (November 2003) indicated that among fourth-grade children in the United States, 31 percent perform at or above the proficient level in reading and 37 percent perform below the proficient level (Lonigan, 2005, p. 2). By third grade, children from minority backgrounds are overrepresented in every disability category (Samson & Lesaux, 2009).

Did any of this information surprise you? If so, what? Why? How will you use this knowledge to educate and care for the very young?

What Is Assessment?

A fundamental premise of evaluation is the concept of "value added"; in other words, did the program contribute significantly to every learner's language growth and development? Over the years, many different methods have been used to answer this and related questions.

Assessment is "an integral component of the curriculum, with results used to guide teaching, identify concerns for individual children, and provide information to improve and guide interventions. Assessment methods need to be . . . developmentally appropriate, culturally and linguistically responsive, tied to children's daily activities, supported by professional development, and inclusive of families" (National Association for the Education of Young Children [NAEYC] & National Association of Early Childhood Specialists in State Departments of Education [NAECS/SDE], 2003, p. 3). This explanation makes an important distinction between assessment *of* learning and assessment *for* learning (Popham, 2006; Stiggins & Chappuis, 2006). Assessment *of* learning implies that you are measuring how much learning already took place; and assessment *for* learning implies that you are using the results of an assessment to make instructional decisions and optimize the learning of every child (Edwards, Turner, & Mokhtari, 2008; Wortham, 2005). Assessment *of* learning usually seeks to compare one child, school, or country with another while assessment *for* learning is used to figure out how best to support each and every child's progress.

Ultimately, both types of assessment—large-scale comparisons and reports of each child's progress—are necessary. Figure 13.1 provides an overview of the different assessment options available to early childhood educators.

Assessment includes, but is not limited to, tests. In the vignette that follows, you will learn about a teacher who uses assessment to support children's learning.

Collaboration with Families and Professionals

Standards in Education
Assessment is one of the most controversial aspects of early childhood education. Visit the site Fair Test at www.fairtest.org to review the National Forum on Assessment's *Principles and Indicators for Student Assessment Systems.*

Dyanne is a student teacher working with a kindergarten class. The class teacher tells her that one of the students, Chelsea, is selectively mute. Dyanne knows from her language arts course that *selective mutism* describes a condition in which the child refuses to talk in social situations despite being capable of speech.

Dyanne finds additional information from the Selective Mutism Foundation (www.selectivemutismfoundation.org). She learns that there are two categories of children with selective mutism: (1) children with underlying receptive and expressive language disorders and (2) children with anxiety disorders. The type of selective mutism observed during the preschool years is more often a language disorder, while mutism during school years is more likely to be anxiety related. Psychic trauma usually is not the underlying cause.

Gathering information in different contexts is extremely important (e.g., recording the child's speech) because the child sometimes will talk in a different settings. The teacher and student teacher enlist the help of Chelsea's family to get a recording of her speech at home. Chelsea does not talk much at home, but she does speak in a whisper to her family members, the family cat, and her teddy bear.

| FIGURE 13.1 | Language Assessment Continuum |

	Formal (most structured)		Informal (least structured)
	Norm-Referenced Assessment	Criterion-Referenced Assessment	Observation/ Documentation
Purpose	To rank or compare one child's performance on a set of test items with that of peers	To assess the child's performance on specific objectives or tasks	To study an individual child's overall performance
Basic assumption	The whole is the sum of its parts	The whole can be analyzed as components	The whole is more than the sum of its parts
Focus	Attempts to measure products or outcomes	Attempts to create a profile of the child's competencies to be used in planning instruction	Attempts to investigate a language skill holistically
Data	Usually quantitative (raw scores, percentages, etc.)	Diagnostic/ prescriptive	Usually descriptive and naturalistic
Examples	Readiness tests, achievement tests	Developmental profiles	Anecdotal records, portfolios, displays of children's work

Through collaboration with the speech/language pathologist, psychologist, Chelsea's family, and Chelsea's pediatrician, Dyanne learns that a combination of family therapy, speech therapy, and behavior modification is recommended in Chelsea's case. About this Dyanne says, "Now I see how important it is to study children's language in a comprehensive way before planning an intervention."

Contributions and Consequences

- *Contributions of the teacher:* What role did Dyanne, the student teacher, play in this situation?
- *Contributions of the family:* How did the family support the child and get involved?

- *Contributions of other professionals:* How did professional organizations contribute to addressing Chelsea's needs?
- *Consequences of collaboration:* How might this story have ended differently if the adults had never reached consensus?

Overview of Assessment

Brain and Language
Research suggests that when a child experiences intense emotions, logical thinking can be disrupted and fear can interfere with academic performance (Amsterlaw, Lagattuta, & Meltzoff, 2009). What are the implications of these findings for testing practices?

PEARSON
myeducationkit

Go to the Assignments and Activities section of Chapter 13 in MyEducationKit and complete the activity entitled "The Pros and Cons of High-Stakes Standardized Testing."

As described by Johnson et al. (1995), many language arts teachers are

> caught in conflicts among belief systems and institutional structures, agendas, and values. The point of friction among these conflicts was assessment, which was associated with very powerful feelings of being overwhelmed, and of insecurity, guilt, frustration, and anger. Assessment, as it occurs in schools, is far from a merely technical problem. Rather, it is deeply social and personal. (p. 359)

Assessment affects the lives of children, teachers, and programs. In fact, children's test scores are being used in many states to evaluate *teacher* effectiveness and to rank schools (Guilfoyle, 2006; Meier & Woods, 2004; Popham, 2006). As Berghoff (1997) explains:

> The elementary school teachers with whom I work are constantly under pressure to get students to achieve high test scores on standardized tests that are given by the school district.

This is a problem for them, because the tests do not assess much of what they teach. Students are expected to read short, contrived passages and find the main idea or the cause and effect pattern in the story. In class, these students read whole books and talk about complex sets of issues. In the conversations about testing in this district, the validity of the tests is not up for discussion. The tests are a fact of life. (p. 321)

Figure 13.2 summarizes the concerns, levels, and targets of assessment.

Traditional Testing

In this climate of change concerning assessment practices, early childhood professionals need to be knowledgeable about assessment issues and the array of assessment options that can provide a more complete picture of young children's language abilities (Division for Early Childhood, 2007; Galper & Seefeldt, 2009). This is particularly important for young children with various risk factors that may affect their performance on tests (Cabell, Justice, Zucker, & Kilday, 2009). Even when tests are well constructed and used appropriately, it is difficult to assess young children's language abilities through traditional testing methods, for several reasons (see Bracken & Nagle, 2006).

FIGURE 13.2 Concerns, Levels, and Targets of Assessment

Main Concerns of Teachers

- *Individual progress in learning.* How are individual children acquiring the knowledge, developing the understanding, and mastering the skills we judge as valuable for them?
- *Social dynamics of the classroom.* How are important social relationships—teacher to child, child to teacher, child to peers, and families to schools—being initiated, sustained, and facilitated in positive ways?
- *Progress of the classroom community as a whole.* How are the dynamics created by a complex network of children contributing to the achievement of broad classroom or program academic and social goals? How does the social life of this classroom contribute to grander social goals, such as the children's sense of their common good in a democratic society?

Levels of Assessment

- *Instructional.* Teachers meet needs of students or class, make grouping decisions, grade students, evaluate instruction, and evaluate themselves as teachers.
- *Instructional leadership and support.* Principals evaluate programs, allocate resources, and evaluate teachers; other administrators such as curriculum coordinators evaluate program quality; counselors and psychologists identify children with special needs and suggest support systems.
- *Policy level.* Superintendents evaluate programs and principals and allocate resources; school boards evaluate programs and superintendents; state departments of education evaluate programs, as do citizens and legislators.

Main Targets of Assessment

- *Problem solving.* Students can use their knowledge to reason and solve problems.
- *Skills acquisition.* Students are able to develop and demonstrate important skills.
- *Generating products.* Students use their skills to create high-quality products.

Sources: Merritt & Dyson (1992); Stiggins & Chapuis (2006).

Inexperience   Generally speaking, young children are not familiar with testing procedures and often do not realize the importance of a test. In everyday experience, for example, people ask children questions because they do not know the answers (e.g., "Where did you put your shoes?" "Is Daddy's car in the driveway?"). In a testing situation, just the reverse is true. Children are asked *display questions*, or questions to which the adults already know the answers. One mother described how her daughter's response to display questions affected the preschooler's test performance:

> I took Terri, my 5-year-old daughter, to school for kindergarten readiness testing. On the way home, I said, "What were some of the questions they asked you?" Terri replied, "A teacher had pictures on little cards and she held them up for me to look at. Then she said, 'What is this?' One was a picture of a bird." "And what did you say?" I asked.

"I didn't say anything," Terri answered. "I figured if that big lady doesn't know it's a picture of a bird, I'm not telling her."

Children may not understand that they are expected to answer a question even if it does not pertain to them and even if the person administering the test already knows the answer. Due to the increased pressure on teachers to show that they are exerting a positive influence on children's test scores, even very young children are being coached in how to be better test takers and drilled on practice items that mimic the format of important tests.

Nonresponse   If a child gives no response to a test item, this does not necessarily mean that he or she does not know the answer. There are many possible explanations. The child may not understand the procedure or may be worried about making a mistake. It could also be that the child feels uncomfortable with the person administering the test.

Consider the experience of Jenny, a bright, talkative kindergartner. Her parents have been informed that she is being recommended for speech therapy, and they are taken aback. When they ask Jenny what happened at school, she says, "A weird man I never saw at school before took me out of my room and into a little closet. He had a hole cut in the back of his hair (The man was bald!), and he was wearing a Mickey Mouse watch. He asked me lots of questions, but he was a stranger, so I didn't answer." A nonresponse is usually scored as an incorrect answer, so a shy or reticent child's ability may be greatly underestimated by tests (Brassard & Boehm, 2007).

Cultural Bias   Suppose that you were going to travel to a distant city to compete in a marathon, and you heard that one of your major competitors had been practicing on that course every day. It would seem like your competitor had an advantage. In testing, when one group of children has the edge over another, it is referred to as *cultural bias*. A blatant example of cultural bias would be to administer a test in English to a child who is newly immigrated and just learning to use English as a second language. In the United States in the 1970s, this is exactly what occurred with many Spanish-speaking students; they were placed inappropriately in special education based on their low scores on tests administered in English. It is important to be particularly cautious when using and interpreting standardized test results with English language learners (Ballantyne, Sanderman, & McLaughlin, 2008; Gottlieb, 2006; Naughton, 2005; Roseberry-McKibbin & O'Hanlon, 2005).

Artificiality   A child may be able to circle the picture that corresponds to a word spoken by an adult or supply the missing word in a simple analogy, but this will not tell us whether he or she can initiate a conversation with an adult or negotiate a dispute over a toy with a peer. Formal tests do tell us something about children's language, but it is not enough (Gullo, 2005; Koralek, 2004).

Because language is a social instrument, it is important to assess language use in natural settings, rather than rely exclusively on the contrived situations required by standardized tests. A young child's language behaviors in different settings can be surprisingly different. Fonda, a solemn, subdued first-grader, rarely spoke at school, yet her mother described the very opposite behavior at home. On further investigation, it was discovered that Fonda's cousin had really frightened her about going to first grade by telling her that "If you talk or you're bad, you'll go to the principal's office and he has this GREAT BIG paddle that REALLY HURTS." As a result, Fonda was afraid to be herself at school. When Fonda was mistreated by peers at school, she said and did nothing. By the time she arrived home, she was often angry, frustrated, bursting to talk, and aggressive toward her little brother. If Fonda had not been observed across several social settings, she might have been incorrectly labeled as "language delayed" because the test provided just one sample of behavior.

Test Construction   Paper-and-pencil tests for young children are limited. Actually, just a few types of tasks typically are found in the items on standardized tests of children's literacy:

> Phonemic awareness (e.g., "Are these sounds the same or different?")
>
> Alphabet recognition (e.g., "Find the letter *b* in the row and circle it.")
>
> Phoneme/grapheme correspondence (e.g., "Write the letters you hear in the word *bat*.")
>
> Responding to pictures (e.g., "Mark the picture in the row that begins with *s*.")
>
> Spelling (e.g., "Find the word *run* in row 2 and circle it.")
>
> Responding to text (e.g., "Read the paragraph and then choose the best title.")
>
> Vocabulary (e.g., "Match each word with its definition.")

Another feature of test construction that puts young children at a disadvantage is the relative length of the testing session. Adults can sit for hours to take an important test, such as the national teacher exam, the Praxis. Tests are not noted for maintaining children's interest, so few tests are longer than 10 to 20 minutes. Longer tests are broken up into a series of shorter testing sessions on different days, but the drawback is that some children may be absent from school when portions of the test are administered.

To understand the problem with a short test, suppose that someone gave you a choice of two exams: one that included 100 items, worth 1 point apiece, and one that included 10 items, worth 10 points apiece. Most of us would probably choose the first test, operating on the assumption that there would be less likelihood of receiving a low score by missing just one item. The same principle applies in some tests for young children. Because there are so few items in all, getting just a few more right or wrong can greatly affect the total score. A child's reading proficiency, for instance, could be assessed as a full year lower due to errors on a few test items.

Response Format   The response format refers to the different ways that very young children can answer test items. Because young children are unsophisticated test takers, they usually respond to items on a group-administered paper-and-pencil test in simple ways, such as circling the correct answers; putting an *X* on an object, shape, or letter; or drawing a line to connect two items that belong together. When a group of first-graders took a test that required them to mark the *correct* answer with an X after spending most of the year putting an X over the *wrong* answer, there was considerable confusion, which had an adverse effect on their test scores.

Rationale for Testing   If tests for young children have so many drawbacks, then why do we continue to use them? There are at least four reasons:

1. *Time and money.* Without a doubt, the large-group paper-and-pencil test is faster to administer, easier to score, and takes less time than testing each child individually. Educators rely on formal tests because they are the most expedient way to get some indication of children's language abilities. Figure 13.3 lists some of the literacy tests commonly used with young children.

2. *Credibility.* Because tests are developed through research studies and statistical techniques, they are official looking and technical. Moreover, if the scores are high, tests give educators facts and figures that seem impressive—"hard" evidence that can be reported to the public and touted as evidence of program effectiveness.

3. *Anonymity.* No one wants to be the bearer of bad news and tell a parent that his or her child is far behind most peers in language development. When families want to

---

FIGURE 13.3 Tests of Literacy for Young Children

Clinical Evaluation of Language Fundamentals–Revised (CELF-R)

Comprehensive Test of Phonological Processing

Concepts of Print; Sand and Stones (Clay, 2000)

Developing Skills Checklist

Dynamic Indicators of Basic Early Literacy Skills (DIBELS)

Early Literacy Skills Assessment (ELSA) (an individually administered reading task)

Get Ready to Read! (GRTR!) screening tool

Peabody Picture Vocabulary Test–Revised (PPVT-R)

Preschool Comprehensive Phonological and Print Processing (Pre-CTOPPP)

Preschool Word and Print Awareness assessment

Test of Early Reading Ability–2 (TERA-2)

Test of Early Reading Achievement, 3rd edition (TERA-III)

Test of Phonological Awareness (TOPA)

Woodcock-Johnson, 3rd edition (WJ-III)

Woodcock Reading Mastery Test–Revised (WRMT-R)

For additional information, see Burke & Hagan-Burke (2007); Burke, Hagan-Burke, Kwok, and Parker (2009); Marston, Pickart, Reschly, Heistad, Muyskens, and Tindal (2007); National Clearinghouse for English Language Acquisition (2006); Niemeyer and Scott-Little (2001). For information online, see www.serve.org.

know why their child has been categorized in a particular way, school personnel can point to the test score instead of saying that it is their collective professional judgment. Tests provide *cutoff scores* that are used to determine eligibility for services, such as a tutoring program or enrollment in a program for gifted and talented students.

4. *Comparability.* Because a standardized test uses the same items, administration procedures, and scoring techniques, students' average scores can be used to compare one school with others locally, regionally, and nationally. States use the test scores to decide which schools are high-performing and document that they are achieving state standards. The federal government then uses these test scores to make funding decisions. Test scores can determine which schools get federal funding, which ones are under pressure to improve, and which ones are taken over by the state and closed. Clearly, tests involve high stakes in today's educational climate. Nevertheless, testing has a place in education, just as knowing a person's temperature or blood pressure can assist a doctor in making a diagnosis.

Performance Assessment

It is particularly important to gather information about the child's language at home and in the community (often supplied by the parents) and to observe the child at school during interactions with adults and peers, both in formal and informal settings (Cohen, Stern, Balaban, & Gropper, 2008). *Alternative assessment* refers to any form of measuring what students know or are able to do other than traditional standardized tests. The following assumptions and attributes characterize informal types of assessment—also referred to as *performance assessment*, *authentic assessment*, and *classroom-based assessment:*

- Students are active participants, rather than passive subjects.
- Evaluation and guidance occur simultaneously and continuously.
- Processes as well as products are evaluated.
- Development and learning need to be recognized and celebrated.
- Multiple indicators and sources of evidence are collected over time.
- Results of the assessment are used to plan instruction, improve classroom practice, and optimize children's learning.
- The assessment process is collaborative among parents, teachers, children, and other professionals (Isenberg & Jalongo, 2009; Puckett, Black, Wittmer, & Petersen, 2008; Stiggins, 2007).

In general terms, the alternative assessment tools that you will need in your repertoire are observation, portfolios, and documentation.

Observation

Observation, both planned and spontaneous, is used by teachers to become more informed about children (McAfee & Leong, 2006). Observing allows teachers to get to know students as individuals, with talents and abilities uniquely their own (Cohen, Stern, Balaban, & Gropper, 2008). Through thoughtful observation, teachers

PEARSON
myeducationkit™

Go to the Assignments and Activities
section of Chapter 13 in MyEducationKit
and complete the activity entitled
"Children with Special Needs."

familiarize themselves not only with the academic aspects of children's development but also with social, emotional, physical, and cultural influences on learning. Many circumstances, both in and out of school, influence learners, and observing paints a clearer picture than testing alone ever could.

Use of observations across time (Brassard & Boehm, 2007) has consistently been recognized as the *primary approach* for assessing the learning needs and educational progress of young children with or at risk of disability (Enz & Morrow, 2009; Meisels & Atkins-Burnett, 2005). The observations of a competent, reflective practitioner are an essential part of early childhood assessment. In most child-care settings, teachers are observing children on a continual basis to make decisions about programming, individual child development, and the possible need for more in-depth assessment if a child is not developing as expected (Baldwin, Adams, & Kelly, 2009). In fact, studies show that teachers are exceptionally good at predicting which children will need additional language support in future years (Samson & Lesaux, 2009). Including a method for recording information gained throughout the observational process is an important component of the data-gathering approach (Watts, O'Brian, & Wojcik, 2004). Figure 13.4 offers suggestions on making observations and writing anecdotal records.

Eli is enrolled in a college course on young children's play. After obtaining permission from each child's parent or guardian, Eli videotapes the children's play in a program for 3- to 5-year-olds and analyzes the tapes based on 10 types of language that young children use during sociodramatic play (Garvey, 1984). The following observations are part of Eli's class project, a classroom-based observational study of children's play behaviors:

1. *Definition of situation.* Two girls are playing with puppets and one says, "This is a talent show."

2. *Assignment of roles.* Two preschool girls resolve conflict over which roles they will play by creating new ones:

> **Lea:** I want to be the mom.
>
> **Marilee:** I do, too.
>
> **Lea:** Well, pretend we're sisters.
>
> **Marilee:** Okay.

3. *Defining location.* A 5-year-old boy slides up to the teacher's desk on his belly and tells her, "Ms. Ruggiero, I'm a python, and I'm a really mean snake. I am 12 feet long and this fat (gestures with hands). Uh-oh—I have to go back to my hole 'cause some mean dogs are chasing me" (slithers back under the table).

4. *Specifying the action plan.* While playing Mommy and Baby Lion, one child says to the other, "Let's growl, okay?"

5. *Assigning props.* A child is holding a plastic apple. "Remember that story 'Snow White and the Seven Dwarfs'? Well, I'm the mean old witch who goes around poisoning everyone. This is my poison apple."

FIGURE 13.4   Anecdotal Records of Children's Language Learning

Anecdotes are brief episodes of behavior stated in behavioral terms that: (1) provide detailed information about literacy tasks, (2) include direct quotations from the children, and (3) emphasize observable behavior related to listening, speaking, reading, and writing behaviors of young children.

Conversely, anecdotes should *not* use derogatory labels (e.g., "She's just a sloppy writer") and should *not* make inferences ("He's really happy about his writing"). Rather, they should describe what children *can* do in a positive tone ("She was practicing her writing") and report behavior that can actually be observed (J. said, "Hey, look at this! I wrote a story!"). Anecdotes are a way of documenting that real learning is taking place. Note in the following example of an anecdote that it provides specific information and includes verbatim comments from the children.

Time: 9:00 a.m.   Grade Level: First grade

Date: October 16   Setting: Small Group

While the teacher is reading aloud to the children using a big book, a child asks, "What's that?" and points to the period at the end of the sentence. Another child comments that "It looks like a dot" and the teacher explains that it is a dot, a very special kind of dot that "tells you to take a little rest when you are reading." She demonstrates how the story would sound by reading a few sentences without punctuation and then tells them that the mark is called a period. Later, when the children are doing their own writing, I observe several children using periods at the ends of their sentences; some seem to be getting carried away and putting a period after each word, rather than at the end of a sentence. One child reads his paper out loud to try and figure out where the "little rest" belongs: "Cleo . . . yeah, I should put one there. I have a Calico cat named Cleo who sleeps in my bed with me at night one time she . . . Wait! I need to rest back there" (he puts a period between "night" and "one").

Recommended Resources

Bentzen, W. R. (2008). *Seeing young children: A guide to observing and recording behavior* (6th ed.). Albany, NY: Delmar/Cengage.

Cohen, D. H., Stern, V., Balaban, N., & Gropper, N. (2008). *Observing and recording the behavior of young children* (5th ed.). New York: Teachers College Press.

6. *Correcting operating procedure and refining the script.*

Anna: You be the baby, and I'll be the mommy.

Shelley: Can I have some candy?

Anna: Okay, as much as you want.

Shelley: But Anna, you are the mommy. You have to give me what's *good* for me.

Anna: I know. You can have a lot.

7. *Rejecting others' performance.* Tomas and Kent have built an airport with blocks and are ready to begin "landing aircraft." Throughout the building process, Kent keeps asking if he can fly into the airport and Tomas keeps telling him "Not yet."

> **Tomas:**   Coming in for a landing!
>
> **Kent:**   Can I come in now?
>
> **Tomas:**   Yeah!
>
> **Kent:**   (He comes in for a crash landing and knocks down one corner of the airport.)
>
> **Tomas:**   No! Not that kind!

8. *Invoking rules relating to the real (versus the pretend).* Selma and Jenny are playing school; Selma is the music teacher, and Jenny is the student.

> **Selma:**   I clap with sticks, and you clap with your hands. (Jenny follows these instructions.) These sticks are magic, and if I rub them over your hands, you'll clap faster.
>
> **Jenny:**   Teachers don't really have magic sticks, do they?

9. *Termination of and/or transition from one organizing theme to another.* "I'm sick of playing school. Let's play bugs, you know, like the movie."

10. *Commenting on the interpersonal climate in the group.* The class has just finished a unit on friendships, and the boys are using some of the techniques that they learned through role-play:

> **Kurt:**   Will you play with me?
>
> **Chad:**   Sure! You're such a nice, nice guy.
>
> **Kurt:**   I like you, too. (Turns to another child.) You're really fun. Do you want to play? (Child nods yes.) (Talking to the teacher) We're all friends, and we're playing.

Through his observations, Eli has gained a more thorough understanding of each child's language strengths.

Portfolios

Classroom *portfolios* are organized, purposeful collections of learners' work that tell the story of their efforts, progress, and achievement in a given area. Creating portfolios provides an alternative to drill worksheets, standardized tests, and other measures that document skill attainment (Seitz & Bartholomew, 2008).

As a first step in using portfolios, the teacher needs to consider the goals for the program. A portfolio often contains work samples, systematic observations, anecdotal records, checklists or inventories, rating scales, and interviews that are keyed to the program goals (Helm & Katz, 2000; Helm, Beneke, & Steinheimer, 2007). Portfolios offer a wonderful opportunity for students, parents, and teachers to actually experience the growth of a child

Research and Report

When children acquire social skills they generally have more positive attitudes toward school, perform better academically, and score higher on measures of overall adjustment (Jalongo, 2007). Find out more about children's social skills, particularly a characteristic called self-regulation, which refers to the ability to control impulses and behave in socially appropriate ways (Boyer, 2008; Post, Boyer, & Brett, 2006). How is self-regulation developed?

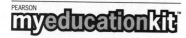

Go to the Assignments and Activities section of Chapter 13 in MyEducationKit and complete the activity entitled "What is Learning?"

rather than only seeing a score on a test (Downs & Strand, 2006; Espinosa, 2005; NAEYC & NAECS/SDE, 2003).

Documentation

The concept of *documentation* is borrowed from the early childhood schools in a municipality of Italy called Reggio Emilia (Wurm, 2005). The founders of these world-renowned programs believe that children have many different "languages," or ways of expressing themselves, and that it is the role of the school to provide the materials, opportunities, and adult/peer support for each child to demonstrate what he or she has learned.

Young children can represent what they are learning in many different ways, so documentation incorporates such methods as carefully arranged exhibits of children's art, captioned photographs of projects, videos of performances, and hypermedia productions on the computer—all of which furnish concrete evidence of children's most significant accomplishments (Hendrick, 2004; Helm, Beneke, & Steinheimer, 2007).

In addition to providing richly detailed descriptions of children's growth as language learners, using various methods of documentation is highly motivating because it enables students to make their learning visible to others, such as family members (Seitz, 2008; Stacey, 2009). Because projects and exhibitions provide tangible outcomes of learning, children can learn to take pride in their accomplishments and strive for excellence.

Evaluating Language Arts Programs

As a teacher of young children, your primary area of interest is the progress of each child in the program. Yet not all types of assessment focus on one child's progress. Large-scale assessments can evaluate particular programs (e.g., the kindergarten language arts program at a school or district) and even be applied at the policymaking level (e.g., a national evaluation of Head Start). Figure 13.5 summarizes ways of evaluating programs.

Teacher Concerns and Basic Strategies

Basically, teachers use six criteria for assessing children's work (Potter, 1985):

1. *Correctness* or *compliance* with instructions is used when a convergent answer is expected. A teacher might say, for instance, "Yes, Luz, the word *cat* does end with a *t*."

| FIGURE 13.5 | Perspectives on Language Arts Program Quality |

Physical Environment

- Are there enough books in the library?
- How much time is devoted to language arts curriculum?
- Is there a reading corner? Listening center? Writing center?
- Are literacy materials incorporated into children's play?

Children's Experiences

- Are children growing in confidence as users of language?
- What adaptations have been made to ensure that all children can fulfill their potential as communicators?
- Do children look forward to literacy activities?
- Are there opportunities for extended conversations with teachers and peers?

Teachers' Experiences

- Are teachers' basic needs being met through adequate salary and health care benefits?
- Are they treated with respect by colleagues and supervisory personnel?
- Is there support for their ongoing professional development in the language arts?

Parents' and Families' Experiences

- Do parents and other family members feel welcome at the school or center?
- Is there regular two-way communication between teachers and families?
- Can families rely on the educational system for literacy support?

Perceptions of the Program by the Community and Society

- How is the literacy program viewed in the community? In the region?
- Is there a general agreement that the program is supporting children's development and preparing them for more productive lives?
- Does it compare favorably with other early childhood programs nationwide?

Source: Katz (1993).

Infants and Toddlers
Higher levels of television and screen entertainment time and low physical activity levels interact to increase psychological distress in young children. A longitudinal study of infants from birth to age 3 showed TV viewing before age 2 does not improve a child's language and visual motor skills (Hamer, Stamatakis, & Mishra, 2009).

2. *Practical workability* applies a set of standards based on appropriate outcomes. A teacher might encourage a child by observing, "LaKisha, your lift-the-flap book really works."

3. *Aesthetic standards* are applied when beauty is the criterion. A teacher might say, "Saad, I notice that the illustrations for your story are very colorful."

4. *Evidence of creativity* is the standard when the product or process is evaluated on the basis of originality. A third-grade teacher

Go to the Assignments and Activities section of Chapter 13 in MyEducationKit and complete the activity entitled "Graphing with Jellybeans."

might remark, "Jeremy, I could imagine just what the planet that you invented would be like when I read your story."

5. *Speed* evaluates the work in terms of the time it takes to complete the task. A first-grade teacher might say, "Everyone put your name on your paper, and let's get started."

6. *Model of product* or *process* is used if a model or finished product prepared either by the teacher or a peer serves as the standard for desired work. A second-grade teacher might say to the group, "You've done a good job making your own book cover out of fabric, like the ones I showed you from last year's class."

Classroom Activities to Assess Progress

There are activities throughout this book that can be used as informal assessment methods—for example, the directed listening/thinking activity (DLTA) and discussion web (Chapter 4); K-W-L Plus (Chapter 5); word walls and e-sorts (Chapter 7); talking drawings (Chapter 10); assessing reading attitudes, interests, and motivation (Research-Based Strategies, pp. 323–324); home language surveys (ELLs, pp. 325–326); and using wordless books as an assessment tool (Links with Literature, pp. 324–325). To view a wide variety of teaching and assessment activities, visit www.teachervision .fen.com. Search by grade level first and then by topic.

Child's Language History   Interviewing someone who has had major responsibility for the care of a child over an extended period of time can be an important source of information. Consider some of the following questions:

1. When did _____ begin to talk? What were _____'s first words? First sentences?
2. Could you describe any particularly memorable examples of _____'s language? Can you, for instance, recall any specific situations when
   • You were amused or surprised by something the child said and told others about it?
   • You incorporated a word or expression invented by a child into your own speech?
   Why do you think these incidents were so memorable?
3. What fingerplays, songs, rhymes, stories, books, or activities did _____ enjoy as an infant, toddler, or preschooler?
4. Did _____ ask to hear the same song, rhyme, or story over and over again? Which one?

5. Did _____ ever pretend to read? (Please describe.) Memorize a poem, song, or book?

6. Has _____ attended any special programs (such as storytime at the library)?

7. Has _____ begun to read? When and where did _____ first learn to read?

8. Does _____ scribble, draw, or write? What kinds of things does he or she write? Do you have any samples that you can share?

9. All learners face challenges. As you think about this child's progress in school, is there anything that might have a negative effect on the child's performance in school?

10. All children have gifts and talents. What areas of particular strength have you noticed in this child?

Participation Chart   As you discuss a book or a topic with a small group of children, check off their names when they contributed and jot down their comments. Particularly for repeated read-alouds, this gives you a record of participation and evidence of how their thinking has developed.

Cloze Activities   The cloze strategy is a test of children's comprehension. It consists of a story from which key words have been omitted and the child has to use knowledge gained from reading thus far to fill in the blanks. To see examples of cloze stories, visit www.enchantedlearning.com and click on the free Sample Pages for Prospective Subscribers; then select Cloze.

Graphic Organizers   Asking children to fill in a blank graphic organizer after listening to or reading a text is a check on their comprehension. For free copies of many different graphic organizers, see www.eduplace.com/graphicorganizers.

Observation Forms   Visit the Teacher Vision website (www.teachervision.fen.com). Begin searching by grade level and then choose "printables" and "observation." The site allows free printouts of three items.

Reading Log   Children should maintain a record of what they have read. You may want to create a grid with the date on the left-hand side. At the top, give children an opportunity to rate the difficulty of the books they selected or how much they enjoyed them using clip-art smiley faces ranging from smiling to frowning (Barone & Xu, 2008).

Class Checklists   One simple-to-use form of classroom-based assessment is a checklist. Type all of the children's names along the left-hand side and identify a skill—for instance, knowledge of the alphabet—as the focus. Across the top, list various skills and enter the date when certain milestones have been achieved below. For example, an early skill might be "knows first letter of his/her name," an intermediate skill might be "identifies some letters," and a more difficult skill would be "matches lowercase and uppercase letters."

Conclusion

The most important thing to remember about assessment is this: Never make a major decision using one small bit of information. One test score may tell you something, but it doesn't tell you very much. It is educational malpractice to use the results of a test to label a child and diminish that child's opportunities as a result of that label. Assessment should have positive outcomes for children.

Perhaps this seems overstated, but it happens to children every day. Consider, for example, the second-grade teacher who administers an end-of-unit reading test. The teacher decides on the basis of that test score alone to place certain children in a "low" reading group, where they remain all year. As the year progresses, it becomes apparent that some children are more advanced than other members of their group. But it would be too difficult for any of these children to catch up with the more advanced group, or there aren't enough students at the in-between level or not enough instructional time for the teacher to form a fourth group. As a result

of one test, these students are deprived of appropriate instruction.

Any conclusions drawn about a child's language ability should be based on data about his or her language, not just on one occasion but on numerous occasions, not just during a test but also during normal conversation, not only at school but also at home, and not only in interactions with adults but also in interactions with peers. It is only by looking for patterns within and across these contexts that we can begin to glimpse children's true language abilities.

PEARSON
myeducationkit To check your comprehension on the content covered in this chapter, go to the MyEducationKit for your book and complete the Study Plan for Chapter 13. Here you will be able to take a chapter quiz and receive feedback on your answers.

Research-Based Literacy Strategies

Assessing Reading Attitudes, Interests, and Motivation

Children in the early elementary grades tend to have positive attitudes about reading, but those attitudes diminish as they go through elementary school (Headley & Dunston, 2000). In addition to using observations or interviews, teachers can assess children's reading attitudes, interests, and motivation through surveys or questionnaires.

The Children's Motivations for Reading Scale (Baker & Scher, 2002) is a combination of several previously developed scales. Here are some sample items:

Enjoyment
1. I like to read.
2. I like to be read to.
3. I like to look at books by myself.

4. I get bored when the teacher reads stories.
5. I think reading is a good way to spend time.
6. I like to get books for presents.
7. I think reading is boring/fun.

Value
1. I think books can be used to find answers to questions.
2. I think I will need to know how to read to do well in school.
3. I think people can learn new things from books.
4. I think people can find things out from magazines and newspapers.

Perceived Competence
1. I think I will do well in reading next year.
2. Reading is easy/hard for me.
3. I think I will be a good reader.

Library Related

1. I like to get books from the library.
2. I like to go to the school library.

Electronic Literacy Assessment, Feedback, and Management

Reading with understanding is an essential outcome, and computers can be used to assess comprehension (Paris & Stahl, 2004). These programs have become increasingly sophisticated and offer several advantages, such as immediate feedback on students' answers to comprehension questions that prompts them to review portions of the text if they did not get the answer correct. In addition, students can self-test on books read at home, and some programs generate take-home reports for teacher and parent use.

Because these programs have a large number of questions, a child's reading level can be quickly ascertained. For children who are experiencing difficulty with reading, it is possible to revisit the same book without taking the same test. A few of the computerized tests also offer recommendations for teachers and maintain each child's work in an electronic portfolio.

Text-to-Speech Software

An electronic reader, one that converts print into spoken words, has great potential for supporting children's learning. One study found that using text-to-speech (TTS) software improved comprehension by 7 percent on average and that the gains were greater for poorer readers (Disseldorp & Chambers, 2003).

Consider this advice about using TTS:

1. TTS is often complex, so everyone needs a training period.
2. Formal planning should precede purchase, so that electronic readers become a regular and frequent component of the curriculum.
3. Consider the large amount of time necessary to scan in texts that are not digitized.
4. Develop a formal library operation to save and make available relevant documents.
5. Provide ongoing resources for teachers to examine and evaluate potential websites relevant to their students' needs.
6. Recognize that students will not be able to function independently with the electronic readers. Teachers or staff must be readily available to provide guidance and help.

An example of TTS is ReadPlease, which puts electronic text into a text box and reads it aloud using voice synthesis. There are also so-called talking word processors, such as TextHelp, Co-Writer, Write: Outloud, Textreader, IntelliTalk, TalkWrite (info@resourcekt.co.uk), KidWorks, Accelewrite, Talking Word for Windows, Talking PenDown, The Writing Set, ULTimate Reader, and Kurzweil's sophisticated system.

Links with Literature

Using Wordless Books as Assessment Tools

What Is a Wordless Book?

Wordless or almost wordless books are stories told through illustrations. Researchers have concluded that when children use the detailed illustrations found in wordless books as a prop for producing an oral or written story, their stories tend to be more elaborate (Norton, 2008). In the following example, Dianesha, age 6, has developed a script to accompany the pictures in the humorous wordless picture book *The Bear and the Fly*, by Paula Winter (1976), in which the father bear makes a huge mess of his house while attempting to kill a pesky fly that appears while the bear family is having dinner, but the fly escapes, unscathed.

Dad Bear: Everyone get back. I'm going to hit a fly.

Girl Child Bear: Dad's going to kill a fly?

Child Bear: Go! Go! Kill it.

Dad Bear: Whoops! I think I missed it.

Child Bear: There went dinner.

Dad Bear: Uuhh!

Mom Bear: You missed! That's my head you're hitting.

Child Bear: Hey, Dad, it's flying up my nose!

Dad Bear: I'm going to kill you, fly.

Child Bear: Dad! You hit me too!!!

Dad Bear: Ohhhh, I'm MAD. That's it—I'm gonna get you!

Mom Bear: (Knocked out) Naaapp.

Dad Bear: I'm going to hit you with a chair. Naah, I think I'll stand on a chair and hit you with a flyswatter. Uh-oh, I can't keep my balance. Ohhh noooo OHH NO.

Fly: (In a tiny voice) I'm going out the window—bye!

Wordless books range from very simple, like this one, to rather abstract and complex, such as Chris Van Allsburg's (1996) *The Mysteries of Harris Burdick* or David Weisner's (1999) *Sector 7* (an imaginary trip to the place where clouds are made) . This makes them ideal for adapting to individual needs. In addition, English language learners can use the illustrations in a wordless book such as *The Red Book* (Lehman, 2004) to produce texts in two languages, with the support of parents and families.

When using wordless books as an assessment tool, select several that are suited to the child's developmental level and then allow the child to choose. It is very important to give the child an opportunity to look through all of the pictures before expecting him or her to formulate a story. If the child wants to go through more than once, or look back at specific illustrations before (or while) dictating or writing the story, this is perfectly acceptable.

A child's ability to generate a story with the support of a wordless book can provide a valid measure of a student's narrative comprehension (Paris & Paris, 2003). Analyze the child's story in response to the illustrations for the following elements:

• Was the child able to use prior knowledge to make sense out of the wordless book? Does the story demonstrate an understanding of the pictures, the overall sequence, and key events in the plot?

• Is there evidence of story language, of specific words or phrases that are used in stories such as "Once upon a time" or "The End"?

• How did the child demonstrate knowledge about the ways of the storyteller (e.g., changing voice for different characters, conveying emotions through facial expressions)?

• Does the child relate the illustrations in the wordless book to personal experiences and/or incorporate them into the story?

• Does the child's original story in response to the pictures demonstrate the child's basic understanding of the theme, motif, or moral of the story? (adapted from Rasinski, 2004)

For more about activities to accompany wordless books, see http://picturingbooks.imaginarylands .org/resources/wordless.html. For a list of wordless books, visit www.lfpl.org/kidspages/booklists/ wordless.htm.

Some recently published wordless books include, for younger children, *Peep!* (Luthardt, 2004), *Carl Goes to Daycare* (Day, 2002), *Busy, Busy Mouse* (Kroll, 2004), *Once upon a Banana* (Armstrong, 2006), and, for older students, *Arrival* (Tan, 2007), *Rainstorms* (Lehman, 2007), *Flotsam* (Weisner, 2006), and *Hot Air: The (Mostly) True Story of the First Air Balloon Ride* (Priceman, 2006).

ELLs

Home Language Surveys

Comprehensive language assessment needs to consider children's language at home as well as in school. This is particularly important for ELLs because their proficiency in their native language may be far in advance of their abilities to use English (Paez, DeTemple, & Snow, 2000). Home language surveys consist of simple questions for families that guide teachers in deciding the optimal level of support in L1 for the child to acquire the second language of English (Ballantyne, Sanderman, & McLaughlin, 2008). A home language survey or family language history is designed to answer the basic question, What does the child know and in what language? Studies of infants, toddlers, and preschoolers suggest that parents' and families' reports on their children's language development are useful and reasonably reliable (Hamilton, Plunkett, & Schafer, 2000; Kummere, Lopez-Reyna, & Hughes, 2007; Paterson, 2000; Thal, O'Hanlon, Clemmons, & Fralin, 1999). That is, when bilingual parents'

reports on their toddlers' language were compared with videotaped samples of the children's language, researchers concluded that parents provided reasonably reliable information about their children's language behaviors (Paterson, 2000).

Using materials from the Illinois State Board of Education (2008), which offers a home language survey that has been translated into 20 languages, and from Restrepo and Silverman (2001), work in groups to design a simple set of questions to get information from parents and families about their young children's language use.

How Do I ...
Get Started with Differentiating Instruction?

Differentiation refers to the strategies that teachers use to adapt the curriculum so that all children can experience success (Lapp, Fisher, & Wolsey, 2009). These modifications to instructional strategies and the overall curriculum are particularly important in inclusive settings (Cook, Klein, & Tessier, 2008) and in work with English language learners (Rothenberg & Fisher, 2007). Differentiated instruction is based on the assumption that the most effective teaching practices are those that consider all learners in a classroom setting and make accommodations in response to academic, cultural, linguistic, and socioeconomic diversity (Santamaria, 2009; Tomlinson & McTighe, 2006).

One way to begin is to think about a range of possible responses from students to a similar activity. For each activity you plan, try thinking along the lines of the basic activity and then consider ways to make it less challenging and more challenging. Use the following two examples to get started. Work with a partner or group to identify several activities and less difficult/more difficult possibilities. Then think about how these might be set up as activities to which children have access in classroom centers.

Activity. Pairs of Opposites

Center. Publishing center

Age range. Kindergarten/primary

Area of development. Cognitive, language, fine motor

Objective. Working with partners, the children will produce pairs of drawings that illustrate word pairs that are opposites.

Materials. Paper and crayons

Procedure. First, the teacher will invite children to demonstrate a pair of opposites. Begin by asking one child to go across the room quickly and then asking another child to go across the room slowly. Next, the teacher will demonstrate *big* and *little* using blocks and then *old* and *new* using toys or other objects. The teacher will lead children in playing a game called Guess the Opposite by giving children one word and asking them to think of opposites they have had experience with—for example, *happy/sad, dirty/clean, hot/cold, day/night, yes/no, up/down, hello/goodbye.* The children's ideas will be written on the chalkboard. Next, the teacher will group children in pairs and distribute one set of paper and crayons to each team of two.

Planning. Assign children to partners so that one child who is drawing representationally is on each team. Ask children to raise their hands when they have decided on an opposite pair to illustrate so that you can make sure they understand the concept before they begin to draw. Children who are having difficulty can select one of the opposite pairs from the chalkboard to illustrate.

Extensions. Children's drawings can be compiled into a class book. Children can create a matching game by drawing pictures of opposites on cards. Books about opposites might be added to the literacy center. A day/night collage that combines drawings, pictures cut out of magazines, and objects to illustrate the activities and moods associated with daytime (on a piece of white paper) and nighttime (on a piece of black paper) can be produced by a small group of children.

Less challenging. Suggest several pairs of opposites to the children; then let each child choose one to illustrate.

More challenging. Invite children who understand the concept well to make a guessing game. One card has a drawing and the word underneath it. The matching card has a question mark on one side and the answer on the back.

Activity. Write around the Room

Center. Writing center

Age range. Kindergarten/primary

Area of development. Language, fine motor

Objective. The children will walk around the room and search for examples of writing. They will be able to write down examples of letters and numerals, other children's names, words, and sentences that they see in their classroom.

Materials. Paper and pencil or crayon for each child. One clipboard.

Procedure. Before the children arrive, the teacher will put written labels on many of the items around the classroom, such as the desk, window, water table, blocks, and so forth. If there are speakers of other languages in the class, these labels will be written in both languages with help from community volunteers. The teacher will assemble the children in a circle and ask them if

they notice anything new. Then children will be invited to look around the room for examples of letters or words. Children will take turns pointing out examples, such as the alphabet, lists of children's names, bulletin boards, book covers, and other written material. The teacher will explain that throughout the day, each child will have an opportunity to write around the room by going around with a clipboard and recording words that he or she has seen.

Planning. Make sure that you demonstrate for the children how this is done. Emphasize that the children's writing can be different—that some might write with scribbles, some might write just the first letter of objects, some might sketch and write, and others might write words and sentences. Encourage each child to try and find one word that other children might have missed.

Extensions. Invite children to work in small groups to illustrate some of the words that they wrote and create a picture dictionary.

During the first week of school, put a big piece of paper up on the wall and ask children to sign in by writing their names. This will give you a quick idea about their prior experiences with writing. Repeat this activity near the middle and at the end of the schoolyear. Put up all the signatures and ask children to compare their progress.

Let children use the clipboard to conduct simple surveys (favorite colors, foods, types of travel). Then compile the information into a simple chart.

Less challenging. Instruct children who may have difficulty forming letters to pretend to write or draw what they see.

More challenging. Have some children draw pictures. Ask the children who have more advanced language abilities to write captions for the drawings to indicate what the figures in the drawings might be saying.

PEARSON **myeducationkit**™   Now go to Chapter 13 in the MyEducationKit (**www.MyEducationKit**
.com) for your book, where you can:

■ Find Chapter Objectives.

■ Complete Assignments and Activities that can help you more deeply understand the chapter content.

■ Extend knowledge with content-specific Web Links.

■ Check your comprehension on the content covered in the chapter by going to the Study Plan. Here you will be able to take a chapter quiz, receive feedback on your answers, and then access resources that will enhance your understanding of chapter content.

References

Adams, M. J. (1990). *Beginning to read: Thinking and learning about print.* Cambridge, MA: MIT Press.

Aiken, J. (1982). *The way to write for children.* New York: St. Martin's.

Aldridge, J., Kirkland, L., & Kuby, P. (2002). *Jumpstarters: Integrating environmental print throughout the curriculum* (3rd ed.). Birmingham, AL: Campus Press.

Allington, R., & McGill-Franzen, A. (2003). The impact of summer setback on the reading achievement gap. *Phi Delta Kappan, 85*(1), 68–75.

Allington, R. L., & Walmsley, S. A. (2007). *No quick fix: Rethinking literacy programs in American's elementary schools.* New York: Teachers College Press.

Alvermann, D. E. (1991). The discussion web: A graphic aid for learning across the curriculum. *The Reading Teacher, 45*(2), 92–99.

American Academy of Pediatrics. (2001). *Kids and television.* Available: www.aap.org

American Psychological Association. (2005). *Violence in the media: Psychologists help protect children from harmful effects.* Available: http://psychologymatters.apa.org/mediaviolence.html

Amsterlaw, J., Lagattuta, K. H., & Meltzoff, A. N. (2009). Young children's reasoning about the effects of emotional and physiological states on academic performance. *Child Development, 80*(1), 115–133.

Anderson, R. C., Hiebert, E. H., Scott, J. A., & Wilkinson, I. A. G. (1985). *Becoming a nation of readers: The report of the Commission on Reading.* Washington, DC: United States Office of Education.

Annett, M. M. (2004). Building foundations for literacy: Program trains parents as reading partners. *The ASHA Leader, 9*(1), 12.

Annie E. Casey Foundation. (2005). *Kids count.* Available: www.kidscount.org

Anthony, J. L., & Lonigan, C. J. (2004). The nature of phonological awareness: Converging evidence from four studies of preschool and early grade school children. *Journal of Educational Psychology, 96*(1), 43–56.

Anthony, J. L., Williams, J. M., McDonald, R., & Francis, D. J. (2007). Phonological processing and emergent literacy in younger and older preschool children. *Annals of Dyslexia, 57*(2), 113–137.

Applebee, A. (1978). *A child's concept of story: Ages two to seventeen.* Chicago: University of Chicago Press.

Aram, D., & Biron, S. (2004). Joint storybook reading and joint writing interventions among low SES preschoolers: Differential contributions to early literacy. *Early Childhood Research Quarterly, 19*(4), 588–610.

Aram, D., & Levin, I. (2002). Mother-child joint writing and story book reading: Relations with literacy among low SES kindergarteners. *Merrill-Palmer Quarterly, 48,* 202–224.

Armbruster, B. B., Lehr, F., & Osborn, J. (2003). *A child becomes a reader.* Portsmouth, NH: Heinemann.

Armington, D. (1997). *The living classroom: Reading, writing, and beyond.* Washington, DC: National Association for the Education of Young Children.

Association for Childhood Education International Diversity Committee. (2008). Diversity education: Respect, equality, and social justice. *Childhood Education, 84,* 158–159. Available: www.acei.org/diversityed_84_3_158f.htm

Au, K. (1993). *Literacy instruction in multicultural settings.* Fort Worth, TX: Harcourt Brace Jovanovich.

August, D., & Shanahan, T. (Eds.). (2008). *Developing reading and second-language learners: Lessons from the Report of the National Panel on Language-Minority Children and Youth.* New York: Routledge.

Ayers, W. (2001). *To teach: The journey of a teacher* (2nd ed.). New York: Teachers College Press.

Baghban, N. (2007a). Immigration in childhood: Using picture books to cope. *Social Studies, 98,* 71–77.

Baghban, N. (2007b). Scribbles, labels, and stories: The role of drawing in the development of writing. *Young Children, 62,* 20–26.

Baker, I., & Schiffer, M. B. (2007). The reading chair: All interest areas need books so spread those books around. *Young Children, 62*(3), 44–49.

Baker, L., & Scher, D. (2002). Beginning readers' motivation for reading in relation to parental beliefs and home reading practices. *Reading Psychology, 23*(4) 239–269.

Bakhtin, M. (1981). Discourse in the novel. In C. Emerson and M. Holquist (Eds.), *The dialogic imagination: Four essays by M. Bakhtin* (pp. 259–422). Austin: University of Texas.

Baldwin, J. L., Adams, S. M., & Kelly, M. K. (2009). Science at the center: An emergent, standards-based, child-centered framework for early learners. *Early Childhood Education Journal, 37*(1), 71–77.

Ballantyne, K. G., Sanderman, A. R., & McLaughlin, N. (2008). *Dual language learners in the early years: Getting ready to succeed in school.* Washington, DC:

National Clearinghouse for English Language Acquisition. Available: www.ncela.gwu.edu/resabout/ecell/earlyyears.pdf

Bandura, A. (1997). *Self-efficacy: The exercise of control.* New York: Freeman.

Barbarin, O., Bryant, D., McCandies, T., Burchinal, M., Early, D., Clifford, R., et al. (2006). Children enrolled in public pre-K: The relation of family life, neighborhood quality, and socioeconomic resources to early competence. *American Journal of Orthopsychiatry, 76*(2), 265–276.

Barclay, K. (2009). Click, clack, moo: Designing effective reading instruction for children in preschool and early primary grades. *Childhood Education, 85*(3), 167–172.

Baron, N. S. (2005). Dick and Jane meet HTML. *Language Sciences, 27*(1), 137–142.

Barone, D. M., & Xu, S. H. (2008). *Literacy instruction for English language learners pre-K–2.* New York: Guilford.

Barton, B., & Booth, D. (1990). *Stories in the classroom: Storytelling, reading aloud, and role playing with children.* Portsmouth, NH: Heinemann.

Barton, P. E. (2004). Why does the gap persist? *Educational Leadership, 62*(3), 9–13.

Barton, P. E., & Coley, R. J. (2007). *The family: America's smallest school.* Princeton, NJ: Educational Testing Service.

Bauer, C. F. (1983). *This way to books.* New York: H. W. Wilson.

Bauer, C. F. (1987). *Presenting reader's theater.* New York: H. W. Wilson.

Bauer, C. F. (1993). *New handbook for storytellers.* Chicago: American Library Association.

Baumann, J. F., Kame'enui, E. J., & Ash, G. E. (2003). Research on vocabulary instruction: Voltaire redux. In J. Flood, D. Lapp, J. R. Squire, & J. M. Jensen (Eds.), *Handbook of research on teaching in the English language arts* (pp. 752–785). Mahwah, NJ: Lawrence Erlbaum.

Baxendell, B. W. (2003). Consistent, coherent, creative: The 3C's of graphic organizers. *Teaching Exceptional Children, 35*(3), 46–53.

Bayless, K. M., & Ramsey, M. E. (1990). *Music: A way of life for the young child.* New York: Macmillan.

Beals, D. E. (2001). Eating and reading: Links between family conversations with preschoolers and later language literacy. In D. Dickinson & P. O. Tabors (Eds.), *Beginning literacy with language: Young children learning at home and school* (pp. 75–92). Baltimore: Paul H. Brookes.

Bear, D. R., Invernizzi, M., Templeton, S., & Johnston, F. (2007). *Words their way: Word study for phonics, vocabulary, and spelling instruction* (4th ed.). Upper Saddle River, NJ: Prentice Hall.

Beck, I. L., McKeown, M. G., & Kucan, L. (2002). *Bringing words to life: Robust vocabulary instruction.* New York: Guilford.

Beck, I. L., McKeown, M. G., & Kucan, L. (2008). *Creating robust vocabulary: Frequently asked questions and extended examples.* New York: Guilford.

Bennett-Armistead, V. S., Duke, N. K., & Moses, A. (2006). *Literacy and the youngest learner: Best practices for educators of children from birth to 5.* New York: Scholastic.

Berger, E. H. (2007). *Parents as partners in education: Families and schools working together.* Upper Saddle River, NJ: Prentice Hall.

Berghoff, B. (1997). Living a literate life. *Language Arts, 74*(5), 316–324.

Bergman, O. (2005). Wait for me! Reader control of narration rate in talking books. Available: www.reading-online.org/articles/art_index.asp?HREF=bergman/index.html

Best, R., Floyd, R., & McNamara, D. (2008). Differential competencies contributing to children's comprehension of narrative and expository texts. *Reading Psychology, 29*(2), 137–164.

Bettelheim, B. (1976). *The uses of enchantment: The meaning and importance of fairy tales.* New York: Knopf.

Biemiller, A., & Slonim, N. (2001). Estimating root word vocabulary growth in normative and advantaged populations: Evidence for a common sequence of vocabulary acquisition. *Journal of Educational Psychology, 93*(3), 498–520.

Birbili, M. (2006). Mapping knowledge: Concept maps in early childhood education. *Early Childhood Research & Practice, 8*(2). Available: http://ecrp.uiuc.edu/v8n2/birbili.html

Bishop, D. V., & Snowling, M. J. (2004). Developmental dyslexia and specific language impairment: Same or different? *Psychological Bulletin, 130*(6), 858–886.

Bissex, G. (1980). *GYNS at work: A child learns to read and write.* Cambridge, MA: Harvard University.

Blass, E. M., Anderson, D. R., Kirkorian, H. L., Pempek, T. A., Price, I., & Koleini, M. F. (2006). On the road to obesity: Television viewing increases intake of high-density foods. *Physiology and Behavior, 88*, 587–604.

Block, C. C., & Israel, S. E. (2004). The ABCs of performing highly effective think-alouds. *The Reading Teacher, 58*(2), 154–167.

Bloome, D., Champion, T., Katz, L., Morton, M. B., & Muldrow, R. (2001). Spoken and written narrative development: African American preschoolers as storytellers and story makers. In J. L. Harris, A. G.

Kamhi, & K. E. Pollock (Eds.), *Literacy in African American communities* (pp. 45–76). Mahwah, NJ: Lawrence Erlbaum.

Bodrova, E., & Leong, D. (2007). *Tools of the mind: The Vygotskian approach to early childhood education.* Upper Saddle River, NJ: Merrill/Prentice Hall.

Bond, G. L., Tinker, M. A., Wasson, B. B., & Wasson, J. B. (1994). *Reading difficulties: Their diagnosis and correction* (7th ed.). Boston: Allyn & Bacon.

Bond, M. A., & Wasik, B. A. (2009). Conversation stations: Promoting language in early childhood classrooms. *Early Childhood Education Journal, 36*(6), 467–473.

Bonoti, F., Vlachos, F., & Metallidou, P. (2005). Writing and drawing performance of school-age children. *School Psychology International, 26*(2), 243–256.

Bornstein, M. (Ed.). (2009). *Handbook of parenting: Biology and ecology of parenting, Volume 2* (2nd ed.). Mahwah, NJ: Lawrence Erlbaum.

Bouchard, M. (2001). *ESL Smart! Ready-to-use life skills and academic activities for grades K–8.* Bloomington, IN: Center for Applied Research in Education.

Boyd, D., & Bee, H. (2010). *The growing child.* Boston: Allyn & Bacon.

Boyer, E. (1996). 5 priorities for quality schools. *Education Digest, 62*(1), 4–8.

Boyer, W. (2008). Parental and educator perspectives on young children's acquisition of self-regulatory skills. In M. R. Jalongo (Ed.), *Enduring bonds: The significance of interpersonal relationships in young children's lives* (pp. 23–38). New York: Springer.

Bracken, B. A., & Nagle, R. J. (Eds.). (2006). *The psychoeducational assessment of preschool children* (4th ed.). Mahwah, NJ: Lawrence Erlbaum.

Bradham, E. G., & Brown, C. L. (2002). Effects of teachers' reading-aloud styles on vocabulary acquisition and comprehension of students in the early elementary grades. *Journal of Educational Psychology, 94*(3), 465–473.

Branson, D., Vigil, D. C., & Bingham, A. (2008). Community childcare providers' role in the early detection of autism spectrum disorders. *Early Childhood Education Journal, 35*(6), 523–530.

Brassard, M. R., & Boehm, A. E. (2007). *Preschool assessment, principles and practices.* New York: Guilford.

Braunger, J., & Lewis, J. P. (2005). *Building a knowledge base in reading* (2nd ed.). Portland, OR: Northwest Regional Laboratory.

Brent, R., & Anderson, P. (1993). Developing children's classroom listening strategies. *The Reading Teacher, 47*(2), 122–126.

Brittain, W. (1979). *Creativity, art and the young child.* New York: Macmillan.

Brown, H., & Cambourne, B. (1990). *Read and retell.* Portsmouth, NH: Heinemann.

Brown, L. J., & Jalongo, M. R. (1986). Make parent-teacher conferences better. *PTA Today, 12*(1), 14–16.

Brown, P. M., Rickards, F. W., & Bortoli, A. (2001). Structures underpinning pretend play and word production in young hearing children and children with hearing loss. *Journal of Deaf Studies & Deaf Education, 6*(1), 15–31.

Bruer, J. T. (1993). The mind's journey from novice to expert. *American Educator, 17*(2), 6–15, 38–46.

Bruner, J. S. (2004). *The process of education* (Rev. ed.). Cambridge, MA: Harvard University Press.

Bryan, T., & Burstein, K. (2004). Improving homework completion and academic performance: Lessons from special education. *Theory Into Practice, 43*(3), 213–220.

Burke, M. D., & Hagan-Burke, S. (2007). Concurrent validity of first grade early literacy indicators. *Assessment for Effective Intervention, 32*(2), 66–77.

Burke, M. D., Hagan-Burke, S., Kwok, O., & Parker, R. (2009). Predictive validity of early literacy indicators from the middle of kindergarten to second grade. *The Journal of Special Education, 42*(4), 209–226.

Burningham, L. M., & Dever, M. T. (2005). An interactive model for fostering family literacy. *Young Children, 60*(5), 87–94.

Bus, A. G. (2001). Joint caregiver-child storybook reading: A route to literacy development. In S. B. Neuman & D. K. Dickinson (Eds.), *Handbook of early literacy research.* (pp. 179–191). New York: Guilford.

Bus, A. G., & van IJzendoorn, M. H. (1999). Phonological awareness and early reading: A meta-analysis of experimental training studies. *Journal of Educational Psychology, 91*(3), 403–413.

Butler, D. (1975). *Cushla and her books.* Boston: The Horn Book.

Butler, D. (1998). *Babies need books* (Rev. ed.). Portsmouth, NH: Heinemann.

Byrne, B., Freebody, P., & Gates, A. (1992). Longitudinal data on the relations of word-reading strategies to comprehension, reading time, and phonemic awareness. *Reading Research Quarterly, 27*(2), 141–151.

Byrnes, J. P., & Wasik, B. A. (2009). *Language and literacy development: What educators need to know.* New York: Guilford.

Cabell, S. Q., Justice, L. M., Zucker, T. A., & Kilday, C. R. (2009). Validity of teacher report for assessing the emergent literacy skills of at-risk preschoolers. *Language, Speech, & Hearing Services in Schools, 40*(2), 161–173.

Cabrera, M., & Martinez, P. (2001). The effects of repetition, comprehension checks, and gestures on primary school children in an EFL situation. *English Language Teachers Journal, 55*(3), 281–288.

Calkins, L. M. (2003). *Units of study for primary writing: A yearlong curriculum.* Portsmouth, NH: FirstHand.

Calkins, L. M., Hartman, A., & White, Z. (2005). *One to one: The art of conferring with young writers.* Portsmouth, NH: Heinemann.

Cambourne, B. (1995). Toward an educationally relevant theory of literacy learning: Twenty years of inquiry. *The Reading Teacher, 49*(3), 182–190.

Cambourne, B. (2001). Conditions for literacy learning: Why do some students fail to learn to read? Ockham's razor and the conditions of learning. *The Reading Teacher, 54*(8), 784–786.

Camp, D. (2000). It takes two: Teaching with twin texts of fact and fiction. *The Reading Teacher, 53*(5), 400–440.

Cappello, M. (2006). Under construction: Voice and identity development in writing workshop. *Language Arts, 83*(6), 482–491.

Carasquillo, A. L., & Rodriguez, V. (2002). *Language minority students in the mainstream classroom* (2nd ed.). Philadelphia: Multilingual Matters.

Carnine, D. W., Silbert, J., Kame'enui, E. J., & Tarver, S. G. (2010). *Direct instruction reading* (5th ed.). Upper Saddle River, NJ: Pearson.

Carr, J. F., & Harris, D. E. (2001). *Succeeding with standards: Linking curriculum, assessment, and action planning.* Alexandria, VA: Association for Supervision and Curriculum Development.

Carter, D. R., Chard, D. J., & Pool, J. L. (2009). A family strengths approach to early language and literacy development. *Early Childhood Education Journal, 36*(5), 519–526.

Carter, M., & Curtis, D. (1994). *Training teachers: A harvest of theory and practice.* St. Paul, MN: Redleaf.

Carter, M., & Curtis, D. (2007). *Learning together with young children: A curriculum framework for reflective teachers.* St. Paul, MN: Redleaf.

Cassady, J. C., Smith, L. L., & Putnam, S. M. (2008). Phonological awareness development as a discrete process: Evidence for an integrative model. *Reading Psychology, 29*(6), 508–530.

Cavaretta, J. (1998). Parents are a school's best friend. *Educational Leadership, 55*(8), 12–14.

Center for Media Education. (2009). *Plugging in parents: Websites to help mom and dad.* Available: www.cme.org

Center for Media Literacy. (2007). Five key questions that can change the world: Lesson plans for media literacy. Available: www.medialit.org/pdf/mlk/02_5KQ_ClassroomGuide.pdf

Center for Technology in Education Technology and Media Division. (2005). *Considering the need for assis-tive technology within the individualized education pro-gram.* Columbia, MD, and Arlington, VA: Author.

Center for the Improvement of Early Reading Achievement. (2001). *Putting reading first: The research building blocks for teaching children to read.* Bethesda, MD: National Institute of Child Health and Human Development.

Centers for Disease Control and Prevention. (2010). *Autism spectrum disorders (ASDS).* Available: www.cdc.gov/ncbddd/autism

Chafel, J. A., Flint, A. S., Hammel, J., & Pomeroy, K. H. (2007). Young children, social issues, and critical literacy: Stories of teachers and researchers. *Young Children, 62*(1), 73–81.

Chagnon, L. T. (2004). *Yes, YOU can teach someone to read.* Bloomington, IN: AuthorHouse.

Chang, N. (2000). Reasoning with children about violent television shows and related toys. *Early Childhood Education Journal, 28*(2), 85–89.

Children's Defense Fund. (2008). *The state of America's children.* Washington, DC: Author. Available: www.childrensdefense.org/child-research-data-publications/data/state-of-americas-children-2008-report.html

Chomsky, N. (1988). *Language and mind.* New York: Harcourt Brace and World.

Christakis, D. A., Zimmerman, F. J., DiGiuseppe, D. L., & McCarty, C. A. (2004). Early television exposure and subsequent attentional problems in children. *Pediatrics, 113*(4), 708–713.

Christian, L. G. (2006). Understanding families: Applying family systems theory to early childhood practice. *Young Children, 61*(1), 12–20.

Ciancolo, P. (1984). Illustrations in picture books. In Z. Sutherland and M. C. Livingston (Eds.), *The Scott Foresman anthology of children's literature* (pp. 846–878). Glenview, IL: Scott Foresman.

Cirino, P. T., Pollard-Durodola, S. D., Foorman, B. R., Carlson, C. D., & Francis, D. J. (2007). Teacher characteristics, classroom instruction, and student literacy and language outcomes for bilingual kindergartners. *Elementary School Journal, 107*(4), 341–364.

Clay, M. (1975). *What did I write?* Portsmouth, NH: Heinemann.

Clay, M. M. (1992). *Reading Recovery: A guide for teachers in training.* Portsmouth, NH: Heinemann.

Clay, M. M. (2000). *Concepts about print: What have children learned about the way we print language?* Portsmouth, NH: Heinemann.

Cleaveland, L., & Ray, K. W. (2004). *Writing workshop with our youngest writers.* Portsmouth, NH: Heinemann.

Clements-Stephens, A. M., Rimrodt, S. L., & Cutting, L. E. (2009). Developmental sex differences in basic visuospatial processing: Differences in strategy use? *Neuroscience Letters, 449*(3), 155–160.

Cliatt, M. J. P., & Shaw, J. M. (1988). The story time exchange: Ways to enhance it. *Childhood Education, 64*(5), 293–298.

Clopton, K. L., & East, K. K. (2008a). A list of books about a parent in prison. *Early Childhood Education Journal, 36*(2), 199–200.

Clopton, K. L., & East, K. K. (2008b). "Are there other kids like me?" Children with a parent in prison. *Early Childhood Education Journal, 36*(2), 195–198.

Coates, E. (2002). "I forgot the sky!" Children's stories contained within their drawings. *International Journal of Early Years Education, 10*(1), 21–36.

Cochran-Smith, M. (1986). Reading to children: A model for understanding texts. In B. B. Scheifflim & P. Gilmore (Eds.), *The acquisition of literacy: Ethnographic perspectives* (pp. 35–59). Norwood, NJ: Ablex.

Cohen, D. H., Stern, V., Balaban, N., & Gropper, N. (2008). *Observing and recording the behavior of young children* (5th ed.). New York: Teachers College Press.

Cohen, L. E. (1997). How I developed my kindergarten book backpack program. *Young Children, 52*(2), 69–71.

Cole, E. B., & Flexer, C. A. (2007). *Children with hearing loss: Developing listening and talking, birth to six.* San Diego, CA: Plural Publishing.

Collins, F. M., & Svenson, F. M. (2008). If I had a magic wand I'd magic her out the book: The rich literacy practices of competent early readers. *Early Years: Journal of International Research and Development, 28*(1), 81–91.

Coltrane, B. (2003). *Working with young English language learners: Some considerations.* Washington, DC: ERIC Clearinghouse on Language and Linguistics. (ERIC Digest No. 481 690)

Comber, B. (2003). Critical literacy in the early years. In N. Hall and J. Marsh (Eds.), *Handbook of early literacy* (pp. 355–368). London: Sage.

Comber, B., & Simpson, A. (2001). *Negotiating critical literacies in classrooms.* Mahwah, NJ: Lawrence Erlbaum.

Comer, J. (1998). Lunch with Lois . . . James Comer. *Our Children: The National PTA Magazine, 23*(8), 11–12.

Compton-Lilly, C. (2007). What can video games teach us about reading? *The Reading Teacher, 60*(8), 718–727.

Conteh, J. (2007). Opening doors to success in multilingual classrooms: Bilingualism, code switching and the professional identities of ethnic minority primary teachers. *Language and Education, 21*(6), 457–472.

Cook, R. E., Klein, M. D., & Tessier, A. (2008). *Adapting early childhood curricula for children in inclusive settings.* Upper Saddle River, NJ: Pearson/Merrill/Prentice Hall.

Cook-Cottone, C. (2004). Constructivism in family literacy practices: Parents as mentors. *Reading Improvement, 41*(4), 208–216.

Copple, C., & Bredekamp, S. (2009). *Developmentally appropriate practice in early childhood programs serving children from birth through age 8* (3rd ed.). Washington, DC: National Association for the Education of Young Children.

Coyne, M. D., Kame'enui, E. J., & Harn, D. C. (2004). Beginning reading intervention as innoculation or insulin: First grade reading performance of strong responders to kindergarten intervention. *Journal of Learning Disabilities, 37*(2), 90–104.

Craft Al-Hazza, T., & Gupta, A. (2006). Reading tutor checklist: A guide for supplemental reading support for volunteer tutors. *Preventing School Failure, 50*(4), 15–22.

Crandell, C. C., Flexer, C. A., & Smaldino, J. J. (2004). *Sound-field amplification: Applications to speech perception and classroom acoustics.* Bel Air, CA: Singular.

Creamer, T. S., & Baker, T. K. (2000). Book access, shared reading, and audio models: The effects of supporting the literacy learning of linguistically diverse students in school and at home. *Journal of Educational Psychology, 92*, 23–36.

Crepeau, I. M., & Richards, M. A. (2003). *A show of hands: Using puppets with young children.* St. Paul, MN: Redleaf.

Črnčec, R., Wilson, S., & Prior, M. (2006). The cognitive and academic benefits of music to children: Facts and fiction. *Educational Psychology, 26*(4), 579–594.

Crosse, K. (2007). *Introducing English as an additional language to young children.* London: Paul Chapman.

Cruger, M. (2005). The parent letter. About our kids: A letter for parents by the NYU child study center. *The Parent Letter, 3*(7), 1–2.

Culham, R. (2005). *6 + 1 traits of writing: The complete guide for the primary grades.* New York: Scholastic.

Cummins, J. (2003). Bilingual children's mother tongue: Why is it important for education? Available: www.multiverse.ac.uk/viewarticle2.aspx?contentId=390 and www.iteachilearn.com/cummins/mother.htm

Cunningham, P. (2008). *Phonics they use* (5th ed.). Boston: Allyn & Bacon.

Dailey, K. (2008). Sharing centers. In M. Jalongo, *Learning to listen, listening to learn: Strategies for young children*. Washington, DC: National Association for the Education of Young Children.

Dale, P. (1976). *Language development*. New York: Holt Rinehart & Winston.

D'Angiulli, A., Siegel, L. S., & Serra, E. (2000). The development of reading in English and Italian in bilingual children. *Applied Psycholinguistics, 22,* 479–507.

Daniels, H. (2002). *Literature circles: Voice and choice in book clubs and reading groups* (2nd ed.). York, ME: Stenhouse.

David, J., Onchonga, O., Drew, R., Grass, R., Stuchuk, R., & Burns, M. S. (2006). Head Start embraces language diversity. *Young Children, 60*(6), 40–43.

Davis, P. (2007). Storytelling as a democratic approach to data collection: Interviewing children about reading. *Educational Research, 49*(2), 169–184.

DeBruin-Parecki, A. (2008). Storybook reading as a standardized measurement of early literacy skill development. In A. DeBruin-Parecki (Ed.), *Effective early literacy practice: Here's how, here's why* (pp. 1–14). Baltimore: Paul H. Brookes.

DeBruin-Parecki, A. (2009). Establishing a family literacy program with a focus on interactive reading: The role of research and accountability. *Early Childhood Education Journal, 36*(5), 381–460.

DeHaven, E. P. (1988). *Teaching and learning the language arts* (3rd ed.). Boston: Little, Brown.

De Marrais, K. B., Nelson, P. A., & Baker, J. H. (1994). Meaning in mud: Yup'ik Eskimo girls at play. In J. L. Rooparine, J. E. Johnson, & F. H. Hooper (Eds.), *Children at play in diverse cultures* (pp. 179–209). Albany, NY: SUNY Press.

Denton, C., Parker, R., & Jasbrouck, J. E. (2003). How to tutor very young students with reading problems. *Preventing School Failure, 48*(1), 42–44.

Denton, K., West, J., & Walston, J. (2003). *Reading—Young children's reading and classroom experience: Findings from The Condition of Education 2003.* Washington, DC: National Center for Education Statistics,

Dickinson, D. K., & Neuman, S. B. (2006). *Handbook of early literacy research, volume 2.* New York: Guilford.

Dickinson, D. K., & Snow, C. E. (1987). Interrelationships among prereading and oral language skills in kindergartners from two social classes. *Early Childhood Research Quarterly, 2*(1), 1–25.

Disseldorp, B., & Chambers, D. (2003). *Selecting the right technology for students in changing teaching environment: A case study.* Available: http://crpit.com/Published-PapersNJS.html

Division for Early Childhood. (2007). *Promoting positive outcomes for children with disabilities: Recommendations for curriculum, assessment and program evaluation.* Missoula, MT: Author.

Dixon, S. D. (2008). Language is everywhere! Universally designed strategies to nurture oral and written language. *Young Exceptional Children, 11*(4), 2–12.

Doake, D. (1986). Learning to read: It starts in the home. In D. R. Torrey & J. E. Kerber (Eds.), *Roles in literacy learning: A new perspective* (pp. 2–9). Newark, DE: International Reading Association.

Donohue, C., Fox, S., & Torrence, D. (2007). Early childhood educators as eLearners: Engaging approaches to teaching and learning online. *Young Children, 62*(4), 34–40.

Downs, A., & Strand, P. (2006). Using assessment to improve the effectiveness of early childhood education. *Journal of Child & Family Studies, 15*(6), 671–680.

Dreher, M. J. (2003). Motivating struggling readers by tapping the potential of information books. *Reading & Writing Quarterly, 19*(1), 25–39.

Dugan, J. (1997). Transactional literature discussions: Engaging students in the appreciation and understanding of literature. *The Reading Teacher, 51*(2), 86–96.

Duke, N. K. (2003). Reading to learn from the very beginning: Information books in early childhood. *Young Children, 58*(2), 14–20.

Duke, N. K., & Kays, J. (1998). "Can I say 'once upon a time'?": Kindergarten children developing knowledge of information book language. *Early Childhood Research Quarterly, 13*(2), 295–318.

Dwyer, J., & Neuman, S. B. (2008). Selecting books for children birth through four: A developmental approach. *Early Childhood Education Journal, 35*(6), 489–494.

Dyson, A. H. (1988). *Multiple worlds of child writers.* New York: Teachers College Press.

Dyson, A. H. (1993). *Social worlds of children learning to write in an urban primary school.* New York: Teachers College Press.

Dyson, A. H. (2006). On saying it right (write): "Fix-its" in the foundation of learning to write. *Research in the Teaching of English, 41*(1), 8–44.

Dyson, A. H. (2007). School literacy and the development of a child culture: Written remnants of the "gusto of life." In D. Thiessen & A. Cook-Sather (Eds.), *International handbook of student experiences in elementary and secondary school* (pp. 115–142). Dordrecht, The Netherlands: Kluwer.

Dyson, A. H. (2008a). On listening to child composers: Beyond "fix-its." In C. Genisi & A. L. Goodwin (Eds.), *Diversities in early childhood education: Rethinking and doing* (pp. 13–28). New York: Routledge.

Dyson, A. H. (2008b). Research directions: The Pine Cone Wars: Studying writing in a community of children. *Language Arts, 85*(4), 305–316.

Dyson, A. H., & Smitherman, G. (2009). The right (write) start: African American language and the discourse of sounding right. *Teachers College Record, 111*(4), 973–998.

Early Childhood and Literacy Development Committee. (1985). *Literacy development and pre-first grade.* Newark, DE: International Reading Association.

Easterbrooks, S. R., Lederberg, A. R., Miller, E. M., Bergeron, J. P., Connor, C. M., & McDonald, C. (2008). Emergent literacy skills during early childhood in children with hearing loss: Strengths and weaknesses. *Volta Review, 108*(2), 91–114.

Ediger, M. (2008). Psychology of parental involvement in reading. *Reading Improvement, 45*(1), 46–52.

Edwards, C. P., & Willis, L. M. (2000). Integrating visual and verbal literacies in the early childhood classroom. *Early Childhood Education Journal, 27*(4), 259–265.

Edwards, P. A. (2009). *Tapping the potential of parents: A strategic guide to boosting student achievement through family involvement.* New York: Scholastic.

Edwards, P. A., Turner, J. D., & Mokhtari, K. (2008). Balancing the assessment *of* learning and *for* learning in support of student literacy achievement. *The Reading Teacher, 61*(8), 682–684.

Egan-Robertson, A., & Bloome, D. (Eds.). (1998). *Students as researchers of culture, language, and their own community.* Creskill, NJ: Hampton Press.

Eihorn, K. (2001). *Easy & engaging ESL activities and mini-books for every classroom.* New York: Scholastic.

Eisenberg, L. S., Fink, N. E., & Niparko, J. K. (2006). Childhood development after cochlear implantation. *ASHA Leader, 11*(16), 5, 28–29.

Ellis, R. (2007). Educational settings and second language learning. *Asian EFL Journal, 9*(4), Article 1. Available: www.asian-efl-journal.com/Dec_2007_re.php

Engle, S. (1995). *The stories children tell: Making sense of the narratives of childhood.* New York: W. H. Freeman.

Enz, B. (2006). Phonemic awareness: Activities that make sounds come alive. In C. Cummmins (Ed.), *Understanding and implementing Reading First initiatives: The changing role of administrators* (pp. 18–33). Newark, DE: International Reading Association.

Enz, B. J., & Morrow, L. M. (2009). *Assessing preschool literacy development: Informal and formal measures to guide instruction* . Newark, DE: International Reading Association.

Enz, B. J., Prior, J., Gerard, M. R., & Han, M. (2008). Exploring intentional instructional uses of environmental print in preschool and primary grades. In A. DeBruin-Parecki (Ed.), *Effective early literacy practice: Here's how, here's why* (pp. 15–24). Baltimore: Paul H. Brookes.

Erickson, K. A., & Hatton, D. (2007). Expanding understanding of emergent literacy: Empirical support for a new framework. *Journal of Visual Impairment and Blindness, 101*(5), 261–277.

Erickson, K. A., Hatton, D., Roy, V., Fox, D., & Renne, D. (2007). Early intervention for children with visual impairments: Insights from individual cases. *Journal of Visual Impairment & Blindness, 101*(2), 80–95.

Ernst-Slavit, G., & Mulhern, M. (2003, September/October). *Bilingual books: Promoting literacy and biliteracy in the second-language and the mainstream classroom.* Available: www.readingonline.org/articles/ernst-slavit

Erwin, E., & Morton, N. (2008). Exposure to media violence and young children with and without disabilities: Powerful opportunities for family-professional partnerships. *Early Childhood Education Journal, 36*(2), 105–112.

Espinosa, L. M. (2005). Curriculum and assessment considerations for young children from culturally, linguistically, and economically diverse backgrounds. *Psychology in the Schools, 42*(8), 837–853.

Essa, E. L. (2006). *Introduction to early childhood* (5th ed.). Belmont, CA: Delmar/Cengage.

Estrem, T. L. (2005). Relational and physical aggression among preschoolers: The effect of language skills and gender. *Early Education and Development, 16*(2), 207–231.

Evers, A. J., Lang, L. F., & Smith, S. V. (2009). An ABC literacy journey: Anchoring in texts, bridging language, and creating stories. *The Reading Teacher, 62*(6), 461–470.

Faber, A., & Mazlish, E. (1999). *How to talk so kids will listen & listen so kids will talk.* New York: Collins.

Feder, K., & Majnemer, A. (2007). Handwriting development, competency, and intervention. *Developmental Medicine & Child Neurology, 49*(4), 312–317.

Federal Interagency Forum on Child and Family Statistics. (2006). *America's children: Key indicators of child well-being, 2006.* Available: http://childstats.gov

Federal Interagency Forum on Child and Family Statistics. (2008). *America's children: Key national indicators of well-being, 2008.* Available: http://childstats.gov

Feeney, S., Moravcik, E., Nolte, S., & Christensen, D. (2009). *Who am I in the lives of children?* (8th ed.). Upper Saddle River, NJ: Merrill/Pearson.

Fenson, L., Dale, P. S., Reznick, J. S., Bates, E., Thal, D. J., & Pethick, S. J. (1994). Variability in early communicative development. *Monographs of the Society for Research in Child Development, 59*(5), 173.

Fernald, A., Perfors, A., & Marchman, V. A. (2006). Picking up speed in understanding: Speech processing efficiency and vocabulary growth across the 2nd year. *Developmental Psychology, 42*(1), 98–116.

Field, J. (2001). Finding one's way in the fog: Listening strategies and second-language learners. *Modern English Teacher, 9,* 29–34.

Fields, M. V., Groth, L., & Spangler, K. (2007). *Let's begin reading right* (6th ed.). Upper Saddle River, NJ: Merrill/Prentice Hall.

Fillmore, L. W. (1991). When learning a second language means losing the first. *Early Childhood Research Quarterly, 6*(3), 23–346.

Fillmore, L. W. (1997). Luck, fish seeds, and second-language learning. In C. P. Casanave & S. R. Schecter (Eds.), *On becoming a language educator: Personal essays on professional development* (pp. 29–38). Mahwah, NJ: Lawrence Erlbaum.

Fillmore, L. W., & Snow, C. E. (2002). What teachers need to know about language. In C. A. Adger, C. E. Snow, & D. Christian (Eds.), *What teachers need to know about language* (pp. 7–54). McHenry, IL and Washington, DC: Delta System/Center for Applied Linguistics.

Fingon, J. (2005). The words that surround us. *Teaching PreK–8, 35,* 54–56.

Firth, U. (2006). Resolving the paradoxes of dyslexia. In G. Reid & J. Wearmouth (Eds.), *Dyslexia and literacy: Theory and practice* (pp. 45–68). Chichester: John Wiley & Sons.

Fisch, S. M. (2004). *Children's learning from educational television.* Mahwah, NJ: Lawrence Erlbaum.

Fisher, A. (2008). Teaching comprehension and critical literacy: Investigating guided reading in three primary classrooms. *Literacy, 42*(1), 19–28.

Fisher, B., & Medvic, E. (2000). *Perspectives on shared reading: Planning and practice.* Portsmouth, NH: Heinemann.

Fisher, D., Flood, J., Lapp, D., & Frey, N. (2004). Interactive read-alouds: Is there a common set of implementation practices? *The Reading Teacher, 58*(1), 8–17.

Forman, G. (1999). Instant video revisiting: The video camera as a "tool of the mind" for young children. *Early Childhood Research & Practice, 1*(2). Available: http://ecrp.uiuc.edu/v1n2/forman/html

Foster, W. A., & Miller, M. (2007). Development of the literacy achievement gap: A longitudinal study of kindergarten through third grade. *Language, Speech, & Hearing Services in Schools, 38*(3), 173–181.

Foundation for Child Development. (2008). How can we improve the education of America's children? *Foundation for Child Development Newsletter.* Available: www.fcd-us.org/issues/issues_show.htm?doc_id=447076

Fountas, I. C., & Pinnell, G. S. (1996). *Guided reading: Good first teaching for all children.* Portsmouth, NH: Heinemann.

Fox, S. (1997). The controversy over Ebonics. *Phi Delta Kappan, 79*(3), 237–241.

Freeman, Y., & Freeman, D. (2002). *Closing the achievement gap: How to reach long term and limited formal schooling English language learners.* Portsmouth, NH: Heinemann.

Freire, P. (1970). *Pedagogy of the oppressed* (M. B. Ramos, Trans.). New York: Continuum.

Friedland, E. S., & Truesdell, K. S. (2004). Kids reading together: Ensuring the success of a buddy reading program. *The Reading Teacher, 58*(1), 76–79.

Friedmann, E., Thomas, S. A., & Eddy, T. J. (2000). Companion animals and human health: Physical and cardiovascular influences. In A. L. Podberscek, E. S. Paul, & J. A. Serpell (Eds.), *Companion animals and us: Exploring the relationship between people and pets* (pp. 125–142). New York: Cambridge University Press.

Fromkin, V., Rodman, R., & Hyams, N. (2006). *An introduction to language* (8th ed.). New York: Holt.

Gadzikowski, A. (2007). *Story dictation: A guide for early childhood professionals.* St. Paul, MN: Redleaf.

Gaffney, J. S., Ostrosky, M. M., & Hemmeter, M. L. (2008). Books as natural support for young children's literacy learning. *Young Children, 63*(4), 87–93.

Gallas, K. (1994). *The languages of learning: How children talk, write, dance, and sing their understanding of the world.* New York: Teachers College Press.

Gallas, K. (1997). Story time as a magical act open only to the initiated: What some children don't know about power and may not find out. *Language Arts, 74*(4), 248–254.

Galper, A. R., & Seefeldt, C. (2009). Assessing young children. In S. Feeney, A. R. Galper, & C. Seefeldt (Eds.), *Continuing issues in early childhood education* (3rd ed., pp. 329–345). Upper Saddle River, NJ: Merrill/Pearson.

Garcia, E. (2008). *Para nuestros niños: Achievement gaps in early education.* Presentation at English-Language Learners Symposium (ETS-Sponsored), Princeton, NJ. Available: www.ets.org/media

Gardner, D. (2005, January). Ten lessons in collaboration. *Online Journal of Issues in Nursing, 10*(1), manuscript 1. Available: www.nursingworld.org/MainMenuCategories/ANAMarketplace/ANAPeriodicals/OJIN/TableofContents/Volume102005/No1Jan05/tpc26_116008.aspx

Gardner, H. (1980). *Artful scribbles: The significance of children's drawings.* New York: Basic Books.

Garvey, C. (1984). *Children's talk.* Cambridge, MA: Harvard University Press.

Gay, G. (2000). *Culturally responsive teaching: Theory, research, and practice.* New York: Teachers College Press.

Genesee, F., Lindholm-Leary, K., Saunders, W., & Christian, D. (2005). English language learners in U.S. schools: An overview of research findings. *Journal of Education for Students Placed at Risk, 10*(4), 363–385.

Genesee, F., Lindholm-Leary, K., Saunders, W. M., & Christian, D. (Eds.). (2007). *Educating English language learners: A synthesis of research evidence.* Cambridge, UK: Cambridge University Press

Genishi, C. (1988). *Young children's oral language development.* Urbana, IL: ERIC Clearinghouse on Elementary and Early Childhood Education.

Genishi, C., & Dyson, A. H. (2009). *Children, language and literature: Diverse learners in diverse times.* New York: Teachers College Press.

Gersten, R., Baker, S. K., Shanahan, T., Linan-Thompson, S., Collins, P., & Scarcella, R. (2007). *Effective literacy and English language instruction for English learners in the elementary grades. IES practice guide.* Princeton, NJ: What Works Clearinghouse.

Gest, S. D., Holland-Coviello, R., Welsh, J. A., Eicher-Catt, D. L., & Gill, S. (2006). Language development sub-contexts in Head Start classrooms: Distinctive patterns of teacher talk during free play, mealtime and book reading. *Early Education and Development, 17*(2), 293–315.

Geva, E., & Yaghoub-Zadeh, Z. (2006). Reading efficiency in native English-speaking and English-as-a-second-language children: The role of oral proficiency and underlying cognitive-linguistic processes. *Scientific Studies of Reading, 10*(1), 31–57.

Gibbons, P. (2002). *Scaffolding language, scaffolding learning: Teaching second language learners in the mainstream classroom.* Portsmouth, NH: Heinemann.

Gill, S. (2006). Teaching rimes with shared reading. *The Reading Teacher, 60*(2), 191–193.

Gillanders, C., & Jiménez, R. T. (2004). Reaching for success: A close-up of Mexican immigrant parents in the USA who foster literacy success for their kindergarten children. *Journal of Early Childhood Literacy, 4*(3), 243–269.

Glazer, J. I., & Giorgis, C. (2008). *Literature for young children: Supporting emergent literacy, ages 0 to 8* (6th ed.). Upper Saddle River, NJ: Merrill/Prentice Hall.

Glazer, S. M. (1998). *Assessment IS instruction: Reading, writing, spelling, and phonics for ALL learners.* Norwood, MA: Christopher-Gordon.

Goh, C., & Taib, Y. (2006). Metacognitive instruction in listening for young learners. *ELT Journal: English Language Teachers Journal, 60*(3), 222–232.

Goldin-Meadow, S., & Rowe, M. (2009). Differences in early gesture explain SES disparities in child vocabulary size at school entry. *Science, 323*(5916), 951–953.

Gollnick, D. M., & Chinn, P. C. (2008). *Multicultural education in a pluralistic society* (8th ed.). Upper Saddle River, NJ: Merrill/Prentice Hall.

Gomez, M. L., & Grant, C. A. (1990). A case for teaching writing: In the belly of the story. *The Writing Instructor, 10*(1), 29–41.

González, N., Moll, L. C., & Amanti, C. (2005). Introduction: Theorizing practices. In N. González, L. C. Moll, & C. Amanti (Eds.), *Funds of knowledge: Theorizing practices in households, communities, and classrooms* (pp. 1–28). Mahwah, NJ: Lawrence Erlbaum.

Gonzalez-Mena, J. (2008). *Diversity in early education programs: Honoring differences* (5th ed.). Boston: McGraw-Hill.

Gonzalez-Mena, J. (2009). *The child in the family and the community* (5th ed.). Upper Saddle River, NJ: Merrill/Pearson.

Gonzalez-Mena, J., & Eyer, D. W. (2008). *Infants, toddlers, and caregivers* (8th ed.). New York: McGraw-Hill.

Good, L. (2005–2006). Snap it up! Using digital photography in early childhood. *Childhood Education, 82*(2), 79–85.

Goodman, K. S. (1982). *Language and literacy: The selected writings of Kenneth S. Goodman.* G. V. Gollasch (Ed.). Boston: Routledge & Kegan Paul.

Goodman, K. S., & Goodman, Y. M. (1979). Learning to read is natural. In L. B. Resnick & P. A. Weaver (Eds.), *Theory and practice of early reading* (pp. 137–155). Mahwah, NJ: Lawrence Erlbaum.

Gordon, R. G., Jr. (Ed.). (2005). *Ethnologue: Languages of the world* (15th ed.). Dallas, TX: SIL International. Available: www.ethnologue.com

Goswami, U. (2001). Early phonological development and the acquisition of literacy. In S. B. Neuman & D. K. Dickinson (Eds.), *Handbook of early literacy research* (pp. 111–125). New York: Guilford.

Gottlieb, M. (2006). *Assessing English language learners: Bridges from language proficiency to academic achievement.* Thousand Oaks, CA: Corwin Press.

Graves, D. H. (1994). *A fresh look at writing.* Portsmouth, NH: Heinemann.

Green, C. R. (1998). This is my name. *Childhood Education, 74*(4), 226–231.

Gregory, G. H., & Chapman, C. (2007). *Differentiated instructional strategies: One size doesn't fit all* (2nd ed.). Thousand Oaks, CA: Corwin Press.

Grover, S., & Hannegan, L. (2005, May). Not just for listening. *Book Links, 14,* 16–20.

Guilfoyle, C. (2006). NCLB: Is there life beyond testing? *Educational Leadership, 64*(3), 8–13.

Gullo, D. (2005). *Understanding assessment and evaluation in early childhood education* (2nd ed.). New York: Teachers College Press.

Gutierrez, K., & Larson, J. (1994). Language borders: Recitation as hegemonic discourse. *International Journal of Education Reform, 3*(1), 22–36.

Ha, F. Y. L. (2009). From foot to shoes: Kindergartners', families' and teachers' perceptions of the project approach. *Early Childhood Education Journal, 37*(1), 23–33.

Hale-Benson, J. E. (1986). *Black children: Their roots, culture, and learning style.* Baltimore: Johns Hopkins University Press.

Haley, J., & Hobson, C. D. (1980). Interviewing: A means of encouraging the drive to communicate. *Language Arts, 57,* 497–502.

Hall, K. M., & Sabey, B. L. (2007). Focus on the facts: Using information texts effectively in early elementary classrooms. *Early Childhood Education Journal, 35*(3), 261–268.

Hall, L. J. (2009). *Autism spectrum disorders: From theory to practice.* Upper Saddle River, NJ: Pearson/Merrill.

Halliday, M. A. K. (1975). *Explorations in the functions of language.* London: Edward Arnold.

Halsall, S., & Green, C. (1995). Reading aloud: A way for parents to support children's growth in literacy. *Early Childhood Education Journal, 23*(1), 27–31.

Hamer, M., Stamatakis, E., & Mishra, G. (2009). Psychological distress, television viewing, and physical activity in children aged 4 to 12 years. *Pediatrics, 123,* 1263–1268.

Hamilton, A., Plunkett, K., & Schafer, G. (2000). Infant vocabulary development assessed with a British communicative development inventory. *Journal of Child Language, 27*(3), 689–705.

Haney, M. (2002). Name writing: A window into the emergent literacy skills of young children. *Early Childhood Education Journal, 30*(2), 101–105.

Harding, N. (1996). Family journals: The bridge from school to home and back again. *Young Children, 51*(2), 27–30.

Harris, V. (Ed.). (1997). *Using multiethnic literature in the K–8 classroom.* Norwood, MA: Christopher-Gordon.

Hart, B., & Risley, T. R. (1995). *Meaningful differences in the everyday experience of young American children.* Baltimore: Paul H. Brookes.

Hart, B., & Risley, T. R. (2003). The early catastrophe: The 30 million word gap by age 3. *Education Review, 17*(1), 110–118.

Hart, M. (1987). *Fold-and-cut stories and fingerplays.* Belmont, CA: Fearon.

Harvey, B. (2001). Supporting family diversity. *School-Age Notes, 21*(12), 1, 3.

Harvey, S., & Goudvis, A. (2007). *Strategies that work: Teaching comprehension to enhance understanding.* Portland, ME: Stenhouse Publishers.

Hawkins, M. R. (2004). Researching English language and literacy development in schools. *Educational Researcher, 33*(3), 14–25.

Hay, I., & Fielding-Barnsley, R. (2007). Facilitating children's emergent literacy using shared reading: A comparison of two models. *Australian Journal of Language & Literacy, 30*(3), 191–202.

Hayes, D., & Ahrens, M. (1988). Vocabulary simplification for children. *Journal of Child Language, 15,* 457–472.

Headley, K., & Dunston, P. (2000). Teachers' Choices books and comprehension strategies as transaction tools. *The Reading Teacher, 54*(3), 260–269.

Heath, S. B. (1983). *Ways with words: Language, life, and work in communities and classrooms.* New York: Cambridge University Press.

Heath, S. M., & Hogben, J. H. (2004). Cost-effective prediction of reading difficulties. *Journal of Speech, Language, and Hearing Research, 47,* 751–765.

Heller, M. F. (2006). Telling stories and talking facts: First graders' engagements in a nonfiction book club. *The Reading Teacher, 60*(4), 358–369.

Helm, J. H., Beneke, S., & Steinheimer, K. (2007). *Windows on learning: Documenting young children's work* (Rev. ed.). New York: Teachers College Press.

Helm, J. H., & Katz, L. G. (2000). *Young investigators: The project approach in the early years.* New York: Teachers College Press.

Hendrick, J. (Ed.). (2004). *Next steps toward teaching the Reggio way.* Upper Saddle River, NJ: Prentice Hall.

Hendrick, J., & Weissman, P. (2009). *The whole child: Developmental education for the early years.* Upper Saddle River, NJ: Merrill/Prentice Hall.

Hickman, P., Pollard-Durodola, S., & Vaughn, S. (2004). Storybook reading: Improving vocabulary and comprehension for English-language learners. *The Reading Teacher, 57*(8), 720–730.

Hiebert, E. H., & Raphael, T. E. (1998). *Early literacy instruction*. Fort Worth, TX: Harcourt Brace.

High, P. C., LaGasse, L., Becker, S., Ahlgren, I., & Gardner, A. (2000). Literacy promotion in primary care pediatrics: Can we make a difference? *Pediatrics, 105*(4), 927–934.

Hills, T. W. (1987). Hot housing young children: Implications for early childhood policy and practice. Urbana, IL: ERIC Clearinghouse on Elementary and Early Childhood Education. (ERIC Digest No. EDO-PS-87-4)

Hipple, M. (1985). Journal writing in kindergarten. *Language Arts, 82*(3), 255–281.

Hohm, E., Jennen-Steinmetz, C., Schmidt, M., & Laucht, M. (2007). Language development at ten months: Predictive of language outcome and school achievement ten years later? *European Child & Adolescent Psychiatry, 16*(3), 149–156.

Holdaway, D. (1979). *The foundations of literacy*. New York: Ashton.

Holum, A., & Gahala, J. (2001). *Critical issue: Using technology to enhance literacy instruction*. Naperville, IL: North Central Regional Educational Laboratory. Available: www.ncrel.org/sdrs/areas/issues/content/cntareas/reading/li300.htm

Hood, M., Conlon, E., & Andrews, G. (2008). Preschool home literacy practices and children's literacy development: A longitudinal analysis. *Journal of Educational Psychology, 100*, 252–271.

Hooper, S. R., & Umansky, W. (2009). *Young children with special needs* (5th ed.). Upper Saddle River, NJ: Merrill/Pearson.

Hoskin, J., & Herman, R. (2001). The communication, speech and gesture of a group of hearing-impaired children. *International Journal of Language & Communication Disorders, 36*, 206–209.

Houck, F. A. (2005). *Supporting English language learners: A guide for teachers and administrators*. Portsmouth, NH: Heinemann.

Howard, S., Shaughnessy, A., Sanger, D., & Hux, K. (1998). Let's talk: Facilitating language in early elementary classrooms. *Young Children, 53*(3), 34–39.

Huck, C. S., Kiefer, B., Hepler, S., & Hickman, J. (2003). *Children's literature in the elementary school* (8th ed.). New York: McGraw-Hill.

Hudson-Ross, S., Cleary, L. M., & Casey, M. (1993). *Children's voices: Children talk about literacy*. Portsmouth, NH: Heinemann.

Hughes, T. (1988). Myth and education. In K. Egan & D. Nadaner (Eds.), *Imagination and education* (pp. 30–44). New York: Teachers College Press.

Hunsaker, R. A. (1990). *Understanding and developing skills of oral communication*. Englewood, CO: Morton.

Hunt, T., & Renfro, N. (1982). *Puppetry in early childhood education*. Austin, TX: Nancy Renfro Studios.

Hurless, B., & Gittings, S. B. (2008). Weaving the tapestry: A first-grade teacher integrates teaching and learning. *Young Children, 63*(2), 40–49.

Hurtado, N., Marchman, V., & Fernald, A. (2007). Spoken word recognition in Latino children learning Spanish as their first language. *Journal of Child Language, 34*(2), 227–249.

Hutchinson, J. M., Whiteley, H. E., Smith, C. D., & Connors, L. (2003). The developmental progression of comprehension-related skills in children learning EAL. *Journal of Research in Reading, 26*(1), 19–32.

Hyman, S. L., & Tobin, K. E. (2007). Autism spectrum disorders. In M. L. Batshaw, L. Pellegrino, & N. J. Roizen (Eds.), *Children with disabilities* (6th ed., pp. 326–343). Baltimore: Paul H. Brookes.

Hymes, D. (1971). Competence and performance in linguistic theory. In R. Huxley & E. Ingram (Eds.), *Language acquisition: Models and methods*. New York: Academic Press.

Hyson, M. (2008). *Enthusiastic and engaged learners: Approaches to learning in the early childhood classroom*. New York: Teachers College Press..

Imhof, M. (2002). In the eye of the beholder: Children's perception of good and poor listening behavior. *International Journal of Listening, 16*, 40–56.

Innis, H. (1951). *The bias of communication*. Toronto: University of Toronto Press.

International Listening Association (ILA). (2008). Facts on listening. Available: www.listen.org

International Reading Association and the National Association for the Education of Young Children. (1998). Learning to read and write: Developmentally appropriate practices for young children. *The Reading Teacher, 52*(2), 193–216.

Isbell, R. (2008). *The complete learning center book* (Rev. ed.). Beltsville, MD: Gryphon House.

Isenberg, J. P., & Jalongo, M. R. (2009). *Creative thinking and arts-based learning: Preschool through fourth grade* (5th ed.). Upper Saddle River, NJ: Merrill/Pearson.

Israel, S. E. (2008). *Early reading first and beyond: A guide to building early literacy skills*. Thousand Oaks, CA: Corwin.

Iverson, J. M., & Goldin-Meadow, S. (2005). Gesture paves the way for language development. *Psychological Science, 16*, 367–371.

Jalongo, M. R. (1992). 12 answers to parents' questions about their young child's reading. *PTA Today, 17*(4), 16–19.

Jalongo, M. R. (Ed.). (2004a). *The world's children and their companion animals: Developmental and educational significance of the child/pet bond.* Olney, MD: Association for Childhood Education International.

Jalongo, M. R. (2004b). *Young children and picture books: Literature from infancy to six* (2nd ed.). Washington, DC: National Association for the Education of Young Children.

Jalongo, M. R. (2007). Beyond benchmarks and scores: A reassertion of the role of motivation and interest in academic achievement. *Childhood Education.* Available: www.acei.org/motivPosPaper.pdf

Jalongo, M. R. (2008a). Editorial: "Enriching the brain": The link between contemporary neuroscience and early childhood traditions. *Early Childhood Education Journal, 35*(6), 487–488.

Jalongo, M. R. (2008b). *Learning to listen, listen to learn: Building essential skills in young children.* Washington, DC: National Association for the Education of Young Children.

Jalongo, M. R., Dragich, D., Conrad, N. K., & Zhang, A. (2002). Using wordless picture books to support young children's literacy growth. *Early Childhood Education Journal, 29*(3), 167–177.

Jalongo, M. R., & Li, N. (2010). Young English language learners as listeners: Theoretical perspectives, research strands, and implications for instruction. In O. Saracho & B. Spodek (Eds.), *Language and cultural diversity in early childhood.* Greenwich, CT: Information Age Press.

Jalongo, M. R., & Ribblett, D. (1997). Supporting emergent literacy through song picture books. *Childhood Education, 74*(1), 15–22.

Jalongo, M. R., & Stamp, L. N. (1997). *The arts in children's lives: Aesthetic experiences in early childhood.* Boston: Allyn & Bacon.

Jensen, E. (2006). *Enriching the brain: How to maximize every learner's potential.* San Francisco: Jossey-Bass.

Johnson, D. (2003). Web watch—Audiobooks: Ear-resistible! *Reading Online, 6*(8). Available: www.reading online.org/electronic/elec_index.asp?HREF=webwatch/audiobooks/index.html

Johnson, D. W. (1972). *Reaching out: Interpersonal effectiveness and self-actualization.* Englewood Cliffs, NJ: Prentice Hall.

Johnson, P., et al. (1995). Assessment of teaching and learning in literature-based classrooms. *Teaching and Teacher Education, 11*(4), 359–371.

Johnson, S. M. (2006). *Finders and keepers: Helping new teachers survive and thrive in our schools.* San Francisco: Jossey-Bass.

Johnston, S. S., McDonnell, A. P., & Hawken, L. S. (2008). Enhancing outcomes in early literacy for young children with disabilities: Strategies for success. *Intervention in School & Clinic, 43*(4), 210–217.

Jones, E., & Nimmo, J. (1999). Collaboration, conflict, and change: Thought on education as provocation. *Young Children, 54*(1), 5–10.

Judge, S. (2006). Constructing an assistive technology toolkit for young children: Views from the field. *Journal of Special Education Technology, 21*(4), 17–24.

Jukes, I., Dosaj, A., & Macdonald, B. (2000). *Net savvy: Building information literacy in the classroom* (2nd ed.). Walnut Creek, CA: AltaMira Press.

Justice, L. M., & Kaderavek, J. (2002). Using shared storybook reading to promote emergent literacy. *Council for Exceptional Children, 34*(4), 8–13.

Justice, L. M., Kaderavek, J. N., Xitao, F., Sofka, A., & Hunt, A. (2009). Accelerating preschoolers' early literacy development through classroom-based teacher-child storybook reading and explicit print referencing. *Language, Speech, & Hearing Services in Schools, 40*(1), 67–85.

Justice, L. M., Meier, J., & Walpole, S. (2005). Learning new words from storybooks: An efficacy study with at-risk kindergartners. *Language, Speech, & Hearing Services in Schools, 36*(1), 17.

Justice, L. M., Pence, K., Bowles, R. B., & Wiggins, A. (2006). An investigation of four hypotheses concerning the order by which 4-year-old children learn the alphabet letters. *Early Childhood Research Quarterly, 21*(3), 374–389.

Justice, L. M., Pullen, P. C., & Pence, K. (2008). Influence of verbal and nonverbal references to print on preschoolers' visual attention to print during storybook reading. *Developmental Psychology, 44*, 855–866.

Kaderavek, J., & Justice, L. M. (2005). The effect of book genre in the repeated readings of mothers and their children with language impairment: A pilot investigation. *Child Language Teaching & Therapy, 21*(1), 75–92.

Kainz, K., & Vernon-Feagans, L. (2007). The ecology of early reading development for children in poverty. *Elementary School Journal, 107*(5), 407–427.

Kanaris, A. (1999). Gendered journeys: Children's writing and the construction of gender. *Language and Education, 13*(4), 254–268.

Kara-Soteriou, J., Zawilinski, L., & Henry, L. A. (2007). Children's books and technology in the classroom: A dynamic combo for supporting the writing workshop. *The Reading Teacher, 60*(7), 698–707.

Karchmer, R. A. (2001, May). Gaining a new, wider audience: Publishing student work on the Internet. *Reading Online, 4*(10). Available: www.readingonline.org/electronic/elec_index.asp?HREF=/electronic/karchmer/index.html

Katrusic, S. K. (2009). The forgotten learning disability: Epidemiology of written-language disorder in a population-based birth cohort (1976–1982), Rochester, Minnesota. *Pediatrics, 123*(5), 1306–1313. Available: http://pediatrics.aappublications.org/cgi/content/abstract/123/5/1306

Katz, L. G. (1988). *Early childhood education: What research tells us.* Bloomington, IN: Phi Delta Kappa.

Katz, L. G. (1993). *Five perspectives on quality in early childhood programs.* Urbana, IL: ERIC Clearinghouse on Elementary and Early Childhood Education. (ERIC Document Reproduction Service No. ED 351 148)

Katzir, T., Youngsuk, K., Wolf, M., O'Brien, B., Kennedy, B., Lovett, M., et al. (2006). Reading fluency: The whole is more than the parts. *Annals of Dyslexia, 56,* 51–58.

Keat, J. B., Strickland, M. J., & Marinak, B. (2009). Child voice: How immigrant children enlightened their teachers with a camera. *Early Childhood Education Journal, 37*(1), 13–21.

Kenner, C., Ruby, M., Jessel, J., Gregory, E., & Arju, T. (2007). Intergenerational learning between children and grandparents. *Journal of Early Childhood Research, 5*(3), 219–243.

Kim, J. (2004). Summer reading and the ethnic achievement gap. *Journal of Education for Students Placed at Risk (JESPAR), 9*(2), 169–199.

Kindler, A. (2002). *Survey of the states' limited English proficient students and available educational programs and services 2000–2001 summary report.* Washington, DC: National Clearinghouse for English Language Acquisition & Language Institution Educational Programs.

Kirk, E. W., & Clark, P. (2005). Beginning with names. *Childhood Education, 81*(3), 139.

Kirkland, L. D., & Patterson, J. (2005). Developing oral language in primary classrooms. *Early Childhood Education Journal, 32*(6), 391–395.

Kissel, B. (2008a). Apples on train tracks: Observing young children re-envisioning their writing. *Young Children, 63*(2), 26–32.

Kissel, B. (2008b). Promoting writing and preventing writing failure in young children. *Preventing School Failure, 52*(4), 53–56.

Kletzien, S. B., & Dreher, M. J. (2004). *Informational text in K–3 classrooms: Helping children read and write.* Newark, DE: International Reading Association.

Kliewer, C. (1995). Young children's communication and literacy: A qualitative study of language in the inclusive preschool. *Mental Retardation, 33*(3), 143–152.

Knecht, H., Nelson, P., Whitelaw, G., & Feth, L. (2002). Structural variables and their relationship to background noise levels and reverberation times in unoccupied classrooms. *American Journal of Audiology, 11,* 65–71.

Knobel, M., & Lankshear, C. (2003). Researching young children's out-of-school literacy practices. In N. Hall, J. Larson, & J. Marsch (Eds.), *Handbook of Early Childhood Literacy* (pp. 51–65). London: Sage.

Knopf, H., & Swick, K. (2008). Using our understanding of families to strengthen family involvement. *Early Childhood Education Journal, 35*(5), 419–427.

Kobrin, B. (1988). *Eyeopeners! How to choose and use children's books about real people, places, and things.* New York: Penguin.

Kobrin, B. (1995). *Eyeopeners II.* New York: Scholastic.

Koenke, K. (1988). Handwriting instruction: What do we know? *The Reading Teacher, 40*(2), 214–228.

Kohn, A. (1996). *Beyond discipline: From compliance to community.* Alexandria, VA: Association for Supervision and Curriculum Development.

Konecki, L. R. (1992). *"Parent Talk": Helping families to relate to schools and facilitate children's learning.* Bloomington, IN: Phi Delta Kappa. (ERIC Document Reproduction Service No. ED 342 745)

Kontos, S., & Wilcox-Herzog, A. (1997). Teachers' interactions with children: Why are they so important? *Young Children, 52*(5), 4–12.

Koralek, D. (Ed.). (2004). *Spotlight on young children and assessment.* Washington, DC: National Association for the Education of Young Children.

Koskinen, P. S., Wilson, R. M., Gambrell, L. B., & Neuman, S. B. (1993). Captioned video and vocabulary learning: An innovative practice in literacy instruction. *The Reading Teacher, 47*(1), 36–43.

Kostelnik, M. J. (Ed.). (1991). *Teaching young children using themes.* Glenview, IL: GoodYear.

Kostelnik, M. J., Soderman, A. K., & Whiren, A. (2007). *Developmentally appropriate curriculum: Best practices in early childhood education* (4th ed.). Upper Saddle River, NJ: Merrill/Prentice Hall.

Kostelnik, M. J., Whiren, A. P., Soderman, A. K., & Gregory, A. (2008). *Guiding children's social development and learning.* Belmont, CA: Delmar/Cengage.

Krashen, S. D. (1997). *Every person a reader: An alternative to the California Task Force Report on Reading.* Portsmouth, NH: Heinemann.

Krashen, S. D. (2001). More smoke and mirrors: A critique of the National Reading Panel Report on Fluency. *Phi Delta Kappan, 83*(2), 119–123.

Krashen, S. D. (2003). *Explorations in language acquisition and use.* Portsmouth, NH: Heinemann.

Krashen, S. D. (2004). *The power of reading: Insights from the research.* Portsmouth, NH: Heinemann.

Kummere, S. E., Lopez-Reyna, N. A., & Hughes, M. J. (2007). Mexican immigrant mothers' perceptions of their children's communication disabilities, emergent literacy development, and speech-language therapy program. *American Journal of Speech-Language Pathology, 16*(3), 271–282.

Kupetz, B. N., & Green, E. J. (1997). Sharing books with infants and toddlers: Facing the challenges. *Young Children, 52*(2), 22–27.

Labbo, L. D., Eakle, A. J., & Montero, M. K. (2002, May). Digital language experience approach: Using digital photographs and software and a Language Experience Approach innovation. *Reading Online*, 24–43. Available: www.literacythroughphotography .com/digital_photography.htm

Labbo, L. D., Love, M. S., Prior, M. P., Hubbard, B. P., & Ryan, T. (2006). *Literature links: Thematic units linking read-alouds and computer activities.* Newark, DE: International Reading Association.

La Fontaine, H. (1987). *At-risk children and youth: The educational challenges of limited English proficient students.* Presented at the Summer Institute of The Council of Chief State School Officers, Washington, DC.

Lamme, L. L. (1984). *Growing up writing: Sharing with your children the joys of good writing.* Washington, DC: Acropolis.

Lane, H. B., & Wright, T. L. (2007). Maximizing the effectiveness of reading aloud. *The Reading Teacher, 60*(7), 668–675.

Langer, J. A. (1994). Focus on Research: A response-based approach to literature. *Language Arts, 71*(3), 203–211.

Langer, J. A. (2002). *Effective literacy instruction: Building successful reading and writing programs.* Urbana, IL: National Council of Teachers of English.

Laosa, L. M., & Ainsworth, P. (2007). *Is public pre-K preparing Hispanic children to succeed in school?* (Policy Brief No. 13). New Brunswick, NJ: National Institute for Early Education Research.

LaParo, K. M., & Pianta, R. C. (2000). Predicting children's competence in the early years: A meta-analytic review. *Review of Educational Research, 70*(4), 443–483.

Lapp, D., Fisher, D., & Wolsey, T. D. (2009). *Literacy growth for every child: Differentiated and small group instruction, K–6.* New York: Guilford.

Larson, J., & Peterson, S. (2003). Talk and discourse in formal learning settings. In N. Hall, J. Larson, & J. Marsh (Eds.), *Handbook of early childhood literacy* (pp. 301–314). London: Sage.

Lau, C., Higgins, K., Gelfer, J., Hong, E., & Miller, S. (2005). The effects of teacher facilitation on the social interactions of young children during computer activities. *Topics in Early Childhood Special Education, 25*(4), 208–217.

Laverick, D. M. (2008). Starting school: Welcoming young children and families into early school experiences. *Early Childhood Education Journal, 35*(4), 321–326.

Lee, S. (2006). Using children's texts to communicate with parents of English-language learners. *Young Children, 61*(5), 18–25.

Lee, S., Huh, M., Jeung, H., & Lee, D. (2004). Receptive language skills of profoundly hearing-impaired children with cochlear implants. *Cochlear Implants International: An Interdisciplinary Journal, 5,* 99–101.

Lehman, B. A. (2007). *Children's literature and learning: Literary study across the curriculum.* New York: Teachers College Press.

Leland, C. H., & Harste, J. C. (1994). Multiple ways of knowing: Curriculum in a new key. *Language Arts, 71*(5), 337–345.

Lemke, M., & Gonzales, P. (2006). *U.S. student and adult performance on international assessments of educational achievement: Findings from the condition of education 2006.* Washington, DC: National Center for Education Statistics.

Lerner, J. W., Lowenthal, B., & Egan, R. W. (2003). *Preschool children with special needs: Children at risk, children with disabilities* (2nd ed.). Upper Saddle River, NJ: Merrill/Pearson.

Leung, C. B. (2008). Preschoolers' acquisition of scientific vocabulary through repeated read-aloud events, retellings, and hands-on science activities. *Reading Psychology, 29*(2), 165–193.

Levin, D. E. (1999, November). Children's play: Changing times, changing needs, changing responses. *Our Children*, 8–11.

Levin, G. (1983). *Child psychology.* Belmont, CA: Wadsworth.

Levin, I., & Bus, A. G. (2003). How is emergent writing based on drawing? Analyses of children's products and their sorting by children and mothers. *Developmental Psychology, 39,* 891–905.

Levy, R. (2009). "You have to understand words . . . but not read them": Young children becoming readers in a digital age. *Journal of Research in Reading, 32*(1), 75–91.

Lewis, B., Freebairn, L., & Taylor, H. (2002). Correlates of spelling abilities in children with early speech sound disorders. *Reading & Writing, 15*(3/4), 389–407.

Lewis, M., & Jackson, D. (2001). Television literacy: Comprehension of program content using closed captions for the deaf. *Journal of Deaf Studies and Deaf Education, 6,* 43–53.

Liebert, R. E. (1991). The Dolch list revisited: An analysis of pupil responses then and now. *Reading Horizons, 31,* 217–227.

Lightbown, P. (2000). Classroom SLA research and second language teaching. *Applied Linguistics, 21*(4), 431–462.

Lima, C. W., & Lima, J. A. (2008). *A to zoo: Subject access to children's picture books.* (8th ed.). Westport, CT: Bowker.

Lindsey, K. A., Manis, F. R., & Bailey, C. E. (2003). Prediction of first-grade reading in Spanish-speaking English-language learners. *Journal of Educational Psychology, 95*(3), 484–494.

Linebarger, D., Kosanic, A., Greenwood, C., & Doku, N. (2004). Effects of viewing the television program Between the Lions on the emergent literacy skills of young children. *Journal of Educational Psychology, 96*(2), 297–308.

Linquanti, R. (1999). Fostering academic success for English language learners: What do we know? (Section 5: English language acquisition and academic success: What do we know?). Available: www.wested.org/policy/pubs/fostering/know.htm

Loban, W. (1976). *Language development: Kindergarten through grade twelve.* Urbana, IL: National Council of Teachers of English.

Lonigan, C. J. (2005). Development and promotion of early literacy skills: Using data to help children succeed. Available: www.ncld.org/content/view/485/456246

Lotherington, H., Holland, M., Sotoudeh, S., & Zentena, M. (2008). Project-based community language learning: Three narratives of multilingual story-telling in early childhood education. *Canadian Modern Language Review, 65*(1), 125–145.

Love, A., Burns, M. S., & Buell, M. J. (2007). Writing: Empowering literacy. *Young Children, 62*(1), 12–19.

Lovel, K. (1968). Some recent studies in language development. *Merrill-Palmer Quarterly, 14,* 123–138.

Lovett, M. W., DePalma, M., Frijters, J., Steinbach, K., Temple, M., Benson, N., & Lacerenza, L. (2008). Interventions for reading difficulties: A comparison of Response to Intervention by ELL and EFL struggling readers. *Journal of Learning Disabilities, 41*(4), 333–352.

Lu, M. Y. (2000). Language development in the early years. (ERIC Document Reproduction Service No. ED 446 336). Available: www.vtaide.com/png/ERIC/Language-Early.htm

Lukens, R. (2006). *A critical handbook of children's literature* (7th ed.). Boston: Allyn & Bacon.

Lund, J. R. (1991). A comprehension of second language listening and reading comprehension. *Modern Language Journal, 75*(2), 96–204.

Lundsteen, S. W. (1993). Metacognitive listening. In A. D. Wolvin & C. G. Coakley (Eds.), *Perspectives on listening* (pp. 106–123). Westport, CT: Greenwood.

Lynch, J. (2000). *A cry unheard: New insights into the medical consequences of loneliness.* New York: Bancroft Press.

MacGregor, D. (2004). Literacy software saves struggling readers. *T.H.E. Journal, 32,* 52–53.

Mackey, B., & White, M. (2004). Conversations, collaborations, and celebrations: How the school library media specialist can shape early literacy instruction. *Knowledge Quest, 33*(2), 30–33.

Madej, K. S. (2003). Towards digital narrative for children: From education to entertainment, a historical perspective. *Computers in Entertainment, 1*(1), 12.

Magnuson, K. A., & Waldfogel, J. (2005). Early childhood care and education: Effects on ethnic and racial gaps in school readiness. *Future of Children, 15*(1), 169–196.

Malach, D. A., & Rutter, R. A. (2003). For nine months kids go to school, but in summer this school goes to the kids. *The Reading Teacher, 57*(1), 50–54.

Malaguzzi, L. (1994). Tribute to Loris Malaguzzi. *Young Children, 49*(5), 55.

Mallory, B. R., & Rous, B. (2009). Educating young children with developmental differences: Principles of inclusive practice. In S. Feeney, A. Galper, & C. Seefeldt (Eds.), *Continuing issues in early childhood education* (3rd ed., pp. 278–302). Upper Saddle River, NJ: Merrill/Pearson.

Manis, F. R., Lindsey, K. A., & Bailey, C. E. (2004). Development of reading in grades K–2 in Spanish-speaking English-language learners. *Learning Disabilities Research and Practice, 19*(4), 214–224.

Mann, V. A., & Foy, J. G. (2007). Speech development patterns and phonological awareness in preschool children. *Annals of Dyslexia, 57*(1), 51–74.

Manning, M. (2005). Reading aloud. *Teaching PreK–8, 35,* 80–82.

Manyak, P. C. (2008). Phonemes in use: Multiple activities for a critical process. *The Reading Teacher, 61*(8), 659–662.

Marchman, V., & Fernald, A. (2008). Speed of word recognition and vocabulary knowledge in infancy predict cognitive and language outcomes in later childhood. *Developmental Science, 11*(3), 9–16.

Margolis, R. (2001). The best little library in Texas: The Terrazas Branch Library is the winner of the Giant Step Award. *School Library Journal, 47*(1), 54–58.

Marsh, J., Brooks, G., Hughes, J., Ritchie, L., & Roberts, S. (2005). *Digital beginnings: Young children's use of popular culture, media, and new technologies.* Sheffield, UK: University of Sheffield. Available: www.digitalbeginnings.shef.ac.uk

Marston, D., Pickart, M., Reschly, A., Heistad, D., Muyskens, P., & Tindal, G. (2007). Early literacy measures for improving student reading achievement: Translating research into practice. *Exceptionality, 15*(2), 97–117.

Martin, L. E., & Thacker, S. (2009). Teaching the writing process in the primary grades. *Young Children, 64*(4), 30–35.

Martin, W., & Porac, C. (2007). Patterns of handedness and footedness in switched and nonswitched Brazilian left-handers: Cultural effects on the development of lateral preferences. *Developmental Neuropsychology, 31*(2), 159–179.

Mason, J., & Au, K. (1998). *Reading instruction for today.* Reading, MA: Addison-Wesley.

Maxim, G. (1989). *The very young: Guiding children from infancy through the early years* (3rd ed.). Columbus, OH: Merrill.

Mayer, K. (2007). Emerging knowledge about emerging writing. *Young Children, 62*(1), 34–40.

McAfee, O., & Leong, D. (2006). *Assessing and guiding young children's development and learning* (4th ed.). Boston: Allyn & Bacon.

McBride, B. A., & Rane, T. R. (1997). Father/male involvement in early childhood programs: Issues and challenges. *Early Childhood Education Journal, 25*(1), 11–16.

McCable, P. C., & Meller, P. J. (2004). The relationship between language and social competence: How language impairment affects social growth. *Psychology in the Schools, 41*(3), 313–321.

McCarthey, S. J. (2000). Home-school connections: A review of the literature. *Journal of Educational Research, 93*(3), 145–153.

McCaslin, N. (2006). *Creative drama in the classroom and beyond* (8th ed.). Boston: Allyn & Bacon.

McClelland, M. M., Acock, A. C., & Morrison, F. J. (2006). The impact of kindergarten learning-related skills on academic trajectories at the end of elementary school. *Early Childhood Research Quarterly, 21*(4), 471–490.

McConnell, S. (1993). Talking drawings: A strategy for assisting learners. *Journal of Reading, 36*(4), 260–269.

McCormick, L., Loeb, D. F., & Schiefelbusch, R. (2002). *Supporting children with communication difficulties in inclusive settings: School-based language intervention* (2nd ed.). Boston: Allyn & Bacon.

McDevitt, T. M. (1990). Encouraging young children's listening. *Academic Therapy, 25*(5), 569–577.

McGee, L. (2007). *Transforming literacy practices in preschool: Research-based practices that give all children the opportunity to reach their potential as learners.* New York: Scholastic.

McGee, L. M., & Morrow, L. M. (2005). *Teaching literacy in kindergarten.* New York: Guilford.

McGee, L. M., & Richgels, D. J. (2007). *Literacy's beginnings: Supporting young readers and writers* (5th ed.). Boston: Pearson/Allyn & Bacon.

McGee, L. M., & Schickendanz, J. A. (2007). Repeated interactive read-alouds in preschool and kindergarten. *The Reading Teacher, 60*(8), 742–751.

McGee, L. M., & Ukrainetz, T. A. (2009). Using scaffolding to teach phonemic awareness in preschool and kindergarten. *The Reading Teacher, 62*(7), 599–603.

McInnes, A., Humphries, T., Hogg-Johnson, S., & Tannock, R. (2003). Listening comprehension and working memory are impaired in attention-deficit hyperactivity disorder irrespective of language impairment. *Journal of Abnormal Child Psychology, 31*(4), 42.

McKeough, A., Bird, S., Tourigny, E., Romaine, A., Graham, S., Ottmann, J., & Jeary, J. (2008). Storytelling as a foundation to literacy development for aboriginal children: Culturally and developmentally appropriate practices. *Canadian Psychology, 49*(2), 148–154.

McMaster, K. L., Kung, S., Han, I., & Cao, M. (2008). Peer-assisted learning strategies: A "Tier 1" approach to promoting English learners' response to intervention. *Teaching Exceptional Children, 74*(2), 194–214.

McMullen, M. B. (1998). Thinking before doing: A giant toddler step on the road to literacy. *Young Children, 53*(3), 65–70.

McNair, J. C. (2007). Say my name, say my name! Using children's names to enhance early literacy development. *Young Children, 62*(5), 84–89.

McName, A., & Mercurio, M. L. (2007, Spring). Who cares? How teachers can scaffold children's ability to care: A case for picture books. *Early Childhood Research and Practice.* Available: http://ecrp.uiuc.edu/v9n1/mcnamee.html

McNeill, J. H., & Fowler, S. A. (1996). Using story reading to encourage children's conversations. *Teaching Exceptional Children, 28*(4), 43–47.

McTavish, M. (2007). Constructing the big picture: A working class family supports their daughter's pathways to literacy. *The Reading Teacher, 60*(5), 476–485.

McVicker, C. J. (2007). Young readers respond: The importance of child participation in emerging literacy. *Young Children, 62*(3), 18–22.

Meacham, A. N. (2007). Language learning and the internationally adopted child. *Early Childhood Education Journal, 34*(1), 73–79.

Mediatore, K. (2003). Reading with your ears. *Reference & User Services Quarterly, 42*(4), 318–323.

Meesook, K. (2003). Cultural and school-grade differences in Korean and white American children's narrative skills. *International Review of Education, 49,* 177–191.

Megee, M. (1997). Media literacy: The new basic. *Emergency Librarian, 25*(2), 23–26.

Mehler, J., & Kovacs, A. M. (2009). Cognitive gains in 7-month-old bilingual infants. *Proceedings of the National Academy of Sciences of the United States of America, 106*(16), 6556–6560.

Meier, D. (2009). (Ed.). *Here's the story: Using narrative to promote young children's language and literacy learning.* New York: Teachers College Press.

Meier, D., & Woods, G. (Eds.). (2004). *Many children left behind: How the No Child Left Behind Act is damaging our children and our schools.* Boston: Beacon Press.

Meisels, S. J., & Atkins-Burnett, S. (2005). *Developmental screening in early childhood: A guide* (5th ed.). Washington, DC: National Association for the Education of Young Children.

Melhuish, E. C., Phan, M. B., Sylva, K., Sammons, P., Siraj-Blatchford, I., & Taggart, B. (2008). Effects of the home learning environment and preschool center experience upon literacy and numeracy development in early primary school. *Journal of Social Issues, 64*(1), 95–114.

Melson, G. F. (2003). Child development and the human-companion animal bond. *American Behavioral Scientist, 47*(1), 31–39.

Mendelsohn, D. J., & Rubin, J. (1995). *A guide for the teaching of second language listening.* San Diego, CA: Dominie Press.

Menyuk, P. (1988). *Language development: Knowledge and use.* Glenview, IL: Scott Foresman.

Merritt, S., & Dyson, A. H. (1992). A social perspective on informal assessment: Voices, texts, pictures, and play from a first grade. In C. Genishi (Ed.), *Ways of assessing children and curriculum: Stories of early childhood practice* (pp. 94–125). New York: Teachers College Press.

Michael, M., & Sengers, P. (2003). *Narrative intelligence.* Amsterdam: John Benjamins.

Millard, E., & Marsh, J. (2001). Words with pictures: The role of visual literacy in writing and its implications for schooling. *Reading, 35,* 54–62.

Miller, P. (2004). *Reaching every reader: Promotional strategies for the elementary school library media specialist.* Worthington, OH: Linworth.

Minkel, W. (2000). Digital audiobooks can help kids learn. *School Library Journal, 46*(10), 24.

Mistrett, S. (2004). Assistive technology helps young children with disabilities participate in daily activities. *Technology in Action, 1*(4), 1–8.

Mistrett, S. G., Lane, S. J., & Ruffino, A. G. (2005). Growing and learning through technology: Birth to five. In D. Edyburn, K. Higgins, & R. Boone (Eds.), *Handbook of special education technology research and practice* (pp. 273–308). Whitefish Bay, WI: Knowledge by Design.

Mogharreban, C. C., & Bruns, D. A. (2009). Moving to inclusive pre-kindergarten classrooms: Lessons from the field. *Early Childhood Education Journal, 36*(5), 381–406.

Mol, S. E., Bus, A. G., & DeJong, M. T. (2009). Interactive book reading in early education: A tool to stimulate print knowledge as well as children's oral language. *Review of Educational Research, 79*(2), 979–1007.

Mol, S. E., Bus, A. G., DeJong, M. T., & Smeets, J. H. (2008). Added value of dialogic parent-child book readings: A meta-analysis. *Early Education and Development, 19*(1), 7–26.

Moline, S. (1995). *I see what you mean: Children at work with visual information.* York, ME: Stenhouse.

Moll, L., Amanti, C., Neff, D., & González, N. (2005). Funds of knowledge for teaching: Using a qualitative approach to connect homes and classrooms. In N. González (Ed.), *Funds of knowledge: Theorizing practices in households and classrooms* (pp. 71–88). Mahwah, NJ: Lawrence Erlbaum.

Montecel, M. R., & Cortez, J. D. (2002). Successful bilingual education programs: Development and the dissemination of criteria to identify promising and exemplary practices in bilingual education at the national level. *Bilingual Research Journal, 26,* 1–22.

Moore, E. S., & Lutz, R. J. (2000). Children, advertising, and product experiences: A multmethod inquiry. *Journal of Consumer Research, 27,* 31–48.

Moore, R. A., & Ritter, S. (2008). "Oh yeah, I'm Mexican. What type are you?" Changing the way preservice teachers interpret and respond to the literate identities of children. *Early Childhood Education Journal, 35*(6), 505–514.

Moravcik, E. (2000). Music all the livelong day. *Young Children, 55*(4), 27–29.

Morgan, P., & Fuchs, D. (2007). Is there a bidirectional relationship between children's reading skills and reading motivation? *Exceptional Children, 73*(2), 165–183.

Morgan, P. L., & Meier, C. R. (2008). Dialogic reading's potential to improve children's emergent literacy skills and behavior. *Preventing School Failure, 52*(4), 11–16.

Morrow, L. M. (2001). Literacy development and young children: Research to practice. In S. L. Golbeck (Ed.), *Psychological perspectives on early childhood education: Reframing dilemmas in research and practice* (pp. 253–279). Mahwah, NJ: Lawrence Erlbaum.

Morrow, L. M. (2008a). Creating a literacy-rich classroom environment. In A. DeBruin-Parecki (Ed.),

Effective early literacy practice: Here's how, here's why (pp. 1–14). Baltimore: Paul H. Brookes.

Morrow, L. M. (2008b). *Literacy development in early childhood: Helping children read and write.* Boston: Allyn & Bacon.

Morrow, L. M., Woo, D. G., & Radzin, A. (2000). Implementation of an America Reads tutoring program. *Reading Online, 4*(4). Available: www.readingonline.org/articles/art_index.asp?HREF=/articles/morrow/index.html

Mosco, M. (2005). Getting the information graphically. *Arts & Activities, 138*(1), 44.

Moseley, D., & Poole, S. (2001). The advantages of rime-prompting: A comparative study of prompting methods when hearing children read. *Journal of Research in Reading, 24*(2), 163–173.

Mosenthal, P. (1983). Defining good and poor reading— The problem of artificial lampposts. *The Reading Teacher, 39*(8), 858–881.

Moses, A. M. (2009). Research in review: What television can (and can't) do to promote early literacy development. *Young Children, 64*(2), 62–89.

Moss, B. (2002). *Exploring the literature of fact: Children's nonfiction trade-books in the elementary classroom.* New York: Guilford.

Moutray, C. L., & Snell, C. A. (2003). Three teachers' quest: Providing daily writing activities for kindergartners. *Young Children, 58*(2), 24–28.

Mui, S., & Anderson, J. (2008). At home with the Johars: Another look at family literacy. *The Reading Teacher, 62*(3), 234–243.

Mundell, D. (1987). *Mental imagery: Do you see what I say?* Oklahoma City: Oklahoma State Department of Education.

Murkoff, H., Eisenberg, A., & Hathaway, S. (2003). *What to expect the first year.* New York: Workman Publishing.

Murphy, J. L., Hatton, D., & Erickson, K. A. (2008). Exploring the early literacy practices of teachers of infants, toddlers, and preschoolers with visual impairments. *Journal of Visual Impairment & Blindness, 102*(3), 133–146.

Myers, P. A. (2005). The princess storyteller, Clara Clarifier, Quincy Questioner, and the wizard: Reciprocal teaching adapted for kindergarten students. *The Reading Teacher, 59*(4), 314–324.

Nakamoto, J., Lindsey, K. A., & Manis, F. R. (2008). A cross-linguistic investigation of English language learners' reading comprehension in English and Spanish. *Scientific Studies of Reading, 12*(4), 352–371.

Narey, M. (Ed.). (2008). *Making meaning: Constructing multimodal perspectives of language, literacy, and learning through arts-based early childhood education.* New York: Springer.

Nation, K., & Snowling, M. J. (2004). Beyond phonological skills: Broader language skills contribute to the development of reading, *Journal of Research in Reading, 27*(4), 342–356.

National Association for the Education of Young Children. (1996a). NAEYC position statement: Responding to linguistic and cultural diversity— Recommendations for effective early childhood education. *Young Children, 51*(2), 4–12. Available in English and Spanish: www.naeyc.org/resources/eyly/1996/03.htm

National Association for the Education of Young Children. (1996b). *Technology and young children—Ages three through eight.* Washington, DC: Author.

National Association for the Education of Young Children. (2005). *Where we stand: Many languages, many cultures: Respecting and responding to diversity.* Washington, DC: Author. Available: www.naeyc.org/about/positions/pdf/diversity.pdf

National Association for the Education of Young Children (NAEYC) & National Association of Early Childhood Specialists in State Departments of Education (NAECS/SDS). (2003). *Early childhood curriculum, assessment and program evaluation: Building an effective, accountable system for children birth through age 8* (Joint position statement). Washington, DC: National Association for the Education of Young Children.

National Capital Language Resource Center. (2008). The essentials of language teaching: Teaching listening. Available: www.nclrc.org/essentiall/listening/liindex.htm

National Center for Education Statistics. (2005). Learner outcomes: Early childhood (Indicator 8). Available: http://nces.ed.gov/programs/coe/statement/s3.asp

National Center for Education Statistics. (2006). *The condition of education 2006.* Washington, DC: Author. Available: http://nces.ed.gov/programs/coe/2006/section4/indicator33.asp

National Center for Education Statistics. (2007). *National Assessment of Educational Progress (NAEP), 2007 Reading Assessment.* Washington, DC: Author. Available: http://nces.ed.gov/nationsreportcard/nde

National Center for Education Statistics. (2008). *The condition of education 2008.* Washington, DC: Author. Available: http://nces.ed.gov/programs/coe/2008/section1/indicator06.asp

National Clearinghouse for English Language Acquisition. (2006). *Which tests are used commonly to determine English language proficiency?* Washington, DC: Author. Available: www.ncela.gwu.edu/files/rcd/BE021790/Which_Tests_Are_Used.pdf

National Council of Teachers of English. (2005). Early literacy (Online resources). Available: www.ncte.org/collections/earlyliteracy

National Council of Teachers of English and the International Reading Association. (1996). *Standards for the English language arts*. Urbana, IL, and Newark, DE: Authors.

National Early Childhood Accountability Task Force. (2008). *Taking stock: Assessing and improving early childhood learning and program quality*. Available: www.policyforchildren.org/pdf/Task_Force_Report.pdf

National Early Literacy Panel. (2008). *Developing early literacy: A report of the National Early Literacy Panel*. Jessup, MD: National Institute for Literacy.

National Early Literacy Panel. (2009). *Developing early literacy*. Jessup, MD: National Institute for Literacy. Available: www.nifl.gov/nifl/publications/pdf/NELPReport09.pdf

National Education Association. (2007a). NEA's Read across America program. Available: http://nea.org/readacross

National Institute on Deafness and Other Communication Disorders. (2009). *Statistics on voice, speech, and language*. Bethesda, MD: Author. Available: www.nidcd.nih.gov/health/statistics/vsl.asp

National Institute on Media and the Family. (2009). Facts. Available: www.mediafamily.org/facts/facts.shtml

National Reading Panel. (2000). *Report of the National Reading Panel: Teaching children to read: An evidence-based assessment of the scientific research literature on reading and its implications for reading instruction*. Washington, DC: National Institutes of Health.

National Research Council, Committee on Early Childhood Pedagogy. (2001). *Eager to learn: Educating our preschoolers*. Washington, DC: National Academies Press.

National Task Force on Early Childhood Education for Hispanics. (2007). *Para nuestros niños. Expanding and improving early education for Hispanics: Main Report*. Tempe, AZ: Author. Available: www.ecehispanic.org

Naughton, S. (2005). Preschool issues concerning English language learners and immigrant children: Curricula and assessment issues. Available: www.nasbe.org/projects/early_childhood/ncela.gwu.edu/expert/faq/25_tests.htm

Nelson, K. (1999). The psychological and social origins of autobiographical memory. In L. E. Berk (Ed.), *Landscapes of development: An anthology of readings* (pp. 97–107). Belmont, CA: Wadsworth.

Nelson, K. (2007). *Young minds in social worlds: Experience, meaning and memory*. Cambridge, MA: Harvard University Press.

Nelson, K. E., Aksu-Koc, A., & Johnson, C. E. (Eds.). (2001). *Children's language: Developing narrative and discourse competence*. Mahwah, NJ: Lawrence Erlbaum.

Nelson, O. (1989). Storytelling: Language experience for meaning making. *The Reading Teacher, 42*(6), 386–390.

Nelson, P., Kohnert, K., Sabur, S., & Shaw, D. (2005). Classroom noise and children learning through a second language: Double jeopardy? *Language, Speech, and Hearing Services in Schools, 36*, 219–229.

Nemeth, K. (2009). Meeting the home language mandate: Practical strategies for all classrooms. *Young Children, 64*(2), 36–42.

Neuman, S. B. (2004). Hear, Hear! Listening for the sounds that make up words is an essential step on the road to reading and writing. *Scholastic Parent & Child, 11*(4), 22.

Neuman, S. B. (2006). The knowledge gap: Implications for early education. In D. K. Dickinson & S. B. Neuman (Eds.), *Handbook of early literacy research, volume 2* (pp. 29–40). New York: Guilford.

Neuman, S. B. (2009). *Changing the odds for children at risk: Seven essential principles of educational programs that break the cycle of poverty*. Westport, CT: Praeger.

Neuman, S. B., Caperelli, B. J., & Kee, C. (1998). Literacy learning, a family matter. *The Reading Teacher, 52*(3), 244–252.

Neuman, S. B., Roskos, K., Wright, T., & Lenhart, L. (2007). *Nurturing knowledge: Building a foundation for school success by linking early literacy to math, science, art, and social studies*. New York: Scholastic.

Neumann, M., Hood, M., & Neumann, D. (2009). The scaffolding of emergent literacy skills in the home environment: A case study. *Early Childhood Education Journal, 36*(4), 313–319.

Neumann, M. M. (2007). *Up Downs: A fun and practical way to introduce reading and writing to children aged 2–5*. Sydney, Australia: Finch.

New Jersey Education Association. (1997). Making the most of meetings with family members. *NJEA Review, 71*, 24–29.

Newman, A. P., & Beverstock, C. (1990). *Adult literacy: Contexts and challenges*. Newark, DE: International Reading Association.

Newman, K. (2005). The case for the narrative brain. *Proceedings of the second Australasian conference on interactive entertainment* (pp. 145–149). Sydney, Australia: University of Technology, Creativity and Cognition Studios Press.

Newman, R. (1996–1997). Turning catalog clutter into creative learning. *Childhood Education, 73*(2), 103–104.

NICHD Early Child Care Research Network. (2000). The relation of child care to cognitive and language development. *Child Development, 71*, 960–980.

Nichols, S. (2007). Children as citizens: Literacies for social participation. *Early Years: Journal of International Research & Development, 27*(2), 119–130.

Nicolopoulou, A., & Richner, E. S. (2007). From actors to agents to persons: The development of character representation in young children's narratives. *Child Development, 78*(2), 412–429.

Nielsen, D. C., & Monson, D. L. (1996). Effects of literacy environment on literacy development of kindergarten children. *Journal of Educational Research, 89*(5), 259–271.

Niemeyer, J., & Scott-Little, C. (2001). *Assessing kindergarten children: A compendium of assessment instruments.* Greensboro, NC: SERVE. Available: www.serve.org

Nieto, S. (2002). *Language, culture, and teaching: Critical perspectives for a new century.* Mahwah, NJ: Lawrence Erlbaum.

Norris, E., Mokhtari, K., & Reichard, C. (2002). Children's use of drawing as a pre-writing strategy. *Journal of Research in Reading, 21*(1), 69–74.

Northwest Regional Educational Laboratory. (2003). Overview of second language acquisition theory. Available: www.nwrel.org/request/2003may/overview.html

Norton, D. E. (2008). *Multicultural literature: Through the eyes of many children* (3rd ed.). Upper Saddle River, NJ: Prentice Hall.

Nutbrown, C., Hannon, P., & Morgan, A. (2005). *Early literacy work with families: Research, policy and practice.* Thousand Oaks, CA: Sage.

Nyberg, J. (1996). *Charts for children: Print awareness activities for young children.* Glenview, IL: GoodYear.

Nyland, B., Ferris, J., & Dunn, L. (2008). Mindful hands, gestures as language: Listening to children. *Early Years: Journal of International Research and Development, 28*(1), 73–80.

Obiakor, F. E., & Algozzine, B. (2001). *It even happens in "good" schools: Responding to cultural diversity in today's classrooms.* Thousand Oaks, CA: Corwin Press.

Oczkus, L. (2009). *Interactive think-aloud lessons: 25 sure-fire ways to engage students and improve comprehension.* New York: Scholastic.

Ofcom. (2008). *Media literacy audit: Report on UK children's media literacy.* Available: www.ofcom.org.uk

Office for Standards in Education. (2008). *Every language matters. An evaluation of the extent and impact of initial training to teach a wider range of world languages.* London: Author.

Ogbu, J. (1988). Class stratification, racial stratification, and schooling. In L. Weis (Ed.), *Class, race, and gender in American education* (pp. 106–125). Albany: State University of New York Press.

Ogle, D. (1986). K-W-L: A teaching model that develops active reading of expository text. *The Reading Teacher, 36*(9), 564–570.

Ollila, L. O., & Mayfield, M. I. (1992). *Emerging literacy: Preschool, kindergarten, and primary grades.* Boston: Allyn & Bacon.

Olsen, G. W., & Fuller, M. L. (2007). *Home-school relations: Working successfully with parents and families* (3rd ed.). Boston: Allyn & Bacon.

Ostrosky, M., Gaffney, J., & Thomas, D. (2006). The interplay between literacy and relationships in early childhood settings. *Reading & Writing Quarterly, 22*(2), 173–191.

Otto, B. (2008). *Language development in early childhood: Reflective teaching for birth to age eight.* Upper Saddle River, NJ: Pearson.

Ouelette, G. P., & Senechal, M. (2008). A window into early literacy: Exploring the cognitive and linguistic underpinnings of invented spelling. *Scientific Studies of Reading, 12*(2), 195–219.

Ovando, C. J., Collier, V. P., & Combs, M. C. (2005). *Bilingual and ESL classrooms: Teaching in multicultural contexts* (4th ed.). New York: McGraw-Hill.

Padak, N., & Rasinski, T. (2007). Is being wild about Harry enough? Encouraging independent reading at home. *The Reading Teacher, 61*(4), 350–353.

Paez, M. M., DeTemple, J. M., & Snow, C. E. (2000). *Home language and literacy exposure index.* Unpublished manuscript, Harvard Graduate School of Education, Cambridge, MA.

Pailliotet, A. W., Semali, L., Rodenberg, R. K., Giles, J. K., & Macaul, S. L. (2000). Intermediality: Bridge to critical media literacy. *The Reading Teacher, 54*(2), 208–219.

Palmer, R., & Stewart, R. (2005). Models for using nonfiction in the primary grades. *The Reading Teacher, 58*(5), 426–434.

Papalia, D. E., Olds, S. W., & Feldman, R. D. (2007). *A child's world: Infancy through adolescence* (11th ed.). New York: McGraw-Hill.

Paquette, K. (2007). Encouraging primary students' writing through children's literature. *Early Childhood Education Journal, 35*(2), 155–165.

Paquette, K. R., Fello, S. E., & Jalongo, M. R. (2007). The talking drawings strategy: Using primary children's illustrations and oral language to improve comprehension of expository text. *Early Childhood Education Journal, 35*(1), 65–73.

Paquette, K. R., & Rieg, S. A. (2008). Using music to support the literacy development of young English language learners. *Early Childhood Education Journal, 36*(3), 227–232.

Parette, H. P., Blum, C., & Boeckmann, N. M. (2009). Evaluating assistive technology in early childhood education: The use of a concurrent time series probe approach. *Early Childhood Education Journal, 36*(5), 393–401.

Parette, H., Boeckmann, N., & Hourcade, J. (2008). Use of writing with Symbols 2000 software to facilitate emergent literacy development. *Early Childhood Education Journal, 36*(2), 161–170.

Parette, H., Hourcade, J., Boeckmann, N., & Blum, C. (2008). Using Microsoft PowerPoint to support emergent literacy skill development for young children at-risk or who have disabilities. *Early Childhood Education Journal, 36*(3), 233–239.

Parette, H., Hourcade, J., Dinelli, J., & Boeckmann, N. (2009). Using Clicker 5 to enhance emergent literacy in young learners. *Early Childhood Education Journal, 36*(4), 355–363.

Parette, H. P., Peterson-Karlan, G. R., Wojcik, B. W., & Bardi, N. (2007). Monitor that progress! Interpreting data trends for assistive technology decision-making. *Teaching Exceptional Children, 41*(1), 22–29.

Paris, A. H., & Paris, S. G. (2003). Assessing narrative comprehension in young children. *Reading Research Quarterly, 38*(1), 36–76.

Paris, S., & Stahl, S. (2004). *Children's reading and comprehension assessment.* Mahwah, NJ: Lawrence Erlbaum.

Park, E., & King, K. (2003). Cultural diversity and language socialization in the early years [Electronic version]. *Digest, 3*(13). Available: www.cal.org/resources/Digest/0313park.html

Parke, T., & Drury, R. (2001). Language development at home and school: Gains and losses in young bilinguals. *Journal of International Research and Development, 21,* 117–121.

Parker, E. L., & Pardini, T. H. (2006). *The words came down: English language learners read, write, and talk across the curriculum, K–2.* Portland, ME: Stenhouse.

Parks, S., & Black, H. (1992). *Book 1: Organizing thinking: Graphic organizers.* Pacific Grove, CA: Critical Thinking Press and Software.

Patera, M., Draper, S., & Naef, M. (2008). Exploring Magic Cottage: A virtual reality environment for stimulating children's imaginative writing. *Interactive Learning Environments, 16*(3), 245–263.

Paterson, J. L. (2000). Observed and reported expressive vocabulary and word combinations in bilingual toddlers. *Journal of Speech, Language & Hearing Research, 43*(1), 121–128.

Patterson, C. J. (2006). Children of lesbian and gay parents. *Current Directions in Psychological Science, 15,* 241–244.

Patterson, E., Schaller, M., & Clemens, J. (2008). A closer look at interactive writing. *The Reading Teacher, 61*(6), 496–497.

Pearman, C. J. (2008). Independent reading of CD-ROM storybooks: Measuring comprehension with oral retellings. *The Reading Teacher, 61*(8), 594–602.

Pena, D. C. (2000). Parent involvement: Influencing factors and implications. *Journal of Educational Research, 94*(1), 42–54.

Pence, K., Justice, L., & Wiggins, A. (2008). Preschool teachers' fidelity in implementing a language-rich curriculum. *Language, Speech, and Hearing Services in Schools, 39,* 329–341.

Perfetti, C. A. (2007). Reading ability: Lexical quality to comprehension. *Scientific Studies of Reading, 11*(4), 357–383.

Peterson, C. R., & Roberts, C. (2003). Like mother, like daughter: Similarities in narrative style. *Developmental Psychology, 39*(3), 551–562.

Pettito, L. A., & Marentette, P. F. (1991). Babbling in the manual mode: Evidence for the ontogeny of language. *Science, 251,* 1493–1496.

Peyton, M. R., & Jalongo, M. R. (2008). Make me an instrument of your peace: Honoring religious diversity and modeling respect for faiths through children's literature. *Early Childhood Education Journal, 35*(4), 301–303.

Phelps Deily, M. E. (2009). *The Education Week guide to K–12 terminology.* San Francisco: Jossey-Bass.

Phillips, B. M., & Lonigan, C. J. (2009). Variations in the home literacy environment of preschool children: A cluster analytic approach. *Scientific Studies of Reading, 13*(2), 146–174.

Phillips, L., Norris, S., & Anderson, J. (2008). Unlocking the door: Is parents' reading to children the key to early literacy development? *Canadian Psychology, 49*(2), 82–88.

Piaget, J. (1959). *The language and thought of the child* (M. Gabain & O. R. Gabain, Trans.). London: Routledge & Kegan Paul. (Original work published 1926)

Piaget, J. (1963). *The origins of intelligence in children.* New York: Norton.

Pierce, K. M. (1990). Initiating literature discussion groups: Teaching like learners. In K. G. Short & K. M. Pierce (Eds.), *Talking about books: Creating literate communities* (pp. 177–198). Portsmouth, NH: Heinemann.

Plourde, L. (1989). Teaching with collections. *Young Children, 44*(3), 78–80.

Popham, J. W. (2006). Assessment for learning: An endangered species? *Educational Leadership, 63*(5), 82–83.

Post, Y., Boyer, W., & Brett, L. (2006). A historical examination of self-regulation: Helping children now and in the future. *Early Childhood Education Journal, 34*(1), 5–14.

Postman, N. (1982). *The disappearance of childhood.* New York: Dell.

Potter, F. (1985). "Good job!" How we evaluate children's work. *Childhood Education, 61*, 203–206.

Proctor, C. P., August, D., Carlo, M. S., & Snow, C. (2006). The intriguing role of Spanish language vocabulary knowledge in predicting English reading comprehension. *Journal of Educational Psychology, 98*(1), 159–169.

Puckett, M. B., Black, J. K., Wittmer, D. S., & Petersen, S. H. (2008). *The young child: Development from prebirth through age eight* (5th ed.). Upper Saddle River, NJ: Merrill/Prentice Hall.

Purdy, J. (2008). Inviting conversation: Meaningful talk about texts for English language learners. *Literacy, 42*(1), 44–51.

Putnam, L. R. (Ed.). (1995). *How to become a better reading teacher: Strategies for assessment and intervention.* Upper Saddle River, NJ: Prentice Hall.

Quintero, E., & Rummel, M. K. (1996). Something to say: Voice in the classroom. *Childhood Education, 72*(3), 146–151.

Quintero, E. P. (2009). *Critical literacy in early childhood education: Artful story and the integrated curriculum.* New York: Peter Lang.

Ranker, J. (2009). Learning nonfiction in an ESL class: The interaction of situated practice and teacher scaffolding in a genre study. *The Reading Teacher, 62*(7), 580–589.

Rashid, F. L., Morris, R. D., & Sevcik, R. A. (2005). Relationship between home literacy environment and reading achievement in children with reading disabilities. *Journal of Learning Disabilities, 38*(1), 2–11.

Rasinski, T. V. (2004). *Assessing reading fluency.* Honolulu, HI: Pacific Resources for Education and Learning.

Raths, L. E., Wassermann, S., Jonas, A., & Rothstein, A. M. (1986). *Teaching for thinking: Theory, strategies and activities for the classroom.* New York: Teachers College Press.

Ratner, N. K., & Olver, R. R. (1998). Reading a tale of deception, learning a theory of mind? *Early Childhood Research Quarterly, 13*(2), 219–239.

Read, S., Reutzel, D. R., & Fawson, P. C. (2008). Do you want to know what I learned? Using information trade books as models to teach text structure. *Early Childhood Education Journal, 36*(3), 213–219.

Reeves, A. (1995). Tote bags: An innovative way to encourage parent-child interaction while learning a second language. In M. Matthias & B. Gulley (Eds.), *Celebrating family literacy through intergenerational programming* (pp. 81–84). Olney, MD: Association for Childhood Education International.

Resnick, L. B., & Snow, C. E. (2009). *Speaking and listening for preschool through third grade.* (Rev. ed.). Newark, DE: International Reading Association.

Reutzel, D., Jones, C. D., Fawson, P. C., & Smith, J. A. (2008). Scaffolded silent reading: A complement to repeated oral reading that works! *The Reading Teacher, 62*(3), 194–207.

Reyes, I., & Azuara, P. (2008). Emergent biliteracy in young Mexican immigrant children. *Reading Research Quarterly, 43*(4), 374–398.

Reynolds, M., & Wheldall, K. (2007). Reading Recovery 20 years down the track: Looking forward, looking back. *International Journal of Disability, Development & Education, 54*(2), 199–223.

Rhodes, J. A., & Milby, T. M. (2007). Teacher-created electronic books: Integrating technology to support readers with disabilities. *The Reading Teacher, 61*(3), 255–259.

Rice, P. S. (2002). Creating spaces for boys and girls to expand their definitions of masculinity and femininity through children's literature. *Journal of Children's Literature, 28*(2), 33–42

Richardson, M. V., Miller, M. B., Richardson, J. A., & Sacks, M. K. (2008). Literacy bags to encourage family involvement. *Reading Improvement, 45*(1), 1–9.

Riches, C., & Genesee, F. (2007). Literacy: Cross-linguistic and crossmodal issues. In F. Genesee, K. Lindholm-Leary, W. M. Saunders, & D. Christian (Eds.), *Educating English language learners: A synthesis of research evidence* (pp. 64–108). Cambridge, UK: Cambridge University Press.

Richgels, D. J. (2001). Invented spelling, phonemic awareness, and reading and writing instruction. In S. B. Neuman & D. K. Dickinson (Eds.), *Handbook of early literacy research* (pp. 142–158). New York: Guilford.

Richgels, D. J. (2003). *Going to kindergarten: A year with an outstanding teacher.* Lanham, MD: The Scarecrow Press.

Richgels, D. J. (2008). Practice to theory: Invented spelling. In A. DeBruin-Parecki (Ed.), *Effective early literacy practice: Here's how, here's why* (pp. 1–14). Baltimore: Paul H. Brookes.

Richmond, J., & Nelson, C. A. (2007). Accounting for change in declarative memory: A cognitive neuroscience perspective. *Developmental Review, 27*(3), 349–373.

Ridley, S. M., McWilliam, R. A., & Oates, C. S. (2000). Observed engagement as an indicator of program quality. *Early Education and Development, 11*(2), 133–145.

Riley, J., & Burrell, A. (2007). Assessing children's oral storytelling in their first year of school. *International Journal of Early Years Education, 15*(2), 181–196.

Riojas-Cortez, M., Flores, B. B., Smith, H., & Clark, E. R. (2003). Cuentame un cuento [tell me a story]: Bridging family literacy traditions with school literacy. *Language Arts, 81*, 62–71.

Ritter, G. W., Barnett, J. H., Denny, G. S., & Albin, G. R. (2009). The effectiveness of volunteer tutoring programs for elementary and middle school students: A meta-analysis. *Review of Educational Research, 79*(1), 3–38.

Roberts, E. (1984). *The children's picture book*. Cincinnati, OH: Writer's Digest Books.

Roberts, T. A. (2008). Home storybook reading in primary or second language with preschool children: Evidence of equal effectiveness for second-language vocabulary acquisition. *Reading Research Quarterly, 43*(2), 103–130.

Robinshaw, H. (2007). Acquisition of hearing, listening and speech skills by and during key stage 1. *Early Child Development & Care, 177*(6/7), 661–678.

Robinson, J. (1996). Introduction to media literacy education and media literacy bibliography. Indianapolis, IN: Media Action Council. (ERIC Document Reproduction Service No. ED 403 611)

Rogers, C. L., Lister, J. J., Febo, D. M., Besing, J. M., & Abrams, H. B. (2006). Effects of bilingualism, noise, and reverberation on speech perception by listeners with normal hearing. *Applied Psycholinguistics, 27*(3), 465–485.

Rose, J. (2006). *Independent review of the teaching of early reading: Final report*. London: The Rose Review Support Team. Available: www.standards.dfes.gov.uk.rosereview

Roseberry-McKibbin, C., & Brice, A. (2000). Acquiring English as a second language. *ASHA Leader, 5*(12), 4.

Roseberry-McKibbin, C., & O'Hanlon, L. (2005). Nonbiased assessment of English language learners: A tutorial. *Communication Disorders Quarterly, 26*(3), 178–185.

Roser, N. L., & Martinez, M. G. (Eds.). (1995). *Book talk and beyond*. Newark, DE: International Reading Association.

Roskos, K., & Christie, J. (Eds.). (2007). *Play and literacy in early childhood: Research from multiple perspectives* (2nd ed.). Mahwah, NJ: Lawrence Erlbaum.

Rothenberg, C., & Fisher, D. (2007). *Teaching English language learners: A differentiated approach*. Upper Saddle River, NJ: Pearson Education.

Rouse, J. (1978). *The completed gesture: Myth, character and education*. Ringwood, NJ: Skyline Books.

Roush, B. (2005). Drama rhymes: An instructional strategy. *The Reading Teacher, 58*(6), 584.

Rowe, M., & Goldin-Meadow, S. A. (2009). Differences in early gesture explain SES disparities in child vocabulary size at school entry. *Science, 323*, 951–953.

Rubin, R., & Carlan, V. (2005). Using writing to understand bilingual children's literacy development. *The Reading Teacher, 58*(8), 728–739.

Rudd L. C., Cain D. W., & Saxon T. F. (2008). Does improving joint attention in low quality child care enhance language development? *Early Child Development and Care, 178*(3), 1–20.

Ruiz, N. T. (1995). A young deaf child learns to write: Implications for literacy development. *The Reading Teacher, 49*(3), 206–217.

Rule, A. C. (2001). Alphabetizing with environmental print. *The Reading Teacher, 54*, 558–562.

Rule, A. C. (2007). Mystery boxes: Helping children improve their reasoning. *Early Childhood Education Journal, 35*(1), 13–18.

Rule, A. C., & Kyle, P. (2009). Community-building in a diverse setting. *Early Childhood Education Journal, 36*(4), 291–295.

Rushton, S., & Larkin, E. (2001). Shaping the learning environment: Connecting developmentally appropriate practices to brain research. *Early Childhood Education Journal, 29*(1), 25–34.

Russell, D. H., Ousky, O., & Haynes, G. B. (1967). *Manual for teaching the reading readiness program* (Rev. ed.). Boston: Ginn.

Sadik, A. (2008). Digital storytelling: A meaningful technology-integrated approach for engaged student learning. *Educational Technology Research and Development, 56*(4), 487–506.

Saffran, J. R., & Griepentrog, G. J. (2001). Absolute pitch in infant auditory learning: Evidence for developmental reorganization. *Developmental Psychology, 37*(1), 74–85.

Sahn, L. S., & Reichel, A. G. (2008). Read all about it! A classroom newspaper integrates the curriculum. *Young Children, 63*(2), 13–18.

Salinger, T. (1995). *Literacy for young children* (2nd ed.). Englewood Cliffs, NJ: Merrill/Prentice Hall.

Salmon, M., & Akaran, S. E. (2005). Cross-cultural e-mail connections. *Young Children, 60*(5), 36.

Samson, J. F., & Lesaux, N. K. (2009). Language-minority learners in special education: Rates and predictors of identification for services, *Journal of Learning Disabilities, 42*(2), 148–162.

Samway, K. (2006). *When English language learners write*. Portsmouth, NH: Heinemann.

Santamaria, L. J. (2009). Culturally responsive differentiated instruction: Narrowing gaps between best pedagogical practices benefiting all learners. *Teachers College Record, 111*(1), 214–247.

Santi, K. L., Menchetti, B. M., & Edwards, B. J. (2004). A comparison of eight kindergarten phonemic awareness programs based on empirically validated instructional principles. *Remedial and Special Education, 25*(3), 189–196.

Santoro, L., Chard, D. J., Howard, L., & Baker, S. K. (2008). Making the *very* most of classroom read-alouds to promote comprehension and vocabulary. *The Reading Teacher, 61*(5), 396–408.

Saracho, O., & Spodek, B. (2006). Young children's literacy related play. *Early Child Development and Care, 176*(1), 707–721

Saracho, O., & Spodek, B. (2007). Oracy: Social facets of language learning. *Early Child Development and Care, 177*(6/7), 695–705.

Saracho, O., & Spodek, B. (Eds.). (2010). *Contemporary perspectives on language and cultural diversity in early childhood.* Charlotte, NC: Information Age Publishing.

Saracho, O. N. (2008). A literacy program for fathers: A case study. *Early Childhood Education Journal, 35*(4), 351–356.

Sawyer, R. (1998). *The way of the storyteller: A great storyteller shares her rich experience and joy in her art and tells eleven of her best-loved stories.* New York: Penguin.

Schaller, A., Rocha, L. O., & Barshinger, D. (2007). Maternal attitudes and parent education: How immigrant mothers support their child's education despite their own low levels of education. *Early Childhood Education, 34*(5), 351–356.

Schappe, J. (2005). Early childhood assessment: A correlational study of the relationships among student performance, student feelings, and teacher perceptions. *Early Childhood Education Journal, 33*(3), 187–193.

Scharer, P. L., & Zutell, J. (2003). The development of spelling. In N. Hall, J. Larson, & J. Marsh (Eds.), *Handbook of early childhood literacy* (pp. 271–286). London: Sage.

Schickendanz, J. A. (2008). *Increasing the power of instruction: Integration of language, literacy, and math across the preschool day.* Washington, DC: National Association for the Education of Young Children.

Schimmel, N. (1978). *Just enough to make a story: A sourcebook for storytelling.* Berkeley, CA: Sisters' Choice Press.

Schultz, K. (2003). *Listening: A framework for teaching across differences.* New York: Teachers College Press.

Schulz, M. M. (2009). Effective writing assessment and instruction for young English language learners. *Early Childhood Education Journal, 36*(1), 57–62.

Schulze, A. C. (2006). *Helping children become readers through writing: A guide to writing workshop in kindergarten.* Newark, DE: International Reading Association.

Schwartz, R. M. (2005). Decisions, decisions: Responding to primary students during guided reading. *The Reading Teacher, 58*(5), 436–443.

Schwartz, S., & Bone, M. (1995). *Retelling, relating, reflecting: Beyond the 3R's.* Toronto: Irwin.

Schwartz, W. (1996). Hispanic preschool education: An important opportunity. New York: ERIC Clearinghouse on Urban Education. (ERIC/CUE Digest No. 113; Report No. EDO-UD-96–2)

Scollon, R., & Scollon, S. W. (2000). *Intercultural communication: A discourse approach* (2nd ed.). New York: Wiley-Blackwell.

Scully, P., & Howell, J. (2008). Using rituals and traditions to create classroom community for children, teachers, and parents. *Early Childhood Education Journal, 36*(3), 261–266.

Seifert, K., & Hoffnung, R. (1999). *Child and adolescent development* (5th ed.). Belmont, CA: Wadsworth.

Seitz, H. (2008). The power of documentation in the early childhood classroom. *Young Children, 63*(2), 88–93.

Seitz, H., & Bartholomew, C. (2008). Powerful portfolios for young children. *Early Childhood Education Journal, 36*(1), 63–68.

Semali, L. M., & Hammett, R. (1999). Critical media literacy: Content or process? *Review of Education Pedagogy/Cultural Studies, 20*(4), 365–384.

Semali, L. M., & Pailliotet, A. (Eds.). (1999). *Intermediality: The teachers' handbook of critical medial literacy.* Boulder, CO: Westview.

Shafer, R. (1981). Narration on the psychoanalytic dialogue. In W. T. J. Mitchell (Ed.), *On narrative.* Chicago: University of Chicago Press.

Shagoury, R. (2009). Nurturing writing development in multilingual classrooms. *Young Children, 64*(2), 52–57.

Shamir, A., & Korat, O. (2006). How to select CD-ROM storybooks for young children: The teacher's role. *The Reading Teacher, 59*(6), 532–543.

Shandomo, H. M. (2009). Getting to know you: Cross-cultural pen pals expand children's world view. *Childhood Education, 85*(3), 154–159.

Share, J., Jolls, T., & Thoman, E. (2007). *Five key questions that can change the world: Deconstruction.* Malibu, CA: Center for Media Literacy.

Shonkoff, J. P., & Phillips, D. A. (Eds.). (2000). *From neurons to neighborhoods: The science of early childhood development.* Washington, DC: National Academies Press.

Shulevitz, U. (1985). *Writing with pictures.* New York: Watson-Guptill.

Shulevitz, U. (1989). What is a picture book? *The Five Owls*, 2(4), 49–53.

Shuy, R. (1981). A holistic view of language. *Research in the Teaching of English, 15*, 101–111.

Siemens, L. (1994). "Does Jesus have aunties?" and "Who planned it all?" Learning to listen to big questions. *Language Arts, 71*(5), 358–360.

Sinclair, D. (1996). Media literacy: Elementary, my dear TL. (ERIC Document Reproduction Service No. EJ 536 240)

Singh, L., & Singh, N. C. (2008). The development of articulatory signatures in children. *Developmental Science, 11*(4), 467–473.

Sipe, L. R. (2008). *Storytime: Young children's literary understanding in the classroom.* New York: Teachers College Press.

Sitarz, P. G. (1997). *Story time sampler: Read alouds, booktalks, and activities for children.* Englewood, CO: Libraries Unlimited.

Skouge, J. R., Rao, K., & Boisvert, P. C. (2007). Promoting early literacy for diverse learners using audio and video technology. *Early Childhood Education Journal, 35*(1), 5–11.

Smart Television Alliance. (2009). *TV gone wrong.* Available: www.smarttelevisionalliance.org

Smith, C. (2008). How can parents model good listening skills? Available: www.rusd.k12.ca.us/parents

Smith, C. B. (2003a). The importance of expository text: Reading and writing. Bloomington, IN: ERIC Clearinghouse on Reading, English, and Communication. (ERIC Document Reproduction Service No. ED 480 886)

Smith, C. B. (2003b). *Skills students use when speaking and listening.* Bloomington, IN: ERIC Clearinghouse on Reading, English, and Communication. (ERIC Document Reproduction Service No. ED 480 895)

Smith, F. (1983). *Essays into literacy.* Portsmouth, NH: Heinemann.

Smith, F. (2003). *Unspeakable acts, unnatural practices: Flaws and fallacies in "scientific" reading instruction.* Portsmouth, NH: Heinemann.

Smith, F. (2006). *Reading without nonsense* (4th ed.). New York: Teachers College Press.

Smith, L., Borkowski, J., & Whitman, T. (2008). From reading readiness to reading competence: The role of self-regulation in at-risk children. *Scientific Studies of Reading, 12*(2), 131–152.

Smolkin, L., & Donovan, C. (2000). *The contexts of comprehension: Information book read alouds and comprehension acquisition.* Ann Arbor, MI: Center for the Improvement of Early Reading Achievement. (ERIC Document Reproduction Service No. ED 450 351)

Sneddon, R. (2008a). Magda and Albana: Learning to read with dual language books. *Language and Education, 22*(2), 137–154.

Sneddon, R. (2008b). Young children learning to read with dual language books. *English Teaching: Practice and Critique, 7*(2), 71–84.

Snedeker, J., & Trueswell, J. C. (2004). The developing constraints on parsing decisions: The role of lexical-bases and referential scenes in child and adult sentence processing. *Cognitive Psychology, 49*, 238–299.

Snow, C. E., Burns, M. S., & Griffin, P. (Eds.). (1998). *Preventing reading difficulties in young children.* Washington, DC: National Academies Press.

Snow, C. E., Griffin, P., & Burns, M. S. (2005). *Knowledge to support the teaching of reading: Preparing teachers for a changing world.* New York: John Wiley & Sons.

Snow, C. E., & Ninio, A. (1986). The contracts of literacy: What children learn from learning to read books. In W. Teale & E. Sulzby (Eds.), *Emergent literacy: Writing and reading* (pp. 116–138). Norwood, NJ: Ablex.

Snyder, T., & Hoffman, C. (2003). *Digest of educational statistics 2002* (NCES 2003–060). Washington, DC: National Center for Educational Statistics, U.S. Department of Education.

Solvie, P. (2007). Leaping out of our skins: Postmodern considerations in use of an electronic whiteboard to foster critical engagement in early literacy lessons. *Educational Philosophy & Theory, 39*(7), 737–754.

Song, H., & Fisher, C. (2005). Who's "she"? Discourse prominence influences preschoolers' comprehension of pronouns. *Journal of Memory and Language, 52*, 29–57.

Sonnenschein, S., Baker, L., Serpell, R., & Schmidt, D. (2000). Reading is a source of entertainment: The importance of the home perspective for children's literacy development. In K. A. Roskos & J. F. Christie (Eds.), *Play and literacy in early childhood: Research from multiple perspectives* (pp. 125–137). Mahwah, NJ: Lawrence Erlbaum.

Sorgen, M. (1999, June). *Applying brain research to classroom practice.* Materials presented at the University of South Florida Brain/Mind Connections Conference, Sarasota, FL.

Soto, L. D., Smrekar, J. L., & Nekcovei, D. L. (2001). Preserving home languages and cultures in the classroom: Challenges and opportunities. *Directions in Language and Education, 13.* Available: www.ncbe.gwu.edu/ncbepubs

Souto-Manning, M. (2007). Immigrant families and children (re)develop identities in a new context. *Early Childhood Education Journal, 34*(6), 399–405.

Spandel, V. (2008). *Creating writers through 6-trait writing assessment and instruction* (5th ed.). Boston: Allyn & Bacon.

Spewock, T. (1991). Teaching parents of young children through learning packets. *Young Children, 47*(1), 28–30,

Spodek, B., & Saracho, O. N. (1993). *Language and literacy in early childhood education* (Yearbook in Early Childhood Education, Volume 4). New York: Teachers College Press.

Spooner, S. A. (2004). Preschoolers, computers, and school readiness: Are we on to something? *Pediatrics, 114*, 852–853.

Stacey, S. (2009). *Emergent curriculum in early childhood settings: From theory to practice.* St. Paul, MN: Redleaf.

Stadler, M., & Ward, G. (2005). Supporting the narrative development of young children. *Early Childhood Education Journal, 33*(2), 73–80.

Stahl, S. A. (2003). How words are learned incrementally over multiple exposures. *American Education, 27*, 28–29.

Stanford, P., & Siders, J. A. (2001). E-pal writing! *Teaching Exceptional Children, 34*(2), 21–24.

Stauffer, R. (1975). *Directing the thinking-reading process.* New York: Harper & Row.

Stead, T. (2002). *Is that a fact?* York, ME: Stenhouse.

Stelmachowicz, P. G., Hoover, B. M., Lewis, D. E., Kortekaas, R. W., & Pittman, A. L. (2000). The relation between stimulus context, speech audibility, and perception for normal-hearing and hearing-impaired children. *Journal of Speech, Language, and Hearing Research, 43*, 902–914.

Stephen, C., & Plowman, L. (2003). Information and communication technologies in preschool settings: A review of the literature. *International Journal of Early Years Education, 11*, 223–225.

Stephens, K. E. (2008). A quick guide to selecting great informational books for young children. *The Reading Teacher, 61*(6), 488–490.

Stephenson, A. (2009). Stepping back to listen to Jeff: Conversations with a 2-year-old. *Young Children, 64*(1), 90–95.

Stevens, L., Watson, K., & Dodd, K. (2001). Supporting parents of children with communication difficulties. *International Journal of Language & Communication Disorders, 36*(Suppl.), 70–74.

Stewig, J. W. (1994). *Dramatizing literature in whole language classrooms* (2nd ed.). New York: Teachers College Press.

Stiggins, R. J. (2007). *Introduction to student-involved assessment for learning* (5th ed.). Upper Saddle River, NJ: Prentice Hall.

Stiggins, R. J., & Chappuis, J. (2006). What a difference a word makes: Assessment FOR learning rather than assessment OF learning helps students succeed. *Journal of Staff Development, 27*(1), 10–14.

Stipek, D. (2006). No Child Left Behind comes to preschool. *Elementary School Journal, 106*(5), 455–465.

Stobbart, C., & Alant, E. (2008). Home-based literacy experiences of severely to profoundly deaf preschoolers and their hearing parents. *Journal of Developmental & Physical Disabilities, 20*(2), 139–153.

Stojanovik, V., & Riddell, P. (2008). Expressive versus receptive language skills in specific reading disorder. *Clinical Linguistics & Phonetics, 22*(4/5), 305–310.

Strasburger, V. C., Wilson, B. J., & Jordan, A. B. (2009). *Children, adolescents, and the media* (2nd ed.). Thousand Oaks, CA: Sage.

Strauss, S., & Altwerger, B. (2007). The logographic nature of English alphabetics and the fallacy of direct intensive phonics instruction. *Journal of Early Childhood Literacy, 7*(3), 299–319.

Strickland, D. (2004). Working with families as partners in early literacy. *The Reading Teacher, 58*(1), 86–89.

Strickland, D. S., & Morrow, L. M. (1989). Interactive experiences with storybook reading. *The Reading Teacher, 42*(41), 322–324.

Strommen, L. T., & Maters, B. F. (1997). What readers do: Young children's ideas about the nature of reading. *The Reading Teacher, 51*(2), 98–107.

Strother, D. B. (1987). Practical applications of research on listening. *Phi Delta Kappan, 68*, 625–628.

Stuber, G. M. (2007). Of primary interest. Centering your classroom: Setting the stage for engaged learners. *Young Children, 62*(4), 58–59. Available: www.journal.naeyc.org/btj/200707

Suarez, D. (2003). The development of empathetic dispositions through global experiences. *Educational Horizons, 81*, 180–182.

Sulzby, E. (1985). Children's emergent reading of favorite storybooks: A developmental study. *Reading Research Quarterly, 20*, 458–481.

Sundem, G., Krieger, J., & Pikiewicz, K. (2009). *Ten languages you'll need most in the classroom: A guide to communicating with English language learners and their families.* Thousand Oaks, CA: Corwin.

Swanborn, M. S. L., & de Glopper, K. (2002). Impact of reading purpose on incidental word learning from context. *Language Learning, 52*(1), 95–117.

Swick, K. J. (2007). Empower foster parents toward caring relations with children. *Early Childhood Education Journal, 34*(6), 393–398.

Swick, K. J. (2009). Promoting school and life success through early childhood family literacy. *Early Childhood Education Journal, 36*(5), 403–406.

Sylva, K., Scott, S., Totsika, V., Ereky-Stevens, K., & Crook, C. (2008). Training parents to help their children read: A randomized control trial. *British Journal of Educational Psychology, 78*(3), 435–455.

Tabors, P. O. (2008). *One child, two languages: A guide for early childhood educators of children learning English as a second language.* Baltimore: Paul H. Brookes.

Tabors, P. O., & Snow, C. E. (2001). Young bilingual children and early literacy development. In S. B. Neuman & D. K. Dickinson (Eds.), *Handbook of early literacy research* (pp. 159–178). New York: Guilford.

Teale, W. H., Paciga, K. A., & Hoffman, J. L. (2007). Beginning reading instruction in urban schools: The curriculum gap ensures a continuing achievement gap. *Reading Teacher, 61*(4), 344–348.

Teale, W. H., & Sulzby, E. (2003). Emergent literacy: New perspectives. In R. D. Robinson, M. C. McKenna, & J. M. Wedman, *Issues and trends in literacy education* (3rd ed., pp. 129–144). Boston: Allyn & Bacon.

Temple, C., Martinez, M., Yokota, J., & Naylor, A. (2001). *Children's books in children's hands: An introduction to their literature.* Boston: Allyn & Bacon.

Terry, C. A. (1989). Literature: A foundation and source for learning to write. In J. Hickman & B. E. Cullinan (Eds.), *Children's literature in the classroom: Weaving Charlotte's web* (pp. 49–57). Norwood, MA: Christopher-Gordon.

Thal, D. J., & Flores, M. (2001). Development of sentence interpretation strategies by typically developing and late-talking toddlers. *Journal of Child Language, 28*(1), 173–193.

Thal, D. J., O'Hanlon, L., Clemmons, M., & Fralin, L. (1999). The validity of a parent report measure of vocabulary and syntax for preschool children with language impairment. *Journal of Speech, Language, and Hearing Research, 42,* 482–496.

Thomas, M. S. C. (2003). Limits on plasticity. *Journal of Cognition & Development, 4*(1), 99–125.

Thomas, W. P., & Collier, V. P. (2002). *A national study of school effectiveness for language minority students' long-term academic achievement.* Santa Cruz, CA: Center for Research on Education, Diversity & Excellence. Available: http://crede.berkeley.edu/research/llaa/1.1pdfs

Tizard, B., & Hughes, M. (1984). *Young children learning.* Cambridge, MA: Harvard University.

Tomlinson, C. A., & McTighe, J. (2006). *Integrating differentiated instruction and understanding by design: Connecting content and kids.* Alexandria, VA: Association for Supervision and Curriculum Development.

Tomopoulos, S., Valdez, P., Dreyer, B., Fierman, A., Berkule, S., Kuhn, M., & Mendelsohn, A. (2009). Is exposure to media intended for preschool children associated with less parent-child shared reading aloud and teaching activities? *Ambulatory Pediatrics, 7*(1), 18–24.

Tompkins, G. E. (2008). *Language arts: Patterns of practice* (7th ed.). Upper Saddle River, NJ: Prentice Hall.

Torgesen, J. K. (2002). The prevention of reading difficulties. *Journal of School Psychology, 40*(1), 7–26.

Torrance, N., & Olson, D. R. (1985). Oral and literate competencies in the early school years. In D. R. Olson, N. Torrance, & A. Hildyard (Eds.), *Literacy, language and learning: The nature and consequences of reading and writing* (pp. 256–284). London: Cambridge University.

Tracey, D. H., & Young, J. W. (2007). Technology and early literacy: The impact of an integrated learning system on high-risk kindergartners' achievement. *Reading Psychology, 28*(5), 443–467.

Trawick-Smith, J. (2009). *Early childhood development: A multicultural perspective* (5th ed.). Upper Saddle River, NJ: Prentice Hall.

Trepanier-Street, M. L., & Romatowski, J. A. (1999). The influence of children's literature on gender role perceptions: A re-examination. *Early Childhood Education Journal, 26*(3), 155–159.

Tsao, Ya-Lun. (2008). Using guided play to enhance children's conversation, creativity and competence in literacy. *Education, 128*(3), 515–520.

Turbill, J. (2003, May). Exploring the potential of the digital Language Experience Approach in Australian classrooms. *Reading Online, 6*(7), 41–52. Available: www.readingonline.org/international/inter_index.asp?HREF=/International/Turbill7/index.html

Turner, J. C. (1997). Starting right: Strategies for engaging young literacy learners. In J. T. Guthrie & A. Wigfield (Eds.), *Reading engagement: Motivating readers through integrated instruction* (pp. 183–204). Newark, DE: International Reading Association.

Uribe, M., & Nathenson-Mejia, S. (2008). *Literacy essentials for English language learners: Successful transitions.* New York: Teachers College Press.

U.S. Bureau of the Census. (2003). Language use and English-speaking ability: 2000. *Census 2000 brief.* Washington, DC: Author. Available: www.census.gov/prod/cen2000/doc/sf3.pdf

U.S. Department of Education. (2007). *Digest of education statistics.* Washington, DC: Author. Available: http://nces.ed.gov/programs/digest/d07

U.S. Department of Education, National Center for Education Statistics. (2000). *America's kindergartners.* Washington, DC: Author.

Van Allen, R. (1976). *Language experience in communication.* Boston: Houghton Mifflin.

Vandergrift, L. (2006). Second language listening: Listening ability or language proficiency? *The Modern Language Journal, 90*(1), 6–18.

Vandewater, E. A., Rideout, V. J., Wartella, E. A., Huang, X., Lee, J. H., & Shim, M. (2007). Digital childhood: Electronic media and technology use among infants, toddlers, and preschoolers. *Pediatrics, 119*(5), e1006–e1015.

VanSchuvver, J. M. (1993). *Storytelling made easy with puppets.* Phoenix, AZ: Oryx Press.

Varley, P. (2002). As good as reading? Kids and the audiobook revolution. *Horn Book Magazine, 78*(3), 251–263.

Vartuli, S., & Rohs, J. (2008). Selecting curriculum content that stimulates thought. *Early Childhood Education Journal, 35*(5), 393–396.

Vasquez, V. M. (2000). Negotiating a critical literacy curriculum with young children. *Research Bulletin of Phi Delta Kappa International, 29,* 7–10.

Vasquez, V. M. (2003). *Negotiating critical literacies with young children.* Mahwah, NJ: Lawrence Erlbaum.

Vestergaard, H. (2005). *Weaving the literacy web: Creating curriculum based on books children love.* St. Paul, MN: Redleaf.

Viadero, D. (2004, May 5). Reading books is found to ward off "summer slump". *Education Week, 23*(34), 12.

Vigil, C., & Robinson, J. (1997). The big bad wolf and stereotype and bias in the media. (ERIC Document Reproduction Service No. ED 403 613)

Viguers, R. H. (1974). *Storytelling and the teacher.* Washington, DC: National Education Association.

Villareale, C. (2009). *Learning from the children: Reflecting on teaching.* St. Paul, MN: Redleaf.

Visu-Petra, L., Cheie, L., & Benga, O. (2008). Short-term memory performance and metamemory judgments in preschool and early school-age children: A quantitative and qualitative analysis. *Cognitie, Creier, Comportament/ Cognition, Brain, Behavior, 12*(1), 71–101.

Vygotsky, L. S. (1962). *Thought and language.* Cambridge, MA: MIT Press.

Walton-Hadlock, M. (2008). Tots to tweens: Age-appropriate technology programming for kids. *Children & Libraries: The Journal of the Association for Library Service to Children, 6*(3), 52–55.

Washburn-Moses, L. (2006). 25 best internet resources for teaching reading. *Reading Teacher, 60*(1), 70–75.

Wasik, B. A., Bond, M. A., Hindman, A. H., & Jusczyk, A. M. (2007, April). The impact of a teacher professional development intervention on Head Start children's language and pre-literacy development. In M. McKeown (Chair), *Fostering development among teachers and children in literacy, math, science, and social skills.* Paper symposium presented at the biennial meeting of the Society for Research in Child Development, Boston, MA.

Wasserman, L. H. (2007). The correlation between brain development, language acquisition, and cognition. *Early Childhood Education Journal, 34*(6), 415–418.

Watts, E. H., O'Brian, M., & Wojcik, B. W. (2004). Four models of assistive technology consideration: How do they compare to recommended educational assessment practices? *Journal of Special Education Technology, 19,* 43–56.

Webster, P. (2009). Exploring the literature of fact. *The Reading Teacher, 62*(8), 662–671.

Weigel, D. J., Martin, S. S., & Bennett, K. K. (2006a). Contributions of the home literacy environment to preschool-aged children's emerging literacy and language skills. *Early Child Development and Care, 176,* 357–378.

Weigel, D. J., Martin, S. S., & Bennett, K. K. (2006b). Mothers' literacy beliefs: Connections with the home literacy environment and pre-school children's literacy development. *Journal of Early Childhood Literacy, 6*(2), 191–211.

Weitzman, C. C., Roy, L., Walls, T., & Tomlin, R. (2004). More evidence for Reach Out and Read: A home-based study. *Pediatrics, 113,* 1248–1254.

Welsch, J. G. (2008). Playing within and beyond the story: Encouraging book-related pretend play. *The Reading Teacher, 62*(2), 138–148.

West, S., & Cox, A. (2004). *Literacy play: Over 300 dramatic play activities that teach pre-reading skills.* Beltsville, MD: Gryphon House.

Whitin, D. J., & Piwko, M. (2008). Mathematics and poetry: The right connections. *Young Children, 63*(2), 34–39. Available: www.journal.naeyc.org/btj/200803

Wiener-Margulies, M., & Rey-Barboza, R. (1996). Toddlers' speech and cognitive effort. *Journal of Genetic Psychology, 157*(1), 65–76.

Wigfield, A., & McCann, A. D. (1996–1997). Children's motivations for reading. *The Reading Teacher, 50*(4), 360–362.

Wiggins, D. G. (2007). Pre-K music and the emergent reader: Promoting literacy in a music-enhanced environment. *Early Childhood Education Journal, 35*(1), 55–64.

Wilcox-Herzog, A., & Ward, S. L. (2009). Measuring teachers' perceived interactions with children: A tool for assessing beliefs and intentions. *Early Childhood Parenting Collaborative, 6*(2). Available: http://ecrp .uiuc.edu/v6n2/herzog.html

Wiles, J. (2004). *Curriculum essentials: A resource for educators* (2nd ed.). Boston: Allyn & Bacon.

Wilford, S. (2008). *Nurturing young children's disposition to learn.* St. Paul, MN: Redleaf.

Williams, A. (2007). Storytime model for large groups: Implications for early literacy. *Children & Libraries:*

The Journal of the Association for Library Service to Children, 5(2), 27–29.

Wise, J., Sevcil, R., Morris, R., Lovett, M., & Wolf, M. (2007). The relationship among receptive and expressive vocabulary, listening comprehension, prereading skills, word identification skills, and reading comprehension by children with reading disabilities. *Journal of Speech, Language, and Hearing Research, 50*(4), 1093–1109.

Wohlwend, K. E. (2008). Kindergarten as nexus of practice: A mediated discourse analysis of reading, writing, play, and design in an early literacy apprenticeship. *Reading Research Quarterly, 43*(4), 332–334.

Wood, R., Rawlings, A., & Ozturk, A. (2003). Towards a new understanding: The "Books Alive! Multimedia Project." *Reading: Literacy and Language, 37*(2), 90–93.

Wortham, S. C. (2005). *Assessment in early childhood education* (4th ed.). Upper Saddle River, NJ: Merrill/Prentice Hall.

Wrobleski, L. (1990). A tip from a teacher: The writer's briefcase. *Young Children, 45*(3), 69.

Wurm, J. (2005). *Working in the Reggio way: A beginners' guide for American teachers.* St. Paul, MN: Redleaf.

Xu, S. H., & Rutledge, A. L. (2003). Chicken starts with ch! Kindergartners learn through environmental print. *Young Children, 58*(2), 44–51.

Yaden, D. (1988). Understanding stories through repeated read-alouds: How many does it take? *The Reading Teacher, 41*(6), 556–560.

Yaden, D. B., & Paratore, J. R. (2002). Family literacy at the turn of the millennium: The costly future of maintaining the status quo. In J. E. Flood, D. Lapp, J. Jensen, & J. Squire (Eds.), *Research in English and the language arts* (pp. 532–545). Mahwah, NJ: Lawrence Erlbaum.

Yates, B. L. (2000). Media literacy and attitude change: Assessing the effectiveness of media literacy training on children's responses to persuasive messages within the framework of the Elaboration Likelihood Model of persuasion. *Dissertation Abstracts International, 61*(08A), 2976.

Yeoman, E. (1999). "How does it get into my imagination?" Elementary school children's intertextual knowledge. *Gender and Education, 11*(4), 427–440.

Yokota, J. (Ed.). (2001). *Kaleidoscope: A multicultural booklist for grades K–8* (3rd ed.). Urbana, IL: National Council of Teachers of English.

Yopp, H. K., & Yopp, R. H. (2006). *Literature-based reading activities* (4th ed.). Boston: Pearson.

Yopp, H. K., & Yopp, R. H. (2009). Phonological awareness is child's play! *Young Children, 64*(1), 12–21.

Yopp, R. H., & Yopp, H. K. (2004). Preview-Predict-Confirm: Thinking about the language and content of informational text. *The Reading Teacher, 58*(1), 79–83.

Zager, D. (2004). *Autism spectrum disorders: Identification, education, and treatment* (3rd ed.). Mahwah, NJ: Lawrence Erlbaum.

Zaslow, M., & Martinez-Beck, L. (2006). *Critical issues in early childhood professional development.* Baltimore: Paul H. Brookes.

Zeece, P., Harris, B., & Hayes, N. (2006). Building literacy links for young children. *Early Childhood Education Journal, 34*(1), 61–65.

Zeece, P. D., & Wallace, B. M. (2009). Books and good stuff: A strategy for building school to home literacy connections. *Early Childhood Education Journal, 37*(1), 35–42.

Zelasko, N., & Antunez, B. (2000). *If your child learns in two languages: A parent's guide for improving educational opportunities for children acquiring English as a second language.* Washington, DC: National Clearinghouse for Bilingual Education.

Zhang, X., & Tomblin, J. B. (2000). The association of intervention receipt with speech-language profiles and social-demographic variables. *American Journal of Speech-Language Pathology, 9*(4), 345–357.

Zhou, S. (2008). Interactive storytelling. *Innovation, 8*(3), 14–15.

Zucker, T. A., & Invernizzi, M. (2008). My eSorts and digital extensions of word study. *The Reading Teacher, 61*(8), 654–658.

Zygouris-Coe, V., Wiggins, M. B., & Smith, L. H. (2004). Engaging students with text: The 3–2–1 strategy. *The Reading Teacher, 58*(4), 381–384.